THE ARMY WIFE

THE
ARMY
WIFE

THIRD REVISED EDITION

By

Nancy Shea

NEW YORK

HARPER & BROTHERS

PUBLISHERS

TO ARMY BRIDES

of

TODAY and TOMORROW

Library of Congress catalog card number: 53-11859

CONTENTS

ACKNOWLEDGMENTS

HUNDREDS of Army wives and many officers have been gracious and interested enough since this book was first written in 1941 to contribute current information over the years in order to keep each edition up to date. For this present edition, acknowledgments are particularly extended to Brigadier General Frank Dorn, Office of the Chief of Information, Department of the Army, to Major Vernon Pizer, and to Major Edwin C. Gibson of the Magazine and Book Branch of the Public Information Division.

I also wish to express my sincere appreciation to Captain G. Keith, SigC (MI) U. S. A., for his interest and helpful suggestions and for reviewing certain parts of the manuscript.

I am particularly grateful to Mrs. Charles Barth, Official Cadet Hostess at the U. S. Military Academy, and to Major George S. Pappas for reviewing the chapter on West Point.

I am also indebted to the Armed Forces Hostess Association for giving such a realistic picture of the modern Army wife's lot in Washington and overseas.

I wish to thank the Heraldic Branch, Office of the Quartermaster General, and the Military Attaché Branch of G-2 for giving particular chapters a final check.

Acknowledgments are also extended to:

Maj. Gen. Arthur W. Pence and Mrs. Pence	Capt. Hugh O'Brien
	Capt. W. H. Teal
Brig. Gen. Marshall S. Carter	Mrs. W. E. Crist
Brig. Gen. Eugene McGinley	Miss Patricia Donegan
Col. Richard H. Agnew	Mrs. E. F. Harden
Col. Albert R. Dreisbach	Mrs. E. R. Heiberg
Col. W. J. Haberer	Mrs. W. A. Huntsberry
Chaplain (Lt. Col.) Wayne Hunter	Mrs. E. M. Lewiecki
Col. Lowell Knight	Mrs. Edgar Riquier
Col. W. Douglas Paschall and Mrs. Paschall	Mrs. C. W. Sampson
	Mrs. Edward H. Underhill
Col. Rodham C. Routledge	Mrs. Joseph Walyus

My sincere appreciation to Evelyn R. Collins, my secretary, for her co-operation, excellent typing, and fine secretarial assistance.

NANCY BRINTON SHEA

INTRODUCTION

THE United States Army today is a dynamic organization constantly adapting itself to changing world conditions. Political, economic, and sociological forces at home and abroad are influencing its character to such an extent that I feel this third revised edition of *The Army Wife* might best be presented in loose-leaf form.

While yielding to certain demands for practicality and streamlining, however, the Army maintains important and vital traditions as the Senior Service. Therefore, it is to the interest of every Army wife to keep informed as to her responsibilities and to be alert to changes.

Since you selected this book to read, I presume you are already an Army wife or at least a potential Army wife. If so, you must be prepared to meet all types of women who are the wives of our fine American men serving as career soldiers in many lands. You will also share with foreign-born brides the pleasures and obligations of military life.

Our modern Army is a senior partner among the peace-loving nations of the world who are joined against alien and hostile barbarism. Its mission is primarily one of training and maintenance, working more in tactical units and spread less thinly than before. In short, it is an Army again . . . in the more generally accepted sense of the term.

THE ARMY TEAM

You are wondering where you fit into the over-all picture in national and mutual defense and just what part you play on the National Security Team as an Army wife. I assure you that you are not only a significant factor in your husband's career but an important though "silent" member of the team. In these times great emphasis is placed on "teamwork," be it in production, industry, or national defense. It is the keynote of success in all military planning. In the individual Service family, again it is teamwork and loyalty between a military man and his wife that spell success.

vii

The career soldier and his wife as well as the career officer and his wife have definite responsibilities as members of the Army team. Your first loyalty, of course, is to your country. Your second is to the parent unit—your battalion, regiment, division, corps, and Army—and the commanders under whom your husband serves, through the entire chain of command to the Commander-in-Chief, the President of the United States. You will soon find that unity is the theme of this book and the key word is teamwork.

In our new defense system there can be no sovereignty among the integral parts. Neither the Army, Navy, nor Air Force can operate as a completely independent unit. Each is part of the First Team . . . the National and International Champions of Western Civilization.

To Army Brides

This book is addressed to Army brides and to women young in the Service. It is not intended to be a handbook of etiquette except as certain social amenities may be treated differently in the Service. Certainly any young woman of today who has had a normal home background can manage her own household affairs effectively. This is merely a book of common sense as related to Army life which is written in the hope of saving you from learning by the frequently painful trial-and-error method, as the author was forced to do on occasion. I have attempted to give the best of my experience, understanding, and love for the Service to those young women.

There are undoubtedly some mistakes in these pages, but inasmuch as the information is not official and it is presented as a guide to the brides of today and tomorrow, perhaps the errors are not too serious. In matters of etiquette, it may be a question of opinion. If you do not agree, continue as your best judgment may direct. The author in no way wishes to set herself up as an authority. The purpose here is to offer simple, friendly advice, and at this moment I intend to take another liberty:

"Judy O'Grady and the Colonel's Lady"

You will recall that Mr. Kipling once wrote, "Judy O'Grady and the Colonel's Lady are sisters under the skin." Certainly, all Army wives are sisters . . . so in this book I shall include *all* wives—the wife of the Pfc, the NCO wife, and the officer's wife—always mindful that there is *no rank* among wives except by virtue of their husbands' position. The same situation exists in the business world, and in social and diplomatic spheres. Good taste, respect, and sound behavior apply everywhere.

It is always easier for me to have a fictional character in my books, someone to whom I can talk directly; so in this book I will need two characters: Connie, the enlisted man's wife, and Peggy, the officer's wife.

I now introduce you to Peggy Carver, whom some of you already know. She was Lieutenant Theodore Worthing's fiancée in my first book just before Pearl Harbor. She became his Army bride.

And to Constance "Connie" Haigwood, the fiancée of Corporal Anthony Tennant (Tony), U. S. A., and the daughter of Master Sergeant John Haigwood and Mrs. Haigwood.

Army More Democratic

It is no longer possible to tolerate even the implication that Army life is merely an officer's life, and I am much embarrassed that I did not include the soldier's wife in my first book in 1941, just before World War II. This mistake was brought home to me forcibly by a letter I received from the mother of a Harvard graduate whose son enlisted immediately following Pearl Harbor. Having advanced to the grade of sergeant, he married, and his mother presented the bride with a copy of *The Army Wife*, only to find the book was written exclusively for the wives of commissioned officers.

I had a definite guilt complex about this shortcoming, which, in a woman's way, I relieved with tears until my husband became exasperated and suggested I write to the Sergeant's mother, return the price of the book, then promise to write a special book for the soldier's wife. Since 1941 I have been mulling this over, rather a ticklish point, and in 1951, when I wrote *The Air Force Wife*, I included the airman's wife. It worked; the airmen's wives are pleased and I intend to follow the same procedure in this book.

Relations Between Officers and Enlisted Men

Before World War II there was a marked and definite line of demarcation between commissioned and noncommissioned personnel, and in the interests of discipline and leadership this will probably never change. Certainly, fraternizing between officers and enlisted men is never encouraged, as the Army demands certain formalities in officer-soldier relationships. To some, this is an outmoded carryover from the so-called "Middle ages," when an officer was appointed from the aristocracy or landowning squirearchy to lead his "common-ers" into battle. There was a rigid and real distinction between the lord of the manor and the worker then.

American democracy today, however, is a far cry from this medie-val military concept based upon heredity and economic power. Ab-rogating the pomp and privileges of a landed aristocracy, we adhere to the basic principles of a free society which encourages every man to attain a place of distinction by means of hard work and merit alone—not because he was "to the manner born." Education is a help, but *experience* is even more important, and it must not be for-gotten that the spirit of public service, involving certain extra obliga-tions as an American, is the backbone of the Army commission.

The Army wife can point with pride to the fact that her husband is a member of the most democratic army the world has ever known. But at the same time she must recognize that an army is built on dis-cipline and that true discipline demands that there be a definite line of demarcation between officers and enlisted men.

It is for this reason that Department of the Army policy requires officers to wear distinctive insignia, to live apart from the men, and to confine their social contacts in the Army to other officers. Those who call this policy undemocratic fail to recognize the basic principle upon which the dividing line between commanders and subordinates is based.

Everything a commander does is potentially related to some future moment of crisis, when his decision, and his men's readiness to act on it, will mean success or failure for the whole team. This decision may well mean ordering his men to risk their lives, if necessary, in the service of their country. Common sense therefore requires that between the commander who must make this decision and the men who risk their lives to carry it out a final line of separation must be preserved to insure fair and impartial treatment. The basis of this separation is the same in peace and in war, in garrison and on the battlefield, for the commander's responsibility is continuing and all-embracing—it is not one that can be turned off and on in an emer-gency.

Most men instinctively understand and appreciate this line of rea-soning. In fact, they have little respect for the officer who attempts to curry favor by undue familiarity.

This does not mean that the commander-leader is not close to his men. On the contrary, he makes a continuous effort to be on warm and friendly terms with them all; he is their parent, brother, and father-confessor. This relationship is personal, frank, mutual, and cordial, but it is a relationship based on sympathetic understanding rather than social familiarity.

RELATIONS BETWEEN OFFICERS' WIVES AND ENLISTED MEN'S WIVES

I feel it is important early in your married life, Connie, that you, as an enlisted man's wife, understand and accept the relationship, too. Most Army men instinctively understand, so get Tony to present his side of the system to you first. There is nothing snobbish or anti-social about it; so from the beginning be careful not to be supersensitive or to carry the proverbial "chip on your shoulder"! There will be times when you as an NCO wife will work with officers' wives on various post projects; simply be co-operative, polite, and gracious.

One important point to remember is: there is no rank among Army wives, yet a junior wife should always show deference to older women, particularly the commanding officer's wife and the ranking sergeant's wife. This does not mean that you should "bootlick," or that you should have an inferiority complex when dealing with officers' wives. Simply be natural and you will be well received.

ARMY LIFE FROM A WOMAN'S VIEWPOINT

When a young woman finds herself carried away by the glamour of the Service and the charm and dazzle of the uniform, she should pull up short a moment and ask herself a few questions: Will I like Army life? Will we be poor, or fairly well off? Can we raise a family properly on Army pay? What financial security can we look forward to? What are the advantages and disadvantages of Army life?

Of course I realize that it is a foolish waste of time even to suggest such questions to romantic youth; yet they are highly important questions, and much unhappiness might be averted by a young officer or soldier and his fiancée if they could bring themselves to face facts before the wedding day. It is far better to break engagement ties than to suffer and eventually break marriage bonds because the Army wife could not adjust to life in the Service.

When a young woman asks herself, "Will I like Army life?" the answer depends solely upon her individual tastes. If she is spoiled and cannot bear to be separated from her girlhood friends and home, then she won't like Army life. If she enjoys travel, a life in which one moves often and sometimes on a few hours' notice, if she is able to adjust herself to conditions and take whatever comes with a smile, then she will be happy!

"Will we be poor or fairly well off?" You will be poor in this world's goods, my dear. A second lieutenant's base pay is the princely sum of $222.30 per month, and the highest salary that he may ever draw, if he rises to the exalted grade of lieutenant general, is $963.30 minus income tax. A sergeant's base pay is $145.24 per month, while a first sergeant receives $206.39. A corporal draws $122.30. According to the present pay scale, the remuneration may not appear very attractive; however, Army people figure the rewards of service by other standards. There are liberal allowances for quarters when not furnished in kind, and medical attendance, when available, is free for all military families. Since everyone knows to the penny exactly what each grade draws in the way of salary, there is no competitive spending or dressing. It isn't necessary to keep up with the Jones family, and show or pretense by officers and their families is definitely frowned upon in the Army. An officer's commission gives him and his family entree into the best society—something that no amount of money can buy, in some instances, in civil life. Don't expect your life to be a bed of roses or sheltered ease, but with it all there is something mighty attractive about being a "camp follower."

"Can we raise a family on Army pay?" It has been done, and is being done every day, though it takes good management and cooperation. Judging by the great numbers of children on Army posts and those traveling on government transports, one might conclude that the Army is quite prolific.

"What financial security can we anticipate?" Everyone, even youth, is concerned today with old-age security. In the Army a retirement system is offered whereby an officer is retired for life with annual pay equal to 2½ per cent of the annual active duty base and longevity pay of the rank with which he retired, multiplied by the number of years of service credited for longevity pay purposes, but not to exceed a total of 75 per cent of such annual active duty base and longevity pay. An officer is retired at the age of sixty (if in the permanent grade of brigadier general). After more than thirty years' active service, an officer may request retirement. In case of physical incapacity for active service, due to accident or ill health, an officer is retired at an amount equal to the monthly base pay of the highest recognized rank satisfactorily held under a permanent or temporary appointment multiplied by (a) a number equal to the number of years of active service multiplied by 2½ per cent or by (b) the percentage of disability. In either case, however, disability retirement pay shall not exceed 75 per cent of the base pay. If an officer dies while on the active list, his widow will receive a small pension.

An enlisted person can retire after twenty years' service at 50 per cent of the base pay for the grade held at that time; after ten years in the Army Reserve he will be advanced to the highest grade held while on active duty and will then receive 50 per cent of his base pay —a very sound investment indeed!

"What are the advantages and disadvantages of Army life?" Travel is considered one of its advantages. Interesting tours of duty in Alaska, Panama, Puerto Rico, Hawaii, Britain, France, Japan, Germany, Austria, and special details to other countries, with their attendant travel opportunities, are broadening, and the average Army wife welcomes Foreign Service orders. Social entree in Allied countries and association with cultured groups at home are definite assets to both officers and noncommissioned officers. To some, the Service offers the attraction of a disciplined and orderly life.

The disadvantages all seem to hinge on Army pay and the expenses and discomforts of frequent moves. However, the lot of the average Army wife appeared very attractive to a student officer at Fort Leavenworth one day as he looked up gloomily from a map problem over which he had been laboring. Over in the corral he could see his wife and a group of Army women jumping their horses in preparation for a scheduled horse show. Looking out the front window, he enviously watched another group of Army wives starting a golf tournament, and from the tennis courts beneath his windows he could hear the score being called by feminine voices. Mumbling in his beard, and settling down to the grind of studying, he was heard to murmur: "Oh, God! In the next incarnation, please let me come back to Fort Leavenworth as an Army wife."

The average Army wife of even ten years' service has truly lived. There were the war years when she followed her husband from post to post, often living in small overcrowded towns under the most trying rental conditions. Next, the months of loneliness that stretched into years of anxiety, particularly if he was missing in action. Then the harrowing months when later news came that he was interned as a prisoner of war.

An Army wife needs to have executive qualities, because even in peacetime the husband is often away. Not only must she be able to run the household but she must make major decisions and be responsible for the children. She is the most important executive officer her husband will ever have.

Army women laugh a lot, and they have a good deal of fun, believe it or not. Few of them would change places with their sisters who have permanent homes, definite systems, and plans of schooling for their children—although it must be admitted that the "stable, well-ordered life" looks mighty attractive to the Army woman upon occasion.

It took a keen sense of humor to live graciously in a cantonment building at Fort Sill, Oklahoma, ironically known as "The Love Nest." It may not still be occupied today by struggling young lieutenants and their brides, but on a sizzling summer day that I remember, with the thermometer climbing to 115 degrees and an Army range in full steam in the seven-by-nine boxlike kitchen, the china doorknobs grew so hot that I had to use a pot holder to open the kitchen door.

Older Army women love to get together and reminisce. They tell about certain transport trips and rehash old stories of former good times. Each storyteller is a story in herself. One will relate tales of the old days in Mindanao, when Army families lived in nipa shacks. Bordering the jungle the nipa houses were built on stilts, and at night the sentries made their inspections with lanterns, peering under the quarters and hoping not to find two fiery eyes staring out at them. Unfriendly Moros were a menace not to be taken lightly, either. Life was filled with adventure. You may be assured that these thrilling stories lose nothing in dramatic quality by repetition. One well-known story of the old days in the Philippines shows the dependence of enlisted men's and officers' families on each other.

It was the morning after a sleepless night caused by an abscessed tooth. What does a lieutenant's wife do about such things when no dentist is available? Why, she tells the lieutenant, of course, and he tells the sergeant and the sergeant gets a corporal, five privates, four mules, and an old escort wagon. A big wicker chair full of pillows is fastened in the wagon, and the lieutenant's wife, with her tiny baby, is lifted into the chair. The grinning corporal establishes himself on the ruthless edge of the wagon side in order that he may hold the paper Chinese umbrella over the Madonna in the chair. The men are all strapped about with 45's and plenty of ammunition. The whole company of soldiers turns out in the tiny quadrangle shouting "The Spirit of '49." Amidst cheers and laughter, off the "uncovered" wagon swings, jouncing its way up the trail to the base hospital twenty-five miles away.

The average Army woman of thirty years' service at the side of her husband has lived an ever changing role, with or without servants, with or without social contacts, with or without conveniences, with or without her personal friends, and nearly always financially overburdened. She has lived in foreign countries, in small towns and in large cities, on tiny posts out in the great open spaces and on huge posts near metropolitan centers. She knows firsthand the rigors of an Alaskan winter, the humidity and heat of a Panamanian summer. She has been through disaster: fire, flood, tornado, typhoon, and earthquake.

She prefers the luxury of an electric range, but she can manage about as well (with a few epithets) with green wood and a smoking G.I. stove or a campfire. She is equally at home in a general's set of quarters or a Quonset hut. Even in the Quonset she manages a feminine touch by making up a comfortable bed, and ten to one she will have thought to include a mosquito net, and will hang up a mirror and not forget to set the alarm clock.

She can play the Lady or Judy O'Grady . . . she can eat hamburgers from a counter at bus stops or caviar with the general . . . she can entertain foreign diplomats as easily as intimate friends . . . she enjoys travel, whether by freighter or clipper, by bus or streamliner . . . she is at home eating sukiyaki in Tokyo or dancing the rhumba in Rio. In other words, she is a cosmopolite.

Tension and nervous strain there are in this kaleidoscopic life, and much to discourage and dismay, but at least there aren't many dull moments. The Army woman learns that she must meet each new situation with philosophy, and that adaptability to change strengthens her fiber, stimulates her mentality, and satisfies something in her soul. She remains young at heart; her life is replete with contacts with all types of people, and she is interesting, vital, and fulfilled as a woman.

An Army wife is almost as much in the service of the government as her husband, because she plays an integral part in representing the social and personal aspects of Army life. A well-qualified wife is a great boon to her husband, and although there have been some disasters when wives were not up to what was expected of them, in many cases wives have greatly enhanced the value of their husbands to the government. The government really gets the full-time service of two people for the pay of one. The wife is definitely expected to pull her weight in the boat and in every way to uphold the fine traditions of the Army.

There is something about the Senior Service, some indefinable thrill, that gets into the blood stream, and despite all the trying features and disadvantages the true-blooded Army wife yearns for the uniqueness of post life. The crispness and polish of uniformed men, the haunting sounds of a bugle at night, the excitement of a parade or of an athletic contest, the feeling of pride for her unit, the comfort and security of a noble family at work and at play—all these are hers.

I have greatly enjoyed writing and rewriting these pages about Army life—a subject dear to my heart—and I offer this book to young Army wives of today and tomorrow in the hope that they may become better acquainted with the aims and ideals of the United States Army, in which their husbands have the honor of serving.

NANCY BRINTON SHEA

Chapter I

ARMY ESPRIT DE CORPS

T HE Army has always recognized the important part a wife plays in her husband's career, but since World War II definite steps have been taken by the Department of the Army to "integrate" wives and to make them feel that they "belong." It is important that Army wives today realize that they have a large stake in their husbands' military career and that by their attitude, interest, and adaptability they also play an important part in our national and international security. We are no longer mere "camp followers"!

America is and always has been a peace-loving nation, but we are today living in dangerous and serious times. In olden times only men fought wars, but modern warfare is no respecter of persons, as many Army and Navy wives realized at Pearl Harbor. We are moving into a new era; many changes are necessary and the Army has raised its sights!

MORALE OF ARMY WIVES

The word *morale*, borrowed from the French, denotes a quality prevalent in every successful military organization. It is a spirit built up in the affections, mind, and heart of the individual who is an active leading member in a favored Service. An Army wife is proud of her husband and of the uniform he has earned the right to wear.

Many schools today are taking the long view in offering American girls courses in "G.I. Wifehood" based on the premise that most of today's college women will marry men who are or who will be connected with the Armed Forces. Exploratory courses are being tried so that potential Service brides and WACS-, WAFS- or WAVES-to-be may get a foretaste of what life holds for them if they marry a man in the Service, a veteran, or one who is going to serve.

The co-eds study the history of the Service, rates and rank, base pay and the "extras," see films ranging from drill to combat, and hear lectures by regular officers from the four Services, the Army, Navy, Air Force, and Marine Corps. This non-credit course is de-

signed to teach military wives-to-be something about our Defense
establishment and to break down prejudices against women in the
Service.

This is wise preparation, for future Army wives need to be well
equipped to adapt themselves to a life of constant movement.
Whether social, intellectual, domestic, or athletic activities occupy
the days, keeping busy serves as a buffer against the tension that accompanies Service life. At first, you may regard the regimented or
over-organized structure of life on an Army post as trying, but it
has its psychological worth in cushioning the absences of a mate
away on maneuvers or attending a school where dependents are not
sent, and various other separations which are inevitable.

You are just like every other Army wife if you have spent a sleepless night now and then worrying while your husband is away, living
through imaginary tornadoes, typhoons, and what not; you may even
conjure up a rival in the form of his secretary or the last pretty
visitor on the post. You aren't a normal woman if you haven't worried over many things that have never come to pass. Dawn usually
brings relief from these unjustified anxieties, and of course no real
Army wife would ever think of admitting them to herself, much less
to her husband. It just isn't done.

THE OLD ARMY

I very much like the summing up of the "old Army" by Susie-
Lane Hoyle Armstrong, the wife of an Artillery colonel. She is de-
scended on both sides from families that have been in the Regular
Army for five generations. She has summed up today's challenge to
new Army wives in these words, which appeared in the *Combat
Forces Journal*:

"I do not weep for the 'old Army,' much as I loved it. Each generation is confronted in turn by a newer generation which refers
nostalgically to the 'good old days' their seniors thought so revolutionary! Changes have come as our horizons have broadened, and the
new way is almost always an improvement. But the fine traditions
that form the intangible core of a soldier's career will never vanish."

It is the fine traditions on which the United States Army is built
that make it an honor to serve as an enlisted man or an officer today.
It is also an honor to be an Army wife. You are not only a part but
an important part of the oldest of the military Services. While no
officer, NCO, or enlisted man was ever "made in the Army" by his

wife, many men have been hurt and others helped by their wives
and their attitude toward the Service.

Wives Form a Cross Section, Too

Perhaps no other profession draws such a cross section of wives
as the military. There will be wives with diplomatic and high social
background alongside wives who were former waitresses, beauty operators, secretaries, models, teachers, salesgirls, dancing instructors,
check girls, and high-powered executives. There will also be a sprin-
kling of talent in the form of artists, wives with dramatic ability,
musicians, writers, and of course a large percentage of wives who
were former Army "brats," Navy "juniors," or Air Force "fledglings" who "know all the answers."

Another group will be those from other countries who have married American soldiers and officers. I know of no finer work in international relations that you as an Army wife can perform than to
live amicably with them, sharing your common interests and continuously learning more about their viewpoints.

With most of these young women the chief obstacle, of course, is
our difficult (but magnificent) English language with its regional
dialects, rich idioms, and popular colloquialisms. It must seem next
to impossible to them at first, but once they learn to express themselves, all other things seem to fall into line. These girls laugh a lot,
perhaps to hide their shyness. But underneath, there seems to be a
wistful longing for people who speak their language, who understand their thinking, and who respect their customs and traditions.

Can you imagine the situation reversed and yourself the bride of
a military man in a foreign land, trying to speak his language,
whether French, Swedish, or Japanese; learning, accepting, and being
loyal to the customs and ideals of his country? Their adjustments are
many, but these girls have a great deal to give of themselves and of
the lands from which they came. Let us be kind, courteous, and
understanding, and to all brides in the Army from other countries,
Welcome!

"Judge Not That Ye Be Not Judged"

Under no circumstances, as you well know, does a well-bred person criticize or belittle another's background, birthplace, home environment, or educational advantages. This is in particularly poor taste
if done by the person who "*feels* superior." This type of behavior

comes under the classification of snobbery, and the person who is so unkind is a snob of the first degree. Remember also that a person who brags openly of his underprivileged environment and lack of breeding is also a snob—on the other end of the stick.

I once heard a kindly senior officer's wife give a bride a most beautiful piece of advice, which we could all take to heart. Mrs. Chaney worded it so tactfully that it did not sound like advice at all. She said she did not wonder why this one or that did not do what everyone else did, because it occurred to her that perhaps they might have a dependent aunt or grandmother, or some other hidden expense, which could not be mentioned because of the pride of the person involved, and the additional load made it impossible for them to do too much socially.

I mention this for a definite reason: Later in the book the chapter on entertaining mentions the importance of returning one's social obligations, and I wish to go on record right here that *it is not necessary to return obligations in kind.* Do only what you can afford to do comfortably and conscientiously, but *do something* in some way to show your appreciation.

No one expects a young couple to entertain in social affairs comparable to those given by senior officers and their wives. For instance, a formal dinner given by your commanding officer may be returned by means of an informal buffet supper, a picnic or wiener roast. It isn't what you do; it is the spirit in which you return your obligations that is important. This is what senior officers and their wives appreciate. Don't forget, every general was once a second lieutenant and many generals came up through the ranks from privates. They understand your problems. If it is any comfort to you, senior officers have heavy obligations and sometimes financial problems including hidden expenses, even as you and I.

Never go into debt in order to entertain, or do without something you really need in order to give a party. Both are silly in the extreme, though I suppose we have all done the latter in order to appear popular with our friends or to balance the family budget.

On the other side of the ledger, or if you are in the money, never be critical of the way the other person repays his obligations to you. Give him the benefit of the doubt. A young couple may have to make certain personal sacrifices in order to have you in for even a simple supper. Accept what they offer as graciously as if they had invited you to a formal dinner.

Today, most people are broad-minded about both smoking and drinking. However you feel about it, "judge not" one way or the other. It is as much of an individual problem for the other fellow as it is for you. To judge him or comment on his behavior marks you as provincial. In the final analysis, be kind—in both your thought and your comment!

Adjust to Your Environment

Army men, when they propose marriage to the girl of their dreams, should be careful to make it clear that *duty* comes first—before family, home ties, or anything else. The guiding principle of West Point is: Duty—Honor—Country! Whether your hero told you that in so many words or not, it is true. Actually, you wouldn't have it different. As a famous soldier-poet wrote to his mistress in the seventeenth century, when apparently she complained at his irregular hours and unscheduled departures: "I could not love thee, Dear, so much, loved I not honor more!"

According to the law of averages, desirable stations are bound to be interspersed among the poor ones; so make the best of whatever comes without assuming a martyrlike attitude—and above all, don't secretly blame your husband. If a trailer should be your lot, make up your mind to have the most livable, most attractive trailer on the post. Don't waste time being miserable because Sergeant Brown, who has six children and whom your husband ranks, is assigned the quarters you feel are rightfully yours. Certainly, never show your feelings or make remarks to or about Mrs. Brown. Learn to adjust yourself and be adult.

Also, avoid feeling that your husband does all the work in the company, gets more than his share of K.P. or week-end details away from home. This is something you will be wise to accept in addition to keeping your feelings to yourself, even if it be true.

A smart wife tries to soothe her husband's indignation rather than inflame it, and is careful never to repeat his criticisms, since he may change his mind the next day or at a later date. If your husband is the commanding officer—or, for that matter, if he isn't—it's bad to carry tales of abuse or chitchat from other wives. Treat such matters confidentially.

Perhaps one of the most important problems in adjustment, requiring all the love, patience, and tact of which a wife is capable, is concerned with promotion. Now that the selective system of promotion is in, it is up to a wife to help her husband over the bad time, should he be passed over. Maybe he wasn't in the right place at the right time; perhaps someone more experienced was selected for the job and his turn will come later. Regardless of the reason, a wife should try to keep her husband from feeling bitter about the system. It is very important for a man to keep a good opinion of himself, and his wife's opinion is most important of all to him. If she feels the situation isn't too bad, neither will he!

Ask yourself: Am I adjustable or am I thinking along rear-vision-mirror lines? Socially, life on and off a post for Army personnel has again taken on the status of courteous and gracious living becoming to people of your station in civilian life. Neckties and blouses or coats are worn in clubs and at home; of course your husband does not receive callers with his coat off or sit in the yard in his undershirt or T-shirt.

Club parties and dinner dances are not USO parties; a husband dances with his hostess, his wife, his dinner partner on his right, the guest of honor, the lady on his left, and other lady guests. It's high time to realize that this is not the South Pacific during World War II.

If you are unhappy, your husband is eventually going to be unhappy too. It is not wise, even in a jocular manner, to complain continually about the Service, and it is extremely dangerous to discuss Service gripes with civilians. Outside of the Service, you will notice that your own social status is a thing apart from civilians and that your husband's conversation carries considerable authority, as does yours. To complain to this group about the Army . . . well, just don't. Complaining suggests a lack of restraint, self-control, plain common sense, and maturity. Finally, no good comes to your husband, as such talk reflects on his happiness in his work—and on his choice of a chatterbox for a wife.

A happy, busy wife who shows interest in the Officers' Wives' Club or NCO Wives' Club soon finds herself surrounded by congenial friends. Her mornings may be spent working at the blood bank or on the hospital committee. In the afternoon, it is always easy to form a golf foursome or make up a table for bridge or canasta.

I feel that an Army wife should be interested in what is going on at the post. She need not neglect her home or children, but she should learn the names of key people and what they do and, if feasible and possible, get to know them personally. In this way she can become an alert, well-informed, and well-integrated Army wife.

YOUR UNWRITTEN EFFICIENCY REPORT

Some twenty years ago I had the pleasure of hearing a retiring general officer, Major General Ernest Hinds, give a most interesting talk to a group of Army women. The subject was "The Unwritten Efficiency Report." He pointed out that as an officer chooses the military career as his profession, so does a young woman choose a career in the Service when she becomes engaged to an Army officer.

There are a few sad examples in the Army today of officers who should be holding key commands but who have been passed over. Sometimes the fault lies at the wife's door! If she is the too ambitious type, or the flighty, fourth-Martini, talkative type, she may have hurt her husband's career permanently. Of course, she never meant to, but this is her reputation and unfiled efficiency report. The Army seems to go on the assumption of the old song "Twenty Million Frenchmen Can't Be Wrong."

SOURCES OF OFFICER MATERIAL

As a bride and newcomer into military circles, perhaps you wonder about the officers, their backgrounds, and how they obtained their commissions in the Army.

In our democracy any ambitious and military-minded citizen who is qualified and can meet the prerequisites may compete to win a commission in the Armed Forces.

Commissioned officers for the Regular Army are obtained from:
1. USMA   The United States Military Academy
2. ROTC   Reserve Officers' Training Corps
3. OCS   Army Officers' Candidate School

Others who may become commissioned officers in the Regular Army:

Enlisted men and warrant officers of the Army
Officers on extended active duty
Distinguished graduates of OCS courses
Distinguished graduates of Senior ROTC
Civilians qualified for appointment in Army Medical Service
(doctors, dentists)

Individuals qualified for appointment in Judge Advocate General Department (lawyers)
Individuals qualified for appointment as chaplains
Individuals possessing essential technological background

RESERVE OFFICERS' TRAINING CORPS
AND
THE IMPORTANCE OF ROTC

By far the majority of officers today are commissioned from the ROTC, and both the Army and Air Force depend on ROTC for the vast bulk of their officer corps. In the past, as you probably know, when the Army was a comparatively small organization, it depended almost entirely on the Military Academy for its officer corps, a group it was admirably able to supply.

When the United States declared war on Germany in World War I, there was as usual a mad stampede to outfit and train a citizen army. The number of officers was pitifully inadequate to command this huge army. Something had to be done—and fast; colleges were converted into training schools and camps, turning out commissioned officers in three months who were called "90-Day Wonders."

The idea took hold, and received its first impetus in the passing of the National Defense Act of 1916. However, you may be interested to know that the real origin of ROTC dates back to John Milton, 1608–1674, who wrote a *Tractate* or thesis on "The Linking of Preparation for the Arts of War as Well as Peace in the Educational Program." It fits perfectly our present-day theory of the ROTC.

Norwich University

As early as 1819, Norwich University at Northfield, Vermont, became the first civil educational institution to include military training. The university was founded by Captain Alden Partridge, a graduate and former superintendent of West Point. Lieutenant General E. H. Brooks, U. S. A., is a graduate of Norwich University.

Virginia Military Institute

Virginia Military Institute, founded in 1829 at Lexington, Virginia, was the second civil educational institution to include military instruction in its curriculum. It was founded by Colonel Claudius Crozett, a West Pointer who had served as a professor at the United

States Military Academy. General of the Army George Catlett Marshall and General Thomas Handy are graduates of V.M.I.

The Citadel

Next was The Citadel, Charleston, South Carolina, which was founded in 1842 by the South Carolina legislature. First head of the school was Major William Fair Graham, a graduate of West Point. Major General E. F. Witsell, former Adjutant General of the Army, and others are among The Citadel's distinguished graduates.

A. and M. College of Texas

Texas Agricultural and Military College is the largest military college in the United States. It turns out trained officers in a steady stream and has served the state and nation with distinction, in addition to supplying technicians and engineers required for our continued industrial and agricultural might.

The Morrill Act of 1862—Land-Grant Colleges

On July 2, 1862, President Lincoln signed the Morrill Act, commonly known as the "Land Grant Act," which gave a real boost to the concept of combining military and conventional education. This act provided for the endowment, support, and maintenance of colleges where military science and tactics were part of the curriculum. Many of our largest colleges and universities today were founded as a result of this legislation.

Today, over 250 colleges offer Army-operated ROTC courses. The Air Force ROTC courses are given in 187 colleges and universities, while naval training is operated in 52 colleges.

How it works: College students are enrolled in the basic course upon meeting prescribed mental and physical standards. After completing a basic course, students may apply for enrollment in the advanced course, which is selective. Those who complete the advanced course of two years are obliged to accept a Reserve commission. Resignation is possible at any time before graduation but the student who resigns must return all monies received up to that date. Students receive uniforms and textbooks. Those in the advanced course receive a stipulated per diem pay, and they also receive pay at the six-weeks' summer camp.

Honor ROTC graduates may be offered appointment as officers in the Regular Army.

The Reserve Officer

The end product of the ROTC program is the Reserve officer, that ubiquitous young man who receives a bachelor's degree and a Reserve second lieutenant's commission at the same time. After laying aside cap and gown, he goes out to lead his platoon in remote regions of the world, returning to civilian life after two years, considerably matured and often still wearing his gold bars. Reserve officers did a splendid job in World War II, and many were recalled to active duty the second time for Korean service. They have reflected admirably our oldest military tradition of the citizen-soldier or "territorial officer," who is prepared to leave his hearth and office at a moment's notice in order to fulfill the obligation of his commission.

To the Reserve officer and his wife go some of the benefits of Regular Army status and all of the responsibilities. Promotion is generally slower because his inactive period is lost time as far as "date of rank" is concerned. Added expense for uniforms, moving, the insecurity of his reserve status, and the necessity for readjustment to civil life can cause some tension and anxiety to the wife who is not used to quick changes and who prefers domestic security to travel. Usually a young college girl, she is loyal to the American Army tradition by performing her mission as an officer's wife, wherever her husband goes.

Service Academies

Both the Army and the Navy maintain their own academies. (Until the Air Force establishes its own Air Academy, cadets will continue to be trained at the Military Academy and the Naval Academy as in the past.) The United States Naval Academy is located at Annapolis, Maryland.

The United States Military Academy

The United States Military Academy, West Point, New York, over the years has been the primary source for Regular Army officers and even today sets the standard which most other military schools in the United States follow. Perhaps you noted that many West Point graduates founded or headed the early land-grant colleges, and West Pointers, owing to their rigid training in the military, in diplomacy, and in military courtesy, are in great demand as ROTC instructors.

The United States Military Academy was established in 1802 at West Point, New York, by the Congress of the United States. Its mission is to instruct and train the corps of cadets so that each graduate will have the qualities and attributes essential to his progressive and continued development throughout a lifetime career as an officer in the Regular Army.

The Military Academy is under the direct supervision and control of the Department of the Army. The corps of cadets is divided into four classes. Foremost among the qualities which the Military Academy instills in its graduates to distinguish them from others is *character*; the corps operates on the honor system.

Although the Academy was founded on March 16, 1802, its early years were a bit haphazard! It was a very unpopular post, because of the bitter winters, windy and white, and the torrid summers, damp and sticky. (The climate hasn't changed.) The few Artillery troops were both ill clothed and ill housed. The initial law establishing the Military Academy authorized ten cadets and five officers. The system by which the cadets were governed was chaotic, to say the least. Cadets were under scarcely any discipline. Married men were allowed to attend, also partially incapacitated veterans, and all were housed in decrepit barracks with straw mattresses on the floor. Uniforms were a matter of choice. Finally, through lack of interest and appropriations, the cadet strength had dropped to only one cadet and one officer in 1812. About this time, Congress took a hand in reorganizing the Academy on a firmer basis. The Academy began to expand. Nevertheless, education and discipline were still sketchy and there was a bitter rivalry between the cadets and the soldiers on the post. Cadets took perverse delight in throwing pillows from their windows at harassed instructors walking by outside.

"FATHER OF THE MILITARY ACADEMY"

In 1817, a young brevet major, Sylvanus Thayer, arrived at the troubled post to take over. He had hard going at first, as the cadets were difficult to reform and his new rules rankled. They organized a committee to defend what they considered their rights, so the new superintendent, without hesitation, had several cadets tried by court-martial for insubordination. Upon completion of the first case it looked as if the cadets would win their point, as the court-martial de-

cided it had no jurisdiction over the cadets. However, the Attorney
General ruled that cadets were subject to the Articles of War and
were under the jurisdiction of a court-martial. This famed decision
left the Major completely and irrevocably in charge.

Since that time, West Point has carried on in the Thayer tradition.
West Point is rich in tradition. It was built and has grown on a foundation of service to country. Its motto is: Duty—Honor—Country.
It is the cradle of the Eisenhowers and the MacArthurs, the Ridg-
ways and the Twinings, the Gruenthers, the Wymans, and the Mc-
Auliffes, and all West Point graduates who have served the nation
well in peace and war.

From time immemorial, brass buttons and a uniform have made a
strong appeal to the feminine sex, and there is an unforgettable
thrill to being a "cadet girl." You, as a young junior-miss reader,
may still receive that long-hoped-for invitation to spend a week-end
at West Point . . . or if you are already married in the Army, perhaps you will get a vicarious thrill out of my suggestions to our girl,
Peggy, on her first visit to West Point as a cadet girl.

Peggy—As a Cadet Girl

Life is too wonderful for Peggy; the morning mail brought Ted's
invitation for the week end at West Point. But in the next moment
doubt and a million and one questions dart through Peggy's mind.
Clothes, the paramount question in every woman's mind. What does
one wear at West Point? Peggy's bank balance is devastatingly low
at this point, and the trip will have to be carefully planned and managed on a shoestring. Her roommate, she remembers, spent a week end
at West Point, but Sheila is such a vague sort of person.

Upon a second perusal of Ted's letter, she notes that he has made
a reservation for her at the United States Hotel Thayer. Thank
heaven for that, but it sounds expensive. Also, he mentions that Mrs.
Charles Barth is the official hostess, and that she is charming to all
the visiting "femmes." That is at least reassuring, but Peggy's diffi-
culties have just begun.

(From now on, Peggy, I shall talk directly to you.)

To begin with, West Point is rather inaccessible, unless you plan
to motor; incidentally, a car will prove a great convenience during
your visit, as the distances between focal points on the reservation
are quite long. Many visitors prefer to use the modern streamlined
busses of the Mohawk Coach Lines, which operate between New

York City and West Point, via Haverstraw and Bear Mountain State Park. In addition to providing a comfortable, pleasant two-hour trip, they follow a scenic route of great beauty.

The Saturday morning trains, busses, and private cars are filled with week-end visitors: college girls, subdebs, probably a few young careerists. I assure you the competition will be keen; so look your best. First impressions are important and lasting, even among women.

Do not expect your host to meet you, because he will probably be in class or standing inspection. Very probably Ted explained in his letter that, because of official duties, he would not be on hand to welcome you, to help with your suitcase, or to sign you in at the Thayer. Also, he should have mentioned that he cannot be reached by telephone. By letter, the two of you should arrange a meeting place beforehand. If you are staying at the Hotel Thayer, allow yourself time to unpack and press out wrinkles of all the clothes you plan to wear during the week end in order to facilitate quick clothes changing later on. Your cadet host may feel uncomfortable about the fact that he cannot offer you more assistance, but he will appreciate your cheerful willingness to fall in with the system. Above all, realize that punctuality is of utmost importance, so make a definite effort to meet him *on time*.

THE U. S. HOTEL THAYER

The United States Hotel Thayer offers excellent accommodations and actually caters to the young women visitors of cadets. A new wing has been built, of dormitory type, which provides excellent accommodations at very low rates. There are pressing rooms adjoining, where ironing boards and irons are provided. River-view suites with one and two bedrooms, also parlor, plus a Congressional Suite are available. During the week ends from September 1 to June 1 accommodations are in great demand by parents and guests of the cadets. The general public is urged to plan visits to West Point during the weekday period whenever possible. The dining facilities are splendid, featuring superior cuisine and serve at table-d'hôte meals.

The United States Thayer Hotel is owned and operated by the government. It is important to make reservations through the cadet, particularly for June week. Cadets have definite limits in the hotel. These usually include the lobby, reception rooms, and terrace. Cadets are not allowed above the mezzanine and may not use the elevators. Requests for week-end reservations should be submitted at least two weeks in advance by the cadet. Because the space available is not sufficient for the many requests received, reservations for Plebe Christmas and June Week are made on the basis of a drawing held by the cadets.

In the old days all cadet girls were accompanied by their mothers or a personal chaperon, but now it is accepted custom and perfectly proper for young ladies to go to the Military Academy alone. They could not be more thoroughly chaperoned if they were in the charge of Mrs. Grundy herself. While at the hotel they are under the direct supervision of the hotel hostess who lives there. The private homes in Highland Falls, where paying guests are received are conducted according to the highest moral standards. Otherwise the hostesses would lose their source of revenue. There is absolutely no impropriety in going "solo," but naturally it is more pleasant to go with a friend or a group of girls.

Should you have no hotel reservation, go to Grant Hall and present yourself to Mrs. Barth. If you have a hotel reservation, go to the Thayer and get settled. If your cadet has not mentioned a meeting place, he takes it for granted that you will meet him at Grant Hall. Mrs. Barth, the official cadet hostess, will be waiting in her sitting room, which is located on the balcony at Grant Hall. There will be a cadet officer of the guard on duty sitting behind a desk crowded with phones and poop sheets. He will phone your request that Ted meet you in the visitors' room.

If time hangs heavy, take a look at the Tudor Gothic interior of the building. The cadets are very proud of their reception room and they will be flattered at your interest. The room is paneled in oak throughout and the windows are Gothic with diamond-leaded panes. There is an air of elegance and charm in a beautiful setting at West Point, where romance still remains gallant, chivalrous, and real.

CLOTHES

Clothes, the all-important subject! Every woman knows that nothing can make or mar a week end for the feminine sex more completely than clothes—or should I say the lack of suitable clothes? Remember this: The Hudson Valley is very cold in winter and can be very, very hot in summer. Include a pair of comfortable walking shoes, and in winter, galoshes. High-heeled cut-out sandals may be the last word where town cars and taxis are available, but at West

Point, where walking is the style, these will handicap you at the start as a hobbling nuisance with your cadet. Especially so when he is anxious to see the kickoff and you are already late—when seconds count.

Try to limit your luggage to one piece, but if this is impossible, at least reduce your clothes and your luggage to a minimum. Estimate your own strength, because you will probably have to carry your own bags. By careful planning as you pack it is possible to eliminate many nonessentials.

Bear in mind that West Point is conservative; the Academy is steeped in tradition and good taste. Bare midriffs, slacks, shorts, or Bikini bathing suits are not considered good taste. Either motoring or going by train, you will probably wear a tailored suit, carrying a topcoat or a fur coat. Your prettiest evening dress is for the hop on Saturday night, and with it you can wear your fur coat or topcoat as an evening wrap. An evening dress is a necessity, as most of the hops are formal except tea hops. You will find the following notice posted in your room: "Regulations require that all guests taking an active part in the cadet hops at West Point be in evening dress. Any dress which could be worn to a tea dance or any afternoon function is not appropriate for the cadet hops. Your escort will appreciate your cooperation." A guest arriving at Cullum Hall in an inappropriate frock would cause her host embarrassment. In a very tactful and diplomatic manner, with the true West Point touch, he would, no doubt, suggest that they take seats in the balcony and observe the dancers from that vantage point.

Summing up: One sports outfit, one daytime dress appropriate for dining at the hotel on Sunday at noon, and one evening dress should see you through a week end.

THE WEEK END

The average week end will go something like this: Usually there is some athletic event on Saturday afternoon . . . a football game, hockey, or tennis matches; or, upon your first visit, your host may want to show you West Point. In this case you will no doubt wind up on "Flirtation Walk," where, if you are the O.A.O. or "One and Only" girl, you will be escorted down the path leading to the river bank. Here is located the famous "Kissing Rock." It is a huge boulder that seems to be hanging by an eyelash, and the tradition is that, unless you confer upon your escort the kiss for which he has been longing, this great rock will come crashing down and send you both and the whole Military Academy to perdition. Needless to add, the story is a clever invention of cadets! To date, the time-worn Kissing Rock has never toppled, nor has the Military Academy felt the slightest tremor; but not so long ago a young lady toppled off it while surreptitiously watching her sister pledge her troth to a cadet.

When a cadet takes his sister, cousin, or the One and Only of his "wife" or roommate to this romantic spot, he always escorts the fair maid along the upper path of Flirtation Walk, thereby omitting the Kissing Rock. Of course, it is to be assumed that no "drag" would be so bold as to suggest the lower path, no matter how badly she wished to visit the famous rock.

All the girls at West Point are known as "femmes." A particular date, or a girl who has been invited up especially, is called a "drag." You are a "drag"!

If you are particularly affluent, you may wish to invite your cadet to dinner as your guest at the hotel; and you will feel well rewarded as he appears resplendent in his full-dress uniform and white gloves. You can tactfully arrange beforehand to have the dinner check put on your bill. This dinner invitation is not expected or necessary; so do not feel obligated to extend it, especially on your first visit. The cadet mess is exceptionally good, and the men enjoy the food there. Should you wish to ask your cadet to have dinner with you at the hotel Sunday noon, you should ask him in advance, so that he can get a "D.P." (dining permit). Times have changed, cadets are now allowed to carry money, and your cadet may invite you to have dinner with him, if time and the state of his pocketbook permit.

If you plan to meet after dinner, take a taxi to Grant Hall, where Ted will be waiting for you in the visitors' room, to take you to the early movie. It is a short walk, and he will have tickets. After the movie, you will walk to the hop, which will be held either at Cullum Hall or in the old gymnasium. One of the "musts" here is that you go through the receiving line with your escort. In the receiving line there will be the cadet hop manager, one officer and his wife, perhaps more. Your escort gives your name to the cadet hop manager, who in turn introduces you to the officer's wife and to the officer. The hop manager presents you as Miss Carver. Shaking hands with each person in the receiving line, you say, "How do you do?" or "Good evening," and *smile*. It is just as necessary for a girl to give a firm handshake, with character in it, as for a man. Of course, no bone-crushing clasp is considered feminine, even if you are in the lady-golf-pro class. A lady always makes the overture of shaking hands with a gentleman. Again, seniority counts; a drag should not offer her hand first to an older woman. An insincere smile is just as indicative of a person's character as a clammy, cold-fish handshake. Courtesy to elders is a sound social investment. Don't greet your hosts as if they were inanimate objects; neither is it necessary to gush. Simply be natural, pleasant, and sincere.

West Point belongs to the old school, and even at the dances there prevails a dignified, old-fashioned formality which is rather refreshing after the boisterous, rowdy balls given at some colleges today. And don't think that it doesn't set some of the femmes back on their heels! Those whom it sets too far back usually don't receive a second invitation. However, regardless of the strict rules and conventions, girls still love to go to West Point.

The drags themselves, whether they realize it or not, are closely observed. The superintendent and the tactical officers at West Point regard it as important that cadets have the proper feminine associates. The fiancée of the yearling today will probably be the officer's wife of a few years hence. She has a definite responsibility, and she should be socially acceptable. This does not mean that she must be wealthy, a member of the Junior League or a Bryn Mawr M.A.; but it does mean that she must fit in. She must be poised and well versed in the social amenities, able to adjust herself, to conform to conditions, and to be at ease in any situation that may arise. She should know how to dress on all occasions and how to conduct herself at all times as a lady. Her future in Army circles may depend upon the impression she makes as a cadet girl.

West Point cadets are conspicuous for their gallantry, their good manners, and the way they treat every visiting femme, regardless of her looks, her social antecedents, and her deportment. However, the latter must be above reproach. Drinking is taboo, and there are special regulations in regard to smoking.

The old system of program dances is still in vogue at West Point. Each hop consists of twelve dances, and when you arrive at the dance your program already will have been filled out for you by your cadet. Make a point of keeping your engagements and dances, re-

gardless of your interest. Evening hops begin at nine o'clock and
end at midnight. The receiving line is in formation one hour and a
half after the hop begins, and cadets are expected to take their guests
through it. In the Army, punctuality is of utmost importance. No
one is fashionably late. Should you be invited to dinner at seven
o'clock, your cadet will be on hand in plenty of time to escort you
so that you may arrive on the stroke of seven. Not one minute before
or one minute after. Don't bring discredit on your host by forcing
him to be late. *Official Courtesy and Customs of the Service* specifically states that "a gentleman is always strictly punctual at all social
engagements." Ladies must be equally so.

When the hop is over, busses and taxis will be waiting at Cullum
Hall, the gym, or wherever the dance is held, and the approved procedure is that guests take transportation at the hop building. Grant
Hall is closed and deserted at this hour of night, so don't expect to
pick up transportation there. You might as well pile in, and share a
taxi with five or six other visiting girls back to the hotel.

On Sunday morning you may go to church or sleep late, but do
not expect to see Ted until after church. The Catholic services are
at 8:00, 9:00 and 10:00 A.M.; the Protestant services are at 9:00
and 11:00 A.M. Regardless of your religious preference you should
make a point of attending chapel once, at least. It is an inspiring
service.

The stately chapel of gray granite hangs over the Hudson like a
great gray eagle clinging to a cliff. Inside, stone arch after stone
arch follows down the nave in stately procession. Old battle flags,
torn by bullets, stained by rain and mud and blood, tarnished by
time, form a tragic and glorious arch over the lads seated beneath.
It is as if the ghosts of old warriors hovered above with hands out-
stretched in solemn benediction. The stained-glass windows, presented by each graduating class, pierce the gray monotone of the
stone walls like so many rainbow jewels.

The organ peals, that most glorious of all organs, the clear, strong
young voices of over a thousand young men sing, then follows the
low rumble of subdued male voices repeating the Cadet Prayer.

It is an unforgettable service!

Before—and after—Sunday dinner at the hotel, the cadets and
their drags usually gather in the ballroom, where they dance to a
jukebox. Others go to the movie or band concert or visit the

Weapons Room. Some take a walk or a swim, depending on the season.

JUNE WEEK AND GRADUATION

To the ladies who come up in June,
We'll bid a fond adieu,
Here's hoping they'll be married soon,
And join the army, too.
—"Army Blue"

June Week is filled with parades, sometimes as many as three in one day. At any hour of the day, in honor of visiting dignitaries, there will boom forth cannon salutes that almost make you jump out of your skin. The military bands work overtime, and in the evenings dance music issues from Cullum Hall, the gym, and the terrace at the hotel.

Thousands of visitors attend the graduation exercises. The address is always given by some public figure, such as the Secretary of Defense, the Chief of Staff, or even the President. As the diplomas, carrying with them the bachelor of science degree, are given out, in order of rank or class standing, the graduates are cheered and applauded. The honor student, the athletic heroes, and the lowest-ranking man in the class, known as the goat, receive the greatest applause.

If you are one of those who have come prepared with bridal attire for a wedding in the West Point chapel, June Week will take on an added importance and glamour for you. One could wish no more for you and your young lieutenant than that your whole lives should be one continuous June Week!

FOR YOUR INFORMATION

It is no part of the task undertaken in writing this book to provide a chapter on the history of the Army. However, I feel that the young woman who hopes to become or is an Army wife should have some knowledge of the background of that branch of the military Service in which her husband will spend the best years of his life and for which he may even give his life. In accomplishing this worth-while objective she will be wise to read the official *History of the Army,* which is obtainable at any Army library on any of our world-scattered posts.

The more you read and the more you observe and learn about the
Army—its early beginnings, hardships and struggles, its outstanding
heroes, its customs and traditions, the changes of today in modern
warfare, the change-over from horse cavalry to armor, the use of
paratroop divisions—the better-integrated career wife you will become. The Army's record is filled with many brilliant examples of
courage, daring, patience, loyalty, professional skill, and self-sacrificing devotion to duty—a record of which all Americans can be
proud!

The Army is a progressive Service that is always planning for the
future safety and defense of the American nation, a force whose
mission is to defend against attack, and if necessary to annihilate its
attackers.

A Thumbnail Sketch of the United States Army

(Notes from *Troop Topics*, D.A. Nos. 20–144 and 20–159)

The United States Army was founded on June 14, 1775, and is
the oldest element of the Armed Forces. In other words, our Army
is actually older than the United States itself, since it was formed
before we became a free nation on July 4, 1776. It is our Senior
Service, having traditions associated with the best of Britain's most
ancient and distinguished regiments.

General Washington's Army

After much debate, on June 14, 1775, Congress voted to establish
ten rifle companies, the first troops to fight in the name of all the
colonies, and these became our first "regular" Army units. On July 3,
1775, General George Washington took command of the newly-
formed Continental Army. The story of that Army's setbacks and
victories during the next eight years is the story of our beginning as
a free and independent nation.

Washington's command probably never numbered more than
35,000, and there were times when his forces dwindled to less than
4,000 men. There were few professional soldiers, but what was most
trying and troublesome was the enlistment of convicts, Loyalists, prisoners of war and deserters from the enemy. In May, 1777, Washington protested to Congress against the buying of convict servants
by recruiting officers. Such recruits, he declared, were absolutely un-
reliable. The southern States lightheartedly relieved themselves of

criminals by compelling them to serve time as Continental soldiers. Washington spoke repeatedly for six years against the use of deserters and prisoners. But he recognized exceptions in the case of Pulaski's and Armand's independent corps and German volunteers . . . exceptions which lowered the general morale and involved both civil and military authorities in no end of trouble.

(This may or may not have been the reason why "convicts, feeble minded and members of the Army" were denied the right to vote until 1942.)

The defeat of Cornwallis at Yorktown marked the end of fighting in the Revolutionary War. Soon after the fighting stopped, the Continental Congress disbanded most of the Continental Army, authorizing only a force of eighty men—twenty-five privates to guard the stores at Fort Pitt, and fifty-five to guard the stores at West Point. These eighty men are important in our nation's history. Without them we could not say that our Army has served without a break since 1775. The eighty-man Army soon had to be expanded again when new military problems arose with hostile Indians.

WAR OF 1812

The War of 1812, in which freedom of the seas was one of the main issues involved, also included much land fighting. American naval power was established in that war and naval victories like that of Admiral Perry in the Battle of Lake Erie were especially important. One of the decisive land battles, the Battle of New Orleans, was fought two weeks after the treaty ending the war had been signed. This was because of the slowness of communications in those days.

MEXICAN WAR, 1846–1848

In 1846 a dispute arose with the government of Mexico resulting from our annexation of Texas, which had been a part of Mexico before declaring itself a free state. A related dispute was the question of where the border between Mexico and the United States should be located. This was our first war on foreign soil and American troops performed much better than in the Revolution and in the War of 1812. One reason was better leadership and training of the soldiers and their commanders. The United States Military Academy had been founded in 1802, and the Mexican War was the first in which large numbers of experienced professional officers were available among the younger men.

CIVIL WAR, 1861–1865

Between the end of the Mexican War and the beginning of the Civil War, most of our army of 15,000 men were kept busy on western frontiers with Indian campaigns and protecting our settlements. The Civil War was our costliest war in lives and that tragic struggle almost split the United States into two separate countries. Americans now honor the heroes of both sides.

SPANISH-AMERICAN WAR, 1898

In 1898, the American people became sympathetic with the efforts of the people of Cuba to win independence from Spanish rule. The actual declaration of war came when the *Maine*, an American battleship, was blown up in Havana Harbor. In the land and sea battles that followed, Spanish rule in the Americas and Far East ended. Cuba became independent; Spain ceded Puerto Rico, the Philippines and Guam to the United States, and we agreed to pay Spain twenty million dollars. We lost some 5,000 soldiers from disease, mainly yellow fever, against less than 500 killed in enemy action.

In 1900 Major Walter Reed of the Army Medical Corps and twenty enlisted men who served as "guinea pigs" on Major Reed's team proved that yellow fever was carried by a mosquito, and developed the means of stamping it out. Their achievements led indirectly to another accomplishment . . . completion of the Panama Canal.

WORLD WAR I

The first World War began in 1914, but the United States remained neutral until April 6, 1917. We entered the war on the side of the Allied Powers (France, Great Britain, and other countries) opposing Germany and other countries known as the Central Powers. Our three big problems were:

1. The Army had to get enough men to fill the units needed to make up an expeditionary force of four million men.
2. Thousands of officers in addition to Regular and Reserve officers were needed to train the new soldiers. Officer training camps turned out 50,000 lieutenants the first year.
3. The expeditionary force had to be supplied.

Most historians agree that the tide of battle was turned by the entry of our troops in the fight. One hundred twenty thousand soldiers died in this war. An armistice was signed November 11, 1918. Then came twenty years of troubled peace.

In the '20's and '30's our Army got steadily smaller; its weapons and equipment became obsolete; its fighting skill suffered from lack of essential training. The Army lacked money to correct these conditions. By 1939, when Hitler's armies marched into Poland and set off World War II, the United States was not even a third-rate military power.

WORLD WAR II, 1941–1945

The surprise Japanese aerial attack on Pearl Harbor December 7, 1941, found us unready for history's greatest war, which lasted four years. Millions of people, military and civilian, died and the cost in money has been estimated at one and one-third trillion dollars. Many of us saw some of that war personally. A total of fifteen million Americans served in the Armed Forces, and more than ten million served in the Army.

THE GREAT DEMOBILIZATION, 1945–1946

Our country has generally sharply reduced the size of its Army after each war. For instance, after the Revolutionary War, the Army was cut to eighty men for a short time. Our Army of 1945, the greatest ever assembled by any nation, was reduced from eight million strong to two million men in less than nine months. One year later, it had been reduced to one million men. The end of the fighting did not end our Army's duties overseas, however.

POSTWAR RESPONSIBILITIES, 1945–19——

In Germany and Japan our Army governed the former enemy peoples for a time, after which it helped them form their own free governments to replace the defeated dictatorships that had brought them only ruin and misery. In these and other countries our Army helped to feed and care for millions of needy and homeless peoples, victims of war's destruction.

1950 . . . KOREA

On June 25, 1950, the Republic of Korea was suddenly invaded by Communist armies of Soviet-sponsored North Korea. American troops stationed in Japan were the first to answer the call of the United Nations for aid to the South Koreans. Some of the hardest and most heroic fighting in our nation's history has taken place in the Korean mountains and rice paddies. Many Americans who have fought in Korea were veterans of World War II, who again answered their country's call to serve the cause of freedom.

In summing up: this makes us part of the long unbroken line of brave men whose service and sacrifice we remember in names like Valley Forge and Yorktown, New Orleans, Chapultepec, Gettysburg, San Juan Hill, the Marne and Chateau-Thierry, Bataan and Corregidor, Oran and Casa Blanca, Salerno and Anzio Beach, Utah and Omaha Beaches, Leyte and Luzon, the Ardennes Forest and Okinawa. The newest names include Pusan, Seoul, Pork Chop and Heartbreak Ridge. And this is far from being a complete list . . . there isn't room for all the remembered and famous places of World War II alone.

In 1775 the mission of the Army was to win freedom; today, the mission is to defend freedom.

Chapter II

ARMY ENGAGEMENTS

NOW that it has happened to you—this magical thing called falling in love—the moon has never seemed so beautiful, the stars so twinkling, the sun so radiant. You are floating on Cloud Twenty-one! Everything and everybody is wonderful!

From the first moment your engagement ring is slipped on your finger, begin planning *together*. The most romantic and happy days of your life are just ahead. The engagement period with all the joyous anticipation of the wedding day is a time that later you will recall with pleasure.

Perhaps you received your engagement ring only last night. It may be a miniature of his college class ring, a miniature of a West Point ring, the traditional diamond engagement ring—or with great sentiment your fiancé may have had the stone of his grandmother's or mother's engagement ring reset for you. Modern engagement rings may bear anything from a star sapphire to a square-cut emerald, one stone or a cluster of stones. It may be an *n*th of a carat or a soda-bottle chip, but if there is true love and romance the wedding band will encircle your happiness.

In days past, the engagement ring was not worn in public until the formal announcement of the engagement. Now it may be worn at any time. Some girls prefer to forgo an engagement ring and choose an elaborate diamond wedding ring with an accompanying jeweled guard ring. The guard ring is called an "eternity ring" and, while bought at the same time as the other rings when the double-ring ceremony is used, is presented and donned on the day after the wedding.

"MARRY IN HASTE, REPENT AT LEISURE"

Of course you didn't accept the first man who proposed to you. Or if you did, it wasn't at the immature age of seventeen or eighteen. It's a smart girl who completes her education and specializes in some practical field with a good background in home management—even though her young lieutenant or corporal is wildly beseeching her to leave it all and go overseas with him or off into the wild blue yonder.

A noted marriage counselor says, "In wiser and more ripened societies—societies not so close to the adventurer, pioneer or explorer stage—there is such a thing as being engaged. It is a recognized experience and a very pleasant one." Be engaged to each other for a while. It is a good testing period. Take a year out instead of hurrying breathlessly to the altar. Enjoy each other's friendship and companionship in the recognized and dignified status of being engaged. Perhaps there would be fewer trips to Reno if young people would take time to learn what interests, hopes, and amusements they share. The engagement period is a good time to become well acquainted with each other's ideals, tastes, and faults. (Of course, my darlings, I realize that I am wasting both my time and yours if you are so in love that the wedding date is already set.)

Connie and Peggy, I am assuming that you are well-adjusted young women and are contemplating marriage for keeps. Few couples marry without having had several down-to-earth quarrels, when the true character usually asserts itself. One should know exactly what kind of person he is choosing. Far better to find this out before the wedding day than afterwards. And you'll sleep much easier, too, if your love has seen you at your worst once or twice—and still loves you.

Your whole future depends upon your selection of the right man! The engagement period is one of the happiest, yet one of the most serious, phases in your life. Take plenty of time to think it out carefully. If you are a religious person, pray for guidance. Prayer, whatever one may think of it as a religious instrument, is after all one of the best psychological devices in the world for clarifying issues. Do the best thinking you can; be sure this isn't just a romantic crush because he looks so handsome in his new uniform; be sure that you've been absolutely honest with yourself and with him—and you need have no misgivings about your decision. If after serious consideration you discover you don't love him enough, for instance, to make some pretty basic sacrifices of your own pleasures for him, then do not hesitate to break the engagement. It takes strength of character, but it is the only sensible thing to do. Don't be a coward and let anyone persuade you to undertake a lifetime job that you can see is marked ahead with milestones of unhappiness.

I doubt if ever there was a thinking bride who at the last moment, or certainly at some time during the engagement, did not have a few qualms about the engagement, her choice of a mate, and marriage. This is only a natural reaction. Believe me, the man worries too! But when you've thought it through, relax and enjoy it.

Make your prenuptial dates treasures of memory that you both will always cherish. It is a woman's world again, your fiancé fell in love with you because you are *you*. He is the center of your world, just as you are the center of his. Let no person or outside influence interfere with the beautiful design for living that you two have planned for the rest of your lives. Earn the right to your happiness, and let nothing deprive you of it!

In these days, young people seem to make up their own minds about marriage. It is a long way back to the gay nineties when fathers customarily delivered speeches about honorable intentions after a young man had called three times. Today the two principals make up their minds first, and the bride tells her parents about the engagement afterwards.

It is still customary in the best circles, however, for an officer to call on the girl's father or mother or whoever is head of the family and ask for the girl's hand in marriage. Most parents today are so conditioned to obeying the wishes of their offspring that it is very unlikely disapproval will be voiced.

Your dad may wonder, "Is he good enough for our girl?" Your mother's heart may sink at the prospect of orders that will necessitate your going to Manila, Tokyo, Guam, or Istanbul. But ten to one you can depend upon your family to be good sports. Outwardly at least, they will voice approval at your new-found happiness regardless of how they really feel about giving you up.

If you are definitely a home girl and have a family complex, then I should advise you not to marry in the Army because you are probably the worrying type and will be miserable, besides bringing unhappiness to your husband. If your parents wish you to make a wealthy marriage and you agree, don't choose an Army man.

If the engagement is approved by the girl's parents, then the young officer or soldier should acquaint his parents with his intentions if he has not already done so. Letters will have undoubtedly been exchanged, and if he and his parents are close they will have read between the lines and won't be too bowled over with the news. Usually the boy's mother writes to the girl or her mother. If the young man is an orphan, his nearest relative should take his parents' place and perform this act of courtesy for him. Before a formal announcement is made of the engagement, these social amenities should be carried out and a definite understanding reached between the two families.

ENGAGEMENTS AND MARRIAGE OF SOLDIERS

There are no longer regulations governing the marriage of enlisted personnel. However, a soldier in the grade of E-1, E-2, E-3, and E-4, unless he has an outside income, should think twice before asking the girl of his dreams to marry him. A Pfc, Pvt-1, or Pvt-2 does not draw enough money to care for anyone except himself. If more regard and discretion were used the number of dependency and hardship cases among families of enlisted men in the lower four grades would be reduced . . . but not even the Army can stop love! Of course, for the married men who are drafted it is a different story, and to these the Red Cross, Welfare Society, and Army Mutual Aid Society are always ready to extend a helping hand in emergencies.

Overseas there are definite marriage regulations for all Army personnel. For instance, soldiers must submit an application for marriage to the appropriate commander who is authorized to approve such applications. Young couples should always consult a chaplain when planning marriage, even if you don't plan to have him marry you. He can be of invaluable practical assistance in getting your license, birth certificate, blood tests, and in finding out about rules concerning marriage ages, parental consent, waiting periods, etc. It should be noted that families of enlisted soldiers below the top three pay grades are not transferred at government expense.

YOUR ARMY CHAPLAIN

Today, premarital counseling is the accepted practice. Often the chaplain you consult about your wedding will not be the clergyman who will perform the ceremony. This is of primary importance in the case of a second marriage or marriage to a divorced person. Many clergymen will not perform such a marriage at all, some will require proof of the innocent party, some will need a waiting period, and proof that the divorce is final should be required by any clergyman.

At the present time, premarital counseling is encouraged by nearly all churches and required by some. The form which this counseling takes depends upon the requirements of the church and the practice of the individual clergyman.

The same policies which apply to the civilian clergyman apply to the Army chaplain. In other words, the Army chaplain conducts marriage ceremonies under the following provisions: "A chaplain may perform the marriage rite provided he complies with the civil law of the place where the marriage is to be solemnized and provided all parties concerned have complied with the requirements of the denomination the chaplain represents, and with any direction that may have been issued by the military command or higher headquarters."

THE ANNOUNCEMENT

Several days before the announcement is to appear in the paper, the bride's mother either telephones the various daily papers or sends a written signed notice to the society editors. Most papers require a signed statement in order to avoid future trouble in the way of lawsuits. Depending upon the social prominence of the families, reporters and photographers will be sent out to get more information. At the same time, a signed copy of the engagement announcement should be sent to the Service periodicals—*The Army, Navy and Air Force Journal*, 1701 Connecticut Avenue, N.W., Washington, D.C., and *The Army Register,* 511 Eleventh Street, N.W., Washington, D.C.

Announcement of engagement for Service journals:

Mr. James Prentiss Carver and Mrs. Carver (or Mr. and Mrs. James Prentiss Carver) announce the engagement of their daughter, Margaret Jean, to James Theodore Worthing, Lieutenant, United States Army, son of Mr. and Mrs. Charles Louis Worthing of San Francisco, California.

Miss Carver attended Ward Belmont, Nashville, and also graduated from Vassar. Lieutenant Worthing is a graduate of the U. S. Military Academy, 1936, and is stationed at Fort Sam Houston, San Antonio, Texas.

Local papers often carry a much more elaborate announcement, especially in the deep South where families are closely connected. Everyone is a cousin or related by marriage ties, so a complete family history is given by the papers of both the bride and the groom if they are of social prominence.

The officer may wish to have the announcement of the engagement in his home paper; so he should be consulted. Arrangements should be made for extra copies of the papers in which the announcement appears.

Should the bride's parents be dead, her engagement is announced by her grandparents, a guardian, an uncle, or any other relative, even

by an older brother or sister. Under no circumstances should the
groom's family make the newspaper announcement, nor should engraved announcements of the engagement be sent. Old friends and
relatives should be told of the engagement before it appears in the
papers.

If for any reason, after the engagement has been announced in the
newspapers, the bride changes her mind or circumstances arise which
convince her the engagement is a mistake, then a second announcement must be sent to the newspapers. An engagement is always
broken and announced by the girl regardless of the reason, never by
the man. A little delay in sending the second notice might be wise,
in view of the bride's variability. (She might change her mind again.)
The second announcement follows closely the form of the first:

Mr. and Mrs. James Prentiss Carver of Atlanta, Georgia, announce that
the engagement between their daughter, Miss Margaret Jean Carver, and
Lieutenant James Theodore Worthing has been broken by mutual consent.

Don't announce your engagement farther ahead than six months;
life is too uncertain! If it is an engagement of short duration, then
allow the announcement to be made not less than six weeks before
the wedding date.

Nine out of ten girls today skip the announcement party, but go
ahead if this bit of fanfare will make you happy. Being a prospective
bride puts you on a sort of pedestal, out of the realm of mundane
things. Your family stands ready to give you the moon, and your
relatives and friends are also standing by to help you make all your
plans and dreams a success.

A formal white wedding is a once in a lifetime affair. Ever since
you were a babe in arms your mother has been dreaming dreams of
you on your wedding day. Don't let her down now. Be your gayest,
happiest self; consult and make your plans with her. Listen to family
ideas from your grandmother and aunts; you may think them old-
fashioned, but then isn't marriage? Your mother will get a vicarious
thrill in reliving her engagement days through your happiness. That
is why it is so much easier on you and everyone concerned if you do
not rush the wedding date. Reserve some time for yourself to relax,
and be wary, in the weeks before the big event, of letting your engagement pad take on the semblance of a railroad timetable. In all of
this wedding welter don't treat the bridegroom as the forgotten man!

SHOWERS

Parties of this sort always seem to spring into popularity when there is a war in the offing. Why, no one seems to know, unless it is war hysteria.

At any rate, showering is not to be greatly encouraged. Brides should limit their shower parties to two and never accept a third. Usually the same friends are asked, as only one's intimate friends are supposed to be invited. It is never given by any member of the bride's immediate family, but may be given by a close friend of hers or of her mother's. More than two shower gifts, in addition to a wedding present, run into money, and there is usually criticism, whether voiced or not. Certainly it is inconsiderate and not in good taste for the bride to impose on her friends; so if someone insists upon giving a party for you, let it be a luncheon or tea, but by all means veto a shower.

Should your hostess consult you in regard to the type of shower and the guest list, choose a shower that will not burden your friends. A stocking shower, handkerchief shower, or kitchen shower is much easier on the pocketbooks of your young friends than a lingerie or linen shower. The latter might be given by an older friend, which will include the older set and many of your mother's friends, whose budgets for this sort of thing are more expansive. But remember: Keep it down to two and no more.

As in the case of announcement parties, the hostess at a shower may let her ingenuity assert itself in any way she chooses. Sometimes the gifts are all heaped on a table or a teacart; she may have her attractive young daughter or son present the gifts; or if there are only a few guests and gifts, the presents might be hidden and a treasure hunt conducted. The leads should be very simple or the honoree will become confused and enjoy neither originality nor party.

When the bride opens her gifts, she must be very gracious and thank each person who has brought her a present. She must be careful not to give extravagant praise to one person's gift and be lukewarm over a lesser gift.

PERSONAL TROUSSEAU

If you are fortunate enough to know where your fiancé will be stationed the first year of your marriage, consult a bridal counselor concerning the type of wardrobe you will need. If it is to be foreign duty, you will have some general idea of the type of clothes. But don't overstock. Orders are often changed without notice and sometimes en route.

The first thing to do is to make an inventory of the clothes you have in your wardrobe, then another memo or shopping list to cover lingerie, hose, accessories (belts, purses, scarves, jewelry, gloves, shoes), blouses, coats, suits, daytime dresses, evening dresses, rain gear, and luggage.

Naturally your wedding dress and your going-away outfit will be highlights of your personal trousseau. The latter should be a suit or costume that you can and will be proud to wear for seasons to come. Have a nucleus of substantial clothes such as well-tailored suits; use the fur coat you have on hand. Styles change overnight, so buy only the essentials and save your money for future wardrobe necessities when you have to replace the trousseau you chose for Washington with a less formal summer wardrobe suitable for the tropics. It gives one a comfortable feeling to have a wardrobe fund for the first year so as to be able to replenish and to buy a new dress in the current style when you feel the need.

On most Army posts the women wear exactly two types of clothes —sports clothes, either the spectator or active type, and evening clothes. In a city or on a post near a city, daytime dresses and suits are needed for luncheons, teas, and informal dinners, in addition to formal evening dress.

The following list is given as an average wardrobe for the Army bride. She may add to or change the list to suit her personal preferences, her pocketbook, or the climatic conditions.

  1 topcoat or fur coat
  1 evening wrap
  1 raincoat; umbrellas
  3 evening dresses
  2 dinner dresses
  2 short dinner dresses suitable for cocktails
  3 pairs evening slippers
  1 or more suits
  Blouses, sweaters
  3–4 summer sports dresses
  2 winter dresses of wool or jersey
  Day shoes, golf shoes, accessories
  1 winter dressing gown, warm mules
  1 summer dressing gown, scuffies
  1 lovely negligee or 1 hostess gown or pajamas

2 bed jackets
6 nightgowns or pajamas
6 pants
6 brassières
6 slips
3 girdles
1 dozen pairs of stockings, various weights

Any number of interchangeable skirts, long and short, with jackets, blouses, and sweaters will add variety to your wardrobe. If you are the "pinafore" type, clever combinations can be devised with extra blouses and skirts. Beach clothes, shorts, slacks, swim suits, robe, beach bag may be important in your trousseau.

Study the fashion magazines. Plan your trousseau with the help of one of the experienced stylists or consultants that all large stores provide. Window-shop first; look about thoroughly, watch sales; then use common sense, make up your mind, know what you want, how much you intend to spend, and start out to shop. Everyone knows that the shopper on a small budget who must dress inexpensively has to be far more exact than the shopper who has unlimited money to spend. Keeping the wardrobe sparse, and adding to it when a definite need comes along, is far more exciting than buying everything at once and growing tired of it. It is odd, but a cheap dress with fairly good accessories will look fine while an expensive dress with cheap accessories will look cheap.

If you can sew a fine seam, you can cut the cost of your trousseau considerably. I repeat, however, do not stock up with a large amount of clothes. Fashions change quickly, and it is a far nicer feeling to have the money in your bank balance for wardrobe emergencies that will surely arise.

To this trousseau list you may add countless sets of lingerie or double the outlay of clothes if your taste and circumstances permit. It will probably be the only time in your life when you will spend so much money at one time on lingerie; but don't go on a lingerie-buying jag. Try to keep in mind that these pre-wedding days, redolent of lily of the valley, will be followed by bread-and-butter days when you may have to tub your lovelies in a Laundromat. It will not be good to wake up with a laundry headache and yards of point d'esprit that will never look the same until it is fluted again at an expensive French hand laundry.

Learn to buy by brand names when you are shopping for quality lingerie. This means you can buy with confidence in whatever city you happen to be; though name-known lingerie isn't necessarily the lowest in price, you can be sure the money you spend is getting the most, dollar for dollar. For example, it is wiser to buy three good slips than six cheap ones, because the good slips not only will outlast the others but will give pleasure in wearing.

The selection of your lingerie should not be totally emotional or from the *femme fatale* point of view! You are entitled to make it a bit out of this world, but don't forget it must lead your day-by-day life with you. And life may be rugged at your first station! If Germany or Alaska is in the cards as a winter honeymoon, include some warm flannel pajamas in your most becoming pastel shades; also, long red flannels of the gay-nineties variety come in some amusing styles.

The most subtle compliment you can pay your fiancé is to plan your trousseau to please him. By now you have a pretty good idea what type of clothes he admires, so strive to complete his dream picture of you. There are certain things which military men like in women's clothes, and one thing they ordinarily don't like is anything that resembles a uniform or clothes regimentation.

Smart formal evening gowns are in order, and the more the better because on a small base you see the same people over and over. Breath-taking effects may be obtained with a minimum amount of good material, some fine ribbon, and flowers if you can sew. Not too minimum, or the breath-taking will be actual as well as figurative! It is wisdom not to spend too much or pay store prices for evening clothes unless you have an outside income or a rich fairy godmother.

Regardless of where you go, lay in a good supply of sturdy, comfortable shoes. Beware of clothes which need constant pressing and the ministrations of an expert cleaner. Take a dim view of the weather and go prepared with attractive rain gear.

If you can afford it, include one really super coat of peach-bloom camel's hair in palest lime, peppermint pink, tomato red, or café-au-lait beige. You can use it for every occasion, from sports right through the evening over your prettiest dance frock.

Army men like:

1. Sleek fit which shows off the figure. They are accustomed to well-tailored uniforms, and they are really quite observant as to the fit of clothes that are supposed to fit, such as suits. They know the cut, line, and curves of bathing suits, too.
2. Gay, colorful hats . . . but not absurd, extreme creations.

3. Dainty, lacy, effeminate collars and immaculate cuffs. This is in direct contrast to the drabness of their O.D. uniforms.
4. Crisp house frocks at breakfast . . . rather than negligees with trains. The prettiest negligee in the world is under a dreadful handicap in the kitchen.
5. Dainty, attractive organdy aprons, crisp as lettuce in the kitchen, not the cellophane or Hoover variety!
6. Simple, smart, up-to-date costumes, but not extremes in fashion.
7. Feminine fripperies, such as froufrou lacy jabots, garden hats, full skirts, furs, snow-white gloves, sheer hose, and high-heeled slippers. Southern men particularly like and often comment on these bits of feminine apparel.
8. Neatness: All the little points of good grooming are appreciated.
9. Good tweedy sports clothes; English oxfords and no fancy jewelry with tweeds.
10. Sensibly dressed women of whom they can be proud; overdressed women embarrass their escorts as well as their hostesses . . . and themselves. The smart woman knows the occasion, and knows what is proper to be worn. If in doubt, it is always better to underdress, simply, but effectively.

Planning your trousseau is fun and a joyous event; every detail of the bridal outfit and the accompanying trousseau must be exactly right. It will almost all be new, shining, and beautiful. Enjoy every moment of it, and plan to treat your wedding day as the beginning of your romance, not the end of it. The bride has illusions, visions, and hopes . . . even as you and I!

LUGGAGE

One of the musts in your trousseau is attractive, durable luggage, preferably of the airplane variety. Airplane luggage is the lightest and most durable on the market today. There are many good name brands.

Your wedding luggage should match; however, do not discard odd suitcases as they will be perfect for cross-country moves later by car. Your wedding luggage may include a combination hat and shoe trunk; the large size for large hats will prove a joy. These usually come with a tray to be used for accessories and lingerie. A sky-robe case with hangers, similar to the cross-country bag aviators use, saves arrival pressing. That plus a generous-sized train box or make-up box should be adequate for the honeymoon trip. Learn early in the game to travel light and plan your trousseau accordingly.

Your luggage, as much as your own appearance, represents you to your fellow travelers, so smartness is worth striving for. Remember, a good appearance is most important. It is a custom as well as a requirement that officers present a good appearance at all times; wives are expected to do likewise.

LINENS

"Trousseau" is a French word, meaning the little *trousse* or bundle which it was customary for the bride to carry to the house of her husband. Today the word has come to mean the bride's personal wardrobe and her household linens.

The list given may seem sketchy to your grandmother and even your mother, who had "hope chests" full of embroidered linens on which they spent their leisure time, but it should prove adequate for the needs of the average young couple.

Buy the best linens you can afford; good linens last indefinitely. It seldom pays to economize on this item. You'll be disillusioned with a bargain the first time it is laundered, because its beauty washes away with the sizing on its first trip to the tub.

White linens are the safest buy, though color co-ordination is increasingly a decoration must, and linens today are available in luscious pastel shades which make them very tempting. All that can be said is that it is a question of taste rather than of an accepted standard.

For 1 Double Bed	*For 2 Single Beds*
6 sheets 90″ x 108″	12 sheets 72″ x 108″
12 pillowcases 45″ x 38½″	12 pillowcases 45″ x 38½″
2 heavyweight blankets 80″ x 90″	4 heavyweight blankets 72″ x 90″
1 lightweight blanket 80″ x 90″	2 lightweight blankets 72″ x 90″

For 1 Bathroom

6 large absorbent bath towels 26″ x 50″
8 regular bath towels 24″ x 46″
6 small Turkish towels, easy to launder, 16″ x 27″
6 small linen towels, guest size
12 washcloths
3 bath mats

Percale or supercale sheets and pillowcases are very durable, although real linen is equally long-lived. However, the latter is too expensive for most budgets. Here is something about sheets: be sure to buy them long enough, so that there is plenty to tuck in, and to fold well over the blanket. If your better half has to yank them up around his neck, you can be sure they won't last very well. The more threads to the inch, the smoother, more fine-textured the sheet. Pillowcases should fit easily, but not so snugly that they will soon be splitting the seams.

A down-filled comforter, the Carlin or Eleanor Beard variety of exquisite beauty, might be added with a gift check. Handmade quilts are also a most welcome gift to the bride's trousseau. You may add blanket covers, mattress covers, and bedspreads, as you wish, to the list given.

Linens last longer, seem fresher, if you follow a regular rotation plan. The easy way to remember is to stack the freshly laundered sheets, towels, pillowcases at the bottom of each pile in your linen closet.

For the bride with a larger budget, I suggest planning your linens to include two or three bedrooms with corresponding bathroom linens as they will always stand you in good stead. Linen is usually the victim of a grinding process of slow attrition, and the better the quality, the longer its life.

You may mark your linen with either a monogram or an initial. Perhaps you are a gambler, and don't want to mark it at all. If you do, it is usually done by hand, though today machine-monogrammed bath towels, facecloths, and bath mats are popular. Avoid funny or would-be-cute ideas. They get as tiresome after a bit as an old shoe tied to your bridal chariot in the second week of the honeymoon.

Table Linen

1 linen damask dinner cloth, 8 or 12 matching napkins
1 buffet or supper cloth with 6 napkins, 8 or 12 preferred
1 luncheon or tea cloth, 8 napkins (12 preferred)
2 luncheon place-mat sets (17 pieces)
2 breakfast cloths, 4 napkins
2 bridge sets, 2 tray sets
Place mats, 4 sets; can be linen, Indian head, straw, or plastic

For the Kitchen

6 glass towels	6 dishcloths
6 hand towels	12 dish towels

A FINAL WORD!

As to your trousseau and wedding, you can have it as simple or as elaborate as you wish, my dear! This day of days comes only once in your life, and all brides naturally should be pampered. However, regardless of your income, limit your personal trousseau to the present necessities.

The happiest solution is for you and your mother to go to a bridal consultant at your favorite large store. She will have a list of trousseau needs, and nothing pleases her more than to work out the wardrobe problems of a bride going to distant shores. Explain your position honestly, tell exactly what part of the budget you wish to allot to the wedding, then the amount for your trousseau and all that goes with it. This service is free, believe it or not!

There is a new idea afoot called "The Trousseau Club" which provides an easy way to acquire linens and has proved a boon to many girls who work before marriage. Certainly, this budget plan of acquiring luxury linens should be paid for by you before your wedding since your trousseau "hope chest" is considered part of your dowry and what you are supposed to contribute to your new home.

Chapter III

THE MILITARY WEDDING

HERE COMES THE BRIDE!

A MILITARY wedding differs slightly from the usual formal wedding. There is nothing more glamorous, however, than a full military wedding, with the handsome groom, his best man, and his brother officers as groomsmen all in full dress or evening dress, wearing the traditional Army blues. Gold braid, gold belts, dazzling epaulets, brilliantly lined evening capes, and flashing sabers make a wonderful background for beautiful bridesmaids in gowns of delicate shades and the exquisite bride in her white wedding dress. The whole scene resembles a court of yesteryear and takes on a note of brilliance.

Decide first of all with your family what type of wedding you will have, whether formal, military, semiformal, or informal. Try to plan it without spending your father's next year's income or leaving your mother with a nervous breakdown. Next, your fiancé included, decide on the date and time. June is the traditional bride's month, though April and May are popular and the autumn season is increasingly fashionable. It is not appropriate or in good taste to plan a large church wedding to take place during Lent, Holy Week, or Advent (the three weeks preceding Christmas). Marriage license bureaus carry on a thriving business every day of the year, however, so the month and date is up to your personal taste and convenience.

An invitation is always a nicer compliment than an announcement. The only thing that an announcement explains is, as Emily Post says, that "you were not invited to the wedding"; however, there are circumstances in which the latter is preferred. For example, when a wedding is limited to the family and close friends, or when a date has to be set at the last minute, announcements should be sent to the friends both near and far who will be interested in the happy news. The bride and her mother should consult a good stationer and decide

39

upon the style and type of engraving, paper, etc. Be open to suggestions, but avoid fads in engraving styles, and, even if you have to
forgo some necessity in your trousseau, insist upon engraved invitations or announcements.

It is a good idea to request that the envelopes be sent to you ahead
of the invitations or announcements so that you can have them
addressed and ready.

This is also a good time to order your calling cards. You will need
them in returning calls at your first post. In the rush of the wedding
plans you may forget to order them; so take this opportunity and you
will be glad to have them on hand. Officers always have their own
personal cards for calling purposes; so yours should read, simply:
"Mrs. James Theodore Worthing." Avoid using initials or abbreviations; for instance, neither "Mrs. James T. Worthing" nor "Mrs.
J. Theodore Worthing" is in good taste. The entire name should
appear on a visiting card.

If you want to have new cards made, they should read "Lieutenant
and Mrs. James Theodore Worthing." The old Army used to call a
lieutenant "Mister" on social occasions, but during World War I it
became the vogue to address him by his official title at all times. Either
form is correct, though the old Army usage was preferred by everyone
except the lieutenants. Individual calling cards are still proper, though
joint cards are being used more and more, for calling. They were
formerly used when sending flowers to funerals, or gifts, etc.

WEDDING INVITATIONS

There are two forms for wedding invitations. For church invitations the form is "request the honour of your presence." If the wedding is to be at a club or in the home, the form is "request the pleasure of your company." Tradition demands the British spelling of
honour.

Before the invitations can be ordered, the bride's mother must consider the date and the hour of the wedding and speak to the clergyman about reserving the church.

The hour for the ceremony varies in different localities. In the East,
either high noon or the later afternoon about half-past four or five
o'clock are the fashionable hours for a formal wedding. In the South
and West, perhaps owing to the climate, late afternoon and evening
weddings are the traditional preference. The ceremony is usually followed by a reception with dancing or a wedding supper.

The proper form for an invitation to the church ceremony is:

Mr. and Mrs. James Prentiss Carver
request the honour of your presence
at the marriage of their daughter
Margaret Jean
to
James Theodore Worthing
Lieutenant, United States Army
Wednesday, the eighth of October
One thousand nine hundred and forty-one
at five o'clock
St. Paul's Episcopal Church
San Antonio, Texas

The invitation to the breakfast or reception is enclosed in the wedding invitation and reads like this:

Reception
Immediately following Ceremony
29 Arlington Drive
R.S.V.P.

If the reception is to be at the bride's home, probably many who are invited to the church will not receive an enclosed invitation to the reception. Unless it is a garden party or one has an enormous house it would be impossible to invite all the church guests. Most people understand this, but great tact and care must be exercised lest an old friend of either family feel slighted.

Some stationers suggest to the bride the use of engraved thank-you cards; but of course you know that every gift you receive should be answered by a personal note in your own handwriting.

It is not against any rule or regulation for a soldier or noncommissioned officer to have a full military wedding. If he decides to go formal, every man in the wedding should be in uniform with the exception of the bride's father if he is not a military man. If the wedding is to be held in the post chapel, it is customary and proper to talk over your plans with the chaplain and to make all of your arrangements with him.

The kind of wedding is usually decided by the financial and social position of both families or by the rules of the church in which the couple plan to be married. If it is to be a home wedding, it is decided usually by the size of the bride's home.

The traditional wedding is a church ceremony. It is followed by a reception in the home of the bride, or if more convenient at the NCO Club or at a hotel.

The proper form for an invitation to the church ceremony for a noncommissioned officer and his bride reads:

Master Sergeant and Mrs. John Haigwood
request the honour of your presence
at the marriage of their daughter
Constance
to
Corporal Anthony Argyle Tennant
United States Army
Wednesday, the third of June
One thousand nine hundred and fifty-three
at five o'clock
Post Chapel
Fort Benning, Georgia

The person chosen to address the invitations, usually a member of the family who writes the most legible hand, should remember that the inside envelope which holds the invitation should be addressed simply:

Sergeant and Mrs. Brown
or
Captain and Mrs. Paine

Initials are used only on the outer or service envelope in which the invitation is sent through the mail.

Like an invitation to a wedding, an announcement of the wedding should also be engraved (never printed) and sent to the entire visiting lists of both the bride's family and the groom's. It is proper to send an announcement only if no general invitations have been issued to the church.

Mr. and Mrs. John Marshall Hunter
have the honour of
announcing the marriage of their daughter
Mary Helen
to
Mr. George Pitt Thompson
Warrant Officer, United States Army
Wednesday, the third of June
One thousand nine hundred and fifty-three
Arlington, Virginia

THE FULL MILITARY CHURCH WEDDING

I shall now describe an elaborate church wedding, as a standard, in the hope that it will cover any situation that may arise. It is given in detail only as a guide, so that a smaller wedding may be fashioned after it.

We shall assume that the bride-elect is from a very wealthy, socially prominent family. The setting is a historic old cathedral at which the bride's family has always worshiped. Perhaps a bishop will officiate, or some other high prelate assisted by several clergymen. A vested choir with a renowned soloist will furnish the music, and the entire church will be elaborately decorated by a florist. The chancel will be a bower of flowers, and the pews for the families and distinguished guests will be designated by ribbons or sprays of flowers tied to the pew ends. Should the groom be an Army boy and, say, serving in his father's regiment at the time of the wedding, then the colors, that is, the American flag and the regimental flag, might be so placed that the couple stand under them during the ceremony. There will be a colorful canopy or awning leading from street to church, and the florist will provide white canvas for the aisle inside.

WEDDING REHEARSAL

This seems a good place to stress the vital importance of a wedding rehearsal. The bride always directs her rehearsal but never takes part in it, as it is considered bad luck. Someone else is her proxy.

As a rule, before a big wedding, the rehearsal is held in the church a day or so before the wedding. All the ushers and bridesmaids should be there, as well as the bride and groom and the bride's father. The clergyman explains the procedure and each one, except the bride, takes his place and acts out the minister's instructions exactly as he will on the wedding day. By all means have the organist present, and every detail should be explained and practiced until everything moves smoothly. One thing about military weddings is that the officers are usually more at ease than the feminine members of the wedding party; a wedding pageant to them is just another dress parade.

The head usher is the one to set the organist straight about the marching tempo and to see that the whole ceremony moves with military precision . . . if there are no young children in the party to complicate matters. After many repetitions, the entire party should master the art of walking to the wedding march.

The bridesmaids should understand the advantage of walking on a single line, placing the heel at each step on an imaginary mark running down the aisle. Once mastered, this will insure an easy flowing movement instead of the "walking on eggs" gait that so often mars a beautiful wedding. Neither should the bride and her father give the impression of scurrying up the aisle or lingering on "leaden or wobbly feet."

THE WEDDING DAY DAWNS

Formerly bridesmaids collected their bouquets at the bride's home, then proceeded to the church. There they awaited their entrance cue in a room off the vestibule. Today brides usually dress at the church in a room appointed for them off the vestibule. The florist sends the bridal bouquet and the flowers for the bridesmaids to the church, and the bride is dressed by the wedding counselor from a bridal shop. This is a good scheme since it eliminates last-minute details for the bride's mother and sometimes tears and hysteria on the part of members of the family. Should the weather prove inclement, it is added insurance toward a smooth ceremony.

The groomsmen arrive at the church half an hour before the ceremony begins. The officers, having deposited their caps in a room off the vestibule, don gloves and assume their posts at the different aisles.

One officer should take charge as head usher in order that he may be free to escort distinguished and elderly guests, as well as to co-ordinate the duties of the other attendants.

An usher asks everyone whom he does not know whether he is a guest of the bride or of the groom (reminding one, somehow, of the old game of London Bridge). The family of the bride is seated on the left side, the family of the groom on the right.

If the parents of the groom are unable to attend, the groom may invite his commanding officer to sit in the front pew on the right. The wives of married ushers are seated in the second pew on the right.

General officers and commanding officers should always be seated according to their rank; other officers may be seated indiscriminately except for the choice of bride or groom's side. When an usher escorts a lady down the aisle he offers her his arm. If a gentleman has come with her, he walks behind them. When a gentleman is alone, the usher walks beside him.

Few people, except at very large, fashionable weddings, enclose pew cards in the invitations; the seating of guests is much more informal than it used to be.

When all the guests have been seated, the head usher escorts the bride's mother to her seat. She is the last person to be seated. Then the doors are closed and no one is seated during the ceremony. The ushers march in in pairs and station themselves beside the first few pews in the nave of the church.

Next come the bridesmaids in pairs, and at the chancel they also divide and stand on the steps or go up into the chancel. In a large church, it makes a pretty setting if the bridesmaids and ushers alternate and stand on the steps leading into the chancel; or it is equally effective if they proceed to the chancel and await the bride.

The maid or matron of honor is next in the bridal procession and stands on the left at the foot of the steps opposite the best man. If there are flower girls, they precede the ring bearer and separate at the chancel steps, standing in front of the ushers and bridesmaids.

The bride and her father, who have driven to the church together, wait with the bridesmaids until it is time for them to join the procession. The bride enters on her father's right arm—then poor Dad does not have to stumble over a cascade of veil and train to get to his seat. Authorities differ on this point, and for a bride to enter on her father's left arm is equally correct. At the rehearsal try out both entrances. Father will agree with the first plan, whether you do or not; but after all, it is up to you. It is your wedding!

It might ease the strain on your father's nerves and checkbook if, just before the wedding rehearsal or a few days before the wedding when things get tense, someone should present him with Edward Streeter's amusing *Father of the Bride*. Dad may be just as jittery as you are, particularly if you are his first-born or first to leave the home nest, and he is sad over giving you up. Many emotions besides love are enveloped in a wedding!

Church Music

Musical selections should always be of the classical type. Often music played at church weddings is the one false note in a lovely ceremony. During the half-hour preliminary period while the guests assemble, the organist may choose selections from the old masters, such as Wagner's "Evening Star" from *Tannhäuser*, "Largo" from the Fifth Violin Sonata by Bach, or "My Inmost Heart Rejoiceth" by Brahms.

Leave all popular favorites to be played or sung later at the reception, where sentimental tunes can be as light and gay as the dancers desire. In *Vogue's Book of Etiquette* Millicent Fenwick lists the following pieces as basically unfit for a sacrament of the church: "Because," "I Love You Truly," "Oh Promise Me," "Liebestraum," and "Meditation" from *Thais*.

The proper wedding marches are: processional, Wedding March from *Lohengrin* by Wagner; recessional, Mendelssohn's Wedding March. While these are also secular music, both are usually approved by modern churchmen, though not by the Catholic Church.

THE CEREMONY

At the first strains of the Wedding March the bride's mother rises and the assembled guests do likewise. On the first note of the Wedding March the clergyman, followed by the groom and best man, step from the vestry into the chancel. The groom removes his right glove, holds it in his left hand, and stands at the head of the steps to await his bride. It seems more gallant, if there are several steps, for him to go down to the foot of the steps to meet her. The guests like to see him smile as he watches his bride come up the aisle. Some bridegrooms look glum and scared!

When the bride and her father reach the steps of the chancel, the bride is met by the groom. She changes her bouquet to the other hand and puts her right arm through the groom's left arm. Her father moves back, then steps forward again when the clergyman asks, "Who giveth this woman . . . ?" The father then joins his wife in the first pew.

At this point the bride and groom, maid of honor and best man move forward to the altar. The bride hands her bouquet to the maid of honor, and the best man passes the wedding ring to the groom, who in turn hands it to the clergyman. During the ceremony the clergyman returns the ring to the groom, who places it on the bride's finger at the words "With this ring. . . ." In a double ring ceremony, the maid of honor hands the groom's ring to the bride, who places it on his finger as soon as she has received her ring.

After the ceremony is over, the clergyman says a few congratulatory words in which he wishes them happiness; the handsome groom kisses his lovely bride and the recessional music begins. The maid of honor hands the bride her bouquet and straightens her train. The bride and groom leave the chancel, and at the head of the steps they pause a moment.

The bride should appear sweet and serious but not in the least self-conscious. While she does not, obviously, walk with downcast eyes, she meets none of the many eyes focused upon her except, for a fleeting moment, those of her mother. She is supposed to be moving at this point in a sort of luminous daze, and usually it isn't hard to act.

Under no circumstances should the bride and groom race out of the church like a troop of old cavalry horses. Up until this time the wedding has been a dignified and beautiful ceremony. The recessional should be just as stately and solemn as the precessional.

The best man escorts the maid of honor, and the ushers escort the bridesmaids to the vestibule where they break ranks to form the arch of sabers.

It is a nice custom and adds a military note if the head usher returns to escort the bride's mother. Of course, the mother may prefer to walk out with her husband. *All guests wait* for the parents of both the bride and the groom to leave, as there is ample time for this courtesy.

The ushers form in two lines facing each other at the entrance of the church, and stand at attention as the guests file out.

ARCH OF SABERS

Only the bride and groom may pass under the traditional arch of steel; it is not proper for any other members of the wedding party to have this honor.

The arch is formed either on the steps outside the church or on the walk leading to the steps. It is not proper to have the arch formed inside the church, as is shown in the following:

The ancient and traditional ceremony of the bride and groom walking under the arched swords of the officer ushers is always expected. At some weddings you will see this ceremony performed in the church, but never in a Roman Catholic Church. Would you like to know the reason for this? The practice of drawing swords at the altar or in the chancel of the church is entirely wrong. Because of the old law of right of sanctuary and refuge, as well as the very nature of a church, it is considered a flagrant breach of military etiquette to draw a sword in church. The arch should be made outside the church if possible, but if inclement weather or street traffic should prevent this, then the crossing of swords may take place in the vestibule near the door. The senior usher should give the order, "Draw SABERS."— *Naval Customs, Traditions and Usage*, by Vice-Admiral Leland P. Lovette

The flower girls, maid of honor, and bridesmaids wait until the head usher orders: "Return SABERS." *

Everyone loves to see the bride enter her new life under an arch of swords; there is something romantic and beautiful about the ceremony.

The bride's father, if he is not in the Service, wears a morning coat or a cutaway with dark gray striped trousers. Very light gray buckskin gloves are usually worn.

The bride's mother is poised, serene, and radiant. She is the hostess of one of the most important events over which she will ever preside; and while she has all the responsibility of the wedding, she does not seem to take an active part. A bride's mother should have great dignity; she is the lovely mature forecast of her daughter in the years to come. She is the last person to enter before the procession, and she should be becomingly and beautifully gowned. The groom usually sends the bride's mother, also his own mother, a corsage.

Since sabers are no longer regulation, it is to be hoped that each chapel will include sabers in its standard equipment for weddings. No doubt many retired officers would willingly present their sabers to the nearest post chapel, or the sabers might be bought from the chapel fund.

Each Officers' Club and NCO Club should also own a saber to be used in cutting the traditional wedding cake at receptions held at the club by the bride's family. To procure a saber for cutting the cake falls to the lot of the best man, and on some bases he is hard put to produce it.

WEDDING PICTURES

Definite arrangements should be made with the photographer before the wedding that no pictures are to be taken until after the ceremony. An exchange of wedding vows is a sacred rite, and certainly there should be no flashing of photographers' bulbs during the ceremony. As the happy couple walk down the aisle or leave the church is the appropriate time for the photographer to take their pictures.

---

* There are two schools of thought on the arch of sabers. The one stated refers to the Catholic Church and a naval tradition; however, in many Protestant churches the arch of sabers is formed in the center aisle as the bride and groom leave the chancel. After the bride and groom have passed under the arch and while the wedding processional proceeds to the vestibule, the ushers double-time down the side aisles to form a second arch on the church steps. If the weather is inclement, the second arch may be formed in the vestibule.

THE WEDDING DRESS

"Something old, something new
Something borrowed, something blue
And a lucky sixpence in your shoe"

Brides who dress in accordance with this old rhyme (and most brides do) usually wear some treasured heirloom of lace or jewelry and borrow a handkerchief. The blue is often a garter. If your bank is fresh out of sixpences, a shiny new dime will do.

And now to the selection of the *pièce de résistance,* the bride's dress! She is the central figure, it is the big moment of her life and no one can or should try to eclipse her.

Satin is still the classic material for the wedding gown, but sheerest lace is also highly favored. Frosted white organdy and marquisette are two leading fabrics for spring wedding gowns.

For the home wedding white bengaline, velvet, crepe, or any of the summer materials such as organza, *mousseline de soie,* or chiffon are appropriate.

The conservative bride with an eye to the future will choose a dress of such material and style that with slight alteration it can be converted into an evening dress. Sometimes the gown is made so that the train can be detached. If the bride wishes for sentimental reasons to keep her wedding dress, she may make it as elaborate as she wishes.

Often she chooses to be married in her mother's wedding gown, and if there is not too great a difference in style and length, this is a perfect solution. The veil may be of rare lace, an heirloom in the family, or it may be layers and layers of tulle or illusion arranged with orange blossoms, pearls, or shirring.

There is a tendency in modern fashion for brides to choose pastel shades, such as ice blue and petal pink, and this is entirely a personal matter; yet tradition decrees that white is really the color of the wedding gown.

FLOWERS

Although the bride may select the flowers and make arrangements with the florist, the groom pays for:

Flowers sent to the bride
Corsage sent to the bride's mother
Corsage sent to his mother

Corsage for his sisters and hers if they are not in the bridal party
Boutonnieres for his father and the bride's father

Wedding flowers do not have to be orchids or expensive camellias; florists can arrange beautiful effects in less expensive flowers. The bride's family pays for:

All flower decorations for church, home, or club
Flowers for bridesmaids
Flowers for flower girls
Flowers for maid or matron of honor
Fee for the organist and soloist
Fee for the choir

Now for the bride's flowers! Remember, Army men do not earn very much, and you won't want him to spend his all on flowers. Fifteen dollars is the average for the wedding bouquet, and if you go into a huddle with your florist, he will wax enthusiastic and patriotic and, with a few suggestions from you, will arrange something lovely. As a suggestion, how about white gladioli treated like orchids; or tulips with their petals turned back, their leaves forming a fan as a background; or fragrant freesias on top of a prayer book with a shower of satin ribbons, freesias knotted into them; or Easter lilies or calla lilies. Or, for five dollars you should get something heavenly in white sweet peas, camellias, gardenias, or a spray of white lilacs.

A recent bride requested the florist to make her bouquet into sixteen small bouquets, with a beautiful orchid in the center. When she threw her separated bouquet to the waiting bridesmaids, each of them received "a bouquet that is supposed to bring them an early betrothal," and the bride kept the orchid to wear on her going-away suit.

FEES

The groom pays the clergyman. The lowest fee is usually ten dollars, and, depending upon the groom's rank and circumstances, varies from ten to a hundred dollars. The amount is enclosed in an envelope, and the best man gives it to the clergyman in the vestry immediately after the service. An Army chaplain will not accept a fee but often will accept a donation for the chaplain's fund. Naturally the wedding trip and ring are the responsibility of the groom.

GROOM'S GIFT TO BRIDE

This is purely optional and depends upon the groom's financial circumstances. Most second lieutenants in the Army have all they can swing to finance their small part in a wedding. However, if the groom can possibly afford it, a *small* personal gift of jewelry, something she can wear, will have a certain sentimental value. West Pointers often give their brides a pearl-studded "A" pin. If there is an heirloom in the family in the way of a string of pearls, a ring or an old-fashioned pin, or some piece of jewelry which a doting grandmother passed on to her favorite grandson, he may give this to his bride.

BRIDESMAIDS

The bride decides on the number of bridesmaids, their dresses and flowers. Everything should blend with the general theme of the wedding. The bride should take into consideration the financial status of her attendants and make their necessary expenditures as small as possible.

It is customary for the bride to choose her sister, if she has one, as either matron or maid of honor. If there are several sisters, all of them may be included, even as junior bridesmaids. It is a pleasing gesture to invite the groom's favorite sister to be a bridesmaid. If the bride has no sisters, she chooses her most intimate friend as maid of honor.

A bride, if she wants the stage to herself, may have no attendants; she may choose only a maid of honor; or she may also add a matron of honor and four to six bridesmaids, flower girls, and a ring bearer. To have more than six bridesmaids seems a bit theatrical. The days of "show" are happily over, and exhibitions of wealth are not in fashion.

Your bridesmaids will bless you if you select a style and type of dress they can wear a second time without being marked as a member of so-and-so's sextet.

Junior bridesmaids' dresses are usually of some simple material and made in such a way that the little girls may use them afterwards as party dresses.

Lately it has become the fashion for a bride to entertain her bridesmaids with a dinner or supper in her home on the night of the groom's bachelor dinner. If such a dinner is given, this is the time for the bride to present her bridesmaids with some little trinket, and it is nice to give something lasting, no matter how small. Many brides do not bother with the dinner at all, and it is more prevalent in civilian than in Army circles.

THE RECEPTION

The first question in planning the reception is always the hour set for the wedding. If the wedding is at noon, it should be followed by a fairly substantial breakfast or luncheon.

An afternoon or evening wedding calls for lighter refreshments such as champagne or punch, sandwiches if desired, and the wedding cake. The party may be as simple or as elaborate as one chooses; if there is to be dancing an orchestra should be engaged. The groom always dances first with his bride, then with the bridesmaids and maid of honor.

When the guest list is large, the wedding reception is often given at a club or hotel. All the details, such as decorations, menu, music, can be taken care of expertly by the club, and the bride and her mother are relieved of responsibility.

The receiving line, formed near the entrance, includes the parents of the bride, the parents of the groom, the bride, the groom, and then the bridesmaids. The ushers are not in the line, and sometimes the father of the bride prefers to mingle with the guests.

If there is to be a dinner, there is a center table—the bride's table— at one end of which she and the groom are seated. At the opposite end sit the bride's father and the groom's mother, next to him the bride's mother, and, on her right, the groom's father. At the left of the bride's father is seated the clergyman's wife if he has one; if not, then the grandmother of the bride or some close relative. The best man sits on the bride's right, and on the groom's left is the maid of honor; then the ushers and bridesmaids and relatives make up the rest of the table. The wedding cake is the centerpiece, and when it is to be cut, a waiter places it before the bride, or if it is a narrow table she may go to the center and cut the cake. At a large dinner of this sort the bride usually cuts only one slice with her husband's saber. Individual boxes of wedding cake are at each place and are to be taken home by the guests; the bridesmaids are supposed to put them under their pillows and dream of them for good luck.

The other wedding guests are seated at small tables either in the dining room or on the terrace.

As to the menu, the club will be glad to suggest a suitable one. Few people can afford to entertain on a very large scale, so buffet suppers are increasingly popular. Young people like the informality and would much rather have a good orchestra for dancing than a fine dinner. At these parties, the simplest of refreshments are served. All the young ask is that there be plenty of food. Chicken salad in piping-hot rolls, and champagne punch were served at one reception, augmented of course, by coffee, tea, and other beverages. Small cakes, an ice, and mints could be added.

INVITATION TO A POST CHAPEL WEDDING

Every bride naturally wants and should have her wedding at her own home church or in her own home; but the Department of the Army doesn't always take the bride's wishes into consideration. Many Service brides get a thrill out of being married in a military chapel. The wholesale weddings at West Point on Graduation Day attest this fact, but unless you are an Army child or have some close family connection living on the post, it seems more proper to have the groom and groomsmen come to the bride, if possible. No matter how simple your home or how small the home church, unless circumstances over which you have no control direct otherwise it is in better taste for the bride and her family to stage the complete wedding. If you are to be married at your fiancé's station, you should be accompanied by your parents and as many of your immediate family or close relatives as is practicable. If you are an orphan, then your guardian or your closest relative should accompany you.

Facilities are available on a post, and it is possible to have a very lovely wedding. However, decorating the church and all the expenses incident thereto should be borne by the bride's family. Your fiancé may, in your absence, have to make all the plans and arrangements with the Army chaplain, the organist, soloist, or choir; but remember, these expenses are taken care of by the bride's family.

It is a great help and a pleasing gesture if the groom will detail one of his groomsmen to assist the visiting parents in these cases. They come from afar and do not know about florists in the vicinity, how to find the chaplain, or how to go about the hundred and one wedding details that will necessarily come up. There are many things in which they will need help, and sometimes they need transportation.

Some young couples dispense with music and decorations, and have only their families and the officer's brother officers present. He always invites his commanding officer and his wife and any other ranking officers under whose direct command he serves. If he belongs to a regiment, it is customary to send invitations to each officer of the battalion in which he serves, or to each officer of the group of which he is a member.

The post chapel wedding might be followed by a small wedding dinner or reception at the Officers' Club; or this may be omitted. An NCO officer or soldier might arrange for the bride's family to give a wedding reception at the NCO Club.

The Home Wedding

For sentimental reasons, the bride may choose to be married at home or in the home of a relative or close friend. The military theme may be carried out, as in a formal church wedding. Home weddings at dusk, the house lighted by pale candlelight, can be particularly lovely. Spring flowers used in profusion or autumn leaves artistically arranged as a background may take the place of an expensive florist's services. An old-fashioned garden makes a perfect setting for a beautiful wedding.

In these trying times most men, particularly fathers who have the bills to pay, throw up their hands and balk at the mention of a big wedding. No wonder the poor dears are frightened if your plans are to compete with the wealthiest girl in your set; but you can still have a lovely wedding, making it as simple or as elaborate as you choose.

Marriage at Parsonage or Magistrate's Office

This ceremony is not a wedding but merely a marriage. Street clothes are usually worn. The groom may wear uniform, though civilian clothes might be less conspicuous and preferable. An elaborate wedding dress does not seem appropriate, though a small breakfast, luncheon, or dinner is in keeping.

The Home Reception

Properly speaking, the only persons in the receiving line are the bride, the groom, and the wedding attendants. The bride's mother and the groom's mother usually greet guests at the door, while the bride's father and groom's father mingle among the guests. However, there are many solutions to this problem. At a recent military wedding reception at the Officers' Club, both the mothers and the fathers of the bride and groom received with the newly married couple. The bride and groom stood between the two families, and the attendants followed the groom's parents.

At a small home reception the dining table is covered with a white cloth, and it gives a pretty effect to surround the wedding cake with a wreath of green leaves. With champagne glasses or a crystal punch bowl at one end, a coffee service at the other, and plates of sandwiches at the sides the table is complete.

Champagne punch looks its best in a clear crystal punch bowl, and it is the simplest to make of all punches. Simply place a quart of lemon ice or sherbet and a quart of ginger ale in the punch bowl and over it pour two bottles of champagne. The yield is about twenty-four cups.

Of course, champagne or punch is not necessary at all, but it somehow seems to go with weddings. If you prefer a fruit punch with iced tea as a base, then stand by your principles and serve it.

It is customary for the bride to cut the first slice of the bridal cake with her husband's saber, his hand over hers. It is also customary to drink a toast to the bride, usually proposed by the best man. Again the groomsmen draw their sabers together—1. Draw; 2. Sabers— and cross them over the bride's head, while the toast is drunk by all the guests. These parties are usually very gay with music, and if space permits, dancing follows. The groom always dances first with his bride, then with the attendants in the wedding. When the crowd thins, the bride whispers to her maid of honor to assemble the bridesmaids in the hall. They all gather at the foot of the stairs, and about halfway up the bride tosses her bouquet. They all try to catch it, but the lucky one is supposed to be the next one to go to the altar. The bride, accompanied by her mother and bridesmaids, goes up to her room where she changes into her traveling ensemble. The groom goes to a room that has been reserved for him in the bride's home, changes his clothes, and waits until he is summoned and told that the bride is ready. Then they come downstairs together, say good-by to all of the relatives and the remaining guests, and leave. Many young couples wish to keep their wedding trip plans secret; so they skip the leave-taking except of their parents and slip out without the knowledge of the guests. They miss a lot of fun, such as the rice shower or having their car placarded with newlywed signs and old shoes, but perhaps if they are shy they prefer to avoid this fun at their expense.

For the reception at home it is always easier to have a caterer handle the dinner, supper, or refreshments if you can possibly afford it. A reputable caterer brings his own serving men or maids, the food will

be good and perfectly served, and if necessary he can furnish dishes
and extra silver. There is enough excitement in the house, what with
extra house guests and the wedding and all. The catering task is too
much to expect of the bride's mother or any hostess unless it is a great
house with trained servants in abundance.

If you cannot afford to have a caterer, then by all means keep the
refreshments as simple as possible. The wedding cake could be baked
beforehand or ordered, and punch can be made a few hours ahead.

GIFTS TO THE BRIDESMAIDS

The custom of giving gifts to the bridesmaids is gaining in popularity, but it is by no means obligatory. Depending upon the bride's
circumstances, she may give some little trinket, but it is nice to give
something lasting, no matter how small. One recent Army bride gave
each of her attendants a miniature silver pin in the shape of a spoon
that was a replica of her pattern of silver. Evening accessories often
are given, or something that is to be worn in the wedding by the
bridesmaids. Evening bags are popular, as are fans, charm bracelets,
compacts, or some similar trifle. The groom usually gives to his
groomsmen some small gift—studs, links, cigarette cases, or leather
traveling accessories.

WEDDING PRESENTS

If wedding invitations have been sent out three weeks before the
wedding date, gifts will begin to arrive soon thereafter. If announcements are sent, the gifts will arrive probably before you return from
your wedding trip. Provide yourself with a gift book, which can be
bought at any good stationer's, and as each gift arrives, you or your
mother should fill in the date it is received, the article, the name and
address of the donor, where bought, and the date the gift was ac-
knowledged. This is a systematic and methodical way to keep a record,
and it will be a wonderful help when everything seems to arrive at
once and you feel overwhelmed. If the presents start coming in too
fast, put them in a special room and do not open them until you are
free to make a record of them. Thank-you notes are easiest to write
while you are in the first glow of enthusiasm over each wedding gift.
You *must* write a note of thanks to every person who sends a gift. The
omission of this courtesy is the one thing the sender may forgive but
never forget, and your youth will not excuse you. Always mention
the present *specifically* in your note, and if possible tell how you

plan to use it. Try to write graciously and appreciatively, and avoid using the word "little." There is nothing more deflating to the person who has spent his all on your gift than to receive such a note as this after sending, shall we say, a sizable silver salad bowl:

Dear Major and Mrs. Thomas:
Thank you so much for the dear little silver bowl you were so sweet to send us.

Sincerely,

Perhaps the persons who sent it sacrificed something they wanted very much in order to send you a present they hoped would add to your happiness. Of course, you would never be guilty of sending an engraved card of thanks or a typewritten thank-you note.

A thank-you note takes little enough time, for the long and pleasant echo it leaves in people's minds. Don't use stereotyped phrases. Think a moment and put down some fresh phrase that you might use in talking; your thanks should sound not only spontaneous but sincere.

Upon the receipt of a wedding gift, a thoughtful gesture is to detail some member of your family to pinch-hit as your secretary in sending a small printed card to the person who sent the gift, saying their gift arrived, the date of arrival, and that a letter of thanks will follow soon. This is important to many people who like to pay their bills promptly but sometimes are inconvenienced and wonder if the gift was delivered.

The written note must follow, no matter how simple it is. Do your own composing, even though you are no poet. The only excuse for a letter not in the bride's handwriting would be some crippling accident such as a broken hand or wrist.

Sterling silver is the most practical of gifts, and your flat silver is a necessity. Choose a pattern you really like, and one that won't be too expensive when you are ready to add to it. Even if you have to start out with two knives and forks, better to have four of the essential pieces in sterling than round dozens of everything in plated ware. Here is a list of what you should get with the checks you receive, or if relatives ask you frankly what you would like in your pattern of silver:

Flat silver in sterling:

    4 luncheon-size knives and forks
    4 bouillon spoons
    4 butter spreaders

4 salad forks
12 teaspoons
3 large table or serving spoons
1 steak or carving set

Later you can complete your service to twelve, also filling in with iced-tea spoons, cream soup spoons, ice-cream forks, after-dinner coffee spoons and large-size dinner knives and forks.

In hollow ware or a good heavy plate you can use:

1 silver meat platter
1 silver vegetable dish with 2 or 3 compartments
1 silver bread tray
1 or more silver sandwich trays

Of course, some fairy godmother may present you with a silver tea service complete with tray. Be grateful . . . but the first thing to do is to insure it and then relax.

How to Mark Linen and Silver

Formerly only the bride's initials or monogram were used, but today it is considered proper to use the bride's future initials. Simple block letters are considered smart or a single Old English initial.

As for china and crystal, if you have any choice in the matter, select open patterns, in consideration of breakage in frequent moves.

The Second Marriage

A second marriage for a man does not in any way affect the ceremony, but a second marriage for a woman can never be like her first. Many war widows, who had to forgo the formality of a white wedding owing to the exigencies of war, still cherish the idea of a real wedding with white satin dress, train and veil. Everything is against it, my dear!

Since the days of the ancient Romans white has symbolized virginity, and the wearing of it should be reserved for the first-time bride alone. Weddings are formed upon just such charming traditions. It is perfectly proper for a young widow to send out engraved invitations or announcements of her wedding, but the remarriage of a divorced woman or of an older woman is always less elaborate than that of a young widow. The standing rule is, no woman rates two white weddings!

YOUR WEDDING TRIP

Your first journey together, whether your honeymoon is to be for a week end or a month, will be a unique experience you will never forget! There will never be another trip to compare with it, so forget everything once you are on your way and be happy.

After you have discussed finances, and how much your husband not wants but has to spend, then decide what sort of trip you will both enjoy most. Consider your tastes when you map out your honeymoon program.

Of course, at this joyful period in your life you are both filled with starry-eyed good will and eager to agree to anything, but don't forget travel brings out the best in some people, the worst in others. Some people are born sightseers and others would be bored with the Taj Mahal. The only thing worse than being dragged through cathedrals and museums is being forced to follow a foursome around a hilly golf course while wearing high-heeled platform pumps. If you know anything about golf courses, you will know that this is taboo, and an easy out for you.

If you two are like most people, somewhere in the middle between extremes, you should be able to agree on a lovely trip that will be unforgettable. Even if you **aren't** movie-camera enthusiasts be sure to take along a camera.

A motor trip through New England or the Smokies in autumn, concluding with a gay visit in New York attending the theater and a round of night spots, sounds like fun!

WEDDING ANNIVERSARIES . . . SUGGESTED GIFTS

First year .... Paper .... Paper napkins, playing cards, diary, stationery

Second year ..... Cotton .... Organdy bridge or breakfast sets, rag rug, chintz-covered closet boxes, candlewick bedspread

Third year ...... Leather .... Desk portfolio, picture frame, phone book cover

Fourth year ...... Silk .... Blanket cover, pillows, lamp shades

Fifth year ...... Wood .... Wooden salad set, nest of tables, furniture

Wedding Anniversaries . . . Suggested Gifts—*Cont'd*

Sixth year . . . . Iron . . . . Andirons, metal trays, plant
stands, Dutch oven

Seventh year . . . . . Copper . . . . Flower containers, copper kettle,
ornaments

Eighth year . . . . . . Pewter . . . . Candlesticks, trays, ash trays

Ninth year . . . . . . Pottery . . . . Flower containers, garden ornaments, plates

Tenth year . . . . . . Tin . . . . Wastebasket, toile vanity boxes,
trays

Eleventh year . . . . Steel . . . . Carving or game shears, garden
shears

Twelfth year . . . . Linen . . . . Table linens, cocktail napkins,
guest towels

Thirteenth year. . . Lace . . . . Pincushion, tablecloth, boudoir
pillows

Fourteenth year. . . Ivory . . . . Beads, fan, bric-a-brac (heaven
forbid!), figurines

Fifteenth year. . . . Crystal . . . . Glasses for all uses (preferably
plain crystal), bowls, vases, mir-
rors, salad plates

Twentieth year. . . China . . . . Breakfast tray set, dresser set,
dessert plates

Twenty-fifth year. . Silver . . . . Trays, cigarette box, candlesticks,
costume jewelry

Thirtieth year. . . . Pearls . . . . Fruit knives, strand of pearls,
jewelry

Thirty-fifth year. . Jade . . . . Jewelry, or set of jade green
glassware

Fortieth year. . . . . Ruby . . . . Jewelry, colored glass (if you
haven't the price)

Forty-fifth year. . . Sapphire . . . . . Jewelry, again glassware

Fiftieth year. . . . . . Gold . . . . Gold-banded china, glassware
with a gold band

Fifty-fifth year. . . . Emerald . . . . . . "A square-cut one, you deserve"

Seventy-fifth year. Diamond . . . . . "Settle for nothing less than a
tiara"

Chapter IV

CUSTOMS OF THE SERVICES
FOR THE ARMY BRIDE

Over hill, over dale,
As we hit the dusty trail,
And those caissons go rolling along!
                    —Artillery song

W HEN the wedding trip is over and the bride realizes that
        she and her husband are nearing an Army post, the place
        that is to be their first home, she gets a distinct thrill. At
last they arrive and are stopped at the gate by a sentry! If the officer
or NCO is reporting for duty at a new station, he will direct the taxi
to take him to post headquarters or he will drive his own car there.
The enlisted man reports in at the Shipping and Receiving Station.

First, he registers and reports in for duty. Ten to one, the quarters
will not be ready and you will have to stay at the hostess house, a
motel, or a hotel in the near-by town until quarters are available.
None of this procedure is very romantic or what you had pictured.

Shortly after your arrival, it is wise to consult the billeting officer
at post headquarters to see what possibility you may have for
housing on the post. He will also have a list of suitable rentals off the
post, and will prove very obliging in helping you to find a place to
live.

Time marches on, but in the old days of horse cavalry and artillery,
the time of mounted regiments, an Army bride was given a more
colorful reception. As the proud young officer with his pretty bride
approached the post, nervously she asked her husband why there were
so many people at the gate. He smiled, but by this time the colonel
of the regiment, his wife, and many of the officers and their ladies
had surrounded the horse-drawn Doherty wagon or conveyance to

extend a greeting and welcome to the bride. The regimental band immediately struck up "Here Comes the Bride." In the old days, in the mounted branches, the officers greeted the bride and groom by riding out on horseback beyond the post to meet them. Then the officers and ladies of the groom's regiment gathered at the quarters of the commanding officer, where a reception was held and an "Army toast to the bride" was drunk.

Until the next bride arrived, this one was considered the bride of the regiment. She was given the seat of honor at the commanding officer's right at the first large dinner party; often she was in the receiving line, and she invariably got a big rush at the first hop and was the belle of the ball. If the groom had been with the regiment even for only a few weeks, they were given a regimental wedding present, usually a silver platter, a coffee service, or some piece of silver on which was engraved the crest of the regiment. This was always a treasured gift because of the sentiment attached to it.

After the reception, during which the bewildered bride met so many people she was in a complete daze, a few of the groom's closest friends and their wives accompanied the young couple to their new home or quarters. The groom carried his bride over the doorstep, kissing her as he crossed the threshold. The guests, equipped with all the makings for another welcoming toast, stayed for one round of drinks and then departed. Alone at last!

This description of the bride's reception to an Army post was, of course, confined to peacetime!

After World War I, brides and grooms were given an inaugural ride around the post on "a rolling caisson" mentioned in the song above. Later the caisson was supplanted by a decorated jeep or tank equipped with a loud horn, which was blown constantly as the newly-weds made their first tour of the post. Following in the procession of cars, the drivers jubilantly blew their horns so as to acquaint everyone with the fact that it was a bridal procession. Soldiers stopped their work to wave a greeting, Army wives dashed to the windows to get a glimpse, because everyone loves a bride! With the great wartime influx of young officers and their brides, regiments and commands could not possibly carry out these old social customs without permitting their work to suffer. In wartime many of the customs of the Service are necessarily curtailed, and to the bride a great part of the sociability, the tradition, and the glamour is lost.

QUARTERS

"Quarters" is the Army term used for residence, apartment, or dwelling which an officer and his dependents occupy. It may mean anything from a shelter—and I mean literally a shelter, such as a Quonset hut—to a comfortable, palatial home.

If you are not stationed on an Army post, you will probably live in town. This may mean an apartment or a house, a motor court or a trailer!

It is unnecessary to go into the pay scale and variations here, but if you live off the reservation, the term used is "being on commutation." It means the officer must commute from the post to his quarters and receives a rental allowance (which is seldom adequate even if he can find suitable quarters). An officer in the Army is expected to live in a good residental part of a town or city. Generally speaking, it is more desirable to live on a post and forfeit the commutation. Sometimes an officer has a choice; but if there are quarters available, the rule is, they must be occupied.

The average set of quarters on an average post of today for a junior officer, company officer, or NCO consists of a living room, dining room, kitchen, two bedrooms and a bath, and sometimes a maid's room and bath. If the furniture is available, the following pieces are issued: living room—a desk and chair, also a folding table; dining room—dining table, eight chairs (two arm and six side chairs), and a buffet; kitchen—a stove, refrigerator, and kitchen table; bedroom— G.I. cots or beds, mattresses, two dressers, one chiffonier, one dressing table and bench. At least you can get along with this, and you should have to buy very little to be comfortable. A divan, the new sectional type, would be practical, and with several substantial chairs and the addition of lamps, curtains, pictures, and rugs, you will have a very livable set of quarters.

To a bride of my day this would have sounded palatial. My first post was Fort Sill, Oklahoma, and we arrived one cold day in January in a typical Oklahoma dust storm. After the customary festivities of arriving were over, and the guests had gone, I looked around at our quarters with a sinking heart. It was a small four-room box with beaverboard walls and the woodwork painted a deep Java coffee brown, of which my gallant young lieutenant seemed very proud. The eight-by-ten living room contained a fat little heating stove, two barracks chairs, and a rough pine kitchen table. In the bedroom, my husband's faithful striker, Valinchus, had placed two G.I. (government issue) cots or bunks neatly made up with issue sheets and O.D. (olive drab, also issue) blankets. In the one tiny closet he had hung all of the lieutenant's uniforms, and around the room he had made a little fence of his boots. (Vaguely I wondered where my trousseau was to be stored!) The dining room contained a similar pine kitchen table and four barracks chairs, and the six-by-nine kitchen had room only for its one imposing item, an Army coal range.

My husband seemed happy, and proud of our home. He pointed out with pride how much Valinchus had done in his absence. The floors had all been scrubbed and painted, the stoves polished, the windows cleaned; there was a neat woodpile at the back door, and had I noticed the "new window shades"? That was a special favor from the Q.M. (quartermaster) although they were also G.I. I went to sleep that night praying that it would look better in the daylight. It didn't—it was shabbier than ever!

My experiences would make a pioneer woman of the frontier days smile. If you are interested in stories concerning the lives of pioneer women in the old days, I recommend to you *Boots and Saddles*, by Elizabeth Custer, and *Tenting on the Plains*, by the same author. When your lot seems drear, go to the post librarian and ask for some of the books written by officers' wives of frontier days. These brave women fought prairie fires, experienced pestilence, earthquakes, and Indian raids, lived through floods, stagecoach holdups, grasshopper scourges, and mutinies.

A very short bibliography of books written by Army women includes the following:

Reminiscences of a Soldier's Wife, by Ellen McGown Biddle, gives a graphic description of the hardships and terrors to which Army women were subjected during the early days of the settling of the West.

Vanished Arizona, by Martha Summerhayes, wife of General Summerhayes (retired), tells a very amusing and entertaining story of her experiences with Indians, rattlesnakes, and buffalo herds in the wilds of Arizona.

With Custer's Cavalry, by Katherine Gibson Fougera, is dedicated to the memory of Elizabeth Custer and is a fascinating book of memoirs of the late Katherine Gibson, widow of Captain Francis M. Gibson of the famous 7th Cavalry, U.S.A.

Army Letters from an Officer's Wife, by Frances M. Roe, is a humorous and spicy account of the old days.

These books and others that are listed in the Bibliography will furnish entertaining reading for a rainy afternoon, and in addition will give you an insight into the customs of the "old Army."

Another must on your reading list about the old Army days is *The Immortal Wife* by Irving Stone. It is the inspiring story of Jessie Benton Frémont, her ambition for General Frémont, her courage in following him to California and to the ends of the earth. It is a beautiful love story with an Army background.

RANKING OUT AND BEING RANKED OUT

This is an old Army custom that, I am glad to say, is obsolescent today. I shall quote a little incident from Martha Summerhayes' book, *Vanished Arizona*, that will illustrate it:

Arriving at Fort Russell, Cheyenne, Wyoming Territory, in April, 1874, to join my husband's regiment, we were met by two gallant officers in the uniform of the U. S. Infantry, who gave us welcome, and to me, a bride, a special welcome to the Regiment.

One of the officers, Major Wilhelm, who was to be Jack's Company Commander, said that Mrs. Wilhelm expected us to lunch and we were to be their house guests until we were settled. Soon after luncheon, Jack said to Major Wilhelm,

"Well, now I must go and look for quarters; what is the prospect?"

"You will have to turn someone out," said the Major.

About an hour afterwards they returned, and Jack said,

"Well, I have turned out Lynch; but as his wife and child are away, I do not believe he will care much."

"Oh," said I, "I'm sorry we have to turn anybody out!"

The Major and his wife exchanged smiles and the former remarked,

"You must not have too much sympathy; it's the custom of the Service. It's always done, by virtue of rank. They'll hate you for doing it, but if you don't do it, they'll not respect you. After you've been ranked out once, you will not mind turning others out. Army women are accustomed to it."

The commanding officer of each post is free to have his own policy in regard to quarters, but few today believe in "ranking out" an officer, once he is settled, unless it is absolutely necessary. At some posts, like West Point, quarters are reassigned once a year, and there is a general moving day. Should you be ranked out, don't be hurt or insulted; "it's only the System." Remember that quarters are part of your husband's pay, and it is only fair that longevity should count in this regard. When your husband is a field officer, you can expect better quarters. The old R.H.I.P. ("Rank hath its privileges") is applicable here, but it should be followed by "Rank also hath its obligations"!

There's an old Army superstition, "Plant parsley and you'll move." Well, I committed the unpardonable sin of planting parsley, and I moved regularly. Then, on one very undesirable station, I had parsley growing everywhere—in window boxes in the kitchen, in small pots for decoration, and in the flower garden. But the god of superstition turned a deaf ear, and even the W.D. left us unmolested. It may work for you, however!

CALLING

The purpose of the exchange of calls has always been to permit the newcomer to become acquainted. In the old days, calling on small regimental posts was not only an important custom but a *must*. As soon as an officer and his wife were settled, in about two weeks, he posted their visiting card on the bulletin board at post headquarters, which meant that the couple was ready to receive callers. In the meantime, twenty-four hours after arrival the newcomers had made their official and social call on the commanding general and on the officer's immediate superior commanding officers.

On small regimental posts, the social amenities of calling were strictly observed but sometimes resulted in odd situations. Major General H. W. Blakely tells an amusing story:

On one post, a newly married second lieutenant was assigned a small set of quarters when he reported, and he and his bride called promptly on "the chain of command" up through the regimental commander. The colonel and his wife returned the call about a week later, and the colonel casually remarked that he hoped that the bride had met most of the post families. She innocently replied that only two couples had called so far. At officers' call the next day, the colonel made some emphatic remarks about the importance of calling promptly on new arrivals. That evening, the lieutenant was Officer of the Day and absent from his quarters while the bewildered bride did the best she could receiving sixty-three callers in less than two hours. But, she had a good story to tell in later years.

During the war years both official and social calling was curtailed to a great extent, and large receptions took the place of individual social calls. It is interesting to note that in the postwar Army many feel that a combination of a general reception, where a newcomer might meet the personnel of the garrison, and a selective system of personal calling should be worked out. Another school of thought has it that the commanding officer of each post should dictate the policy of social calling. Others dislike calling altogether and would like to see the custom abolished.

Today calling on large posts is almost impossible and is often confined within a regiment or to one's intimate friends. So if no one calls on you at first, don't feel neglected. A large reception at the Officers' Club, nowadays, serves as a general introduction and replaces the excessive number of calls.

When reporting at a new station, an officer should consult the adjutant to find out the policy of calling and returning calls.

At smaller Army installations perhaps the officers and their wives of the group or branch to which your husband is assigned may call.

The Important First Calls

Unless the commanding officer has indicated that he does not wish to be called upon, the new officer and his wife pay a social call upon him and his wife, and also upon the new officer's immediate superior officers. In a regiment, this would include the commanding officer and also the executive officer.

If the post C.O. is a general officer, he may or may not return this call personally. Often he has his aide return calls on the junior officers. Some C.O.'s prefer to set aside one afternoon or evening during which they are "at home" to callers. Others obviate all calling by giving a reception. The latter method is in force today at all large posts.

Receiving Callers

Should callers appear before you are completely settled on your new post, don't feel uncomfortable or apologize. Everyone realizes what settling means, and if you have sufficient G.I. chairs in which to seat your guests, that is all that is necessary. Generally a formal call should last no longer than fifteen minutes, and should be returned within ten days. The customary hours are from seven forty-five until nine o'clock in the evening, Friday and Saturday nights excepted.

For receiving callers in the evening, an officer should be in semiformal dress, wearing a blouse or coat; his wife need not necessarily wear a dinner dress but she should change to something other than the dress she has worn all day. Sports clothes such as shorts or pedal-pushers are a bit too informal to receive callers, don't you think? However, if it is hot and you are receiving in the patio or on the terrace, informal attire might be in order. If there is ever any question in your mind as to the formality required, just be sensible and err on the side of convention.

Should there be a servant on duty, she may answer the door; otherwise it is proper for the officer to go to the door (not his wife, unless she is alone), and his wife rises to greet the guests. The visiting officer introduces himself and his wife to your husband, who in turn will present them to you. The correct formal greeting to an introduction is simply, "How do you do?" When greeting callers in your own home, it is gracious to be a bit more effusive by adding, "We are so glad to have you" or "It is nice of you to come over."

Don't worry about the conversational chitchat! You will probably be asked how you like the Post. If you like it, be sincere and say so; if you loathe it, be noncommittal, yet tactful, because you may change your mind later.

If cards are left there will be two of the visiting officer's, one for the hostess and one for her husband. His wife will leave one card for you. Here is an old-fashioned, easy, and infallible rule to remember about cards: A lady never calls socially on a man; so she leaves a card for each adult woman only. An officer leaves a card for each person called on.*

Returning Calls

Either save calling cards or keep a list of all callers. The latter is a safer method, because sometimes people fail to leave cards, or the cards are lost. In the case of someone you particularly want to find at home, you may leave cards or not and return a second or a third time. You must be careful about returning calls; many older officers attach great importance to this.

How very important first impressions are in the Army! A young officer is the cynosure of all eyes in his regiment, and his bride is equally so in the social circles of the Army. Colonel Moss, in his *Officers' Manual*, says, "You cannot observe with too much care the social customs of the Service, the customs that are so essential to the

---

* It is customary to leave one joint card, and the officer leaves one of his visiting cards for each person called on.

good fellowship, contentment, harmony, and happiness of the garrison."

Having made your call, leave the required number of cards on a card-tray table in the hall. Once you have risen to leave, leave by all means. Say good-by or good night, but don't linger. In the Army, that is called "doing a rug dance."

CALLING CARDS

The selection of calling cards is important and they should be absolutely correct. Often people see your card before they see you, and if your card is peculiar, they may think you are peculiar also. Sometimes they may see your card and never see you at all, in which case you will wish your card to make an especially good impression.

It is best to go to a good engraver, who knows what is in good taste. He will cost no more than a poor one. Good jewelry stores and any large department store should be reasonably satisfactory. Also, there are any number of large firms, such as Tiffany's in New York, Bailey, Banks & Biddle Company and J. E. Caldwell Company, both of Philadelphia, that for years have made a specialty of engraving for Service personnel. Your husband will need a personal card, you will need one, and you will probably want a joint card as well.

USES FOR CALLING CARDS

1. Cards are left at formal calls.
2. A lady leaves cards at a formal tea for hostess and guest of honor.
3. Cards are used to accompany gifts.
4. Cards are left when friends aren't home.
5. Cards are convenient for brief messages or an introduction.
6. Cards are used for PPC calls. PPC written in ink in lower left-hand corner means *Pour prendre congé* (to take leave)
7. Cards are left on calls at hospitals, particularly if one is unable to visit the patient.

If you are stationed on a post where calling is the order of the day, by all means regard it as a pleasant social function and you will enjoy meeting new people. Your first formal call is a get-acquainted call. Just be pleasant. Don't overdo it, stay fifteen minutes, make no excuses about your short stay, but also be careful not to consult your watch at frequent intervals or keep your eye glued on your host's clock.

Leave your cards without comment on the tray or table at the end of your visit. Remember, an officer leaves his card for each adult member of the family; a lady leaves a card for each adult lady member . . . a maximum of three.

The Visit

Under no circumstances should you confuse a visit and a call.
1. A visit may be paid at any time of day or early evening that is convenient to the host.
2. A visit is paid to a neighbor or friend whom you know very well.
3. A visit, as such, is never paid to a stranger or acquaintance.
4. You may wear whatever is suitable.
5. Arrangements may be made in advance by telephone for a visit.
6. You may stay as long as you feel welcome.

More Army Customs and Traditions

"Customs and traditions are like moss—they grow slowly." Custom is defined as established usage, and those customs which endure finally come to be regarded as the common law of society. Like life itself, customs are subject to constant but slow change. New customs are born to supplant the old, usually because they answer man's purpose better and are more practical.

Taboos, or things to avoid doing, are said to linger on much longer even than positive customs. They become unwritten laws which are strictly observed long after the reason for them has disappeared.

The military service bears some resemblance to a hierarchy. Control is exercised by leaders or officers, and subordinates are required to extend an unfailing respect to the authority which issues their orders. The Service never demands personal admiration of a superior officer, but it does demand without equivocation respect for authority and unfailing courtesy to individuals who exercise it.

It may make your path easier if you know something of the current customs and some of the fine old military traditions which have become our heritage. Certainly they have a most important bearing on every officer's and soldier's life and will continue to influence your husband's character and manner of living as long as he is in the Service and even when he is retired. There is enough sound sense and worth in them, too, to warrant some real study of the history of the Armed Services of our country.

The Army today places less emphasis on grade, rank, and position on the promotion list and more upon capacity, character, and demonstrated ability than was once the case. Promotion by selection is being tried out, and this will have a strong effect, in that the senior of today may be the junior of tomorrow. The old system was, "Once a senior, always a senior"—in other words, "The king can do no wrong"—and the death of a senior, or his retirement, was the only step to promotion.

The custom that R.H.I.P. (Rank hath its privileges) will continue to be strong, but in this postwar period *greater emphasis* is being placed upon the responsibility that goes with position. Remember that rank carries its laws and unwritten responsibilities as well as prerogatives: so never be envious . . . it is not all a bowl of cherries! Look around the post and note which husbands have the ulcers. It may make you feel happier about your man's junior status.

TRADITIONS

Army traditions are unwritten rules of conduct based on historical precedent. The value of tradition and custom in the Service as a morale factor is incontestable.

The Army is proud of its history, with its many brilliant examples of courage, determination, professional skill, and self-sacrificing devotion to duty. Its record to date has been excellent. Perhaps this can be attributed in part to the perfect teamwork and training, to the experienced guidance of our leaders, and to the high morale of every soldier.

There are many Army traditions about which you will never hear a verbal expression, yet they are thoroughly ingrained, and a part of every well-rounded Army officer if he is a credit to his Service.

There is the *tradition of being a gentleman*. Certainly an officer and gentleman cannot be created by an act of Congress, even if it is so stated on his commission! An officer may possess all the attributes of education and a certain polish; he may be on his best behavior during the selective process and later; but if he is a phony he will revert to type eventually. Such individuals are among those caught in the elimination process. It is part of the code that officers are expected to be gentlemen. This is manifested in their moral standards, conduct, appearance, and the professional standards they establish in the performance of duty. Gentlemen do not drink to excess; they do not give bad checks; they do not avoid the payment of just bills or speak ill of a lady's reputation in public.

There is the *tradition of loyalty*. An officer must be loyal to the nation he has sworn to protect; he is loyal to his brother officers, his men, and his organization. The loyalty of officers is taken for granted, as is the loyalty of all soldiers.

There is the *tradition of dependability*. An officer's word is invariably believed. He is dependable in all things, both great and small, and his written word or statement should be accepted at its face value.

One of these fine days you may be greatly surprised to hear your husband referred to as a public servant. He is exactly that and more as he fulfills the *tradition of public service*. He goes where he is ordered and performs the tasks which his duties require. In peace he prepares himself and those subordinate to him for war; in war he leads Americans in battle against the enemy.

The *tradition of discipline* and leadership go hand in hand and are deeply ingrained in the mind and heart of the successful officer. He is trained to lead others just as he is trained to be led by others.

I have purposely left one of the finest traditions until last . . . the *tradition of unselfishness*. An officer in command of men always sees that their needs are satisfied before he considers his own comfort. When the good of the Army requires him to forgo doing something which he wants, he does so cheerfully.

You may fit into the picture here without realizing it. Suppose your husband has his heart set on going to school, but instead is ordered to Alaska. Be sympathetic with him in his disappointment, but help his morale by trying to like the idea of going to the new post.

There are Army wives who consider it bad luck for their husbands to try to get their orders changed. I don't know, but I have heard of tragedy following in the wake of changed orders; perhaps it is wise to "swim with the current," take orders as they come, and uphold the tradition of unselfishness.

FORMAL CEREMONIES

Military ceremonies add color to the life of military personnel. Many ceremonies include rendering homage to the national flag or to the national anthem. Everyone loves a parade and band, and at large posts such as the U. S. Military Academy at West Point hundreds of spectators attend.

Retreat is a daily ceremony at all Army posts and is held at a fixed time in the later afternoon. Now this concerns you! Should you be driving your car or bicycling when you hear the bugle, you should dismount and stand facing the flag at attention. At retreat, troops are formed on unit parade grounds. When the trumpet call is sounded, the troops in formation stand at "parade rest." At bases, where there is a saluting cannon, the evening gun is fired, symbolizing the closing of the day's routine duties. At the first note of the national anthem, the organization is brought to attention. The flag is lowered during the playing of the anthem. For a brief space in the busy day all military personnel pause to pay homage to the nation's flag.

Civilians who are present on the reservation during Retreat, including the wives and children of officers and enlisted men, are expected to pay appropriate courtesies. Men should face the flag, stand erect, remove their headdress with the right hand and hold it over the left breast, retaining the position throughout the playing of the anthem or the trumpet call which follows the Retreat gun. *Ladies should face the flag and stand erect.* Vehicles should be stopped and the occupants dismount and pay the courtesies outside the cars.—*Officers' Guide*

PARADES

A military parade is a colorful ceremony at which band and unit colors are present, and officers and men are dressed in their best, literally shining with "spit and polish." Units of command are formed and presented to their commander and pass in review before him.

Spectators are expected to add dignity to the ceremony. Here are a few taboos: There should be no loud talking or unruly behavior; smoking is in poor taste; children are welcome if kept under control; dogs are *not* welcome.

A few *musts*: All spectators pay homage to the flag; all spectators rise should the reviewing officer be a general officer, when the ruffles, flourishes, and general march are sounded, and military personnel salute; all spectators render the courtesy of standing at attention when the color guard reaches a point six paces from the front of their position and hold it until the colors have passed.

Reviews

The object of a review is to provide a ceremony where all may see the men in fighting trim complete with equipment, transportation, and guns. It is less formal than a parade, but the colors are carried the same as in a parade.

Saluting

The origin of the salute goes back to olden days in Europe when freemen were allowed to carry weapons. When they met, each would hold up his right hand to show he had no weapon in it and that they met as friends. In this way, the salute came to be the symbol or sign by which freemen or soldiers might recognize each other. Today it is the symbol of the military profession. It is a friendly greeting and a dignified military gesture. The serfs or slaves in the Middle Ages were not allowed to carry weapons and slunk past the freemen without making any sign.

The *Officers' Guide* urges members of the Army to be meticulous in rendering salutes and in returning salutes from personnel of the sister Services. It adds that "such soldierly attitudes enhance the feeling of respect which all should feel towards comrades in arms."

Salutes are not exchanged in churches, theaters, or public conveyances, or when one is actively engaged in games or carrying articles in both hands. An old custom is that each newly commissioned officer presents a dollar bill to the first soldier who salutes him.

Never hang on an officer's arm when he is likely to be saluting. Only when the going is rough should you take his arm!

Gun Salutes

The internationally accepted national salute is twenty-one guns. Only the President, ex-President or President-elect, rulers of other nations, and members of royal families are given the national salute. All salutes are given in an odd number of guns. Why, no one knows!

Don't be alarmed and think war has been declared if you happen to be awakened some morning by a gun salute. You may hear any of the following on an Army post:

The Secretary of Defense receives a 19-gun salute.

The Secretary of the Army is furnished 19 guns.

Governors and Senators receive a 19-gun salute.

The Undersecretary of the Army receives a 17-gun salute.

The Chief of Staff receives a 17-gun salute.
General of the Army receives a 17-gun salute.
Four-star generals or admirals receive a 17-gun salute.

GUARD OF HONOR

Persons of high rank, either civilian or military, are often received and escorted by a guard of honor. Troops for this detail are selected for their military appearance and superior qualities of discipline. The escort is formed with the band in line opposite the place where the personage is to present himself. Upon his arrival, troops present arms, the band plays appropriate music, and gun salutes are given, after which the guest of honor usually inspects the guard.

When the body of an important person such as the President, the Vice-President, or the Secretary of Defense or State is lying in state, a guard of honor is always furnished. Of course, this will not happen on your base, but it is well to know what is happening if you are in Washington when such an event occurs.

THE FLAG

The American flag stands as a living thing, a symbol of the people, of the land, and of the democratic idea. It is displayed from sunrise to sunset, and to Americans it is the most beautiful flag in the world.

There are four different names for the flag: standard, ensign, color, and just plain flag. Flags flown on Army posts are: garrison flag, used on holidays and special occasions; post flag, used in pleasant weather; color, carried by dismounted units, Air Force, Army Ground Forces; standard, flag used by mounted or motorized units.

CHRISTMAS AND THANKSGIVING DINNER

From olden days it has been the custom for the post commander to visit company messes on Christmas and Thanksgiving. It is also the custom in most organizations for the families of officers and non-commissioned officers to have dinner in the mess, particularly on Thanksgiving Day. Most families prefer to dine at home on Christmas Day. The custom varies among organizations and stations, but some sort of participation and get-together is traditional on these holidays.

ARMY CHRISTMAS TREE

It is a universal Service custom for a post-sponsored Christmas-tree ceremony to be held on Christmas Eve, at which every child within a stipulated age bracket—up to twelve is the usual age—receives a gift. The chaplain is generally in charge, assisted by members of the Woman's Club, who help with the wrapping, tagging, and distribution of the presents.

Sometimes Santa arrives by plane or helicopter, often by sled, and in Hawaii usually in an outrigger canoe. A paratrooper Santa dropped from a plane and was welcomed at one Army post by all the small fry. This Christmas custom is supplemented by a variety of activities such as carol singing, religious activities, or maybe a sleigh ride.

New Year's Call

At some posts it is customary for the Commanding Officer and his staff on New Year's Eve to drop in at the NCO Club during the dinner-dance to wish the non-commissioned personnel "A Happy New Year." It has been a custom throughout the Army that officers make a formal call upon the Commanding Officer on New Year's Day. The manner in which this call is made varies widely between organizations and stations, but it is always announced how it is to be arranged. In the usual case officers are accompanied by their wives when the call is made at the quarters of the Commanding Officer—*Officers' Guide*

The Army-Navy Football Game

Annually, on the last Saturday in November, usually at the Municipal Stadium in Philadelphia, Pennsylvania, the football teams of the United States Military Academy from West Point and the United States Naval Academy from Annapolis meet in a game which creates intense interest from Washington to Tokyo and from Alaska to the Panama Canal Zone.

The cadets from West Point and the midshipmen from Annapolis are transported en masse to this game, and all around the world radio or television sets are turned on. The respective academies alternate in being "host." The corps of cadets and the regiment of midshipmen march from their trains onto the playing field, the organization acting as host marching on first. The spectacle of these fine young men in the gray and blue uniforms is stirring.

Armed Forces Day

The third Saturday in May has been set aside by the Secretary of Defense as Armed Forces Day. In the past, April 6 was Army Day; September 18, Air Force Day; October 27, Navy Day; however, with the unification of the Services, it seems wise and fitting that Armed Forces Day suffice for all.

NAVAL CUSTOMS AND TRADITIONS AN ARMY WIFE SHOULD KNOW

With unification of the Services, one of these fine days you may suddenly find that your husband is ordered to NATO, or to a naval station. It will make your lot a bit easier if you know something of naval customs and traditions beforehand.

The Navy is rightly proud of its history, and its customs and traditions are hoary with age. They date back to the early days when "iron men went down to the sea in wooden ships" (some facetious young ensigns like to reverse this quotation). The value of tradition and custom to military or naval service is incontestable. The worth of ceremony rests mainly upon the fact that it binds us to the past, while at the same time lending an air of dignity and respect to all official relations, at home or abroad. Ceremony is said to be the cement of discipline, and upon discipline the Naval Service rests.

It might be interesting to know something of the Department of the Navy. It is made up of: (1) the Navy Department, which is the executive department in Washington; (2) the Shore Department, which is charged with the field activities; (3) the Operating Forces or sea, air, and shore elements participating in naval operations.

The Marine Corps is one of the most colorful branches of the U. S. Military and Naval Service. There is a popular belief among many Americans that "when the Army and the Navy finally gaze on heavenly scenes they will find the streets are guarded by United States Marines." Many Marine officers are Naval Academy men who upon graduation chose the Marine Corps. The reputation of the Marines as "tough fighting men" and their smart appearance and strong morale appeal to the highest type of American youth. There is no finer body of fighting men in the world.

Would you like to know why Marines are called leathernecks? Well, the name dates back to the early days of the Revolution, to the black-leather stocks which were part of the uniform. Even as late as thirty years ago the inner lining of the collar of the full-dress coat was made of leather so it would stand up.

The standards of the Corps are high as to physique, intelligence, and character. And a Marine loves to say, "It is still possible to be a Marine, if you're *man* enough." Their *esprit de corps* is excellent and their morale is always high.

The Coast Guard is the oldest of the Services. In time of peace it operates under the Treasury Department, but in time of war it is an integral part of the Navy. The Coast Guard motto is *Semper Paratus* . . . Always Ready.

It is a nice compliment to be invited aboard a ship for dinner. In normal peacetime when the ship is in port, Navy wives frequently go on board ship after 4:00 P.M. and remain for dinner. It is customary for Navy couples to invite friends to the officers' mess aboard ship occasionally. The officer of the deck will be standing at the head of the gangplank to receive you. He remains on deck during the period of his watch, which is four hours.

No one in the Navy is fashionably late, so if your invitation states that you are to be at the boat landing at four-thirty, allow plenty of time and arrive at four-fifteen. The officers' motor "launch," the captain's "gig," or if you're lucky the admiral's "barge" will take you out to the ship. When you get there, chances are you will be greeted after introductions with the phrase, "Glad to have you aboard." The proper answer to that, believe it or not and simple as it seems, is "Glad to be aboard."

Never be guilty of calling a battleship a *boat;* nothing hurts the ears of a Navy man so much. The Navy defines a boat as something to be hoisted aboard a ship.

You may be in time to see the ship's colors hauled down at sunset. This corresponds to retreat on military posts and Air Force bases. Visitors stand at attention while two sailors reverently and slowly take down the flag and fold it. On ships having a band, the national anthem is played.

Dinner will be on the dot, usually at six o'clock in the officers' mess, which is in a part of the ship designated as "officers' country." Remember you are the guest of the entire mess, as the expense of guests is prorated among the entire group. The meal will be served by quiet, well-trained attendants, and you will be impressed with the appointments and service.

Heavy old-fashioned silver will bear the Navy seal, beautiful white linen damask will cover the table, and the dinner will probably be something special in your honor, such as Indian curry or rice-tafel. Don't expect to see the captain at dinner, unless he is your host. Ordinarily he eats alone, in silent dignity in his own mess. You will conduct yourself as if you were dining in the home of friends, and after dinner everyone lingers in the mess for a little chat before going to the movies out on deck.

Don't go below to powder your nose because the movie will start as soon as the captain is seated. Be assured he will be on time, and when he arrives someone bellows "Attention" over the public-address system. All the officers stand at attention until he is seated. You remain seated, as ladies never stand in the presence of the admiral unless he is accompanied by ladies. Later, coffee is served in the wardroom, after which the motor launch is brought alongside to take all visitors ashore.

Some Tips on the Navy!

1. In getting into a boat, the ranking officer's lady gets in last. As a rule, the ladies precede the gentlemen, unless circumstances are such that the ladies require assistance, when an officer will precede them. In rough sea, boats can churn around diabolically sometimes when one is trying to secure a footing onto the gangway! A ladder is worse.

2. The senior officer leaves the ship last. He disembarks first. An easy way to remember this is to bear in mind that the senior officer must stumble or crawl over everybody else's legs. This is one time seniority pays off in reverse.

3. Junior officers take the seats nearest the bow.

4. You can distinguish the officer of the deck by the telescope he carries as an insigne of his position, and by his wearing gloves. You say "How do you do?" to him and smile!

5. Gentlemen guests salute the quarterdeck. (Your husband will know what this means and explain to you.) The quarterdeck has been a dignified and sacred area from the earliest days.

6. The starboard side of a ship is always kept clear for senior officers and is always used as the honor side.

Battleships, often called battle wagons, are designed to give punishment, also to take it. It normally takes four years to build one. Battleships are named for states: *California, Missouri, Pennsylvania*. Carriers are the Navy's mobile airfields. A carrier's job is to give punishment, but not to take it. Carriers are named for famous battles or famous men: *Lexington, Saratoga, Franklin D. Roosevelt*. Cruisers are the scouts of the fleet. They are named for cities: *Louisville, Honolulu, Indianapolis*. Destroyers are the trouble boats of the sea and are named after naval officers, enlisted men, and civilians distinguished in the Navy: *Ward, Scott*, etc. Submarines are long-distance scouts. They are named for fish: *Pompano, Perch, Cusk, Gudgeon*.

Women used to be allowed to live on board in the days of sailing ships of the British Navy, but only if they were married to members of the crew. It is to this strange circumstance that we are indebted for the expression "son of a gun." There was a child actually born on board, probably under a gun and only sheltered at birth from the view of the ship's company by a canvas screen. As it was, alas, impossible to tell the paternity of the child, it was called a "son of a gun."

Should you wish to know more about Navy life, I suggest that you read *The Navy Wife*.

AIR FORCE CUSTOMS AND TRADITIONS AN ARMY WIFE SHOULD KNOW

The Air Force is the youngest of the Services, and until June 26, 1947, the Air Corps was a branch of the Army. When the National Security Act was approved by the President, this merger was known as the "Unification Bill." The Air Force has a few of its own customs, but the bulk of them were derived from the Army.

For instance, you might be interested to know that:

Air bases are named for military aviators who lost their lives in combat or in aviation accidents. When you are going to a new base, therefore, it is smart to find out something about the person for whom the base is named. It is quite possible to make a horrible blunder through ignorance in such a matter; on the other hand, such knowledge may be turned to good conversational advantage.

At an Air Force funeral, when a formation is flown, it is timed so that the planes appear over the procession while the remains are being borne to the grave. When the formation is a V of five or seven planes, it is customary to fly less one airplane to indicate a blank file for the deceased flier.

The more information you have about the history and traditions of a place when you get there, the easier it will be to become a part of the community. Don't parade your knowledge, but don't be an ignoramus either. Know the answers even if you don't have to give them often.

VIP's

Very Important Persons or *VIP's* is a term that originated during World War II when such were given priorities in traveling on war business. When traveling in military aircraft they are always on-and-off-loaded first. They are also greeted by the base commander or a reception committee, and on many bases special VIP quarters await them.

Air Force Customs While Traveling in Military Aircraft

1. Passengers, regardless of rank, seniority, or Service, are subject to the orders of the assigned first pilot or airplane commander.

2. Civilian dependents are loaded and unloaded after VIP's, but before officers, regardless of rank.

3. An aircraft carrying general or flag officers is usually marked with a detachable plate carrying stars appropriate to the highest rank aboard. Count those stars!

4. Passengers are expected to observe all safety regulations and not explore the plane. To enter the flight deck or pilot's compartment one should be specifically invited.

5. Unnecessary moving about in the plane causes additional difficulty for the pilot in maintaining his assigned altitude. Passengers who are abnormally active while in the air are designated "waltzing mice," and they aren't popular with airmen.

6. There are regulations against smoking during take-off and landing, and sometimes during flight. Parachute rules must be observed.

7. Airplane flights are dependent upon weather, so the pilot's decision to fly or not to fly is never questioned by passengers. The pilot has a lot of information they don't have.

8. Just as the captain at sea is the last to leave his ship in distress, so in an emergency in the air a pilot cannot leave the controls until all others aboard his aircraft have had an opportunity to bail out. You must obey the pilot's commands, particularly if he orders all passengers to bail out or "hit the silk."

RANK AMONG WOMEN

The only women who have rank in the Service are the WACS, WAFS, WAVES, and Marines; Army and Navy Nurses, Air Force or flight nurses, and Women Medical Specialists. In no way does this include Army, Navy, or Air Force wives. Although there is no rank among Service wives, still a junior officer's wife should always show courteous deference to older women and especially to the commanding officer's wife, though not in a way that smacks of "bootlicking" or currying favor.

This is actually merely one of the first lessons in good breeding (or courtesy) you learned as a child—to have respect for your elders.

During the war years, a very indifferent and objectionable attitude developed among many young people in regard to deference to their seniors. Discipline of the Service came hard to young men, and it was equally hard for their wives. It was considered smart to disregard many of the social amenities and to consider any courtesy that required either mental or physical effort an outmoded custom. As a result, many young wives who failed to observe the social amenities were branded as ill bred, careless, and ignorant. Behavior of this sort reflects upon your husband and, if persisted in, hurts his career.

Let us take another slant to illustrate the importance of courtesy. In the business or professional world, certainly the wife of the president of a university or the wife of a president of a large business corporation is shown a certain deference. The position of the college president's wife or the business executive's wife parallels that of your commanding officer's wife. It is the same difference!

In polite society, special respect is always shown to older people, especially women. A younger woman should rise when introduced to an older woman. As you were taught in childhood, offer your chair or perform any little courtesy that the occasion warrants, but avoid any affectation or show of manners for which you may be criticized.

STAR DUST AND BAR DUST

Promotion came fast during the war, and many very young officers of ability found themselves in command positions. It was not unusual for a captain to become a colonel or in a few instances a brigadier general. Corporals became captains and sergeants advanced to colonel. Some retained their rank after the war, and their wives found themselves likewise in positions of responsibility. Many warrant officers rose to high ranks.

In the give-and-take of life, naturally difficult situations are bound to arise where a senior officer finds himself serving under a young general who was formerly junior to him. This is rarely pleasant on either side, but military men have a way of handling these situations with dignity, tact, and diplomacy. It is the wives in many instances who are bitter and make trouble. Women are different by nature; should a situation such as this ever arise in your experience, try to handle it with all the tact of which you are capable. Should your husband be demoted in rank, never complain or act hurt about it; probably he will be promoted later and you will realize how foolish it was to worry.

At some time you will run across the wife to whom her husband's two silver bars spell exalted rank. You may even meet a wife who is blinded by star dust! It is evading the issue to say that rank-conscious wives do not exist. I like particularly the story of the general's wife in Washington during the war who was asked: "Why don't you wear the miniature of your husband's rank in small diamond stars?" Her enjoyable reply was, "Look, if my husband were a butcher, would I go around wearing a small lamb chop on my shoulder?"

"Wear Your Husband's Rank Proudly in Your Heart, But Never on Your Shoulder" (Marion MacDonald)

Being the wife of the commanding officer is not easy. First of all, it requires great tact, understanding, and a kind heart plus unlimited versatility, and executive ability combined with graciousness. A big order, isn't it?

I sincerely hope that every reader of this book has met at least one commanding officer's wife who has all these qualities. From my own experience of some thirty years, three Army wives stand out in my memory as commanding officers' wives. Each possessed all of the attributes mentioned above. Every young wife should find her ideal, then try to model her life along similar lines. Look for the good, the finest in everyone with whom you are serving and try not to see the faults.

Certainly the wife of the commanding officer, because of her husband's position if for no other reason, must have your respect. The seasoned wife takes her husband's rank and position in her stride. She is proud of him, but never noticeably so. Generally she has worked at his side through the years, but she never forgets that it is *his* position and that the *rank* and *stars* belong to him.

At a social gathering in a private home, officers and their wives remain until the commanding officer has departed. There have been many painful and amusing instances where parties laster far longer than the hosts had planned because the C.O. was enjoying himself. But that's the way it is.

Final Tips and Taboos

By this time, Connie and Peggy, you should consider yourselves briefed on Army customs and traditions. *However:*

1. Whenever you are in doubt on any question, don't hesitate to follow the sensible procedure of consulting the wife of a senior officer.

These older women will be more than glad to help you in any way they can. After all, they had to learn once themselves, perhaps the hard way, and they don't forget that.

2. It is considered unmilitary for an officer to carry an umbrella (except in the Chinese Army).

3. Do not speak of your husband as *the* major or *the* colonel; after all, there are a few others of these ranks in the Army. Merely call him Bob or Jim—and when you want to be formal say "my husband."

4. It is not considered military for officers in uniform to be the motive power for baby carriages. How to get around this one without doing it all yourself is your own business.

5. Most officers in uniform avoid carrying bundles unless absolutely necessary, the reason being that it is difficult to salute. (A woman begins to suspect about here that a man made up these rules!)

6. Promptness is a military must. Never keep anyone waiting unnecessarily . . . or even necessarily. Be particularly considerate in keeping appointments with those who may be a bit in awe of your husband's rank.

7. Avoid gossiping, promoting rumors, or listening to gossip. No good ever comes from malicious talk, and often reputations are torn to shreds. In this regard "Silence is golden." It's a bit easier to start a fire than to put it out, and many people burn down their own houses.

8. Should your husband confide in you or tell you details of official business (which he shouldn't), use tact and common sense in keeping them to yourself. Many a man's Service career has been sidetracked by the indiscreet babbling of his indiscreet wife.

9. Pay attention to small details. Write letters of condolence, congratulation, thanks for gifts and courtesies *promptly*.

10. Don't ever commit the unpardonable sin of airing your military knowledge! Remember the Army is a man's game in a man's world, and just about the time you think you know a little about it you will be embarrassed. About the only safe rule to follow is that of the wise old owl: Listen if and when you must, but give the impression of profound intelligence by keeping your knowledge to yourself.

ORDERS OF THE OLD ARMY

The following orders were found recently among old records in the Pentagon. The orders were posted to troops at Fort Riley, Kansas, October 25, 1842.

Attention to Orders:

ONE. Members of this command will, when shooting at buffaloes on the parade grounds, be careful not to fire in the direction of the Commanding Officer's quarters.

Two. Student officers will discontinue the practise of roping and riding buffaloes.

THREE. Attention of all officers is called to Paragraph 107 Army Regulations in which it provides that officers will wear beards.

Chapter V

LIFE ON AN ARMY POST

A S A BRIDE new to the Army, at first you may feel strange among the military, but with the passing of time, various assignments, and different stations you will come to have an Army wife's feeling of "belonging." It is a wonderful "family feeling." From it should come a loyalty to the Service, a pride in your husband's contribution to the Army which it is good for you to express . . . particularly to your husband. Remember, your positive attitude toward liking the Service is a fine thing for his morale. It will be reflected in his happiness and in his work.

You will find that from the time you are established on a post you will be honestly, completely, unreservedly, and thoroughly welcome. Before, your friends—your very good friends—may have been numbered on your ten fingers; now, they will number in the hundreds and even thousands, both men and women, all of them potentially people who will want to meet you and know you, making your life happy and brilliant. Not a single one who wouldn't, at the drop of a feather, help you in need, cheer you in despair, and above all congratulate you for any good job done.

After even one year's service at a large station like Fort Benning or Fort Sill, it matters not where you may later be stationed, you will inevitably run across someone you have met or known before. If you go to the ends of the earth you will usually find that other Army people have prepared a welcome for you. That is the bond of the Service!

You should understand from the start that while there is nothing the Army will not do for you, though sometimes what's done seems to be done in a mighty peculiar way, you must at all times return that loyalty with your whole heart and mind. Being a successful Army wife is a full-time twenty-four-hour job.

You must accept—and you will learn to in time—the Army on blind faith even when you don't understand it. Later, when you see more of the Service, you will realize why. Also, there will be plenty of times (even as you read these words, perhaps) when that blind

86

faith will be pretty hard to hang on to. But cheer up! There's an old saying, "Misery loves company," and you have plenty of company, believe me. There are thousands of other enlisted men's and officers' brides living on a post for the first time, so you aren't exactly alone. When you get lonely or upset the first time, go see a movie and simmer down, provided there is a movie where you happen to be.

ADVANTAGES OF LIVING ON A POST

Transportation is a major item today, and an officer, NCO, or soldier saves much time and energy if he does not have to drive miles through heavy traffic from his home to the post. Living on the post, he is near his work and saves the cost of transportation.

If quarters are furnished, light, heat, water, and telephone service (at a lowered rental) plus maintenance are included, and prove a great saving. Refrigerators, stoves, Venetian blinds, fans, and heaters are supplied, also standard articles of furniture such as dining-room furniture, desks, chairs, dressers, dressing tables, chests, and G.I. beds or cots, if they are available.

Shopping and marketing are often made convenient by the operating of private concessions under the Post Exchange. Commissaries are operated only where city markets are inaccessible.

On all larger posts laundry and dry-cleaning facilities are available and a few installations have automatic laundries equipped with washers and driers.

A hospital or dispensary is available for dependents in case of emergency treatment.

Banking and post-office facilities are usually provided, while a library, gymnasium, and swimming pool increase the recreational possibilities. A motion-picture theater showing the latest films at low rates is a popular feature of every post.

If the number of children warrants, a school is operated on the post for the preschool, primary, and elementary grades. Transportation is usually furnished older children who attend school off the post.

A chapel and chaplain are available, and usually Protestant, Catholic, and Jewish services are held.

A beauty shop, barber shop, and shoe-shining and repair shop are under the direction of the Post Exchange and are operated for the convenience of personnel.

Tennis courts, bowling alleys, handball courts, volleyball courts, badminton courts, baseball and softball diamonds are located at nearly all posts, and where possible a golf course with clubhouse adds to the pleasure of all golfers stationed at the posts.

The Officers' Club and the NCO Club are in charge of their dances and bingo games, the custom being that a designated group sponsors the weekly or monthly entertainment and is responsible for its success. The mess, bar, family-night buffets, and private parties come under the jurisdiction of the club officer in charge.

The Officers' Wives' Club and the NCO Wives' Club serve as the hub of the Army wives' social life. Other activities are so varied that considerable space has been given to the many aspects later in this chapter. It is every wife's duty not only to join but to take an active interest in the Woman's Club on the post where her husband is stationed.

There is no law making it obligatory for an officer to join the Officers' Club, but he is expected to support the activities of his unit, and according to the *Officers' Guide,* "In peacetime, it would be unheard of for an officer to refrain from membership in the club."

The same holds true for an officer's wife; it is her duty to join and pay her dues, which are usually nominal, whether or not she is able to attend. Understand, there is no regulation or law compelling a wife to join the Woman's Club, but *she is expected to do so!* The NCO wife is likewise expected to join and attend the NCO Wives' Club.

The Over-All Housing Picture

The next five years should see a great change in the housing picture, so take heart! The green light has been given to permanent construction for many posts. Family units with two, three, and four bedrooms are planned and much of the construction will be of multiple-unit, garden-type apartment construction. At some posts individual houses will be built. Beautiful plans are being submitted by architects for government housing, and no doubt the most attractive and most practical ones will be accepted.

The seriousness of the housing situation, and the deplorable plight of many Service families who were living in substandard quarters, plus the unreasonable distances personnel are required to commute, brought the current strenuous attempts to improve things.

It has been proved that a serious shortage of suitable quarters for dependents of military personnel adversely affects the morale of the

Service, causing many highly desirable officers and enlisted men to seek separation or discharge. If your quarters aren't the best, just realize that others are aware of the situation and are working to remedy it.

YOUR FIRST QUARTERS

Let us be optimistic and assume that your husband will be fortunate enough by virtue of his duties to be assigned a permanent set of quarters, or at least a unit consisting of a living room or a living-dining-room combination, a kitchen, and one bedroom, maybe two, with a bath. This is the ultimate. In the next chapter we will go into "Love and Light Housekeeping" and all that goes with living in a "one-room efficiency." There is an expression used among soldiers to bolster up a comrade when the going is so rough it is ludicrous, and I think it is applicable here. If you are lucky enough to draw even the most primitive quarters on a base, even though you have a Park Avenue and Southampton background, don't be surprised if some seasoned joker says to you on your voicing a complaint: "Ah . . . you never had it so good!"

If quarters are assigned to your husband, the rental allowance is deducted from his pay check. There is one general regulation: If quarters on the post are available (desirable or not), they must be occupied. It takes a military board to condemn quarters as unlivable and unfit for occupancy.

IDENTIFICATION

All military dependents over twelve years of age are required to have post passes in their possession. To procure a permanent pass, dependents have to fill out various identification forms; on foreign bases, photographs are usually required and even fingerprints. Regulations differ at various posts.

Soon after your arrival, make a tour of the post and acquaint yourself with the commissary, the exchange, the school, the chapel, post headquarters, post operations, and the base hospital. It will pay off to know where they are when you are in a hurry.

HOUSEHOLD EQUIPMENT

On a permanent post, one very material saving to a young couple is the use of standard types of furniture if and when it is available. All permanent quarters are equipped with stoves and electric refrigerators, two costly items in the budget of newly marrieds.

Dining-room furniture, desks, chairs, dressers, chests, and dressing tables if available are also issued upon request or they may be in the quarters upon your arrival. It is possible even to draw beds, mattresses, and pillows unless you have and prefer to use your own.

Oh yes, I know . . . there are some posts with not a stick of furniture; then be grateful you have a roof and start improvising and using your wedding checks for the necessities. Be it ever so humble, there will never be another place like the G.I. Quonset or the unfurnished quarters where you first set up housekeeping. Nor will there ever be another dinner like the first one you cook and serve, perhaps on a card table or a rough packing box, using your best silver and finest china by way of being festive!

Right off, learn to use your prized possessions every day; don't save for company. Remember, you'll want to keep your husband as long as you do your silver, and he will appreciate and learn to love the cherished things that spell home to both of you, although man-like he may never mention it. By using your sterling silver and wedding presents at the beginning, you and your husband can set a standard of living graciously. It is the little routine things like eating breakfast together and using your spode breakfast service that you will treasure the longest. Do have breakfast with him if possible; it is a wonderful way to start the day with a nice warm togetherness.

MAKE YOUR HOUSE FUNCTIONAL

Men like feminine women but they like functional houses, and a happy household is a synthesis of both. Learn early in the game to make your house work for you rather than being a slave to your house. A functional house is a planned house; it is not filled with useless, small accessories, gadgets, or dust catchers, which require extra work.

You won't be able to do much about the outside of the quarters if you live on a post on which there are rows and rows of duplexes in "tenement tan" or London-gray stucco or maybe a color scheme hideously reminiscent of war camouflage. Simply forget it, and concentrate on the interior. If there is a front porch, your welcome begins there. An unswept entrance, strewn with old newspapers, leaves, or toys is never a very inviting approach.

Make your windows interesting for they are the eyes of your house. There is nothing lovelier than crisp white muslin or organdy curtains, crossed and looped to show a pot of perky cyclamen or blossoming pink azaleas. Never skimp on curtain material. An effect of quality and excellent taste can be achieved with plain cheesecloth if plenty of material is used. Keep your window treatments simple but gay. If the glass is sparkling and there is a blossoming plant as a greeting, no one will confuse your quarters with the other fifty-eight sets in your row. And if they all copy you and dress up their front windows, put a different flowerpot in the window. It's as simple as that!

Your first home is vitally important; it is imperative that you exercise good taste. Remember, with planning it is possible to have an attractive home regardless of your budget.

A FIVE- OR TEN-YEAR PLAN

Today we are living in a changing world; it is wise to face life as it is, to be alert and to have vision. When planning to buy furniture for your first set of quarters, try not to think entirely in terms of just this first house but in terms of what you eventually wish to own. Try to project your life ahead at least five years with numerous moves. But, with your tongue in your cheek, also remember that "three moves are equivalent to a fire."

Your home should be a genuine expression of you, not a rehash of a former era. Furniture should always be selected in relation to the people who are going to use it. Suppose someone parted with Grandma's whatnot as a wedding present for you. Simply skip it and, if you can, tactfully give it right back to the generous donor or store it in a basement where the termites will take care of it for you.

YOUR HOME REFLECTS YOU

Your home is much more than a collection of furniture and fabrics; it is your background. Your living room paints your portrait as a homemaker and is more of an index to your character than any palm reading will ever reveal. There is no doubt that a home has an individual atmosphere just as a person has an individual personality. The moment one steps inside the door of a house one senses something of that atmosphere.

Neatness is attractive in any home but in a small home it is essential. Empty spaces are delightful; clutter is your worst enemy so avoid buying anything because you think it is cute. You will merely wonder what to do with it. The modern trend is toward simplicity in design, bare spaces, plain lines, cheerful color, and lack of fussiness. These things, skillfully managed, help to create a restful atmosphere even in a comparatively tiny house.

Short budgets require disciplined buying, so learn to add a little at a time and have the excitement of collecting truly beautiful things over a period of years.

You don't need "Welcome" on the front door mat if you can achieve hospitality, eagerness, and delight when you respond to a guest's knock or ring. A smile always helps when you answer the door to admit anyone. If you have a dog, teach him to wag his tail in welcome, rather than rush to the front door and frighten the visitor by his ferocious burglarproof manner of barking.

A brilliantly lighted front hall gives a cheery air to the house and sets its tone. Avoid the dimly lit cloister entrance where your guest is in fear lest he trip over a sleeping dog or a recumbent golf bag. Arrange a large bowl of greens such as laurel, magnolia leaves, or ivy in the hall if you can't afford fresh flowers. If you have only one mirror, hang it in the hall over a table or chest. Both you and your guests will enjoy a last-minute glance to give the assurance and poise needed when one goes out to face the world. Remember, too, that your husband spends some time in the place, although of course you never think it's enough. And the man does deserve more consideration. Maybe the following will help.

MASCULINE BILL OF RIGHTS

If you want your man to love his home, study the masculine point of view before you begin to decorate. Let him sketch plans with you. Let him see samples. Have him meet the decorator and *never* commit yourself to heavy expenses without discussing plans with him in advance.

1. A man has a right to man-sized chairs and to solidly built furniture.

2. A man has a right to good reading lamps, large ash trays conveniently placed, and a special place for his books and magazines.

3. A man has a right to a study or bedroom of his own if space permits and he wishes it. His judgment in colors should be respected.

4. A man has a right to privacy in his own home, and he will respect yours in turn. Do not rearrange his personal belongings. Do not use his things without asking his permission. It is said that only the greatest of souls can share fountain pens, razor blades, and umbrellas with equanimity.

5. A man has a right to some luxury of his own kind. He enjoys big spongy bath towels, a good light for reading in bed, a good light for shaving, and a convenient place for keeping his liquor and for mixing drinks.

A Few Dos and Don'ts

1. Do make a plan before buying anything.
2. Don't buy sets or suites of furniture.
3. Do seek advice, but don't accept it indiscriminately.
4. Do develop sales resistance.
5. Don't let your home appear as a pretentious furniture or silver display room.
6. Don't buy even as much as a spoon if there is no need for it.
7. Do avoid bargains, as there is nothing so expensive in the long run.
8. Don't place any piece of furniture cater-cornered.

The Living Room

Your living room can be completely charming without being expensive if you will use your wits and a sewing machine. Of course, not every bride is skilled in using a sewing machine, but this is a good time to begin. Plan your living room to be really lived in. If your husband is six feet three and you are five feet two, select furniture that will fit each of you. Low chairs in which a tiny person can lean back blissfully may be more than a headache to an ex-football player.

Provided the quarters have the usual G.I. furniture, a desk, table, and chairs, you will want at least two comfortable chairs as soon as you can afford them.

A good divan is always expensive, but don't buy a cheap new one. One old Army trick is to use a G.I. cot, upholster the ends with G.I. pillows, and make a well-fitting slip cover for it. If you aren't expert enough as a seamstress yourself, then hire someone to do it. It pays. Don't omit the pillows and plenty of them! One clever bride, with her husband's help, made good modernistic bookcases and end tables out of packing boxes. Often Army women use "target cloth" for curtains. This is usually obtainable through the Ordnance Corps, is very cheap, and dyes beautifully. Until you can afford good rugs such as Oriental or Broadloom, don't buy any. Make string rugs, dyeing them to match your color scheme, or use hooked rugs. Grass rugs or the invaluable *lauhala* mats are in order in the tropics.

When your budget will stand it, invest in a comfortable divan or two love seats for your living room. A good plan is to watch the used-furniture ads in the papers, haunt the secondhand stores, or the antique shops if you are collecting. Or go to the express company and the storage company sales that are usually held twice a year. There you can often pick up really good, well-made, expensive pieces of furniture at your own price. Get a good decorator to come and help you plan your living room. Pocket your pride, tell him what you have to spend, and be honest; then you can take his suggestions and do the best possible.

By all means, consider the new sectional furniture . . . the kind that can be separated and used as individual pieces, or in twosomes form a love seat, or with three or four units make an extra-long sofa on which your husband can stretch full length. The only difficulty is that it appears bulky; however, now it is made of light plastic material.

Never buy faddish furniture or something for the particular house you are occupying. Remember, you may move tomorrow! Avoid massive or very heavy pieces. You will pay excess on every move, and that runs into money. By the same standard, avoid very light, frail furniture, or brittle antiques that won't stand packing and hard moves.

If you buy really good chintz, have it lined as a protective measure. It is wise to consult a good decorator before investing. Even with short windows, make your hangings three yards long so that they will fit any window, any place you may move. When buying material for three windows, it is wise to buy enough for a fourth. Three sets of curtains often prove awkward.

THE DINING ROOM

On almost every post, furniture for the dining room is issued. Should you be compelled to buy it, then a drop-leaf table or a gate-leg table that can later be used in a living room or hall is preferable to a dining set. Odd chairs work out to better advantage later. If there is any possibility of your going to Panama or the Philippines, spend very little on china. An inexpensive set of dishes that can be used in the kitchen later is desirable. If you received your flat silver as a wedding present, and some fairy godmother gave you a silver tea service, start to fill in your silver slowly, buying one good piece at a time. Cheap hollow ware bends badly in moving. We are also assuming that you have a good supply of linen in your trousseau.

Card tables are all right for card playing, but even the strongest and most sturdy are wobbly and rickety for dining. Don't join the card-table-using fraternity except for parties. One clever young couple I know, a sergeant and his bride, chose to take a check rather than silver for a wedding present. After buying the essentials in furniture, there was little left for silver. Since they were to be on the move, they invested in a well-equipped wicker picnic basket. It contained a complete setting of six knives, forks, spoons, etc., in plastic. They claim this answers their needs for the present, until they can start saving for their sterling flatware.

Colorful place mats can make an attractive table. Personally, I loathe paper napkins, and it isn't too much trouble to rinse out small napkins, but that is a matter of personal choice.

Country drug and grocery stores still keep candy in big, square unembellished glass jars. Try buying a pair or two of them. Minus the covers, they are stunning for holding flowers on dining table or sideboard.

If you have a small dining room, a round table not only promotes conversation but saves space. Large folding round tops can be bought to fit over a card table and these will allow for six or eight place settings—in case you have no dining room and have to serve in the one-room efficiency.

THE FUNCTIONAL KITCHEN

Your kitchen is actually a workshop and should be cheerful. I personally like a blue and white Dutch kitchen. Some kitchens in their hospital whiteness, without a touch of color, remind one more of an operating room than of a temple of culinary delight. A touch of color makes most homemakers happier, and a comfortable, low painted chair or rocker where one can sit while preparing vegetables or holding the "littlest one while kissing a hurt" adds inviting charm and hominess.

If you do not have built-in cabinets and work space, don't place your table so far away from the stove that you will need roller skates to do your own cooking. Learn to save steps, to conserve your energy for the more important things, to be easy on yourself.

Buy good utensils and all of the labor-saving devices that you need as you need them and can afford them. A good electric mixer is expensive but worth the price if you go in for cooking in a big way. A high-speed blender is another sound investment when you can afford it.

Insist upon the best in cutlery, as cheap knives cost more in bad tempers than the monetary difference warrants. If your husband is a hunter or fisherman, sooner or later he will get the idea of buying a deep-freeze!

The old-fashioned kitchen was the heart of the home where family and friends were likely to congregate at all hours because it was usually the cheeriest and warmest spot. Next came the narrow, galley-like, up-to-date kitchen, which tended to exclude everybody but the cook, and kept her strictly on her feet. Today, the pendulum is swinging back and in modern homes the larger kitchens provide all the comforts of home; in addition to being the business end of the house, they also welcome company with the greatest charm. This is the type of kitchen where you like to keep a coffee pot on the stove and a full cooky jar on the shelf.

THE BEDROOMS

If G.I. cots are all that you can draw for the bedrooms, cover the bed ends with attractive cretonne or quilted chintz, make a pretty bedspread, and you have a grand decorative disguise. A folding table with a skirt of the same chintz will suffice for a dressing table. One clever bride thumbtacked a foundation of peach sateen to the table, then used a pair of inexpensive dotted net curtains as the overskirt. The ruffled sides formed the valance, and the ruffled ends formed a pretty finish for the front of the table. Padding was used for the top, over which she became "quite extravagant" and put quilted peach satin, and over the whole placed a slab of inexpensive glass; thus she had a beautiful dressing table for a few dollars and a little ingenuity. Wardrobe trunks, slip-covered, often have to serve as wardrobes and chests of drawers.

For the bride who has received a goodly supply of wedding presents, the furnishing and decorating problem is much simpler, especially if she has been thrifty and saved her wedding checks. However, never buy right off! Study your quarters and their possibilities, and remember a good decorator is a wonderful help, but never give him carte blanche unless you can afford it. If you are stationed in or near a city like New York or Washington, some large reputable firm may supply your furnishings on a budget plan. However, this is sometimes dangerous for young people. They get into debt. But that is a vital point that requires special emphasis, and will be taken up later.

Here is a scoop! When you run up against the impossible in a set of Army quarters, or you have to make a garage over into a livable home, or when you can't make up your mind, or if shortages and lack of money flout your best-laid decorating schemes, there is a new service sponsored by *House Beautiful* with Elaine Neal as its consultant. You send her your floor plan, placement of windows, doors, fireplace, if any, and present arrangement of furniture. Include floor dimensions and ceiling height. A snapshot helps if you can send one, and she likes you to tell her something about yourself, your color preferences and taste, and how your family lives. The fee is two dollars per room, and this service is limited exclusively to mail. Address your letter to Elaine Neal, *House Beautiful*, 572 Madison Avenue, New York City, 22, and allow at least three weeks for a reply.

Early in your Army housekeeping you will need to develop a philosophy for living, all your very own. It will pay dividends if you learn early to enjoy and to be grateful for what you have each day, because that elusive tomorrow never comes. Try to see the best in your home each day; it may be a Quonset hut but there are bound to be compensations. There will probably be a view which some millionaire would envy, but no amount of money could buy it because the land belongs to Uncle Sam, and you are his ward for the present. It is your view. Be glad if your quarters are small; your household duties will be less and you can spend more time on other activities you enjoy. Again, should you draw a field officers' set, enjoy that for the time it will be yours. Perhaps you can now have Great-Aunt Susie come for a visit since you have an extra bedroom and bath on the first floor. It may lend itself to a house party, and all of your civilian friends will be impressed and envy you. Just take whatever comes in your stride and you will enjoy the Army!

It is said, and it is practically a scientific fact, that to be loved makes women beautiful, and houses blossom in exactly the same way. If you love your home, whether it is a penthouse or a prefabricated shelter, it will have charm.

Consult your husband and get him interested in the arranging of each set of quarters as you move about from place to place. Encourage his interest and make him feel that he has a part in planning the appearance of your home. Men have good taste and they are prac-

tical. At first he may say he does not know about such things, but
that is because he is diffident. While most Army men dislike depart-
ment-store shopping, perhaps you can persuade him to go along if
you make him feel you really need his help in going to a furniture
store or decorator's shop to buy a rug or a certain piece of furniture.

When buying bedroom furniture, never economize on mattresses
or springs. These two items are far more important than the head
and foot board of the bed. Again, avoid suites. They are the invention of merchandising men and afford an excellent means of selling
more goods. Even if you are new at this housekeeping game, learn
early that the only things that are "for free" are the sky, the air, the
stars, and wild flowers. Don't let a sharp salesman talk you into a
buy which will definitely include inferior springs and a poor mattress and completely wrap you up in a smooth-sounding installment
plan! Beware of sales psychology when purchasing and be alert to
the fact the $98.99 is really $100 plus tax.

Your bedroom should be a "relaxing oasis." The beds should be
placed so that the bright morning light will not awaken a late sleeper
and the night owl's reading lamp will not bother the other person.

Today, you can rest more comfortably than Cleopatra on many
kinds of springs and mattresses. We Americans have learned a great
deal about bed comfort, most of it in the last hundred years. I very
much enjoyed the following story about an American husband, ir-
ritably waiting for his wife to finish shopping, who invented the wire
bedspring. He was Mr. James Liddy of Watertown, New York. According to legend, Mr. Liddy was waiting in his buggy for his wife
to buy dress goods some ten years before the Civil War. Chafing with
impatience to get home and tighten his rope bedsprings (a twice-
yearly task necessary to remove the sag), Mr. Liddy, like many a husband, waited and waited, and finally clambered down to find Mrs.
Liddy.

When he returned, his horse shied suddenly, lunged forward, and
threw Mr. Liddy against the spring buggy seat. Instead of being
bruised, he bounced pleasantly and comfortably. This started Mr.
Liddy thinking. He went home and experimented with buggy springs
for his bed. Result: by 1900 almost everybody was sleeping on coil
bedsprings, and the innerspring mattress was on its way to being
born.

Quiet helps you to relax, deepens your sleep. Here are a few tricks that help cut down noise. Leave a space between your bed and the wall, so that vibrations aren't transmitted to the bed. Put your clock on a tiny felt mat. Carpeting is good as a noise absorber; so are curtains with lots of fullness and body. (Should you build a house, keep bedroom quiet in mind: place your closets between rooms to absorb noise, specify doors without keyholes, and place bedrooms away from the garage and other active and noisy spots.)

You cannot enjoy or be proud of your bedroom if the colors clash, if the furniture is ill assorted, or if the bedroom looks untidy because the bedspreads don't fit or the spreads don't go well with the curtains. Remember, your bedroom is more yours than any other room in the house so don't be hesitant about surrounding yourself with personal possessions that make you happy whenever you see them. For instance, this is the spot for family pictures, a beautiful painting or print, the cigarette box you bought at that funny little shop in Venice. Possessions that bring a flow of happy memories! If you decorate it so that you really like it, the chances are that your family will like it, too. Your bedroom is a V.I.P. in your home (Very Important Place).

As mentioned earlier, men like big comfortable chairs by the right kind of light, table tops and chair arms that glasses won't stain and that are kept free of gimcracks. Put your ivory elephant bridge, if you must have one, somewhere else. Have large, easily cleaned crystal ash trays, a crystal cigarette box large enough for at least one pack of cigarettes, and a lighter kept filled with fuel on a near-by table. If your husband enjoys working at a desk so disordered it looks as if a cyclone had hit it, then try to find a niche for the desk where it is not in public view. It's easier than finding a new husband, and anyone with literary inclinations dislikes heartily having his papers rearranged into orderly stacks.

Everyone appreciates some degree of privacy and a modicum of personal independence. Try to arrange for both your husband and yourself to have one inviolate corner. It may be possible to set aside a corner of a seldom used guest room for your desk or sewing. Should your husband's hobby be woodwork, maybe he would like a portion of the garage for his workbench and tools. These are the little things that sometimes make or break a marriage.

If it is at all possible, have separate dressing rooms and separate closets. You may have your dressing table and clothes closet as fussy with froufrou as you like; but remember that your husband, sharing the bedroom, may enjoy a more conservative room. His dressing room and clothes closet, the latter equipped with detachable slanting shoe racks, large wooden hangers that will keep his uniforms in shape, tie racks, and separate boxes for military headgear, should be done in a monotone accented by a masculine color. Nothing la-di-da here.

LINEN CLOSET AND BATHROOM

A smooth-running household always boasts a well-arranged linen closet. Sheets are stacked in neat piles and confined with attractive ribbon or decorative bands to match the color scheme of the closet. Matching shelf edging with colored shelf paper in a different shade to harmonize adds a pleasing note. Lavender placed between the sheets or a "clove apple" gives the linen a refreshing odor. Lacking a linen closet, you might keep your linens in a special chest. To me there is nothing worse than fumbling around in a dark closet. Brighten your closets not only with color but with high-voltage light bulbs. Keep them bright and in order.

Many bathrooms in government quarters have small linen closets in which to keep towels, bath mats, bath cloths, and similar items. Check these often so that the contents are kept in order and do not avalanche forth when the door is opened—like Fibber and Molly's. If the closets are not ventilated, be sure to rotate the contents frequently and air them well.

If space permits, it is convenient to have bathroom scales and an attractive clothes hamper. Certainly, it goes without saying that everything of a personal nature should be kept out of sight. That means your hubsand's sight as well as that of guests. Many a divorce has gathered its real impetus from the festoons of damp panties, hose, and brassières through which a husband has been forced to battle his way at night in order to brush his teeth. In a bachelor-girl's apartment he thought they were sort of fun. But not as a steady diet!

As to color in bathrooms, someone went overboard in planning quarters of the before-Pearl Harbor vintage. Once in a great while you will draw a conservative black and white tile bath; but for the most part the color combinations are weird! Green and black, yellow and blue, turquoise and black, rose and blue—these are common. The most violent fantasy I ever encountered was a funereal oversize black bathtub, black toilet, and black lavatory. I was depressed for days and marveled at the architect's grim sense of humor in getting it approved. Now, you may understand why all-white bath accessories are recommended for a bride's trousseau. White is the only color guaranteed not to fight with the tile.

THE GUEST ROOM

If you are fortunate enough to have a "spare room" for guests, you can make it do double duty by serving as a study, a sewing room, or a hobby room when it is not occupied.

Every young couple looks forward to the arrival of their first house guests. They are proud of their home, and they want to show off their guest room to the best advantage by making their guest comfortable. First of all, there is the thrill of anticipation and getting ready for the guest.

Here are a few tips that may help you in your preparation. It is nice if you have soft, comfortable, inviting beds and can provide two pillows for each, one soft and one hard pillow. However, if your appointments are too plush, your guest may be tempted into prolonging his stay like "The Man Who Came to Dinner." If it is a G.I. situation as to beds, there isn't much you can do about it except hope that your guest likes a hard, solid tamped-down mattress.

Provide a bedside table even if it is only a painted orange crate or slightly disguised mess stool. It is a sign of welcome to place a small vase of flowers on the table, a tiny silent clock, and some new magazines and an interesting book or two. Provide a good lamp for reading in bed, and a light extra blanket folded at the foot of the bed.

An ordinary table might serve as a desk if it is well equipped with stationery, post cards, several types of stamps, ink, and pen. In the clothes closet, which should be entirely cleared, there should be a good supply of hangers. Matched closet accessories add an attractive touch. A dresser, a chest, or an improvised dressing table plus a comfortable chair which you may lend from your own room during the guest's stay should make the room quite comfortable.

A festive note is achieved by lining the dresser drawers with gay book paper or flowered wallpaper. Plain white shelf paper is better than nothing. Colored desk-size blotters cut to fit the drawers give the effect of a velvet lining. On the dressing table place fresh powder puffs, hairpins, a pincushion with various kinds of pins, needles, thread, and scissors.

Luggage racks are a convenience if you have them and should be improvised if you don't. In the bathroom be sure there are plenty of fleecy, luxurious towels, bath oil, soap, and powder.

The Woman's Club or Officers' Wives' Club

As stated before, the center of social life for Army wives whether living on or off the post is the Woman's Club. On many posts, particularly overseas, a wife upon arrival automatically becomes a member of the Woman's Club. It is every wife's duty not only to join but to take an active interest in the Woman's Club.

Overseas, the Wives' Clubs are the core of Army life, both social and philanthropic. Most wives feel the need of belonging to a social group and of being wanted in the group, so Overseas Clubs are always popular and seem to thrive.

There are several definite and good reasons for the promotion of a Woman's Club on each post, and whether or not you consider yourself in the category of a "joiner" or a clubwoman is beside the point. To think of a Woman's Club as only a "bridge club" or as a spot for tea or luncheon and a gossip-fest is decidedly narrow and has no place in the big picture of a woman's place in today's Army.

A happy, busy wife who takes part in the many activities of the Woman's Club on the post is a more interesting person to come home to. She need not neglect her home or children, nor does she have to attend all meetings, but almost anyone can arrange to attend occasionally, at least enough to get acquainted.

Another point is to take part in everything and not to stand back and expect the older wives to do the work. Go along with them and learn as you go by doing whatever you are asked to do. The time may come all too soon when you will be taking their places, and the task of conducting a smooth-functioning club will be your responsibility. Get acquainted with the various committee chairmen and, without being officious, graciously offer your services.

Not only is your Woman's Club the center of many social and humanitarian projects for wives living on the post, but it is of even greater importance to wives living off the post. It may be their only means of getting acquainted with other Army wives; it may keep them from being lonely in a strange city; best of all, it will offer worth-while work in many helpful ways and be their chief social center.

The commanding officer's wife is usually the honorary president, while the acting president is elected by popular vote. If you have any special gift or talent, don't hide it under a bushel! Of course, it is not very good taste to advertise one's accomplishments; if you are an asset, others will soon realize it. It is well to avoid cliques, and to go slowly in picking one's intimate friends, but by signing up for the various activities in which you are interested you will probably find congenial companions, some of whom may grow into lifelong friends.

Bridge

To play a good game of bridge is a social asset, and nothing more quickly reveals a person's good or bad manners than the etiquette displayed at the bridge table. The ideal partner is one who never criticizes or seems even to be aware that a mistake has been made; she recognizes a good maneuver on your part and gives you credit for it whether you win or lose the hand.

That no one likes a poor partner or even a poor opponent goes without saying, so if you have never played bridge it is hardly fair to attempt to learn at a bridge party or a club unless lessons are being given for members. The beginner should either take a few introductory lessons or study the game and then play with friends before joining the Bridge Club. This does not mean you must be expert, but merely that you should know the conventions before playing in a club.

Woman's Club bridge is usually of a sociable, talkative brand, so simply consider it "party bridge"! Do not take your game too seriously or presume to take your partner or opponents to task for a mistake. Many beginning bridge players when criticized by a superior player give up the game entirely and develop an inferiority complex toward it. Unless you are actually in the capacity of a bridge teacher avoid holding post-mortems over someone's delinquencies, even your own.

Also, if you wish to be invited into a foursome, avoid such mannerisms at the bridge table as snapping down a card or bending a trick, or picking it up and trotting it up and down the table. Whistling, humming, drumming on the table, massaging one's face, striking poses, and wandering around the room when one is dummy are all pet offenses that can become unendurable to one's companions. Another annoyance is to have an overconfident opponent throw down his hand saying, "The rest of the tricks are mine," when it is quite possible that they might not have been had the hand been played out. If luck is against you, don't complain; every bridge player has bad days "when he can't lay up a cent." Be a good sport or loser, and philosophically accept the run of bad hands with the good. When you have made a play of poor judgment, the best thing you can say is, "I'm very sorry, partner," and let it go at that.

Playing for stakes is a subject in itself, and you should inquire before accepting an invitation where you know there will be a set game and the players, playing for money, take their game seriously. You can feel free to say, "I'm sorry but I never play for more than a tenth" or whatever is your limit. The average person is equally embarrassed in losing or winning a stake "that matters" and the only answer is to play for one that doesn't.

In most other card games, players seem to be a bit more relaxed than in bridge; however, in any game most important of all is your ability to be perfectly tranquil and cheerful regardless of whether you are winning or losing.

Other Activities

Golf is a very popular sport, and increasingly so among women. If you play, you will naturally join the Golf Club group. If you desire to play, again as in bridge, take lessons before joining in competition. Golf is a strain upon the amiability of the average person, and in no other game except bridge is serenity of disposition so essential. It is said that "he who loses his temper is pretty sure to lose the game."

Bowling, tennis, and swimming appeal to many young wives, and with a sufficient number of groups tournaments, meets, and various good times are planned. If you don't find much doing in your favorite sport, advertise around the post and you'll usually find others with similar interests. Don't always wait for someone to do your organizing. Talk to the recreation officer and cook something up.

If you have histrionic ability or are interested in the theater by all means sign up with the Dramatic Club. It is a group that always has lots of fun. In addition to actors and actresses they always need prompters, make-up artists, and decorators for sets. It is also good fun to work with the Little Theater group in your near-by town, and this participation makes for good spirit between Army personnel and the townspeople.

The Woman's Club usually has its own library, or at least a Reading Club. Both fiction and nonfiction books are available, and visiting authors, interesting paid speakers, and qualified book reviewers often appear on the program during the year.

There are many other activities in which you can engage profitably: art groups with sketching classes, music appreciation, garden groups, and many more too numerous to mention here.

If you are especially trained and good at something find a few congenial souls and start a group yourself under the sponsorship of the Woman's Club. Foreign-language classes often study French, Spanish, Italian, German, and Russian. Fluency in speaking a foreign language will greatly enrich the background of an Army wife and some day may have practical value as well.

Thrift Shop

On many posts, a Thrift Shop is maintained for the purpose of disposing of slightly used wearing apparel, furniture, and household articles. All workers are volunteers, and the money is used to further philanthropic work on the base. This project is usually sponsored by the Woman's Club.

Personnel desiring to sell used articles are asked to bring them to the shop, setting their own price. It is customary for 10 per cent of the consignee's price to be paid to the Thrift Shop; however, many useful articles are donated. When making a change of station and packing day arrives, it is a grand way to clear out all the white elephants, outgrown toys and children's clothes, uniforms, civilian clothes, kitchen utensils, dishes, electrical appliances, and all kinds of furniture.

The Thrift Shop is a glorified Woman's Exchange and highly patronized by brides, some of whom are trying to rid themselves of gimcracks in the way of impractical wedding presents and others who are trying to acquire a few articles of used furniture.

The Nursery and Child-Care Centers

The Woman's Club sponsors and operates a well-staffed nursery on most Army posts. It is maintained to give young mothers a little leisure time for shopping, recreation, or business, and to enable young children to play together and to adjust to other children. In this way young mothers are encouraged to attend club activities. Parents attending dances, parties, movies, or church services are assured the best of care for their small fry at a low rate for an entire evening. A small fee is charged for each additional child; in fact, they come "Cheaper by the Dozen." This activity rates high among the worthwhile projects sponsored by the Woman's Club.

Red Cross

One of the most important activities of the Woman's Club is always the Red Cross. When you are called, do your bit willingly. Even if you can't sew a straight seam, you can wrap bandages or learn to knit. In the Services, for obvious historical and traditional reasons, no Red Cross appeal ever goes unheeded.

Brownies and Girl Scouts

These two worth-while organizations are also sponsored by the Woman's Club on many posts. The Boy Scouts and Cub Scouts are sponsored usually by the Officers' Club; however, Girl Scout leaders and the Cub Scout chairman of Den Mothers serve on the Woman's Club board of governors and have a vote each in policy making.

The President of the Woman's Club

The active president of a Woman's Club has an important job; the honorary president serves purely in an advisory capacity. The active president is usually someone who is personable, has a winning personality, possesses a certain amount of executive ability, and is capable—otherwise she would not have been nominated and elected. Once elected, she is saddled with many responsibilities.

A sincere and earnest Woman's Club president tactfully lets it be known too that she is available for consultation on personal and social problems. In a way she is a senior counselor to all her constituents.

NCO WIVES' CLUB

The Noncommissioned Officers' Wives' Club, its organization, and the operation of a model smooth-running club will be discussed fully in Chapter VI, "Life Off an Army Post."

Chapter VI

LIFE OFF AN ARMY POST

A T MANY large installations today as high as 90 per cent of
Army personnel are required to live off the post. Your life
will parallel the life of your civilian neighbor in many ways,
and you must get along with your neighbors even if it means your
going three-quarters of the way. To get along with others and to work
successfully in a group is part of being adult, so here is your chance.

If you have lived in a civilian community all your life, this should
not be too hard for you. Unfortunately, during World War II and
since, many small towns adjacent to Army installations are guilty of
rent gouging. Gradually, these unfair practices are being eliminated.
However, it shows a poor spirit of patriotism on the part of greedy
landlords.

IMPORTANCE OF CIVILIAN CONTACTS

The Army today is making as big a bid for civilian favor as the
Navy has always done. It is important that we merit the respect of
taxpayers, and that all Army wives do their utmost in promoting cordial relations. By no means am I recommending that you bootlick,
curry favor, or toady to any civilian of wealth, power, or political
influence, but you should show an interest in the civilians where you
are stationed, and it can't be patronizing. You will be expected to
enter into their social activities and community projects; try to be
one of them rather than an outsider, and everyone will profit. Your
husband may be a student at either a Service school or some college;
he may be on duty at an adjacent post but because of the shortage of
quarters be required to live off the post; he may be on duty with the
National Guard or a Reserve unit or serving as an Army Attaché in
a foreign capital.

Army wives sometimes follow the line of least resistance and stick
together in a community, thereby gaining the reputation of being
clannish. It isn't tactful to talk too much about the gaiety of life on

various Army posts where you have lived. Silly chatter of this sort often leaves the impression with civilians that all Army wives think about is the social side of life, which, of course, is far from true.

Should your husband be assigned to a Reserve unit, a National Guard or R.O.T.C. unit, *your* assignment will be to do the best individual public relations job of which you are capable. The Army wife is truly a diplomat without portfolio, however, when her husband serves on a mission to a foreign country. She is the focus of all eyes, and her general behavior at all times must be above reproach. There, in a very real way she is representing the United States of America. She must do it with charm, sincerity, and dignity.

ORDERS

Out of a clear sky some morning, you may pick up the paper and see your husband's orders to service in Tokyo or to a National Guard unit in Salt Lake City, or perhaps to a Reserve unit in Long Beach, California. You may gasp quietly, but hysterics and heroics are out. Remember, your husband is in the Army, and a public servant of the people and the government. Try to like the idea. If you don't, then be a good actress and pretend you do. You can console yourself temporarily by the fact that orders are subject to change and sometimes are changed even while one is en route to the new station. At this point, if you are really down, a little wishful thinking can do no harm, but under no circumstances must you wire your Congressman, my pet!

On the bright side, remember that it is always unwise to start complaining about posts and places you have never seen. Regardless of what you think about your husband's orders, do not commit yourself to such an extent that you may be embarrassed at a later date when perhaps you have changed your mind.

Here are a few facts of Army life that you will be wise to assimilate early in your married life. *Remember always:* the orders are your husband's. Never be guilty of referring to a new assignment as "our orders" unless both you and your husband are in the Service. (There are a few cases, you know.)

Before you have been married very long you may run across some inept Army wife who will say, "When we received orders . . ." or, what is even more painful, "When we get to be sergeants or colonels . . ." The correct form is: "When my husband received his orders," or "When Jack is a colonel," or "When Jim becomes a master sergeant." Beware of the official and editorial "we"! The worst *faux pas* of all is to say, "When we were in command." Don't forget, wives have no rank; they are, as of old, merely "camp followers," regardless of who really wears the trousers at home.

When orders are received today, the soldier or officer sometimes has to report immediately, so he goes on ahead of his family. This has its advantages in that he can sign in at his new station, take care of the hundred-and-one preliminaries, and get started on his new assignment. Since housing is still so critical on or near most posts, a man really has to hunt to find a suitable place for his family to live. If he is alone he can afford to take a little more time and not feel he has to take the first place offered.

The family, especially if there are young children, is better off at the previous base until quarters of some time are available. Living in hotels, eating out, having the children sick and uncomfortable are items that run into money and play havoc with the family budget and disposition.

On overseas assignments, in almost every instance the husband precedes his wife and family, then takes his turn on the roster for transfer of his dependents when quarters are available. The Army authorizes concurrent travel when possible.

POINTERS ON HOUSE HUNTING

Probably the most common outdoor sport in the Army is house hunting! If you are a bride who has never lived on a post your adjustment to a small home of your own in a civilian community will be simple. You can rent if you are lucky enough to find an apartment or a house that is vacant, or you can buy. You may be able to sublet a furnished home or an apartment, but many times, in communities where houses are at a premium, a young couple has been forced to buy; others have actually built their own homes. Either of the last two expedients is a bit risky.

Another plan—say you are on a supposedly three-year National Guard assignment—is to buy a house and remodel it to your taste. The Federal Housing Administration offers some attractive propositions. If you are reasonably sure of even more than a year's duty, it is occasionally a good plan to buy instead of paying rent. Small homes continue to mushroom overnight, many to accommodate the G.I. undergraduates who are said to "come to college complete with wife, baby and bottle sterilizer."

Naturally, the hope of every married couple is to find the ideal apartment or house, with big rooms, low rent, and lots of sunshine and breeze! You may start your hunt by consulting the Billeting Officer at the base or by inquiring at headquarters for listings of rentals and real estate available. If you go to a city rental agency, be sure to choose a reliable one with which you can get in touch at any time. The most common method used in the Service is the grapevine, by which houses are passed on from one Serviceman to another by tipping off his best friend, who in turn has a friend in need of a home. It's a good scheme, too, to check with the adjutant on transfer orders of other personnel.

In choosing a house or an apartment, if you have any choice, it is wise to consider particularly the location. How near is it to the post, the market, the school, church, bus or car line, and recreational facilities? Will the neighborhood be congenial? Are there street lights, sewers, garbage removal, and mail delivery? Often a ducky little dream house is available but it is so far removed from the base that not only will your husband be late in reporting to duty, but the time spent in driving plus the extra transportation cost will make it highly impractical. Or it may be a magnificent eagle's nest reached by a flight of ninety-six steps up which you crawl with your groceries once a day!

If the location is satisfactory, then before considering a lease it is well to check the following: (1) Is the plumbing in good condition? All bowls, faucets, toilets, and toilet seats should be checked for repairs. (2) What type of heating is available? (3) Are stove and refrigerator furnished? These are two costly items. (4) Are screens and storm windows in good condition? (5) Are the laundry facilities satisfactory?

Remember, you must establish clearly through your agent, by agreement with the landlord, exactly what is to be done *before* you move in and who is responsible for whatever repairs are necessary after you move in. You have a right to expect that all walls and woodwork be freshly painted if you are taking it for some time, and you can stipulate that this includes the painting of closets and shelves. Closets should be fitted with poles, the necessary shelves, and lights. There should be at least two base plugs in the living room and one in every other room.

Now I realize that you cannot be too demanding, but you can afford to do a bit of bargaining. Be pleasant but businesslike about the whole proceeding. Have a clear understanding about maintenance items, which include:

1. Utilities—gas, electricity, telephone
2. Heat—usually included in apartment rent
3. Water rates and garbage disposal
4. Care of lawn, grounds, shrubbery

LOOK BEFORE YOU LEASE

Be sure to read the lease carefully. Check every sentence and, as one Army officer suggested, "read the fine print." It is just as important to read a lease painstakingly as it is to read every clause in an insurance policy. In view of the temporary status of Army personnel, most landlords are willing to rent apartments on the basis of one month's occupancy, after which at least ten days' notice is required to terminate the contract.

In leases extending more than a month you should insist on a military clause which reads about like this:
"In case the said ...., Captain, USA, is detached from his present station, this lease may be vacated upon ten days' notice."

Always avoid breaking a lease except under exceptional circumstances, such as orders, death, or something over which you have no control; otherwise it is legally and ethically wrong. In addition, it may bring upon you a lawsuit which might have a serious effect upon a soldier's or officer's record and bring discredit on the Army. Frequently it is possible to sublet or to obtain for your landlord a new client who is willing and glad to take your lease.

Of course, there is something to be said on the side of the landlord, too. Whether we like it or not, many landlords shy away from renting "to those terrible Army people," I am told, because a few large and noisy cocktail parties held in the rented homes of Service personnel elicited unfavorable comments from a civilian community. Criticism is more severe because you are in the service of your government, and high standards of conduct are rightly expected of you. Irresponsible conduct always reflects on the Army, which is not good publicity. Also, it makes it hard for the next young Army man and his wife to rent the house. A neighborly and considerate wife who is always helpful to the civilian wife next door can do much to improve community relations.

If a house or an apartment cannot be found, a room in a hotel or boardinghouse, a motel, a tourist court, or a trailer may have to be the solution. All are designed to make money and most are expensive. The trailer is the only cheap one, and that's not until one recovers from the initial expense. To have rooms in somebody else's home is given the dignified title of "co-operative living." It is not ideal, but if this is your lot temporarily, be sure to have a clear understanding as to your privacy, kitchen privileges, cleaning arrangements, laundry privileges, use of the telephone, and who pays for what and when!

Renting on any basis always presents a few hazards, but the first important point is to know what you can afford to pay. Keep in mind small costs such as tipping in a hotel; extra window washing in an apartment house; the type of janitor, superintendent, doormen, elevator operators; the protection given the apartment against peddlers; and the methods of handling deliveries and mail.

Today the primary essential is sufficient space for your living needs. Even twenty years ago one's home used to be considered a symbol of financial success as much as a shelter. Success took the form of an eight-, ten-, twenty-, or thirty-room house, a mansion with acres of gardens. Fortunately our standards change.

National Housing Act

Before World War II it was customary for the government to furnish public quarters for officers, enlisted personnel, and their dependents. Today, with the great increase of the Army and the relative increase in the number of older, technically trained men in the Service, men who are married and desire a family life, the housing provided by the government has not kept pace with the need. Many soldiers and officers are forced to be separated from their families; many more are living under unpleasant conditions in trailer camps, shacks, tourist cabins, and single rooms—environments which are highly undesirable for bringing up children. Often prices are exorbitant. The effect of such conditions in terms of morale and the reluctance of young men to commence military careers can be readily understood.

Under Title VIII of the National Housing Act the Federal Housing Commissioner is authorized to insure mortgages of private builders for the construction of rental housing on or near military installations against defaults due to deactivation, or curtailment of activities at such installations. An average of $9,000 per family unit is allowed.

The purpose of the Wherry Act is to encourage private enterprise to construct rental housing to serve the needs of personnel at military installations without any cost to the government. However, this act is not the complete answer to military housing problems. Cost of construction at many places is so high that rentals of suitable quarters and utilities in Wherry housing will be substantially greater than the monthly rental, for instance, of $67.50 allowed noncommissioned officers and $75.00 allowed a second lieutenant with dependents, or a warrant officer W-1. For such personnel, public quarters on bases are needed urgently. It is to be hoped that Wherry Act projects will supplement rather than supersede public quarters.

Dorthy Duncan has summed up functional living in these words: "To be comfortable one needs a place in which to eat with satisfaction and content; a place to sleep undisturbed; a place for study, work and undisturbed thought; a place for social recreation and the entertaining of friends; a place in which to make love without interruption!"

Personally, I think home should be a livable background for everyday life in which it is possible for each individual to have living and working privacy. That, to me, includes one's desk as well as one's own bed, bureau or dressing table, and radio. It takes a bit of doing in one room. Even if everything else goes into storage, with these four items I can turn the most bleak motel room into a bed-sitting room with a few decorative touches in pictures, curtains, and attractive bedspreads of a non-bedroom character. But more of this later in the chapter!

LOVE AND LIGHT HOUSEKEEPING

Let us suppose you start your married life off in the smallest of apartments, "the one-room efficiency," or maybe one hotel room, or even a single room which some ambitious householder dignifies by calling an apartment. In this room you will eat, sleep, live, study, work, relax, and entertain, so first of all in addition to being attractive it must be functional. I hope it will be unfurnished, and right off you can start acquiring your own possessions.

First a few notes on color. Be grateful if you draw a landlord who will paint or paper your one room; and be appreciative if he offers to let you choose the color scheme. Remember, color is always important; an unbecoming color scheme can make a hypochondriac of you. So in your one room, have a care!

Can you guess what is the distinguishing feature of your own personal coloring? Your hair, my sweet! There are said to be five natural basic color types: brown hair, blond, red, black, gray (or white). (I refer to the natural blonde, of course, not to the gal with chameleon taste. It is expensive to have to change one's home decorations with each visit to the beauty shop.) For what it is worth to you, a striking brunette with black hair should use bold colors like coral, nasturtium, or fuchsia against ivory walls. It is suggested the redhead go all out for shades of gray-green, or golden yellow. Copper and a white room with accents of turquoise will also enhance her beauty. The girl with the soft brown hair should dabble in pastels and slightly muted or grayed colors. For blondes, soft turquoise, aqua greens, orchid, and pastels are flattering. For the woman whose hair is white or turning silver gray, various tones of soft blues are pretty. She can also use eggplant shades, claret or burgundy, or even a high shade of red; but she should avoid harsh colors and black in her decorations.

Violent colors are usually tiring, while greens and blues are considered restful. Dark-green walls reminiscent of trees and grass are popular at present. Though blue can be a cold color, it is very popular too. Cézanne and Van Gogh were masters of blues, blue greens, and blue violets. We speak of "blue blood" denoting aristocracy; blue ribbons are given as prizes; we have blue delphinium, forget-me-nots, and cornflowers; the sky, the ocean, the lakes are blue. Blue used in small doses and combined with red, white, or yellow can be worked into interesting color schemes. If you have brown hair, get acquainted with all shades of yellow. It is the sun color. Use sunlight curtains; feature daffodils, chrysanthemums, canary birds, oranges, squash, and pumpkins at seasonal times in your decorations. Red will meet you with an open hand; that is why front doors are sometimes painted red. But go easy for it can be a brutal color! The universal caution is to watch the shade of whatever color you choose.

Use the salesman at the paint store as a technical adviser. You also might ask if he has a chart of the Williamsburg colors. Either light- or dark-green walls can prove a dramatic background for living-room furniture. With dark-green walls you will need a light ceiling, usually a pale yellow or butter color. Wallpaper is something else again; some beautiful effects can be achieved with Chinese papers, striped or old-fashioned colonial or Victorian motifs. Let yourself go because you will never have a similar opportunity on an Army post! This need not cost a lot, even if you have to furnish the paint. The labor can be shared with your husband; all you need is good taste, a willingness to work, and a strong back.

In a one-room home it is best to strive for a living-room effect. The bed is usually a day bed, twin day beds, or a couch. There are dozens of convertible davenports or divans on the market, but I have yet to find a really comfortable one that did not take "a man and a boy" to open and close! Day beds are cheaper and much smarter anyway, and two are not too much in a large room either on opposite walls or at right angles with a square community table in the corner between them. You will want a large coffee table, one of those two-person desks perhaps, which might double for a dining table, plenty of built-in or portable bookcases, all of which you and your husband can construct yourselves if either of you has a flair for such things. The most popular and really attractive informal bookshelves today are merely plain boards supported at the ends by stacks of cinder brick. They can be moved or rearranged at will and can be made of practically any scrap lumber available.

Bookshelves can also serve as room dividers, and even the most amateur of home carpenters can construct an exceptionally handsome wrought-iron bookcase with these "makings": You will need a pair of sturdy black mat-finish iron legs (rubber-tipped) and shelf supports, plus all the wood screws necessary for easy assembly. Ingenious cross bars between shelves prevent books from slipping out. You can build any length bookcase you need, from one foot up to five feet, with three standard ten-inch-wide boards. A screwdriver is the only tool required.

Do not economize on the mattresses or springs for your day beds, and for spreads use unbedroomy fabric spreads in a living-room color such as beige or gray corduroy or a chartreuse or maroon chenille. Chests of blond mahogany drawers will take care of your personal clothing, linens and flat silver. It is to be hoped that you will have roomy closets and a dressing room connected with bath; but if not— you are young and you will manage.

Two small rugs, one 5'x7' and one 3'x5' in a harmonizing or neutral shade seem a better choice than investing in an 8'x10' or 9'x12' rug. The small rugs can be used later in bedrooms or a hall. You may want to add mirrors, one good picture, table lamps, occasional tables, but your largest expenditures will be your couch beds and a comfortable chair for each of you.

Probably the biggest news in window treatments today is the popularity of the café curtain. This curtain, borrowed from ubiquitous little restaurants in France, is merely a refinement of the familiar sash curtain. It is easy to launder and to hang, and it is so flexible that it affords plenty of light and air. Café curtains are inexpensive and easy to make. They work well in most contemporary interiors of informal nature and can be used with or without draperies. They can also be used without shades or blinds. Most café curtains are unlined, and they can be made of lawn, dimity, chambray, Shantung, sheeting, gingham, challis, linen, China silk, nylon, or any non-bulky material; for the kitchen, checked toweling is effective. Two tiers of café curtains on the same window are attractive when different colors are employed. Flexibility is the basis of their usefulness, and they should traverse (pull across) easily.

If a furnished or hotel room is your lot, the first thing you will want to do is regroup the furniture for comfortable living. Hotels seem to have a knack for arranging furniture at the most unsociable angles, so that it will look as if the occupants are not on speaking terms. If your stay warrants, you can slip-cover the furniture, remove the mirror from over the dresser, replacing it with a picture since a bedroomy dresser has no place in a room you are trying to make even slightly formal. Again, if you are staying long enough to make it worth while, you can get the hotel to convert the twin beds into day beds or modernistic couches (with the usual palmistry method). Two extra armchairs and unbedroomy spreads for your couches will convert the room into a sitting room.

Most Service wives today do not invest in "overstuffed" furniture, as they find light woods such as maple or bleached mahogany more satisfactory. Rattan from the tropics is used extensively and when well upholstered as to springs and padding is quite comfortable. Wrought iron is attractive but it is heavy to move and on the expensive side if well constructed.

Should your room have an alcove, this can be used for dining. A drop-leaf or gate-leg table or even a desk will prove ideal. Should you also have to cook in this one room, if a Venetian blind does not conceal your stove, refrigerator, and sink, as is customary in a real efficiency apartment, a folding screen will answer the purpose. In this type of one-room apartment a wall bed is usually furnished, and a divan or davenport helps to convert it into a living room.

LOVE IN A COTTAGE

A small house is perhaps the most romantic setting of all for young honeymooners. If you live in a rented house, take as much pride and interest in it as though it belonged to you. Then it will become home.

The suggestions offered in furnishing quarters in Chapter V on a base are applicable to furnishing a "cottage home," except that on a base your cost will be less since the central pieces of furniture will be supplied. If you are starting from scratch, as most young couples do, in order to buy intelligently you will need a plan.

One of the great mistakes brides make is to think they can start out where their parents left off; in other words, they want their first home to be equal to or even better than their girlhood home. There are some things, however, that are essential in this machine age.

Your first must is a stove and next a refrigerator. Try to find a landlord who will supply both, for they are expensive items and terribly unwieldy when it comes time to move. Even if you can sell, you will probably have to take a big loss. If you must buy your own stove, study a good many models before selecting one. Shall it be gas or electricity? The electric stove is cleaner and easier to take care of, but gas is quicker and in some localities cheaper to operate. The stove should have four to six top burners, broiling and baking facilities, and some storage space for cooking utensils. If the stove comes with the house, be grateful even though it is old.

In buying a refrigerator you will again have a choice of electricity or gas. Each has its advantages—and the salesman will tell them to you. Then in some remote place you may have an old-fashioned icebox that has to be serviced by hand. An icebox is one item which you can safely purchase secondhand if you are sure its condition is good. It can be refinished easily by spraying with enamel or plastic paint.

Do not let your impatience to acquire "things" and get your house settled push you into hasty choices. The money end is most important so we will start with financing. First of all, you and your husband will be smart to decide how much you can afford to spend and whether you can spend now or must budget your money over a period of time.

You may finance your necessary purchases by extended credit, for which there will usually be a charge of 6 per cent interest on the unpaid part of the cost price. For instance, you pay one-third of the total price in cash and the balance in one year. Installment firms cover themselves in one of two ways, sometimes by both: (1) carrying charges or interest and (2) higher prices. If you are asked to pay more than 6 per cent interest, you are helping to guarantee the company against loss from other less reliable customers.

If you have proper security, bank financing is the best and, in the final analysis, the least expensive; interest rates are about 3½ per cent. You can borrow from a finance loan company, but its interest rates will be terrific; it is allowed by law to charge as high as 17 per cent so as to cover losses. Again, you are paying for the unreliables.

How to Buy Furniture

Reliable stores will tell you the truth about the quality of furniture. In many states there are requirements that things such as stuffing in pillows, mattresses, and cushions must be graded. Be sure to read the tags. The good qualities are horsehair, cotton and horsehair, and pig's hair, in that order. Kapok does not stand up, but it is commonly used in cheap furniture. Duck and down feathers are also used for cushions and pillows.

Of course, your husband will go along when you buy furniture. He will know all about the wooden structure of the piece, whether the construction is good, and will want to measure and fit it for size and comfort. You will probably find best buys in secondhand furniture in shops run for charity where everything is donated. Patronize your own local Thrift Shop. Auctions, storage warehouse and railroad claim sales are excellent sources for buying reasonably. With some sandpaper and paint you can do wonders.

Remember that slip-cover enchantment for your home is within the scope of every budget, and a well-made attractive slip cover can hide a multitude of sins. But don't go off the deep end by slip-covering to excess. Watch those big flower patterns.

In buying beds, the money should go first of all into comfort. This means a good box spring and mattress. Beware of a cotton-filled mattress. Firm at first, later it will become lumpy. Good mattresses are made of horsehair. Box springs are desirable. Since one-third of our lives is said to be spent in bed, let us choose really beguiling beds that invite us to relax, to stretch, to yawn, and to forget our worries. In the old days in France, the great ladies of the court knew so well that they could look their most bewitching in bed that they entertained their friends at morning sessions called *ruelles* while still reclining among their pillows. This is not recommended for modern times, but it doesn't hurt to make slumber facilities as attractive as possible.

Rugs are judged in three ways: by the depth of the pile, by the blend of the wool yarns, and by the weave. Don't forget, the rug is the foundation of your room and important.

The basic furniture requirements for a living room are: a divan, couch, or sofa, comfortable armchair or chairs, small tables which can be moved easily, bookcase or cases.

For the bedroom: a bed or beds, a storage cabinet for your husband's clothes if closet space is at a premium, a chest of drawers, a dressing table and chair (this, of course, can be improvised from a table or even a shelf, draped by you), one comfortable chair, and a chaise longue if space and budget permit.

Whether you eat in the dining room, living room, or an alcove you must have a substantial table and chairs. Do not buy dining-room or even dinette suites. A drop-leaf table and odd chairs are a better buy.

At the very beginning, simplify your life. No one can tell you what will make you really comfortable except yourself. Your home is where you are going to live, so forget your friends and of what they approve when you begin to furnish and decorate it. Don't try to follow a magazine house or a set pattern; remember, a true home is far more than the furniture it contains. You will be missing a lot of fun if you let a decorator or stranger completely decorate your home for you. Often it is good to call in a decorator for help, but it is also fun to shop around, to visit furniture marts for new ideas, and to patronize secondhand stores.

Good grooming will be as important to the beauty of your home as it is to your own morale. Now that you have your dream cottage arranged to your liking, here are a few pointers on good grooming.

1. Are your pictures hanging at eye level? Are they jolted or out of line?

2. Do all of the lamps have their hats on straight?

3. How about the Venetian blinds? Do they look tipsy? Are they clean?

4. Dusting the books on the shelves is not enough. Do they have good standing posture?

5. Are your magazines arranged attractively? If you want to save old copies, file them somewhere but don't burden your room with them.

6. And now that everything is in line, is it too much in line? Is everything in stiff rows like a bunch of tin soldiers?

HOUSEKEEPING ON WHEELS

Trailer life is becoming more and more popular with Army families. As one wife explained, there is a close camaraderie among trailer owners. A trailer driver will always stop and give help to another trailer owner who is in trouble.

The big question when no quarters are available usually is, "Shall we buy a trailer?" Many wives shy away from the idea, associating it with pioneer life and hardships; however, the modern trailer compares to a small, well-equipped, compact apartment.

If you are a roving spirit, it is an ideal way of living. Whenever I see a trailer stopped on the roadside, I have an overwhelming desire to see the inside arrangement—and believe me, there are some beauties! Recently I saw a cigar-shaped aluminum trailer about thirty feet long, paneled inside with magnolia wood. The kitchen walls were covered with stainless steel.

The front of the trailer was a combination living and dining room carpeted from wall to wall in gray twist carpet. On one side were closets with ample drawer space for linens. Comfortable sofas covered in duran plastic could become extra beds at night, there was a portable radio, a television set, a drop-leaf table for meals, and double fluorescent lights at strategic points. The bath was tiled, and had a lavatory, shower, toilet, and an air-conditioning unit or cooler.

The kitchen was a masterpiece in ingenious storage and a marvel in convenience. There were closets and shelves with racks (Navy style) for securing the dishes and utensils. There was an electric eight-cubic-foot refrigerator and a Monel metal sink with both faucet and hand pump for use when traveling. There were formica-topped counters or cabinets with drawer and shelf space above and underneath. The two bedrooms had good beds equipped with box springs and mattresses. The master bedroom contained a double bed, the boys' bedroom twin island beds which could also be made into bunk beds. There were built-in dressers, night tables, and closets with full-length mirrors. All the rooms were separated by disappearing sliding doors. Colorful awnings gave the appearance of a small country home.

One Army wife in California told me she had lived in a trailer for four years and loved it. Here are some of her suggestions: Shop around before buying a trailer; very modern secondhand ones are to be found. It is well to buy one thirty feet long or more with plenty of closet and storage space. A butane stove is good, and the blower can be used in summer to cool the bedrooms. Hot-water heaters are a help, and the McPherson toilet with a one-inch drain is recommended rather than a three-inch drain which is of no use in many courts. Trailers cost $4,000 up.

Trailer court areas are usually supplied with shower rooms, toilets, and laundry facilities. The overnight charge varies, but in any court weekly and monthly rates can be arranged. In trailer cities in the Midwest where living conditions become too crowded, families in small towns take in trailers for parking on lawns. In this case, trailer occupants often use the bathroom facilities of the house.

The disadvantages of trailer life come mostly in the poor sites for parking, especially in the northern states. Some of the courts have poor drainage and even poorer sanitary facilities; children have no place to play except in the mud. Better trailer camps are found in the southern states, and, needless to add, summertime in a trailer with plenty of outdoor life is preferable to the long snowbound hours of winter. Keeping sand and mud out of a trailer is one of the housekeeper's worries. One ingenious husband hinged a large-size scrub brush to the side of the doorstep, bristle side up! Another suggestion is to nail bottle tops cork side up to a board and place it near the entrance as a shoescraper. Owing to the compactness and lack of floor space in a trailer, one has to learn to take smaller steps from place to place; countless bruises at first convince one that this is true.

The advantages of trailer life are that housekeeping is at a minimum, there is no rent to pay except for the parking cost, utilities are cheap, there are no packing or moving problems when orders come in, and it is an interesting and a different experience.

Each trailer owner adds many little home touches. As one trailer wife explained proudly, for greater privacy she uses zippers on window curtains! Oil-burning heaters are also quite the thing, so if the weather turns cold (even in California or Florida, where it isn't supposed to), you can be comfortable. Some trailers have tiny trap doors in the kitchen floor so the garbage can be dropped through to a garbage can placed below. I saw one trailer in California with a built-in dog kennel. Another had a tiny plexiglass sun-deck dome for tanning the torso. Folding flower boxes that hold pots of gay geraniums and petunias are almost standard equipment now.

Trailer wives, with less housework, have more time to be sociable, more time for their families. Far from being a group who need sympathy they rather feel it for their sisters who when the dreaded orders come must pack up the accumulations of their stay and move on to the unknown and begin the struggle again to get settled. The Army wife who is also the trailer wife merely closes the closets, puts the radio or television set on the floor, and waits for her husband to disconnect the pipes. Then off they go, confident that they will always have a roof over their heads.

The Army, with the opening of the many new trailer parks on the posts, is recognizing this method of living not as a haphazard makeshift but as the ideal home for the man who sees the world. What better way than from his own window!

When Your Husband Is a Student

The Army has adopted a far-reaching program of education which applies to all officers of the Army active and inactive, R.O.T.C. students, and enlisted men of the National Guard and the Regular Army. In this wonderful career program, you can expect your husband to spend at least a third of his service in school. From a wife's point of view, getting an education Army style has definite advantages as well as some disadvantages.

For those who are ambitious and have ability, the Army offers opportunities for advancement. To accomplish its mission, the Army must train individuals not only as combat soldiers but as radio operators, military policemen, personnel management specialists, cryptographers, motion-picture photographers, telephone installers, draftsmen, and in many other specialties as well. Much of the training is given in formal classroom instruction at Army Service schools, training divisions, and replacement training centers. Some jobs are, however, best taught by on-the-job instruction and practical experience. In addition to these two types of in-service training, the Army makes available correspondence courses for officer and enlisted personnel which can be taken through the United States Armed Forces Institute (U.S.A.F.I.). These courses are taken voluntarily in off-duty time.

Warrant officers and enlisted personnel usually indicate to their unit officers their interest in particular courses. Unit officers, after due consideration of both unit requirements and individual abilities of enlisted and warrant officer personnel, select personnel from among those best qualified to attend a particular course in accordance with the established prerequisites of that course. One requirement is that enlisted personnel must have a minimum of nine months to serve upon the completion of school courses.

At these various schools competition runs high. Often there are months of waiting to see if the high educational standards, credits, and other requirements can be met. Students get very tense at times, and that is where a wife's responsibility comes in. One student, a young colonel, remarked, "When the student's home is running smoothly, his grades are good and he does his best work. When illness or taut nerves disrupt the home atmosphere, it shows immediately in his grades."

If there are children, homemaking presents new problems. When Daddy is studying, the children must be quiet, the radio muffled, the conversation kept low, and the mother's disposition even and calm. The pressure of schoolwork makes it impossible for most husbands to do much reading to and playing with the youngsters, so the mother finds she must spend additional time with them.

As one young student's wife explained, "We frequently find ourselves adopting the role of chaplain to our school-wearied husbands. When the pressure gets too great, we must convince the student—and occasionally ourselves—that the goal is worth striving for. A good pep talk is worth hours of study at times, to pull our husbands out of discouragement and depression. We must keep pointing out the value in future years of efforts expended now." A sympathetic, understanding wife is often called upon to use all of her resources, of that I am sure.

Upon arrival at a Service school, civilian college, or university there is the usual problem of finding a place to live for nine months, two years, or even longer. A few fortunates may be assigned quarters on the base, but never count on this good luck!

Some students are forced to commute as far as thirty miles, and their wives often find time hangs heavy until they make a contact with the nearest Woman's Club or NCO Wives' Club. If you are in a university group far removed from any Army post, it is up to you to get a list of other students' wives. Call on them, be friendly and organize a small bridge, canasta, sewing, or knitting club of your own. It will help also to get acquainted with the neighbors, whatever their status.

Should your husband be the only Army officer at the college, cultivate the ability of making friends, and fast! Consult the local newspaper or campus bulletin, see what is offered in your field, then go in pursuit of it. Many wives take courses at the college, studying side by side with their husbands. If your man prefers that you leave him in solitude, for goodness' sake do it. Also, be careful not to arrange social affairs at your home when he is studying, and don't insist that he attend parties with you on his study nights. In other words, grow up!

For short courses, say of three or four months, a student's dependents do not accompany him but remain at their home station. The student lives in B.O.Q., and no doubt it has its advantages. At Service schools, however, where a course is of nine months' or two years' duration, many valuable contacts and friendships are made among the members of the class and their families.

THE NATIONAL GUARD

Since most of the Regular Army is deployed all over the globe— in Alaska, the Pacific, Iceland, Morocco, the Caribbean, England, and Europe—a goodly portion of the burden and responsibility of defending the continental United States rests with the National Guard.

The *Officers' Guide* says: "There can be no greater proof of good citizenship than the willingness of members of our Reserve components to combine their civil vocations with regular military training plus the obligation to serve on active duty in emergency under the conditions prescribed by law. Calls to active duty disrupt the primary vocation and often entail hardships to families. The families of members deserve credit as well as those who wear the uniform."

The present-day National Guard goes back into the dim reaches of history to pre-Revolutionary days when all male citizens able to bear arms comprised a militia. There were the "minutemen" who fought at Lexington. The concept of a citizen-soldiery, as represented today by the National Guard of the United States, is firmly rooted in the Constitution.

The National Guard, the Reserve, and the R.O.T.C. constitute the staying power of the United States. To every National Guard unit or organization at battalion and higher levels the Department of the Army details Army officers and enlisted men to instruct in the latest approved technical and tactical doctrines and correct administrative procedure.

The National Guard has a dual mission:

"To provide a reserve component of the Army of the United States, capable of immediate expansion to war strength, able to furnish units fit for service anywhere in the world, trained and equipped to defend critical areas of the United States against land, seaborne or airborne invasion.

"To provide sufficient organizations in each State so trained and equipped as to enable them to function efficiently at existing strength in the protection of life and property and the preservation of peace, order and public safety, under competent orders of the State authorities."

YOUR HUSBAND'S RESERVE OBLIGATIONS!

And, yours too, I might add! For what affects him affects you, since you are a member of the team. From the time of the Revolution, "minutemen" have played an important part in American history. Reservists in the Armed Forces are our modern minutemen. And they are just as vital to our nation's security today as the original minutemen were in 1776.

World Wars I and II found our Reserve and National Guard, through no fault of their own, lacking strength and equipment and in need of additional training before they could take the field.

After World War II, the National Guard, the Air National Guard, and the Organized Reserve Corps were each reorganized in order to set up a unified Reserve program. On June 24, 1948, the Selective Service Act was passed; it was amended in 1951 and became the Universal Military Training and Service Act. This was followed by the Armed Forces Reserve Act of 1952.

There are seven Reserve components in the Armed Forces of the United States. They are:

1. The National Guard of the United States
2. The Army Reserve
3. The Naval Reserve

4. The Marine Corps Reserve
5. The Air National Guard
6. The Air Force Reserve
7. The Coast Guard Reserve

The former Organized Reserve Corps of the Army consisting of the Officers' Reserve Corps and the Enlisted Reserve Corps are merged by the new law into a single Army Reserve. Everyone ordered to active duty from civilian life is given at least thirty days' notice unless military conditions do not permit.

THE ARMY RESERVE

Its members are Reserve commissioned or warrant officers or Reserve enlisted members of the Army, whether serving with the Army Reserve or the National Guard of the United States. It has the following subdivisions: Ready Reserve, Standby Reserve, and Retired Reserve. Members of the Ready Reserve may be ordered to active duty in an emergency declared by the President, while members of the Standby and Retired Reserve are subject to order to active duty only in a national emergency or war declared by the Congress.

Your husband, whether he is drafted or enlists, will make it his business to find out all the answers, so all you have to do is to realize that he is a good citizen in wanting to protect his country, his home, and you. Give him your full support and be a fine Army wife in making your home as happy and congenial as possible.

Everyone realizes the sacrifices young couples make to serve in the Army Reserve but after all, when the chips are down, you are taking military training to protect *your* country, *your* home, *your* loved ones, and *your* own life when the going gets tough.

The Reserve wife or National Guard wife should have the same attitude toward Service life as the Regular Army wife. In other words, when your husband is ordered to active duty, you are, to all intents and purposes, Regular Army personnel and are entitled to all benefits accorded Regular Army personnel.

When your husband is not on active duty, you are a sort of military-faced civilian because in these times you face the possibility that your husband's status may change to military at any time. You live the life of a civilian, perhaps with only slight contacts with the Service. The Reservist puts in his training sessions at his assigned station, then goes home to become a complete civilian. He is always aware of the fact, however, that he may be recalled to active duty at any time.

In addition to serving his country and the satisfaction derived therefrom, the Reserve wife may wonder what other benefits her husband will receive. First, there will be training and schooling; second, pay for drills and training periods; third, credits for retirement.

RESPONSIBILITY OF AN INACTIVE RESERVE WIFE

If your husband is a Reservist, his obligations are equally important whether he assumed them voluntarily or fell heir to them through the operation of our national laws enacted by Congress. The fact that he is not on active duty does not mean that he is any the less obligated to carry out his part of a contract as a Reservist. As noted above, he receives rather liberal pay for his duty and drill periods. You should realize, however, as does he, that this pay he receives is not his real aim and objective. Improvement in his professional efficiency is the big inducement for him.

For you, the inducement is the knowledge that he is better preparing himself for whatever may be his role in defending his home and country. This should influence you to co-operate in every way toward making his attendance at drills easier and his two-week camp period each year an enjoyable as well as a profitable occasion.

If your husband has to use his vacation period for the two-week camp period, why not pack up the youngsters, provided you can secure accommodations near the camp, and accompany him? In this way, since there will be some extra funds, the whole family can enjoy a change of scene and a vacation.

THE IMPORTANCE OF A WOMAN'S CLUB TO WIVES LIVING OFF THE POST

While a Woman's Club is the center of many social and humanitarian projects to wives living on the post, it is of even greater importance to those wives living off the post. It may be their only means of getting acquainted with other Army wives; it may keep them from being lonely in a strange city; it may offer worth-while work in any number of helpful ways and be their chief social center.

In the preceding chapter much space was given to the activities of the Officers' Wives' Club on a post, so in this chapter special emphasis goes to the NCO Wives' Club and how to organize it.

The Noncommissioned Officers' Wives' Club

On many posts today the NCO Wives' Club functions to bring the wives together in social, philanthropic, and community life. On some posts you may find there is no organization at all, or a poorly attended club in which there is little interest of members and no punch to the entertainment or projects offered. Since Army wives come from every walk of life, their interests are naturally varied, and it is in club life that they can give wide expression to them.

One sergeant's bride explained to me that she was very lonely at their first station. She said that no one even bothered to speak to her. It seems sad and inexcusable that a newcomer joining a post should ever feel lonely. An alert NCO Wives' Club can remedy this situation by setting up a spotters' section or a reception and hospitality committee.

In organizing a club, first of all decide on its name. Next, have your bylaws printed in booklet form, along with the constitution. Club stationery should be purchased; then it might be well to conduct a contest, requesting participants to submit ten rules for a successful club.

This is the winning list submitted by Dorothy Kling, an NCO wife:

L   Learn your bylaws
A   Attend all meetings
D   Deliver dues promptly and cheerfully
I   Invite new members
E   Elect capable officers
S   Submit your suggestions
C   Cancel outside criticism
L   Lend your loyalty
U   Unite in work and fun
B   Be a better member and build a better club

From now on I shall give you notes and suggestions passed on to me by the president of a very successful NCO Wives' Club.

The executive board consisted of eight members: president, vice-president, secretary, treasurer and four committee members. It was voted that all officers stay in office one year instead of six months. Also, a retiring officer was elected vice-president, so she could assist the new president.

A form was made up by the president listing the duties of the various committees:

MEMBERSHIP

Makes an effort to contact newcomers to the post. Invites them to club. Plans projects, games, etc., for increasing membership and helping to get acquainted.

HOSTESS

Introduces new members at meetings. Helps newcomers to feel at home.

SUNSHINE

Sends cards, gifts, to members confined or ill. Calls on absentees, showing interest of club in its members.

ENTERTAINMENT

Selects six hostesses at a time alphabetically. Plans party, decorations and food. Buys prizes. Each member should serve on this committee about once in four or five months.

It was made a club policy early in the year to:

1. Ask for no money other than dues, $1.00 per month.
2. Limit farewell gifts to sum of $3.00.
3. Limit Sunshine gifts to $2.50.
4. Send cards (not gifts) to sick members of less than 3 months' membership.
5. Limit to $1.00 gifts to members leaving (because of transfer) whose membership was less than 3 months.

It was further planned to have some sort of activity at each business meeting except where a large amount of business made it impracticable.

After trial and error the present plan for entertainment committees proved most practical: Six club members were chosen each month alphabetically; one was selected to act as chairman, and the group or committee planned and conducted the social. The president bought a simple dessert for each business meeting and asked for volunteers at the meeting to assist in serving.

A club scrapbook was kept which showed pictures and printed material concerning club activities. It was the president's duty to see that a weekly column appeared in the local papers concerning the club and its members.

The club arranged two evening socials a year to which husbands of the members were invited: a dinner in the fall and a picnic in the spring.

The biggest achievement of the year was the publication of a cookbook. The sale of this book made it possible to buy several pieces of club equipment and to give a large Christmas party which drew 100 per cent attendance.

The assistance of the club was asked for and given in planning the Post Pre-Kindergarten School, Army Mutual Aid, Children's Christmas Party, and Post Nursery.

Club pins were sold to members at a nominal fee.

Practically any book of rules of order (*Robert's Rules of Order,* for instance) will include a model constitution on which you can base your own club constitution. Some NCO Wives' Clubs hold weekly meetings, especially the active groups overseas. The first week of the month a luncheon may be served, followed by bingo; the second meeting is often given over exclusively to games such as bridge, canasta, and pinochle with appropriate prizes; the third may be a Special Activities Day. Classes in sewing, knitting, crocheting, sketching, painting, and ceramics may be introduced, with club members serving as instructors in their especial skill. It is customary for one meeting a month to be given over to a project, such as making two layettes a month. These are turned over to the base chaplain, who distributes them where needed.

The benefit you derive from your club will be in ratio to the enthusiasm, interest, and work you put into it. Don't be timid about joining. It is a base activity which needs your wholehearted support, not so much financially as morally, socially, and in the spirit of friendliness which makes for pleasant and gracious living.

Chapter VII

THE BUSINESS OF OPERATING
AN ARMY HOUSEHOLD

Soup-y, soup-y soup-y
Without a single bean,
Pork-y, pork-y, pork-y
Without a streak of lean,
Coffee, coffee, coffee
The weakest ever seen!
—"Mess Call"

BASIC PRINCIPLES OF HOUSEHOLD MANAGEMENT

SUCCESSFUL Service women are perhaps among the most resourceful, the most versatile, and the most efficient of managers in the field of homemakers. An Army officer's wife *must* be successful if she is ambitious and wants her husband to wear stars some day—on his shoulders, of course!

To be successful combines all the qualities of being a financier, a culinary artist, an interior decorator, an expert in marketing and buying, the perfect hostess, a devoted wife and mother, a social success, and a woman who can make a second lieutenant's pay stretch to the *n*th degree without ever breaking. A pretty big order, isn't it?

But Army women have a knack of being able to do these things and also to make a home out of a Quonset, a nipa shack, or whatever Uncle Sam assigns their husbands as quarters. They learn to take in stride the thing that would play havoc with the average civilian household: the frequent moving or change of station, sometimes upon a few hours' notice.

An Army wife never complains when she has to leave the spring garden she has so painstakingly planted. She smiles and hopes that the family who inherits it will enjoy her pansies, tulips, and hyacinths, and that she may find something growing in her yard at her next station. That is the Service! The only tragedy that upsets the seasoned Army woman is to be separated from her husband.

Most Army homes have an indefinable charm—a charm that reflects the personality of their present owners, regardless of shabby furnishings, bare walls, or lack of servants. There is an inviting atmosphere, a total lack of pretense, and a sincere hospitality that make the guest want to linger.

The old adage, "A rolling stone gathers no moss," is disproved by Army people long in the Service; they are inclined to collect too much in material goods. With the opportunity to collect treasures on foreign service, many of the senior officers make their homes most fascinating and interesting. Some of these houses contain museum pieces and priceless treasures in the form of Oriental rugs, exquisite Chinese handmade linens and embroideries, wonderful collections of silver and china, bronzes, Japanese lacquer, Chinese ancestral scrolls, teak-wood chests and cabinets, and inlaid mother-of-pearl screens that would cost a fortune at home.

To acquire beautiful treasures and lovely furnishings depends on knowing how to spend and to save wisely. The success of Army household organization depends upon one little word: *system.*

System in the Army Household

Every successful business in the world is built upon system, and without system a business does not continue to thrive. The Army household is a business, and the Army wife is the business manager. The keynote of her housekeeping should be "efficiency."

In America women are said to control the purse strings, and Army wives do most of the actual purchasing for the home. Rule One is that, while you may do the buying, your husband is *legally* and *officially* responsible for your debts. A wife's carelessness in financial matters can cause a husband to be court-martialed and dismissed from the Service. Many otherwise happy families have been wrecked on this rock of debt in the matrimonial sea; it is something not to be treated lightly. What you do with your husband's credit is important.

Marriage means more than establishing a love nest. It implies creating a successful home, and a successful home is built by sound financing. Records show that money problems form one of the biggest causes for divorce today, and debt is something that is feared by all officers of the Service. The government instructs its employees that all official bills be paid by the tenth of the month and all other bills not later than the fifteenth of the month.

Your household is a business, and you are its manager. To know where the money is to go is the A B C of business. First of all, as the business manager provide yourself with the proper equipment. If a desk is part of your household furniture, take it over; if you don't have one, set up a bridge table or use the dining-room table. If you are using a roomy desk, have special drawers for files, document boxes, and household inventories. There should also be space for account books, cookbooks, a card catalogue, and a typewriter.

If the bridge table is your lot, you will need two tin boxes: the old-fashioned strongbox type or lockbox, large size, plus a fisherman's tin box for tackle converted to hold desk equipment. Your small box or desk might be equipped with the following:

pens	stationery	scissors	paste
pencils	post cards	tape measure	glue
clips	stamps	checkbook	mucilage
thumbtacks	scratch pads	stapler	ink

Should space be a factor, with your two tin boxes and a shelf or table you can set up your office anywhere. The strongbox should be large enough to hold a loose-leaf binder of standard dimensions— $8\frac{1}{2}'' \times 11\frac{1}{2}''$. In this box you could also keep all the legal papers which it is necessary for you to have at hand at all times.

If you are naturally methodical, half your battle is won. There will quickly be a place for everything and everything will be in its place. To accomplish the maximum in assisting your husband to complete a successful Army career, it is essential that you keep certain records. Some of them must be kept with absolute accuracy, and at first you may consider them unduly extensive; but none is recommended which will not prove to be worth while in insuring against financial embarrassment, in preventing neglect of social obligations, in increasing your future happiness, and in retaining your husband's respect, love, and devotion.

The Army family which earnestly tries to run its establishment on a business basis will find that system and efficiency bring proportionate returns, as they do in a thriving business.

Good Husbandry

Webster defines "husbandry" as the "care of domestic affairs, domestic management; hence, thrift; wise management."

We might go a step further in saying good husbandry is a matter not only of spending the income wisely, but also of making your husband feel happy, both about the income and about that for which you spend it. If, for instance, you furnish your home so that you both find happiness and comfort, you have done your job well. If you furnish it to suit yourself only, in an impractical manner with emphasis on gadgets and in a pastel color scheme that all but sickens your spouse, you have *not* done your job well. He may never complain, but if you are spending his hard-earned money, eventually he may resent your selfishness.

A woman's share of marriage is said to be indefinite; it is truly as large are your imagination! What you make of it will determine what your marriage will turn out to be in five years or twenty. Marriage, however, is not a 90-10 proposition, nor 80-20, nor even 50-50. A good partnership must have mutual understanding and unselfishness plus love and plenty of tolerance. Each side must give 100 per cent— which may be poor arithmetic but is sound sense. The Bible says: "She that is married careth . . . how she may please her husband."

Good husbandry implies that a wife should be thrifty, and not court vulgar extravagance or stupid ease, simply because another supplies her wants. Remember the peasant bride who said to her lover: "Two eat no more together than they eat separately."

THE BUSINESS OF BEING "MRS."

When you became an Army wife, you accepted a definite share of responsibility. You cannot meet this responsibility by love and kisses alone, and whether you are legally experienced or inexperienced you have entered into a partnership business with your husband. Brace yourself, because it is bound to touch on such unromantic things as getting the floors waxed and the windows washed, how much it will cost to give a party, how long a sheet can be expected to wear. If you have an outside income, your business will be run on a large scale, and probably you won't have to worry about the longevity of sheets. If you are like most of us, however, you will have to meet large problems with a small income.

The first need in a good partnership is mutual understanding. In marriage, as in bridge, a team must play the same conventions to avoid going down. The time to bring up money matters and to reach some sort of agremeent is before you trip up to the altar. It will be too late on the honeymoon. For some reason, it is difficult to speak of money matters just after the ceremony. Why, I don't know. Yet in those first few weeks of married life you may form habits and set up standards for keeps—for instance, the habit of living on an irregular amount irregularly handed out.

You will be wise to decide on a joint bank account, and many wives like the idea of having a separate savings account for emergencies. Of course, in the days of *Life with Father* you would have had difficulty putting this across, but today it is easier.

Many girls have had experience in the business world and know the value of a dollar. Certainly, feminine dumbness is not considered cute by men when it comes to money matters. Be most careful never to undermine your husband's confidence in the way you spend money. Unless you keep an eye on the bank balance and a close tab on check stubs you are headed for TROUBLE.

THE FAMILY INCOME

Any method of handling the family income has its obvious advantages and disadvantages. Financing involves making a plan that becomes the backbone of your home. Until you have had five or six months' experience in running a household, it is rather futile to make up a budget. Before a workable budget can be made, it is necessary to have some kind of record of expenditures on which to base it. The past months' accounts may be made the basis for the following month's budget until a fairly definite standard of expenditures has been determined. Perhaps too much is being spent on food and not enough allowed for clothing.

Moving around from place to place as Army people do, plus official trips which the per diem pay never seems to cover, makes it difficult to set up a general budget that will meet all conditions. Standards of living vary with individuals and localities; so the best plan for a young couple seems to be the trial-and-error method. Try out various suggestions as to budgets and settle upon the one that fits your needs, whether in California, Maine, Germany, or Japan.

Merely keeping a neat column of figures in a little black book, whereby you record every expenditure, no matter how trivial, is not as satisfactory as developing a "money sense." Some couples prepare a financial plan indicating all fixed charges, such as rent, food, insurance, savings, payments on a car or furniture, and then divide equally the remainder of the family income between them. Above all, be frank and honest with each other about financial matters.

Army life is filled with emergencies, and every soldier and officer should look ahead and in every way possible make plans to protect his wife and children should the unexpected happen. Certainly, an Army wife should have the power of attorney, so that in an emergency she can dispose of any joint property and transact other necessary business.

In the last war, there were many sad cases of wives left alone with their children without any means of support when their husbands were killed or did not return. Some found themselves with just enough money for a few weeks' food and had no idea where to turn except to the Red Cross or charity.

In Hawaii, many wives and dependents were evacuated on Christmas Day, 1941, some on very short notice. I was fortunate in having two hours' notice. It was not possible to get a check cashed, and, unless one had prepared in advance for just such an emergency, the financial predicament was serious. Many noncommissioned officers' wives were in desperate straits simply because their husbands had always taken care of the finances and they did not have the power of attorney. Do you realize that you cannot even obtain an automobile license if the car is registered only in your husband's name and you do not have the power of attorney? A wife should have joint control of the finances since she is the business manager of the firm.

Many NCO's give their company address as their permanent address, but it is wise to list a permanent home mailing address. If you have no family, arrange with your bank, a lawyer, or a friend whose address could be used if necessary. This is a sensible precaution. A couple who have become separated in an emergency may be reunited through contacting someone at their permanent address.

Plan your budget so that there will be no necessity to ask your husband for money, either for personal or for household needs. Some families follow the "allowance plan"—a household allowance and a personal allowance for the wife and each of the children. The word *allowance* in this case smacks of condescension, which may be proper toward children but is not applicable to the wife or partner. However, this is a mere technicality, and if the housewife approves, this method may be as good as any.

Charge Accounts Versus Cash System

Charge accounts have several advantages: To have a charge account means that your credit standing is good; charge customers receive special service and courtesies—for example, advance notices of sales;

goods may be bought on approval and returned to the store if not satisfactory; the customer has added prestige when she says to the saleswoman, "Please charge it to my account." A disadvantage is that one is likely to buy more than is wise unless the budget is kept firmly in mind. The credit system is fine if you have the strength of will to resist temptation.

One objection to the cash system is that money must always be carried and small change kept on hand. Painstaking accounts of each penny or dollar spent are necessary; otherwise losses and mistakes occur. By carrying large amounts of cash one runs the added dangers of pickpockets, burglars, carelessness, and fire. In large stores it is sometimes hard to get cash returned when a purchase has been mistaken. They prefer you to make another selection of goods or give credit and sometimes refuse to return the money. However, a cash basis is certainly recommended for persons who are inclined to be extravagant.

SAVINGS!

How much money should a young couple save? That really is the $64 question and $64 is undoubtedly the wrong answer. However, early in your planning of a budget together you should set up a savings account even if you can save only $5.00 a month. In every pay bracket, saving is a pretty tough proposition today, what with elevated taxes and the mounting cost of living. For an Army family the best means of saving seems to be insurance.

BORROWING

Never borrow money from friends or relatives. The proper place to borrow money is from a bank. Another form of borrowing is to ask tradesmen or stores to carry your account longer than the customary time. However, it is advisable for young officers, if they are in debt, to send each firm a small amount each month, if only $5.00, toward payment of the account. If you are honest, you will write and explain your difficulty and make an effort to pay something each month. Your credit rating will remain unhurt.

Beware of "loan sharks," and *make it a rule never to endorse* or sign a note for anyone, or ask anyone to endorse a note for you. Endorsing is a vicious custom in the Service. An officer hates to turn down a brother officer who is in financial difficulty, but too much cannot be said about the undesirability of such a legal obligation. If you can afford to lend the actual cash, and care to, it is better than to guarantee to pay a note, no matter how good the "risk" may be.

INSTALLMENT BUYING

A family should have a small savings account before considering buying an expensive item on the installment plan. At all times, in your savings account there should be enough money to take care of two future monthly installments. Emergencies and unexpected expenses have an unhappy way of popping up the second month the installment is due. To agree to installments that make too large a dent in the pay check is obviously foolish. Since you have an assured income and are not in debt, there will be times when it seems wise to buy an expensive item, such as a piano, an automobile, a washing machine, or a refrigerator, on the monthly payment plan. Be sure to find out how much interest you will pay, and the monthly carrying charges.

YOUR BUSINESS LOG

"Log" is a Navy term; it is "a record of facts." It is in no sense a diary and should be kept free of sentiment and mental wanderings. Your log should be a record of events to which, in the future, it may be necessary or desirable to refer in order to refresh your memory. It is especially important when moving from one station to another, or for any day in which there occurs any important or unusual event. It should contain data for at least five years; often it is necessary to check income-tax returns, and sometimes they are subject to a call for verification of statements made in your joint income-tax returns. Notes can be made in a notebook in pencil, then transferred to your log at the first opportunity.

First of all, buy yourself a standard loose-leaf binder. There should be at least six heavy separation sheets, each with a tab to show the nature of the records on the pages immediately following. These tabs should be labeled in order: Automobile, Legal, Financial, Social and Dates (calendar, not social), Inventory.

Here are some of the items you might record in your log:

1. Departure from a permanent station, stating date and hour of departure, means of transportation used, and names of dependents making the trip. Such data are required in making a claim for

reimbursement by the government for the transportation of dependents.

2. Expenses during a trip by automobile from one permanent station to another—for gas, oil, tires, repairs, etc. If your husband, traveling under orders, makes the trip with you in the car, he is entitled to claim as deductions from income his actual travel expenses, i.e., the cost of gas, oil, etc., for a mileage equal to that between stations. If a wife travels without her husband in the car, travel costs are not deductible from the income. Of course, dependents are not considered in determining per diem allowances on a trip.

3. Hotels, motels, and eating places used en route. It is remarkable how often some article of value is left in a place where one has eaten a meal or spent the night. If the name of each place is noted, such lost articles can frequently be recovered.

4. Leases or other written agreements made. Anything of a legal nature should be recorded in general terms and in more specific terms in the legal section of your records.

5. Social obligations incurred and returned. This is for no thought of "any eye for an eye, or a tooth for a tooth," only as a matter of record.

6. Interesting or prominent people you meet. To recall past friendships, nothing is more important than records. Record the names and addresses of people you would like to remember, and they will probably be legion. Here's a tip! Always write down the names of your host's children wherever you visit. When your better half starts out on a cross-country to a distant base mentioning that he may see the O'Connors, be sure to brief him on Mrs. O'Connor's first name and the names of the little O'Connors. It always pays off; and should he be too busy to listen—I always found a little note slipped into my husband's pocket with the necessary data was read and used very gratefuly once he arrived at his destination. Should O'Connor have changed wives, I always tried to remind him of that, too, but not on paper! Husbands have a careless habit of leaving embarrassing notes in the wastebasket, and, as you know, some women are as curious as cats.

7. Important events in family life. These will include engagements, weddings, births, christenings, illnesses, injuries, and deaths. Dates and hours of births and deaths may in later years be of unexpected legal importance.

Automobile Log

Your automobile record should contain a complete identification of your car, including, besides all the data contained in the registration card, its color, equipment such as radio and heater, and identification numbers of tires. Then there will be license data, date of expiration, cost and number . . . of tag. The most important of all is the location of the ownership certificate, from what state the present ownership certificate was obtained and when. You will also want to record auto insurance carried, kind, amount, company, and date of expiration.

Legal Record

In your legal section should be recorded in full any matter which might lead to legal complications, such as:

1. Wills. The date and substance of your latest will and your husband's will should be recorded here, also a statement of where the original wills are kept, preferably in a safe-deposit box at some bank.
2. Leases. The substance of any lease by which you have agreed to rent property from or to another. Copies of leases should be kept with you in your strongbox.
3. Purchases. Notation of property purchased with full description, date, purchase price, down payment, and monthly payment required.
4. Policies—a list of insurance policies carried by you or your husband.
5. Pension data for widow.
6. The date and hour of employing or discharging a servant, in states where an employees' compensation law is in effect.
7. Federal and state income-tax data.
8. Notation of inventory of furniture and equipment of any furnished apartment or house rented by you, and of the checking and release when leaving. Such inventory should be kept in your lockbox.

Also to Be Kept in Lockbox

1. Canceled checks for current year
2. Your power of attorney for your husband
3. Automobile ownership certificate

4. Auto insurance policy
5. Copies of leases
6. Receipts of bills paid with cash
7. Storage or warehouse receipts

SAFE-DEPOSIT BOX

Every family should maintain a safe-deposit box in some bank or trust company vault and should keep in it all legal papers, such as birth and marriage certificates, wills, insurance policies, and other valuable property.

There are three ways in which a title may be taken to a safe-deposit box; each has its merits, and each its disadvantages. The first is individual ownership, in which case the box is absolutely private to the owner; in case of death, it can be entered only in the presence of a representative of the probate court.

The second method is joint tenancy for a husband and wife, in which case either may enter the box independently of the other. However, if either party dies, the box is sealed and may be opened only in the presence of a representative of the state tax commission, the purpose being to discover any assets which may be held subject to inheritance tax.

The third method and probably the best for Service personnel who are married is "individual ownership with appointed deputy." This is similar to the first method except that the box owner appoints a deputy who may enter the box. This method is advantageous to officers and families leaving for occupation duty. A relative or attorney may be appointed as deputy and may open the box in case necessary papers need to be forwarded.

LIFE INSURANCE

Insurance is one of "the first things that come first." Every young soldier, NCO, and Army officer with a wife, and particularly with a wife and family, should provide for their protection before all else. Straight life and endowment insurance is considered a good investment, and here are four good reasons:

1. The investment is as well protected as is humanly possible.
2. Insurance commits you to a plan of saving.
3. It means ready money in case of the death of the earner.
4. It serves as an investment fund against which you can borrow if necessary.

National Service Government Life Insurance for $10,000 is made available to every serviceman on active duty without cost.

How much additional insurance should be carried? This and many other questions do not have a stock answer. They will vary with the individual, his income, and his family needs. Normally, a husband takes out insurance for his wife, who is known as his beneficiary. With the birth of each child, it is well to increase the insurance if possible.

Sometimes a young wife is startled to find that her husband has not changed his policy, made out originally to his family, over to her name. This sense of responsibility is something very basic and fine in your husband's character, certainly not anything to destroy or attack. Unless there is an unusual need in his old home, he will no doubt change over his policies in due time. He should at least be given the chance to do so of his own accord. However, if he is inclined to procrastinate, you might tactfully remind him that you are his new responsibility; but under no circumstances should you make a mercenary issue of it.

To get a clear picture of your husband's insurance program, sit in on the next conference he has with his life insurance agent. The agent will be glad to explain the program, and it is only right that you know your husband's plans and wishes should anything happen to him. Insurance experts advise that, whatever amount of insurance is carried, it be bought with the understanding that in case of death some of the principal, *but not all,* will be paid to the widow at once. Their experience has been that when a widow with little knowledge of how to invest, or handle fairly large sums of money, turns it over to a "friend" to invest, sometimes a charmer of the opposite sex, she loses part or all of the principal. The safest way is simply not to have all that money at one time.

A better plan is to have the major portion of the money paid to her in monthly installments over a certain number of years. This monthly income is distinguished from an annuity in that the latter is more expensive and continues for the lifetime of the beneficiary, while in an insurance benefit the monthly payments end when the amount designated has been paid.

If your husband's insurance policy is set up to pay you a lump sum, you will have the responsibility of investing it wisely enough to have an income from it. This is extremely difficult to do today, and you will probably need the services of a banker, a lawyer, or a broker. All of this is expensive and you will have to make decisions. You will be in a much better position to make these decisions if you and your husband are sensible and talk over your financial affairs frankly during his lifetime. Do not be sensitive about raising the subject. It is for your own good and that of your family. In addition, it will give your husband a certain peace of mind to know that you are provided for in an emergency, and that you will carry out his wishes.

WILLS

The mentioning of a "last will and testament" is a very ticklish proposition in some families, and yet every well-advised officer should talk it over with his wife. Many wives also make wills—a wise precaution if they have certain bequests they desire to make. Personally, I think that every wife should make a will, no matter how little of this world's goods she may have to bequeath. At the time of death, and in the stress and strain of readjustment, often a husband will dispose of, by selling or giving away, valuable possessions that the deceased would wish to be given to particular friends or to members of her own family.

In addition to discussing wills—while it is not a very cheery subject —officers and wives should come to some decision as to where they wish to be buried. If there are children, family burial plots should be considered. An officer should decide where he wishes to be buried and leave written instructions to this effect. He may make one of three choices, subject to local health laws and sanitary regulations: (a) at the place of his death; (b) at his home; (c) in a national cemetery. Where death of an officer occurs suddenly, it is difficult for his widow, stunned by grief, to make important decisions. This extra hardship can be averted if the husband has been thoughtful enough to discuss these important matters during his lifetime.

A will sounds like a formidable instrument. Really it is nothing more than a legal document whereby a person disposes of his property in the manner he wishes.

A testator is the person who makes and leaves a will in force at his death. A codicil is a postscript or an addition to a will that must be executed with the same legal formalities as the will itself. An executor or executrix is the person designated by the testator to carry out the provisions of the will. The wife may be chosen as the executrix of the husband's will or vice versa.

It is well to consult an attorney for the preparation of a will. If this is not possible, then never try to make any but a very simple will. A will must be in writing. The law in most states requires at least three witnesses to a will. The purpose of the subscribing witnesses is that someone will be available who can testify to the authenticity of the testator's signature. Consequently, if the persons who have witnessed the will are not available at the time of the testator's death, difficulty will be experienced in probating the will. Should a witness die or be transferred—say, to foreign service—and not be available, the officer should destroy this will and prepare a new one. Since the authenticity of the signatures of the witnesses must be proved in court at the time of probating the will, care should be exercised in selecting witnesses who will be available to simplify this legal requirement. A will which in its execution does not completely conform to the provisions of the statute law of the state in which it is to be probated is invalid, notwithstanding the intention of the testator.

Short Form of a Simple Will

All of my estate I devise and bequeath to my wife, for her own use and benefit forever, and I hereby appoint her my executrix, without bond, with full power to sell, mortgage, lease or in any other manner dispose of the whole or any part of my estate.

JAMES THEODORE WORTHING

Dated July 1, 1953

Subscribed, sealed, published and declared by James Theodore Worthing, testator above named, as and for his last will in the presence of each of us, who at his request and in his presence, in the presence of each other, at the same time, have hereto subscribed our names as witnesses this July 1, 1953, at the city of Riverside, California.

. . . .

Witness   Address

. . . .

Witness   Address

. . . .

Witness   Address

The marriage of a man and the birth of his child, subsequent to the making of a will by him, have the effect of revoking such a will in many states. A new will must be made.

Joint bank accounts have been mentioned elsewhere. If cash is deposited in the bank in the husband's name only, his wife cannot draw it out of the bank until the will is probated, even though he left it to her by will.

HEALTH INSURANCE

With many government hospitals being inactivated, owing to the economy program, it is impossible in many places for dependents today to receive medical service or hospital care. Everybody wonders about the extra expense (or ought to) involved in a serious illness or in having a baby. It is good sense to write these off in advance by carrying health insurance.

The Blue Cross Hospital Plan of the Associated Hospital Service offers one of the finest types of protection to Service personnel. It (1) covers hospital bills; (2) covers medical-surgical bills while you are hospitalized; (3) covers medical-surgical bills when hospitalization is not required. A patient is allowed to stay in the hospital up to twenty-one days, and maternity cases are kept ten days. The Blue Cross pays the hospital direct, so there is no embarrassment about collecting the money from the insurance company. It is considered the most satisfactory health insurance available.

FIRE AND AUTOMOBILE INSURANCE

Fire insurance is a must in the Service. If your husband does not have the maximum amount to cover your possessions, do not delay getting it. Write at once to the Army Cooperative Fire Insurance Association at Fort Leavenworth, Kansas, for necessary blanks and information. The yearly premiums are nominal, and it is splendid protection.

Automobile insurance, at least against public liability and damage, is imperative. The United Services Automobile Association of Fort Sam Houston is a mutual company of long standing, organized and managed by Army personnel. Its premiums to Service personnel are lower than those of most automobile insurance companies and its service is of the highest. Educational insurance will be covered in Chapter X.

INCOME TAX

It is a common and erroneous belief in civilian circles that Service personnel are exempt from taxes. Under the present federal personal income-tax law a husband and wife may file a joint income-tax return. If the wife has an income from any outside source, she must keep an accurate record of sums received, with the date of receipt and source of such income.

Pay, not allowances, is subject to tax. Allowances include quarters allowance, ration allowance, and per diem.

SHOULD A WIFE WORK?

Homemaking is a full-time job, and a wife should not work unless there is a real need for the money she earns. Of course, there are extenuating circumstances, where an aged or ill parent must be supported, but simply to improve one's standard of living or to buy a piano, silver, or a car is not a very worth-while reason, if such work in any way jeopardizes your home responsibilities.

If you do work, always remember that your husband and your home should come first, and it is not cricket to expect your husband to accept a slapdash sort of housekeeping. Also, never use your job for an alibi. Above all, whatever temptation you may have felt to be a martyr, banish it forever.

While there is no regulation against an Army wife's working on a post, some commanding officers have serious objections, and will not allow it. Before accepting a position of any kind on a base, find out the C.O.'s wishes in the matter. This does not hold true on overseas bases where the extra services of teachers, secretaries, clerical workers, and P.X. personnel prove a blessing.

The reasons against wives' working on the post are obvious. Female workers can prove either a mercy or a nuisance. First of all, a great deal depends upon the attitude of the worker. She must keep her home and personal affairs out of the office, and she must consider all office and official matters *strictly confidential*. If she isn't careful how she talks both *during and after* office hours she will probably be eased out; also she can expect a certain amount of jealousy from the civilian employees, who are too ready to feel that favoritism got her the job. Even at best, a job on a post is not too easy . . . for a married woman!

A young married couple should never scale their living expenses to a double income because if the wife has to stop work they are really stuck. The basic expenses should be the husband's problem; he is the permanent earner and is legally responsible. By basic expenses I mean food, rent, and clothing. If the wife earns extra money, it makes for a better feeling to put it in a joint bank account; "this is the kind of thing that takes two individuals and merges them into a family team."

"Nothing but Money Is Sweeter Than Honey!"

—Benjamin Franklin

It takes will power to save money, but the pleasant satisfaction a bank account gives you more than makes up for the minor self-denials to which you condition your character. There are all sorts of attractive savings plans, which your banker will be glad to recommend. Many Army personnel try to keep the equivalent sum of a month's pay in their savings account for emergencies such as a change of station.

Investments should not be made without consulting your banker or broker. His sound advice may save you many dollars. However, if you have extra money with which to speculate on the stock exchange or "play the ponies," that is your own affair.

An officer's commission gives him and his family entree into the best society—something that no amount of money can buy, in some instances, in civil life. An NCO and his family, also a soldier and his family, can also move in civilian circles with whatever group they find congenial; the fact that he is a member of the United States Army gives him the prestige necessary.

Operation Efficiency

Home management is not a hit-and-miss proposition! It is an important business and requires just as capable handling as any career. Your paramount objective in this business is to keep the two of you comfortable, well fed, and well clothed. The first step in the organization of your household is to plan a schedule suited to your temperament and to your activities.

When all is said and done there are four musts in the daily routine regardless of what you are doing with the rest of the day. They are:

1. Bedmaking
2. Dishwashing, tidying up
3. Meal planning and marketing
4. Preparation of meals

Learn to enjoy doing a good job at your housework; have respect for your job and a mature pride in your home. There is nothing menial in housework if you have a sincere love for and a genuine interest in your home. But remember, to have an orderly, attractive, well-kept home requires daily routine.

I

When You Are Your Own Maid

Depending upon your hours of rising and the time of breakfast, after which you see your hero off to work, two hours should give you ample time to do your daily routine housework thoroughly. Of course, if you stop to finish a detective story or go back to bed for an extra nap, remember to deduct it from your leisure instead of skipping your household duties.

If you want to do a good cleaning job, get set for it by wearing comfortable and practical clothes. With all the good-looking play outfits on the market, you might as well choose an attractive combination such as shorts and shirt, slacks (if you have the figure for them) and shirt, pedal-pushers and shirt, or an attractive utility house dress. There's no point in looking like a scrub woman when it is possible to look pleasing. Here is a check list that may help.

1. After removing breakfast dishes, put butter and cream in refrigerator, then clean living room and dining room. (You may have early-morning callers, and it is disconcerting to have a disordered living room at any time when visitors arrive.) Assemble in a basket anything left in the living room that belongs in the other rooms. A special wastebasket on rollers for papers, discarded flowers, and ashes will save you steps. If you're a soap-opera addict, tune in on your favorite program and enjoy it while you work!

2. Make beds and tidy bedroom and bathroom. Fold towels neatly on racks. Clean lavatory and tub, check supply of soap and toilet tissue. Replace soiled towels with clean ones.

3. Return to the kitchen, check over menu for the day. Check refrigerator for leftovers and, if necessary to market, make list. Prepare vegetables for lunch and dinner and do any long-in-advance cooking preparations for dinner while washing last night's dinner dishes and the breakfast dishes. (Of course, some housekeepers may be horrified at this. For my money, twice a day is enough for any bride to wash dishes. The brides think so, too!) While drying the dishes, perhaps you can tune in on a foods program which will give you ideas in planning your meals and tell you the prices of foods that are in season and plentiful.

4. If it is convenient to market early, this is the best time for good fresh buys and you will beat the crowds. Of course, you will not need to market every day. Once or twice a week should be sufficient.

5. Prepare lunch for yourself on a tray, if your husband does not come home to join you. Wash or stack your dishes; your kitchen will be neater and more inviting if everything is washed before you prepare dinner.

6. Learn to budget your time, so that you can include rest, recreation, personal beautifying, and mental improvement in your "design for living."

7. If your menu calls for a simple dinner which will not require your attention until an hour before mealtime, you will be free until late afternoon. Plan ahead if any food conditioning is necessary such as crisping vegetables for salad and thawing frozen foods. Set your table attractively. Arrange the living room for evening enjoyment, such as laying the fire, adjusting the window shades, and setting out the equipment for making drinks, if your husband wishes to serve a cocktail before dinner.

Dinner should be a restful meal, gracious and peaceful and not interrupted by frequent trips to the kitchen. A weary husband may enjoy a cocktail or highball before dinner, or it may be equally restful for him to have a quiet talk with you as an unhurried companion. Sometimes he may like to listen to the radio, and make informative remarks on the news to you. Even if you don't agree with his views, save your comments until after dinner. A good meal improves a man's disposition. You can make this before-dinner interlude a period of charm and relaxation to which your husband will look forward if you plan intelligently. Have your domestic machinery so well oiled that you can take it easy before dinner.

8. After serving dinner, clear the table, stack the dishes in a covered container. (Never ask your husband to help you with the dishes at night; he has been working for the government all day. If he enjoys drying the dishes and offers to help or to do them, that is something else! Be agreeable and don't fail to be appreciative; but don't expect him to do your work in addition to his own military duties.)

There is nothing effeminate about a man's helping about the house. If your husband likes to cook, surrender the kitchen whenever he offers to take over. Illness or some unforeseen occasion may arise and it is good if a husband is capable of carrying on in your place. I still believe, however, that just as an Army man keeps his job separate from his home life, so should an Army wife keep her housekeeping job separate from her homemaking.

Suggestions on Daily Routine

1. Go over entire quarters daily. Learn to finish one room before going on to another.

2. In your daily care, it is easiest to dust first, straighten, then run your carpet sweeper or vacuum and dry mop.

3. Before going to bed, straighten living-room furniture, put away newspapers, cards, card table; empty ash trays and dispose of glasses so that the sight of the living room will not overwhelm you the next morning. It takes only a minute to empty the contents of the ash trays into a paper bag and to quick-rinse the glasses and bottles; the polishing can wait until morning. Plump up the pillows, open the windows, weather permitting, and you will have a much more cheerful view of life in general the next morning.

In the management of your household, remember that the small decisions are yours. Don't worry your husband with such trivialities as the bakery or dairyman's passing you by; learn to keep these petty annoyances to yourself. No man likes to clutter his mind with such details, and little irritations like these all come in the realm of housekeeping and are the gremlins that beset every housewife. He has his own pet gremlins to contend with in his work, but ten to one he never mentions them to you. Be adult, and do likewise!

Your Weekly Routine

There will be certain days that you may set aside for special cleaning, baking, mending, just as your mother and your grandmother did before you; but it will help greatly if you will be methodical and use a little will power about complying with the routine schedule you make for yourself.

Monday: Regular daily routine plus! Monday spells washday to many housewives; I like the first day of the week to get organized for the days coming up. It is a good day for general cleaning and checking. If the laundry is to be sent out, it should be listed and counted. If it is to be done at home, it will be easier if it is separated. Check and straighten linen closet. Check supplies of all types; bath, kitchen, laundry, and needs of household.

Tuesday: Laundry and part of ironing. Defrost refrigerator.

Wednesday: Thorough cleaning of bedrooms and baths including clothes closets.

Thursday: Mend, remove spots from clothes, brush clothing, clean silver.

Friday: General cleaning of living room, hall, dining room, downstairs closets, and kitchen. Introduce fresh flowers for week end.

Saturday: Market early, then after routine work enjoy the week end with your husband.

HUMAN SERVANTS VERSUS ROBOT SERVANTS

This should be a chapter in itself since it is a very controversial subject today and depends largely upon which side of Mason and Dixon's line you have been reared. It is interesting to note that girls who come from parts of the country where there has always been household help are the last to see the value and advantage of time- and labor-saving mechanisms. The same outlook is shared by men from the South. You and your husband may have to effect a compromise if you hold out for a part-time maid while he favors electrical slaves to wash, iron, clean, and cook for the family.

Or, if your husband is a Southerner and prefers to dole out the cash bit by bit to a gal with a feather duster, then take the advice an older Navy wife once passed on to me. She said, "When you are in a place where servants are plentiful, take advantage of your good fortune and live the life of Riley, because there will be times, my dear, when you will have to wash, iron, cook, raise a family without any help at all."

If you are all for robot servants, then don't worry—in time you will have your innings! Although an electric washing machine, dishwasher, and vacuum cleaner come in the major investment group, most housekeepers today consider a washing machine an absolute necessity. Next in rank as a labor-saving device comes the vacuum cleaner, while an electric dishwasher is the dream of most housewives. Certainly, a young couple can worry along without the mechanical dishwasher and disposal unit until the family is large enough to make dishwashing a burden!

YOUR MAID IS A VIP

If you are fortunate enough to have a full- or a part-time maid today, it stands to reason that you must pay standard wages and have your home equipped with modern appliances and labor-saving devices. If predictions are correct, in another year only one U. S. family in forty will have a full-time maid or household worker.

One of the reasons many young women do not wish to go into domestic service is that they feel there is a social stigma attached to it.

This attitude can be eliminated if you fulfill the following points as an employer:

1. It is mandatory by law that you have social security insurance for household employees. They contribute one-half of the 3 per cent, but as an employer you are responsible for sending in the entire amount to the Collector of Internal Revenue.

2. Arrange specified days and time off.

3. Schedule your maid's work.

Make your maid feel at home and comfortable; the more you can do to make her feel at home, the more permanent and rewarding your association will be. Her room should be attractive. It might be a bed-sitting room and include a comfortable studio bed, a good reading lamp, a desk, a radio, and closet space. Good sense and common decency will make the wise employer look after a maid if she is ill. If there are children in the household, your maid's good nature and dependability contribute enormously to your peace of mind and the happiness of your family. When you choose a maid, you are really choosing a member of the family.

PLANNING MEALS

Menu planning saves time, money, and the need of thinking each day what to have for the next meal. Try making out practical menus for a week and you will be sold on the idea. Always plan meals when you are hungry, not after having eaten a hearty dinner!

It is a good idea to shop personally at least once a week and to become acquainted with your grocer, butcher, and baker at the market where you do most of your buying. If you market at the same grocery regularly enough, the staff will learn your needs and preferences and will value your patronage. You can save money by watching the daily papers for sales of foodstuffs. Stock up on staples and canned goods during sales.

Today, the only advantage in commissary buying is the convenience of shopping on the post, if you reside there. Prices are the same as those of downtown stores. This is true also of Post Exchange concessions.

Place a grocery pad and pencil in a convenient spot in the kitchen and keep a close check on supplies, especially when they are getting low. If you did not receive a cookbook at one of your showers, invest in one immediately. There are hundreds on the market, but one of the most reliable is *The Boston Cooking School Cook Book*, by Fannie Merritt Farmer. *The Joy of Cooking,* by Irma Rombauer, is particularly helpful on meal planning, and one of the newest and best "how to do and know how" books is the *Household Manual,* by Henrietta Ripperger. *The Good Housekeeping Cook Book* is also excellent.

A FEW TIPS ON MARKETING

1. Check your staples once a week. When you open the last bottle of catsup or vinegar, can of coffee or box of salt, list it, and reorder.

2. Have a standing order for milk, butter, and eggs.

3. Don't fail to ask the price of things before you buy.

4. Learn the different cuts and grades of meat. Cheap cuts can be delicious if properly cooked. Ask for the bones that come with all your meat, so you will have the makings of bouillon, soup, or a savory gravy. Save out bits of vegetables here and there, such as celery tops, a carrot, four or five string beans, outside cabbage leaves, and you can make a wonderful vegetable soup. Learn small economies as you go along.

5. Special sales can save you money, but be sure the quality is high even though the price is low. It is usually safe to buy your favorite name brands.

6. Plan your vegetables so that you will use the more perishable items like spinach, lettuce, and tomatoes first. Reserve cauliflower, cabbage, and squash for the last of the week.

7. In buying fresh fruit and vegetables, watch the market. Read the ads; listen to the radio.

8. Give yourself a good course in marketing from books. There is no use learning the hard way when experts have tested and worked out an easy way that is yours for the asking at any library.

Brides of a former era considered food a baffling subject and sometimes boasted that they did not know "how to boil water" or whether lamb chops arrived in a basket or on the hoof. But those silly absurdities no longer exist; in this day of practical living, brides are eager to learn about savings and short cuts in the culinary art. I claim that anyone who can read a cookbook can cook. However, there is a knack to interpreting the cookbook, so work with your mother if you can and learn all of her cooking secrets. If your mother is not the housewifely type, hie yourself to a good cooking school, or take a course in home economics.

You should acquire, one way or another, a fundamental knowledge of the cookery of simple foods and the rudiments of housekeeping. Whether or not you ever have to use this knowledge is beside the point; even on foreign service where you may inherit a well-staffed household your home will function more efficiently if you know a thing or two about cookery and home management.

YOUR EMERGENCY SHELF

In the Army there is no such thing as an unexpected guest. Once he arrives and accepts your invitation to share potluck, it is up to you to use your ingenuity in preparing a good luncheon or dinner. Your emergency shelf will prove the lifesaver. It should be kept well stocked with standard canned goods and a few delicacies that will turn a plain dinner into a company dinner and make your husband marvel at your cleverness. With no mental road blocks as to your culinary ability, a pantry well stocked with the right cans and seasonings, a basic knowledge of the principles of plain cookery, and a true incentive to supply your husband with the food he really likes, you will go far!

Most men like oyster stew, kidney stew, broiled sirloin steak, French fried potatoes or baked potatoes, rib roast of beef, French fried onion rings, green apple pie, and strawberry shortcake. For emergency use, it is a good plan to keep two cans of Madrilene or jellied consommé in the refrigerator along with two packages of frozen vegetables. Your emergency shelf might include:

Canned soups
Canned meats (whole chicken, ham, corned-beef hash)
Canned fish (tuna, salmon, lobster, crabmeat, sardines, caviar, anchovies)
Canned vegetables (peas, mushrooms, asparagus, artichoke hearts)
Canned fuits (pineapple, pears, peaches, apricots, whole greengage plums)
Canned juices (tomato, grapefruit, grape, lime, lemon, orange, sauerkraut)
Crackers, cookies, pretzels, popcorn, peanuts, potato chips in cans, olives,
    pickles, brown bread, sandwich spreads, plum pudding, jellies, pre-
    serves, mints, candy, nuts

Remember that fine food isn't fancy, dressed-up food! A great chef serves dishes as deceptively simple as one of those "plain little black frocks whose price-tag reads $295 at Bergdorf's." Sophisticated food can and should be tempting and beautiful, but never just pretty. To use your imagination is all right, but don't veer over to the tearoom school of thought that puts a banana in a slice of pineapple with a cherry on top and calls it a candlestick salad . . . heaven forbid! Most men loathe fussed-up food, but actually everyone appreciates really first-class food.

Many Officers' Wives' Clubs and several Noncommissioned Officers' Wives' Clubs have been enterprising and ambitious enough to compile plain and fancy cookbooks which they sell to raise money for various charities.

REGIONAL COOKING

An Army wife soon learns the advantages of being a regional cook. Wherever she is stationed, she learns to use the native fruits and vegetables displayed in the markets. The native markets are usually most reasonable and perfectly safe from a sanitary point of view on thick-skinned fruits. In Hawaii, she learns to prepare bananas and breadfruit in interesting ways and finds that papayas and passion fruit make luscious ice cream and sherbet. In Panama she learns to make delectable salads of the better mangoes. In Tokyo she manages delicious tarts from the delicately flavored Japanese plums.

In the Philippines fish and chicken are normally inexpensive, and one can learn much from a native cook. I once mastered the art of boning a chicken from my Chinese cook, but I doubt if I could do it today as it takes almost surgical skill and infinite patience and time. The way an experienced Filipino cook can prepare prawns and any kind of sea food will be something you may wish to learn. Spicy Indian curries with chutney from Java or rice-tafel from Singapore will be recipes you will want to try out and bring home with you. You may acquire a knowledge of making sukiyaki in Japan.

A full-course Chinese dinner starting out with bird's-nest soup and after several hours of eating some eighteen or twenty courses ending with peanut candy will be an experience you will always remember, although I doubt that you will ever have the ambition to try to duplicate it.

In Germany, your *Fräulein* cook may teach you to make pumpernickel, coffeecake, cheesecake, and delicious *Wiener Schnitzel*. In Vienna, you will want to copy pastries which rank next to French pastry, also the Viennese recipes for coffee and hot chocolate. The French are noted for their omelets, soufflés, and wonderful combinations of foods. It is generally admitted that the French cuisine is the basis and model of all good Western cooking. Italian cooking is also wonderful and you will want the recipes for ravioli, spaghetti, and antipasto.

Add to this a knowledge of Panamanian, Puerto Rican, Central and South American cookery and you will end up with an individual style all your own. Your international treasure chest of foods should make you not only a cosmopolitan cook and hostess but an "entertaining lady" as well.

Chapter VIII

ENTERTAINING IN THE ARMY

Then drink, puppy, drink, and let every puppy drink
That's old enough to lap and to swallow;
For he'll grow into a hound and we'll pass the bottle round
And merrily we'll whoop and we'll holloa.
—Army Hunt Song

ENTERTAINING is said to have originated when the first cave lady made a social call on her neighbor and was offered refreshment, perhaps a drink of cool water in a gourd. Since that day, offering refreshment to a guest has come to be regarded as a gesture of hospitality.

Here are a few preliminary ideas which may help you either as a guest or when you are the hostess, and serve to give you poise and confidence. First of all, answer every invitation graciously and promptly. In Service circles, if you arrive even five minutes early, your hostess may not be ready to receive you, though she should be unless something has gone wrong with her last-minute plans. If an unavoidable accident delays you, you should phone if possible, and in any event your hostess will not wait at a formal dinner more than twenty minutes before dinner is announced. When you arrive you are expected to take your place and start your dinner at whatever course is in progress. It is not considered "smart," however, to delay your entrance just because you don't like soup.

The hostess must always be in command of the situation. An attractive table, congenial guests, and good food make up the recipe for a successful party, and if carefully planned it needn't cost a lot, either. Behind every successful party there has been a lot of constructive planning and, though the hostess pains belong to the person giving the party, guests have definite obligations to their hostess. First of all is punctuality; next, if there is a guest of honor, special attention should be paid to the honored one; it is assumed that all invited guests will be courteous and friendly.

Types of Hostesses

Some people are born with a gift for entertaining, some acquire it, and some never get it at all. Regardless of one's willingness to give a successful party, it cannot be achieved without "the know-how and the know-what"—in other words, a good technical knowledge of party giving.

Frank Crowninshield claims that "hostesses resemble mushrooms in that they divide themselves into two wholly antithetical categories: the benign or succulent and the noxious or deadly." It is perfectly easy to detect a hostess of the toadstool variety. The genus has an infinite number of species and subspecies.

At some time in your social career you undoubtedly will be exposed to the "eager beaver" type, the overzealous dinner hostess who begs and begs you to eat something you know will give you a bad night. Poor dear, she is too attentive; and in her eagerness to please she performs like a marionette and succeeds in making everyone uncomfortable.

Then there is the harassed or apprehensive hostess who apologizes for everything, often starting out with her husband. She should remember that her guests would be much less bored or less embarrassed by burned biscuits than they are by hearing about them. An apprehensive hostess can undo even the best-organized party, and she is incapable of enjoying herself at her own party. Believe me, if you act as though you are having a wretched time, your guests will be right with you.

Next come the fussy and the bossy hostesses! They are by no means the same; the fussy hostess is concerned with the details of the party while the bossy hostess is concerned with people, her guests. They are her slaves to order about for the evening. Sometimes she forces them to play intellectual games considerably beyond their mental capacity—games in which invariably she is skilled.

And last of all "untouchable hostesses" we have the exhausted party giver who arouses everyone's sympathy as she struggles through the evening glassy-eyed from her exertion, her face set in a deep-freeze smile. She has really done it up brown, she has thought of everything, she has given her all. But now that the party has begun she is merely a hollow shell of even her former self. The guests make a few abortive and apologetic efforts at gaiety during the evening, and then creep away at an early hour, feeling and looking a bit guilty about the whole thing.

Like most Army wives, I've been lucky enough to see many kinds of entertaining in many different places, and I have met some charming, relaxed, and most gracious hostesses in contradistinction to the toadstool variety. I think perhaps the word "relaxed" is the secret of entertaining. Ostensibly, nothing worries the competent hostess; she makes each guest feel not only that the party is given especially in his honor but that he has done her a great favor in being present.

Some of the nicest as well as liveliest parties I have ever attended were in cramped little quarters that were made gay and brilliant with loving attention and pleasant talk. The raw material of a successful party, never forget, is neither food nor drink—it is people. Perhaps for that reason the quality which above all others makes a good hostess is that of possessing a genuine interest in her friends. Many of us are fond of our friends but we fail to be interested in the little things which go to make up their lives; consequently, we do not make very successful hostesses. I'm sure we would do much better if we quit worrying about our own part of the show, quit thinking of it as "my party," and began honestly to see it as the guests' party.

FORMALITY VERSUS INFORMALITY

Very few formal, well-staffed homes today, in this land or even abroad, can accommodate the *"traditional thirty-four"* guests at one dinner table, or even half that many, in comfort. Formal dinners are so much trouble, so much expense, and require so many servants that even in their heyday they were given by great establishments only three or four times a year. Important hostesses today prefer to give small, frequent semiformal dinners or quite informal dinners. If the occasion really seems to demand a formal dinner, for visiting royalty or such, then a private suite in a hotel, a fashionable restaurant or club is usually the answer. If dining at home seems best, a competent caterer may be engaged who furnishes dishes, silver, complete service, and waiters.

Since formal dinners are given at embassies, and formal official dinners are given throughout the Service, it seems wise to include sections on formal invitations and formal entertaining just in case. At some time you might be required to marshal your forces as a hostess for a formal luncheon or dinner. Ten to one, you will go along your merry way enjoying informality in your entertaining, but there may come a day!

INVITATIONS

In the Army there is a certain informality about extending invitations to small social affairs. However, if the entertainment is of an official nature, such as a reception, a formal at-home, or a dinner in honor of a visiting dignitary, the greatest formality is observed both in extending and in accepting the invitation.

Formal invitations, whether engraved or written by hand, are always in the *third* person. Good usage demands that acceptances and regrets be written in the same person.

The telephone is the means of conveying many invitations; and out of this custom has grown another modern practice, that of sending the reminder card. It is strictly an American institution, and probably a very smart way of recalling to the guest's mind that the invitation was issued by word of mouth, either over the telephone or vis-à-vis. It seems easier to extend the written invitation in the first place. Often the hostess will find it quite a chore to telephone her invitations if the guest list is a long one. What with busy signals, leaving messages for those not at home, and long enforced conversations with those at home, this method takes more time than writing notes. So the written invitation is again finding favor whether it be formal, informal, or written on a visiting card.

In cities, telegrams are rapidly taking the place of telephoned or written invitations. Telephoning one message and fifty names to the telegraph office is a simple matter, and the telegraph company does the rest. For an impromptu party, it is the answer, because everyone not only answers but answers *pronto!*

It is never good form to issue an invitation to a party at another party which you are attending. The people invited may forget your asking them and not show up. Verbal invitations should never be given within earshot of the uninvited.

Few Service people are so formal that they send out engraved invitations for dinner, except on legation duty or in Washington. Blank forms may be filled in, as:

Colonel and Mrs. John Allen Murray
request the pleasure of
Major and Mrs. Henry Addington Barrows'
company at dinner
on Saturday, the tenth of May
at eight o'clock
318 Sumner Place

written by hand.

The partly engraved invitation when used is sent for big dinners of twenty or more and for formal dinners whether large or not. Traditionally, an engraved invitation meant full evening dress, and "Black Tie"—written in the lower corner—indicated an exception to the rule. Today, the black tie is the rule; "White Tie" shows the exception. "Decorations," * as always, means full evening dress. Formal invitations may also be written on any personal writing paper and need not be engraved. A formal invitation is never written entirely across the page, in longhand running style, as an informal invitation is.

The acceptance or refusal should be written within twenty-four hours and should follow the same form as the above. Delays are very annoying to a hostess, and she might like to ask someone else in your stead who has better manners.

Your acceptance, on a good grade of white paper, should read:

Major and Mrs. Henry Addington Barrows
accept with pleasure
Colonel and Mrs. John Allen Murray's
kind invitation to dinner
on Saturday, the tenth of May
at eight o'clock

If it is impossible for you to accept, the form for regret used is:

Major and Mrs. Henry Addington Barrows
regret that they are unable to accept
Colonel and Mrs. John Allen Murray's
kind invitation to dinner
on Saturday, the tenth of May

The Informal Written Dinner Invitation

Dear Mrs. Day:

Will you and Colonel Day dine (or have dinner) with us on Friday, the fourth of June, at seven o'clock?

We shall look forward to the pleasure of having you with us.

Very sincerely,
Helen Adams Carver

---

* The word "Decorations" as used here is only a term and does not refer to military decorations, although, as far as anyone knows, that's where it came from.

The Informal Note of Acceptance or Regret

Dear Mrs. Carver:

Colonel Day and I accept with greatest pleasure your kind invitation to dinner on Friday, the fourth of June, at seven o'clock.

Thank you for your kindness in thinking of us.

Sincerely yours,

Ruth Lallande Day

If you must decline any but a formal invitation, it is imperative to state some valid reason. It is exceedingly ill mannered to decline an informal invitation without offering an excuse.

Dear Mrs. Carver:

We are so sorry that we cannot dine with you on Friday, the fourth of June, as we are motoring to Carmel for the week end.

Thank you for your kindness in thinking of us.

Most sincerely,

Ruth Lallande Day

Visiting-Card Invitations and "Informals"

For luncheons, teas, cocktail parties, buffet suppers, and informal dances notes are seldom written. Visiting or calling cards or "informals" are used:

Wednesday, May 12

at one o'clock

Mrs. James Spencer White

Luncheon   The Town House

or:

Mrs. James Spencer White

Lunch   The Ocean House

One o'clock

Wednesday, May 12   R.s.v.p.

This invitation requires an answer at once, the same as a dinner invitation. It is permissible, but not customary, to place R.s.v.p. on a visiting-card invitation. R.s.v.p. (*Répondez, s'il vous plaît*, "Reply, if you please") on an invitation commands a reply. The hostess does this in order to be sure of the number for whom to make reservations.

The "informal" or "doublecard," on which are engraved the names of the husband and wife, is often used.

Major and Mrs. William Adams Blaine

Cocktails   Officers' Club
5–7   Saturday, May 1

This invitation really requests an answer although people are very lax about answering written invitations to cocktail parties.

A tea:

To meet
Mrs. Martin Lewis
Mrs. William Adams Blaine

Tea   Friday, May 31

This is the informal invitation that does not require a written answer unless you cannot attend. If you are unable to be present, a written note of regret should be sent.

Sometimes a guest arrives unexpectedly and the hostess wonders if she may ask for an invitation for him or her. The answer is, she may not unless the party is both large and informal, such as a cocktail party. No considerate person will ever at the last moment ask a hostess to take an additional woman guest at a formal dinner; think what it would do to a planned seating arrangement!

If it is a buffet supper, the hostess will probably not mind another guest, and if it happens to be a man, and an entertaining one, she may be delighted to have him. Let your intelligence be your guide.

The Telephone Invitation

Usually the Army wife keeps an engagement book or social calendar near her telephone and makes a note of her engagements when she receives them. This also proves a good check when one is making up a guest list.

Formality should be observed in issuing a telephone invitation to older people or to those with whom one is not on familiar terms. For instance, no junior officer's wife should call a senior officer's wife by her first name unless she has been invited to do so. The colonel's wife herself will usually address you formally until she knows you quite well. The conversation will go something like this:

"Mrs. Brandon, this is Ruth Day speaking. Will you and your husband have dinner with us (or with Colonel Day and me) on Saturday evening at eight o'clock at the Officers' Club?"

Your answer might be: "Yes, we'd love to," or "I'm sorry, Mrs. Day, but we are going away this week end."

It isn't necessary to tell where you are going or with whom you have another engagement. Sometimes it is actually much more tactful not to mention names. However, it isn't very polite to say, "We have another engagement," and let it go at that. Your refusal must be gracious and sincere, and if at all possible you should sound sorry.

Invitations should not be left with servants or children, who often get them fouled up; however, you may leave your number and ask to be called. It is not necessary to indulge in long conversations, if you have any choice in the matter.

Needless to add, the telephone is never used to answer a formal written or engraved invitation, though it may be correctly used to reply to a visiting-card invitation such as a luncheon, tea, or cocktail party.

Telephone Etiquette

When answering the telephone, before you know who is calling it is quite correct to say simply "Hello." If you commit yourself by saying, "Mrs. Brandon speaking," you may regret revealing your identity, particularly if it is a stranger who wants to sell you something.

In a social telephone conversation, never say, "This is Mrs. Brandon calling." Say instead, "This is Judith Brandon calling." Should you be calling a business firm, of course, you would say, "This is Mrs. Robert Brandon."

A low-pitched, well-modulated voice is easier to understand over the telephone than a high-pitched, shrill voice. Remember, if the person to whom you are talking is a stranger, your telephone personality is being rated by your speech, your voice, and your telephone manner. You would not be so blunt as to accost a stranger at a party with the inquiry, "Who are you?" It is an equal rudeness to ask on the telephone, "Who is this?" when the desired information might be obtained without offending by saying, "Who may I say is calling?"

Guessing games with names is an infantile practice, and one should identify himself to get the conversation off to a good start. If you say, "This is Judith Brandon," it eliminates the first question of "Who is calling?" and it is a necessary courtesy when you fail to reach the person with whom you wished to speak. There is nothing quite so irritating as to be told "someone" called while you were out.

If you have a servant, teach her the correct form for answering the telephone: "Major Brandon's quarters, the maid speaking." Have a pad and pencil near by and instruct your maid to ask courteously if there is any message, or the caller's number, in case you are away from home. If you are at home, the maid may politely inquire, "Who is calling, please?" so that she may relay the information to you and save you from going to the phone if you are busy at the time.

Your household is judged by the courtesy of your servants and children. Even the most illiterate maid can memorize the above accepted form rather than answering, "Naw, she ain't in." Long conversations over busy government trunk lines are not to be encouraged; there is no excuse for the forty-five-minute chat. It is pure poison when you are on a party line. Among offenders guilty of crippling the telephone service are adolescent boys and girls who do their homework with each other over the telephone, carry on long, silly conversations, and are too lazy to even look up numbers but call Information to save themselves the trouble. Too, young children should not be allowed to answer or to play with the telephone, as a lot of time is wasted trying to make the child understand the message.

THE BRIDE GOES TO HER FIRST ARMY LUNCHEON

What to wear! Every woman knows that nothing can make or mar a party more completely than being suitably or wrongly dressed. Everyone also knows that to be well dressed is to be suitably dressed.

First impressions we make upon others depend entirely upon what we wear and how we wear it; "voice, speech and manners are noted second and character is discerned last of all." A bride at her introductory luncheon wears, depending on the season, either a suit, a pretty spectator-sports linen or packable from her trousseau, or a pretty daytime dress. If the luncheon is given at the Officers' Club and she lives on the base, she may or may not wear her most becoming hat and accessories. Most younger women go hatless on all occasions, but good taste dictates that in town a hat be worn with street clothes in the daytime.

The safest rule of all to follow when in doubt about what to wear is to choose the plainer dress. It is always better to underdress, simply but effectively.

If it is an informal party, such as a bridge luncheon, the guests may be seated at bridge tables and served a plate lunch. Or, if it is buffet the guests may serve themselves, then find places at tables or sit about the lounge informally with their plates in their laps. (Most unsatisfactory unless there is a goodly supply of small tables about.)

After luncheon, the entertainment may take the form of bridge, canasta, mah-jongg, a club meeting, a musicale, a lecture, or something specially planned. If there is no special entertainment provided, guests usually sit around and converse for twenty to thirty minutes, then bid their hostess good-by. If there is a guest of honor everyone makes a point of saying good-by to her.

At a small home luncheon your hostess will greet you at the door and introduce you to the guest of honor, if any, and to any guest you may not know. It really is quite painless, so don't be frightened.

Breakfasts and Brunches

Since informality is the keynote of a Sunday morning or holiday breakfast or brunch, sports clothes seem to be the order of the day. However, if on a Sabbath a young couple dressed in their Sunday best dropped in after attending church, their more formal attire would be quite correct. For churchgoers the twelve-o'clock party is something to look forward to. Sunday is a leisurely day when no one has to do anything (except maybe play golf) or go anywhere except to church. For week-end house guests, a brunch or Sunday morning breakfast over which everyone sits and talks may be an easy way of starting the day agreeably.

"Brunch" is an engagingly hospitable word which starts with breakfast and ends with lunch and means a friendly informal party staged between ten and one o'clock. The food should really be served before twelve-thirty; otherwise the party, not of its own accord but in conformity to social custom, becomes a luncheon and a more elaborate menu should be offered.

Teas and Tea Dances

Afternoon teas may be as formal or as informal as one likes. The simplest variety is tea served to perhaps a half-dozen friends. It centers about a small table, perhaps even a card table, over which is thrown a cover of sheer organdy or fine linen. The hostess usually presides at the small tea table, and if there is no servant one of the younger guests passes the cups of steaming tea, while another may volunteer to pass the sandwiches and cakes. This is known as the intimate tea, and since it comes at one of the most beautiful times of the day, when daylight is softening into dusk, nothing in the world is pleasanter.

Then there is the informal, at-home Tea spelled with a capital T. On this occasion the hostess uses her loveliest tea service and tea cloth. The quarters are shining and at their very best. In other words, everything is on inspection; it is a party for the feminine world.

Wear your dressiest afternoon dress, a gay, large or small hat, and white gloves (if they are in fashion). Carry a cardcase or small purse. If you are returning from town and must wear a suit or tailored outfit, be sure that you are perfectly groomed, that your blouse and gloves are fresh. If you can, add a gardenia, a carnation, or a camellia; it will improve your morale enormously.

The tea table, with a silver tea service at one end and a coffee service at the other, will be presided over by an intimate friend of the hostess or the ranking officer's wife. This is a courtesy usually extended to the C.O.'s wife and the deputy's wife, if they care to serve or pour. Europeans think it a strange custom that we invite friends to pour, asking them to work as hard as a hired servant, but we consider it a great compliment!

After greeting your hostess and the guest of honor, go into the dining room and from the buffet or serving table select a plate, cup, and tea napkin. It is quite proper to have the cups and saucers in front of the deputy hostess who is pouring. The older woman will probably greet you with some pleasantry if she knows you. Otherwise she may simply ask, "How will you have your tea?" Your answer will be, "Strong, with lemon and one lump, please," or "Weak, please; no sugar but quite a lot of cream." You then help yourself to sandwiches, cakes, and confections, which are arranged on the tea table.

Try to have a short visit with your hostess and a few words with the guest of honor, but under no circumstances monopolize their time. All guests converse with one another, whether or not they have been introduced.

A half-hour or forty-five minutes at the most is long enough to stay at a tea of this sort. Thank your hostess, say good-by to the guest of honor and, if you can gracefully do so, to the deputy hostess who served you.

One calling card for your hostess and one for the guest of honor should be left on a tray that will be conveniently placed in the hallway.

Tea dances, given any afternoon of the week but usually on Wednesday, Saturday, or Sunday afternoons, are a popular form of entertainment sponsored by the Officers' Club on many Army posts. They are informal, yet semiformal dress is worn. A cocktail dress either short or of ankle length is appropriate; a costume suit with furs in season or a dressy daytime dress now supplants the sloppy sports clothes affected by the younger set during the war years.

COCKTAIL PARTIES

Six o'clock is considered the smart hour for cocktail parties though many invitations read five to seven. It is the easy way to entertain more friends than one's home should hold for any meal, and unless well planned can deteriorate into a carelessly run event which in the argot of the post is called a "rat race."

Should you be going on to a formal dinner later, plan to arrive late, after six, so that you may wear evening clothes. In cities, and on many posts, the ladies wear afternoon dresses or dressy daytime dresses. The officers wear uniforms, business suits, or dinner clothes if going on to a dinner party.

This is one party where you may drop in at any time between the hours mentioned; you are not expected to stay the entire period of time. From thirty minutes to an hour should be long enough, and make it a point to leave by seven if your invitation says from five to seven, even though you were late in arriving. Your hosts may have a dinner engagement themselves, or they may have split the guest list so the crowd will be staggered rather than staggering.

Thoughtful hosts and hostesses today provide at least one non-alcoholic drink such as tomato juice, Coca-Cola, or ginger ale for those who do not indulge in stronger beverages. This is an indication of good taste and thoughtfulness, since those who for one reason or another do not or cannot take alcohol feel more a part of the party if they are offered and can hold a glass of some kind in hand. Should none but alcoholic drinks be served, then very politely you can say, "No, thank you."

By no means consider yourself out of step just because you don't indulge. Sometimes young people are afraid to say "no" because they fear it may lessen their popularity; but truly, people will respect you for the stand you take, provided you are not rude or critical in regard to the drinking of others, or unfriendly or disapproving in your manner. Remember this: you will be better off if you never drink. This applies equally to officers, enlisted men, and all Army wives. Drinking is an expensive and dangerous habit. Many men have wrecked their military careers by overindulgence; many homes have been broken up by excessive drinking on the part of wives. "Drunkenness is seldom seen among people who make an art of living, and good taste's dictum makes it always safer in everything to underdo, rather than to overdo."

THE BUFFET SUPPER

The buffet supper is one of the most popular forms of entertaining today. Its informality appeals, many more guests can be entertained, and the service is simpler for the hostess. At any social function of this sort it is proper to wear evening dress after six o'clock, though an ankle-length dress or a dinner dress with sleeves, a cape, or jacket (if in fashion) is more appropriate since the occasion is informal. Should a skating party or some informal entertainment be planned following the supper, you should dress accordingly.

Cocktails, if any, are served, and then supper will be announced. Everyone proceeds to the dining room, where the table is attractively arranged with platters of meat, hot dishes, and the salad. Rolls, relishes, and coffee may be passed but often are served from a serving table. Plates, silver, and napkins are arranged for easy service, and if the hostess does not ask deputy hostesses to serve the salad or vegetables the guests help themselves. Color plays an important part in the beauty of the modern buffet table.

Sometimes small tables are set up in the living room, and place cards may even be arranged for special seating. Unless she is incapacitated, a lady should serve her own plate and not expect her escort to make two trips around the table.

One attractive feature of a buffet supper or luncheon, unless places are set, is that women as well as men can feel free to move around if they get marooned with a boring partner. One can always presumably return to the table for a serving, then join another group a short time later.

The cocktail supper held from six until eight is in effect a stand-up buffet supper and is growing in popularity as an entertainment preceding a dance. There is something about going to a dance "cold" that is discouraging, and the man of the family often begs off and has been known to "feign illness" rather than get into formal attire; yet if the couple is invited to a pre-dance cocktail supper or a party warm-up he will go eagerly and be the life of the party!

THE DESSERT BRIDGE PARTY

This "back-to·husband" movement went out of style years ago but on many posts today is being revived! The idea behind it is sound; it is intended to eliminate tea drinking and cake eating late in the afternoon, which in addition to being bad for one's figure are also bad for the housewife's enthusiasm as to cooking dinner for friend husband. Your mother may recall that it was this form of entertainment that gave bridge parties a bad name with husbands back in the twenties!

Each guest goes to the dessert bridge without having eaten midday dessert at home. At the home of the hostess the dining table is set for the dessert course only. If she owns finger bowls and wishes to be fancy, each place setting may include a china plate, on that a glass dessert plate, on that a finger bowl and in it some floating flower petals. The napkin is placed at the left of the fork and the dessert spoon at the right of the plate. A sheer luncheon set of organdy, piña, or lace is used. Runners are no longer considered fashionable, so only the place mats are used.

In front of the hostess is the coffee service, and while the guests are finishing their dessert she pours the coffee and it is handed around the table. After coffee, they begin playing on tables set up in the living room, and the game ends at four or four-thirty. This gives the wives time to arrive home to greet their husbands and to provide a well-cooked substantial dinner; then everyone is happy!

The same type of dress or suit suggested for a luncheon is appropriate for a dessert bridge. It is informal, and therefore not as dressy as a tea.

THE FORMAL DINNER

Once in a while the problem of a formal dinner must be faced and, although at this point you are an invited guest and on the receiving end, still there are certain formalities you should know.

Wear your best dinner dress or formal evening dress. Some women feel that a formal dinner calls for bare backs and bare shoulders, but a gown with a suggestion of sleeves is also apropos. Gloves are always worn to a formal dinner and removed at the table. To me it is barbaric to leave them on the arms, tucking back the hands, suggestive of a surgeon getting ready for an operation!

Your husband will know what to wear: either formal uniform

evening dress or civilian evening dress (tails) or, if he possesses neither, a dinner coat, though the latter is not correct, strictly speaking, except in tropical climates.

A few general officers and ranking officers who maintain well-staffed households entertain formally as in days gone by, but most formal dinners today are given at exclusive clubs or hotels.

The seating at a formal dinner in Service circles is always according to rank, with the exception of the guest of honor. The experienced hostess—and no one except an experienced social leader should attempt to entertain at a formal dinner—will draw up a seating chart. Undoubtedly she will have to consult the official *Register*, and if her husband is helpful he will assist in drawing up the seating arrangements. If there is any question whether Colonel Brown's commission in the Infantry antedates Colonel Foster's in the Engineers, perhaps the adjutant of the post will help out by looking up the correct dates of rank! It is that important.

Your hostess will be standing near the door and will greet you upon your arrival with some gracious remark and a smile of welcome. Remember this: The perfect guest owes his hostess the courtesy of entering into the spirit of the party and should strive to be entertaining and at his best. However, one should not attempt to "take over" or try to be the "life of the party." What most social gatherings need is a few trained listeners, and your popularity will depend upon your poise, your graciousness, and your charm. No man, young or old, is impervious to a beautiful woman who is a good listener. People love to talk about themselves if you can get them to open up. A grim-visaged, crusty old Marine colonel may prove a delightful dinner partner if you are a mind reader and can direct the conversation to his pet hobby. All he needs to have is a pretty and intelligent listener who has the ability to ask the right question at the right time. The bride or young woman in the Army who is a good listener and a close observer can learn more at her first formal dinner party than can be included in this entire book.

Never be late to dinner. If you are invited at eight, be there at eight, not five minutes before or two minutes after. A formal dinner never begins before seven o'clock, and when it is set for this hour, it is because the guests are going on to another entertainment later, such as the opera or the theater. The usual hour for the formal dinner is eight o'clock or eight-thirty. It is a social sin to keep a dinner party waiting!

Your dinner partner is the gentleman on your left, but during dinner be careful to divide your conversation equally between the men on either side of you. Because the host should at the beginning of dinner direct his conversation to the guest of honor on his right, it follows that the other men must turn to the right also. If some one of the guests through thoughtlessness or preference concentrates his attention on the lady on his left, a guest is automatically left out of the conversation at one point or another. Every experienced hostess is familiar with the guest who gazes wildly into space, with the stricken expression of a castaway, while her partners on either side chat vivaciously with other guests. Should you draw for a dinner partner a Sphinx, who wishes to commune with himself and be left alone with his food, that is something else. However, you should make several attempts to engage him in conversation. If that doesn't work, you're on your own. Maybe you can horn in on the couple across the table.

After dinner, the American custom is for the ladies and gentlemen to return to the drawing room or living room for coffee and liqueurs. The European custom is that the men remain behind in the dining room for coffee, cigars, brandy, and talk while the ladies await them in the drawing room.

Guests at a formal dinner which has been followed by conversation alone usually leave at about ten o'clock. As a rule, not everyone leaves at once, but the ranking guest leaves first. The host and hostess rise when bidding their guests good night and go with them to the drawing-room door. As a guest it is enough to say, "Good night, and thank you so much." Then leave. The door dawdler is the bane of everyone's existence.

ENTERTAINING IN ENLISTED CIRCLES

In our new career Army undoubtedly there will be more rapport in the social life among enlisted men and their wives than was true in the early days.

It is agreed that the only way to keep the global peace is on an international basis of friendship. Well, friendship begins at home, and we can all begin with those nearest us. A kind heart, an unselfish nature, and the ability to get on with others are the requisites. There are times when everyone needs a friend or friends; no one is truly self-sufficient in this life.

If giving a dinner for the newly arrived soldier and his bride is too much of a strain financially, then take a try at the suggested tea or coffee idea. You might even ask the lonely wife to walk with you over to the Post Exchange. Put yourself in the bride's place. Think back and recall how strange and ill at ease you felt upon entering Army life. There's nothing so helpful as to be welcomed and made much of, even in a very simple, informal way.

As soon as you entertain your first guests, you will have put down roots. Do not apologize for what you have or don't have. Do only what you can afford, but do it in a friendly, gracious way. Begin by being friendly and kind with your next-door neighbor or the latest bride in the company or someone you have passed over intentionally or unintentionally . . . up until now.

If money is what has curtailed your friendliness, but you are willing to give of yourself, your time and effort, you need not spend one penny. It costs nothing to make a friendly call, to offer to market for a neighbor who has recently come home from the hospital, to sit with a baby while its mother does an important errand, or to carry a small bouquet from your garden when your neighbor's mother arrives for a visit. On the first day new neighbors are moving their furniture in next door, offer to lend them anything they may need but can't find, such as a coffee pot or can opener. Offer to let them use your phone until theirs is connected. So often these things are offered four or five days too late. These are little gifts and acts which money cannot buy. The tiniest thoughtful courtesy can make a mere acquaintance blossom into a fine friendship.

When you bake a delicious angel food, how about sending over a generous wedge to the bride and groom who live across the street, or some homemade ice cream to the cross-country widow whose husband is on an extended TDY? In a one-sided way this comes under the head of entertaining. And not that you should ever expect a return—but it has always been my experience that any of the proverbial bread I have cast upon the waters has always returned to me a club sandwich!

The Corporal and His Bride Are Entertained

Tony arrives one evening quietly excited with the following invitation: (Before you can even open it, he tells you it is from Helen Burton, his master sergeant's wife.)

My dear Mrs. Tennant—or Connie?

I have not been able to reach you by telephone, so I am sending this note to ask if you and Tony will have family dinner with us on Wednesday evening at six-thirty? Afterwards a few friends may drop in. Everyone is anxious to meet you as we are all so fond of Tony. My husband and I are especially anxious to welcome you in our own home.

Very sincerely,

Helen Burton

A cordial, sincere invitation like this should warm your heart, and you hasten to answer. Sending word by Tony that you accept or regret will never do, regardless of the man's point of view! On plain gray or white stationery your reply might be something like this:

My dear Mrs. Burton:

Thank you for your kind invitation to dinner on Wednesday at six-thirty. Tony and I will be most happy to accept. It is so thoughtful and sweet of you and Sergeant Burton to think of us, and I am looking forward with great pleasure to meeting you and all of Tony's friends. Thank you for calling me Connie. It makes me feel I really "belong."

Sincerely,

Constance Tennant

If it is a telephone invitation, you accept Mrs. Burton's kind dinner invitation as graciously as you can without being effusive. Sometimes invitations are extended verbally through the husbands; if this is the case, you can answer the same way. However, should a formal or an informal note be sent, it is proper to reply in kind.

Wear your prettiest short or ankle-length dress, because you will be meeting Tony's friends for the first time and will want to look your best.

Let us assume that Mrs. Burton is an older woman, the motherly type with years of Army experience back of her. She would not classify your first family dinner in her home as anything "fancy" but is only being neighborly, and in her heart she may be hoping someone will be equally kind to her own daughter, who is soon to be an airman's bride.

Introductions

It is important that people be properly introduced to each other, and there are a few simple rules which may make you feel more at ease. One always introduces a man to a woman, a younger person to an older person, and one person to a group. There are several correct ways of making introductions. One may say, "Mrs. Thomas, may I present Sergeant Black?" Names should always be spoken very distinctly, so that they may be understood.

Another form is: "Mrs. Thomas, I should like to introduce Sergeant Black." This is considered less formal than the first form. Or, "Mrs. Thomas, this is Sergeant Black." The name of the person to whom the introduction is being made is always mentioned first.

In the case of introducing a warrant officer, still another form would be: "Mrs. Thomas, do you know Mr. Thompson?"

When introducing members of the family, one avoids using titles as much as possible. For instance: "Mrs. Brown, this is my husband." "Mrs. Paine, may I introduce my daughter, Carolyn?"

A man should always rise when introduced to anyone, and men usually shake hands. A woman may offer her hand or not, but a man never offers his hand first. If a woman extends her hand, under no circumstances can the offered hand be ignored.

As you know, the correct reply to any form of introduction is, "How do you do?" and it is courteous to add the name of the person to whom you are being introduced.

No woman is ever presented to a man, except to the President of the United States, a royal personage, or a dignitary of the church. A hostess always rises to meet or to be introduced to a guest. Otherwise a woman does not rise to be introduced.

A man should never be guilty of introducing his wife as "the little woman," "the wife," "friend wife," or "the missus"; it is equally vulgar for a wife to introduce her husband as "the sergeant," "my man," or "my hubby"!

Another introduction taboo is: "Sergeant Burke, *shake hands* with Sergeant Jones." "May I make you acquainted?" is a form no longer used in introductions.

Introduce and Identify Yourself

Should an officer or enlisted man meet an enlisted man or officer he has not seen in years, he should introduce and identify himself. If there appears any doubt on the part of either, a gentleman should be good enough to set his "amnesia victim" at ease by giving him a clue. It is well to mention your name, maybe a word or so as to the year, etc., you were students at Benning. He will bless you with a light of recognition in his eye. For instance, "Good morning, Colonel Jones . . . I am Sergeant Connors . . . Old 4th Cavalry . . . Border days at Fort Ringold!"

Another snag in introductions crops up when an Army man has taken a new wife. This can be particularly startling in a receiving line!

Mentally you wonder if Mary died, if they were divorced, or just what the score is.

Socially, both men and women should take care to mention their current spouses early in the conversation, just to set the "other fella" straight. This would avoid a lot of mental gymnastics. If you have a new mate, casually say so, mentioning his or her given name. It is best to skip over any unpleasant features in conversation, such as lengthy particulars of illness, death, divorce, or separation.

It is no longer the best form to say, "Pleased to meet you," or "I am pleased to make your acquaintance." Again, the most acceptable form is "How do you do?" You don't need to answer that rhetorical question, of course, but may plunge into conversation at that point.

When one shakes hands it should be with warmth and firmness. A limp hand suggestive of a clammy fish is irritating. However, no one enjoys a bone crusher. Shake hands as though it were a pleasure, but not as though you were a drowning man going under for the third time.

THE BURTONS' FAMILY DINNER

By now you and Tony have arrived in front of the Burtons' quarters, Connie, you in your prettiest, Tony in uniform slicked up with "spit and polish," for this is your first dinner party on a post. You are both excited and should be radiantly happy!

Sergeant Burton is at the front door to welcome you in response to Tony's ring. If the host does not waive the formality of an introduction, Tony will say, "Connie, this is Sergeant Burton. . . . My wife." The words "my wife" are, of course, addressed to Sergeant Burton.

Your host makes the reply: "How do you do, Mrs. Tennant? May I welcome you to our post?" Your answer could be, "I'm happy to be here." By this time you are in the living room, and Mrs. Burton comes forward to extend a warm welcome. She might also present her daughter and son at this time.

After a few minutes of pleasant conversation you are invited in to dinner. Since you are the guest of honor, Connie, you will be placed on Sergeant Burton's right; Tony will be on Mrs. Burton's right. The daughter will be beside Tony, and Charles, the son, next to you.

Helen Burton, excellent cook that she is, might serve first a delicious soup followed by veal scallopini, steamed brown rice, and fresh peas. Sergeant Burton busies himself mixing a tossed salad, his own specialty. There will be hot rolls which give you a nostalgic feeling for your mother's home cooking. Finally you get to the Ozark pudding, another of the Sergeant's specialties. He proudly boasts that it is the President's favorite dessert, and if it is good enough for the President in the White House he feels that he and his guests can struggle along!

Army men really get around the world, and often at great personal sacrifice they manage to bring home beautiful treasures from foreign countries. You and Tony are impressed with the Chinese rugs, scrolls, and exquisite china and linens the Burtons had collected on foreign service before the war. There are batiks from Java, a Satsuma tea set from Japan, a Canton salad bowl from Hong Kong, carved wood lamps from Hawaii, and a tapa cloth from Samoa. But best of all are the fascinating stories of Service life in the Philippines, Hawaii, and Panama with which the Burtons entertain you. They are careful to explain that their possessions had been acquired over a period of some twenty-five years of service, when foreign service prices were low. Even so, it had taken a bit of doing and planning.

Shortly after dinner three more sergeants and their wives drop in to meet Tony's bride. The conversation is stimulating, but the lingo so definitely Army that you decide that Service people have a special language of their own. You are content to be a good listener and do not miss one single hostess gesture on the part of Mrs. Burton.

Later in the evening a large wooden bowl filled with tempting fruit is passed, and with it cheese and crackers. Soon the delicious aroma of Sergeant Burton's wonderful coffee permeates the living room and all the guests move out to the kitchen to serve themselves. During the conversation you learn many things about the post, but you are far more intrigued with Helen Burton's graciousness toward each guest. The light refreshments show that she thought of her after-dinner guests before they arrived and that she planned for them.

TABLE MANNERS

"The standard pattern of table manners is broken down into twenty-three rules," according to the *Vogue Book of Etiquette*. Also the *Handbook and Manual for the Noncommissioned Officer* is used here.

1. "Napkins belong on the lap, except in the case of young children. They should never be tucked under the belt, in the collar or between the buttons of a coat." "Use your napkin when you have to. Don't be afraid to soil it." (*NCO Manual*)

2. One should sit straight but comfortably. Food should be conveyed to the mouth, not the mouth brought down to the food.

3. The arms should move freely in conveying food to the mouth, but when cutting meat they should stay down near the sides instead of giving a spread-eagle effect.

4. "In using a soup spoon, dip the spoon away from you and never put the bowl of the spoon in the mouth; instead put the side of the spoon to the lips and then tilt the spoon slightly." (*NCO Manual*)

5. When one has finished the soup, the spoon is left in the soup plate, handle to the right. If a bouillon cup is used, the spoon is left on the saucer. Never should a spoon be left in a tea or coffee cup. Never, even for one moment, should a spoon be left sticking up out of any kind of cup. " 'Tis best to 'shift one's oar."

6. When anything is served in a cup with a handle or handles, the contents are supposed to be drunk from the cup.

7. All affectations such as crooking the little finger or wiping off the silverware on the napkin (which is an insult to the proprietor of any reputable restaurant, much less one's hostess) should be avoided.

8. In selecting the correct piece of silver for each course, a guest can always observe the hostess and take the lead from her. Otherwise a generally safe rule is to start at the outside and work in.

9. Food should be cut and handled neatly; only one piece of meat or anything else should be cut at a time. It should not be pushed around the plate or messed up with other food.

10. "The knife should always be held in the right hand with the handle in the palm and the index finger along the back of the blade. Never take food to the mouth by means of the knife. After having used the knife never lay it again on the table nor place it with the handle on the table and the tip of the blade on the edge of the plate.

Lay it across the upper half of the plate with the handle to the right and the cutting edge of the blade facing the eater." (*NCO Manual*)

11. "The fork, when used as an aid to the knife in cutting meat or for a similar purpose, should be held in the left hand with the end of the handle resting in the palm, and with the index finger extending along the back. When the fork is used for eating purposes it is held in the right hand, while in European countries the left hand is often used." (*NCO Manual*)

12. When one has finished eating, the fork and knife should be placed across the middle of the plate, handles to the right. The tines of the fork should be turned upward, not downward as in foreign countries, and the edge of the knife blade should be toward the table edge.

13. Bread, toast, rolls, and muffins should always be broken in half or in even smaller pieces before they are buttered or eaten. Never butter a whole slice of bread. Never cut a biscuit, roll, or muffin with your knife.

14. Don't dunk, although it is an approved fashion in lunch wagons. Dunking a whole doughnut into coffee is rated very little above eating with a knife. Gravy or sauces should never be sopped up with bread propelled by the fingers. The right way is to drop a bit-size piece of bread into the plate, spear it with the fork, and then sop up the gravy.

15. One should never talk while having food in one's mouth, and the mouth should always be closed when chewing.

16. Toothpicks should never be used at the table or at any other time or place if other persons are present. To have toothpicks on the table is considered vulgar in the extreme, and their main usefulness is in the serving of canapés.

17. Don't lean back at the table and say, "I'm through." The fact that you have placed your knife and fork horizontally on your plate shows that you are through.

18. Don't push back your plate when finished.

19. Don't encircle your plate with the left arm, clenching your fist while eating with the right hand. Looks as if you are guarding your food!

20. Don't ever put liquid into your mouth if it is already filled with food.

21. Avoid all unnecessary noises in eating and drinking.

22. Fingers should never be used to push food onto the fork.

23. Anything that must be taken from the mouth and put back on the plate is dealt with according to a very simple rule: If it went in on a spoon, it comes out on a spoon (cherry or plum stones, for instance). If it goes in by hand, it comes out by hand (olive pits, grape seeds). Exceptions to this rule might be a fish bone or pieces of shot often found in game; though conveyed to the mouth by a fork, they are taken out by hand.

FIVE OLD-FASHIONED RULES OUTMODED TODAY

1. "Leave a little on your plate for Lady Manners." War and the rationing of food put a sensible end to this affectation. The gospel of the clean plate today is the answer.

2. "Food should be eaten as little as possible with the fingers." This is another silly one, and today sandwiches, fruit, candy, cookies, and other similar foods are eaten by hand. Even fried chicken goes in by manual means in the best of society. Of course, forks should be used for a wedge of sticky cake—chiefly as a protection against being messy.

3. "Reaching across the table is rude." No more. Modern etiquette sanctions any reaching that does not inconvenience other guests.

4. "No one should begin eating until everyone has been served." After one or two others have been served, there is no reason not to begin eating.

5. "The fork must be switched from the left hand to the right hand as soon as each piece of meat has been cut." No longer; today either the Continental or the American method is proper. In other words, use either left or right hand for conveying meat on a fork to one's mouth.

TECHNIQUES FOR EATING FOODS THAT ARE SOMETIMES DIFFICULT TO EAT

Asparagus is definitely not a finger food. It is eaten with a fork.

Artichokes are always eaten with the fingers leaf by leaf. Each leaf is first dipped into sauce. When the center is reached, the thistle part is scraped off with a knife and fork, and the heart is eaten with a fork. It is tricky the first time, and there's always a first time!

Candy, whether offered on a plate or in a box, is always taken with its little paper frill. The main points are not to touch other pieces and not to hesitate so long in choosing that it becomes a national issue. Needless to add, it is reminiscent of boarding-school days and positively barbaric to bite, poke, squeeze, or break candies to investigate the filling and then put them back in the box.

Oysters and clams should never be cut, regardless of their size.

Olives should not be popped into the mouth whole; the flesh should be bitten away until only the stone remains.

French fried potatoes should be eaten with a fork. Shoestring potatoes, on the other hand, are finger tidbits.

Corn on the cob is delicious to taste but not very pleasant to manage. Well, just eat it as neatly and as quickly as possible. The less said the better!

Spaghetti is eaten with a fork only; even in Italy an accompanying spoon is considered bad usage. After spearing a few strands of the wily spaghetti, twist the fork in such a way as to wrap the strands around it neatly, like a cocoon. It is then easy to cut with the side of the fork before eating.

Pickles are eaten with the fingers when served with sandwiches.

Broiled lobster is called a finger food because it is impossible to eat the meat in the claws until they have been cracked and broken. A finger bowl with hot, slightly soaped water should be in attendance.

CONVERSATION

There are as many kinds of conversation as there are kinds of people; however, it might be noted that a good conversationalist is always a constructive listener. The *NCO Manual* says, "One should cultivate alert, accurate, and sympathetic listening in conversation. By all means, one should be able to talk other than 'shop.' Trite expressions, attempts at fanciful language, profanity, coarseness, and bad grammar are the marks of poor manners and bad training."

Nothing so instantly reveals the quality of one's background as speech—the words that are chosen and the way they are pronounced. A beautifully dressed woman wearing sables and dripping with diamonds can reveal her true background the first time she opens her mouth if she says, "Hully gee, I sure got him told off!" "Hold back them drapes, dearie!"

Then there are definite grammatical errors indicative usually of sheer carelessness. Without attempting a lesson in grammar there are a few things that should be emphasized. First, the double negative is in black disgrace—for instance, "I can't do nothin' today." Mixing adjectives and adverbs is a dead giveaway: "She felt very badly" instead of "She felt very bad." Some people use "I" and "me" interchangeably. If the speaker would only think first before saying, "The gift was sent to Jim and I," she would change to "The gift was sent to Jim and me." The test is to take Jim out and use the same pronoun; nobody would ever say, "The gift was sent to I." Then sometimes on the phone we hear, "This is her speaking. I am her," when the correct form is: "This is she speaking. I am she."

Of course, there are exceptional people who despite their lack of education are fine, respected people because they make no pretense. They may say, "I come," "I ain't got no right," and "I done it" and get by—but such boners certainly don't help. Then there is another group of people who have educational advantages but through carelessness, laziness, or the desire to be different make grammatical errors. There is no excuse for them.

Slang is acceptable today if it is fresh and applicable; but to be effective it should be sparingly used. Coarse or profane language is always a social handicap, something akin to dirty fingernails or ears. It must be remembered also that outmoded slang can date the person using it, and it is as unappetizing as a piece of tired celery. I refer to such terms as "23-skiddoo," "kiddo," "could be," or any of the hundreds of phrases coined each year by radio humorists.

Today for anyone who has the will to help himself numerous opportunities are available. Never be ashamed to improve yourself. Invest in a standard grammar and rhetoric and learn the fundamentals you might have missed in school for one reason or another. It is fun for a young couple to study together. Attend a vocational or night school together one or two nights a week, take a course in grammar, rhetoric, or English composition and you will be on your way. Get a small pronouncing dictionary of words in ordinary use and read it word for word, marking and studying any that you use in your conversation and mispronounce. You and your husband can make a contest or game of words, and one excellent practice is to read aloud to each other, looking up the pronunciation and meaning of any word unfamiliar to you. In this way, your vocabulary will grow enormously.

Conversation is a considerate give-and-take, in which one tries to be as interesting as possible to the other person. The first rule for conversational behavior in company is: "Try to say and do only that which will be agreeable to others." The second rule is: "Try to draw the other person out and make him or her interesting." A bore is said to be "one who talks about himself when you want to talk about yourself."

Conversational Taboos at Social Gatherings

1. Vivid details of an operation, illness, death, or funeral
2. Personal jokes of an embarrassing nature
3. Sneering remarks or attitudes
4. Destructive gossip and repetition of scandal
5. Discussion of personal money matters or the price paid for articles
6. Thoughtlessness of the feelings of other or tactlessness
7. Discussion of one's personal affairs with strangers or mere acquaintances
8. And unless the gathering is one of young mothers, forget the children!

SOCIAL TALENTS

There are certain social talents so generally useful that if you have not acquired them, and wish to be a successful Army wife, you should start now. Here they are: The ability to introduce people, acknowledge introductions, accept and pay compliments, express gratitude, and know the few rules of etiquette that are based on consideration for others.

Every Army wife owes it to herself to be competent in at least two social graces. These include being an average or better player in card games (bridge, rummy, canasta, or poker); adeptness in ballroom dancing; ability to play a musical instrument; ability to be socially athletic (golf, tennis, badminton, bowling, table tennis, hiking, riding, swimming). If you are good at any two of these, you will pass muster! If not, get busy and it won't take long. The more strings you have to your bow, the better chance you will have of fitting into a wide variety of situations. And if people—lots of different kinds of people—genuinely like to have you around, your social success, which is so important to your happiness on a post, is assured.

SOCIAL CUSTOMS FOR ARMY BACHELORS

"It's fatally easy and easily fatal for a bachelor to get into the habit of going to other people's parties and not giving any of his own." So says Dorothy Draper—"and if he persists in the habit long enough, he gets the reputation of 'always a guest, never a host.' " So I am including this item in the hope that some generous young Army wife may lend you her book!

Many Army bachelors take all social courtesies more or less as their

due. Well, the Army is shaking down, and, my dear young lieutenant, whether you are aware of it or not, you have certain definite social obligations as a bachelor, and Army hosts and hostesses have a
right to expect certain things of you. Your manners and the way you
handle the social amenities have a distinct bearing on your official
record as "an officer and a gentleman." Here is a brief check list to
start with:

1. If calling is in order, you are expected to make social calls the
same as a married officer. It is a gracious gesture to pay a social call if
one of your married friends or the C.O. has a young-lady guest.

2. When you are invited to a party, you should decline or accept
immediately, not leave the hostess dangling until the day of the party.
It is not good manners to be evasive and say you will let your hostess
know later; it leaves the impression that if nothing more interesting
to do turns up you will consider coming.

3. If you are invited to a dinner party, your social duty is to dance
with your hostess, the lady you escorted, and all the ladies at your
dinner table. (Now this is not just being mid-Victorian; Army wives
have memories like elephants where courteous bachelors are concerned.)

4. Too many bachelors have a "spoiled" attitude, and seem to
think they are doing the hostess a favor when they accept. One bachelor recently waited until the day of the party, then called his hostess,
a general's wife, and asked bluntly, "What time is your party?"—not
then actually accepting or declining either. Have a care on this score,
young man. You may bring a bride to this or some base and be faced
with a similar situation. It is a boorish attitude.

5. Army bachelors have social obligations just as married officers
and their wives have. Sometimes two or three bachelors give a cocktail party or dinner at the club together to repay their obligations.
Keep a check on your obligations.

6. Dinner calls are also a gracious gesture and should be made
within a week after you have attended the party.

7. Should a bachelor officer ask permission of the hostess to bring
his girl to her party—and this should be only if his hostess is a close
friend and the party is large and informal, such as a large cocktail
party—in some way he should show his appreciation of this hospitality . A nice thing to do is to send flowers the morning of the party,
or to send his hostess a corsage. If the hostess for some reason cannot
include the girl, she courteously explains the situation and asks him

to bring her some other time. Having accepted, the bachelor is expected to attend, alone.

8. If the party is being given on the post, and the invited bachelor wishes, it is a courteous thing to ask the hostess if there is any young lady visiting on the post that she would like him to escort to the party.

A bachelor sometimes is diffident about giving a party, but he can always go in on the expense angle with his favorite couple and join them in returning his obligations, provided their guest lists tally well enough. An Army wife might even suggest, if she knows our lieutenant well enough, that it is just about time for him to give a party to return his social obligations, and that she will be delighted to act as his hostess and help in any way she can, if he has no other preference. If you are a sharp young officer, lieutenant, this will be your cue, and once you have had the fun of giving a party at which all the guests have a good time, you will welcome an excuse to give one eventually all by yourself.

RANK IN THE ARMY

Socially, both commissioned and noncommissioned officers are addressed by their proper titles. For instance: "Good evening, General Green," regardless of whether you are addressing a one-, two-, three-, or four-star general.

"How do you do, Colonel White?" No distinction is made between a colonel and a lieutenant colonel; both are called Colonel.

"How are you, Major Brown?"

"It is nice to see you again, Captain Black."

"Thank you, Lieutenant Gray." No distinction is made between a first and a second lieutenant; both are addressed as Lieutenant.

"When did you return, Mr. Miles?" A warrant officer, in any of the four different grades or ranks, is always addressed as Mister. Warrant officers are commissioned officers with all of the allowances and social privileges of the base.

"Good morning, Sergeant." Noncommissioned officers and soldiers are always addressed by their titles. There are four different grades of sergeant—master, technical, staff, and sergeant—but each is addressed as Sergeant. There is no longer a first sergeant.

"Good afternoon, Corporal."

"Good evening, Private Parker." Privates first-class and privates are addressed as Private.

A chaplain is not addressed by his rank, but is always addressed as Chaplain. Medical officers are addressed by their rank.

Of course, it goes without saying that "Mrs. *Colonel* Jones" and "Mrs. *Major* Wright" are as incorrect as "Mrs. *Doctor* Brown" and "Mrs. *Judge* Davis."

HOUSE GUESTS

As the *Officers' Guide* states, "Much has been written about the art of being a good host, but all too little has been written about being a good house guest. Thoughtlessness or ignorance sometimes plays havoc with cherished friendships. Thoughtfulness will cement and strengthen them. As in all other human relationships *good breeding is shown by a proper regard for the rights of others.*"

First of all, no one should feel hurt when a hostess specifies both the time of arrival and the time of departure in the invitation. Sophisticated guests actually want to know what the arrangements are so they themselves can make plans in advance.

The host and hostess should be informed as nearly as practicable of the exact hour of your planned arrival and your departure. Never write or telegraph "Arriving on Thursday." That is too indefinite for your hostess. She may have a bridge or luncheon engagement or a beauty-shop appointment which will raise her metabolism to dangerous levels if she has to do guard duty at home waiting for your arrival. If a guest is this thoughtless and inconsiderate, the hostess is well within her rights to leave a note of welcome saying when she will return, then go on with her original plans.

Of course, there may be extenuating circumstances. If the guest is arriving by car, in accepting the invitation he might say so and add: "We expect to arrive at your home shortly after four on Friday afternoon and must start our return before nine on Monday morning. Thank you again for your kind invitation and we are looking forward with great pleasure to being with you."

Arriving as nearly as possible at the time you have given your hostess. Your delayed arrival may upset her planned entertainment; early arrivals are even less appreciated. Leave when you are expected to, regardless of the good time you are having. Benjamin Franklin put it right on the line when he said, "Fish and house-guests should never be kept over three days."

In these busy days few hostesses, whether in the Army or not, appreciate surprise guests (visiting firemen excepted . . . the welcome mat is always out for your husband's former "wife" or roommate at the Academy, or his buddy in flying school, or the guy with whom he bailed out over Bali, or a former company commander). If circumstances are such that you arrive unannounced or uninvited, be prepared to take potluck and like it. An Army wife appreciates a few hours' notice, at least. That is only cricket!

How to Be a Welcome House Guest

1. A guest must adjust to the conditions of the household. Emily Post says, "You take your meals at their hour, you eat what is put before you, and you get up and go out and come in and go to bed according to the schedule arranged by your hostess. And no matter how much the hour or food or arrangements may upset you, you must appear blissfully content. When the visit is over, you need never enter the house again; but while you are there, you must like it. You must like the people you meet and the things they do. That is the first inviolable law for the guest." She continues in a humorous vein, but she does suggest that you can *always* send yourself a *telegram* and *leave*. Regardless of how uncomfortable the visit has been, however, you must not even by a facial muscle betray to your hosts that you have had anything but a beautiful time when you bid them good-by. Your obligation extends further. Having broken bread in their house, you must never confide to anyone afterwards how desperately wretched you were on your visit.

2. A man guest should keep his things picked up and his room tidy, even though he is unaccustomed to doing so at home! He should leave the bathroom in the same or better condition than he found it.

3. A lady guest should take complete care of her room and be similarly thoughtful about the bath. In a servantless home, she should share in the household work to the extent that is welcome or acceptable.

4. In a servantless home, it is a gracious gesture to offer to take your host and hostess and the children, if you wish and can afford it, out to dinner. If once proffered and declined do not press the invitation.

5. When you leave be certain no personal belongings are left behind for the host to package and mail.

6. Always ask permission to tip a servant. Some hostesses object to the practice. At any rate, be sure to thank the servants for courtesies they have extended.

7. A remembrance to your hosts given either before or after your departure always seems a bit more gracious than to arrive with gifts (like a social passport, as it were). The thoughtfulness of arriving with a little gift for each of the small fry is a nice gesture, however. Children love presents, and the most inexpensive gifts will please them and put you off on the right foot with the juniors.

To a Young Girl:

8. If you are the guest of an Army couple don't expect your social whirl to begin the moment you arrive or feel hurt if your hostess has not been able to provide a new date or some special form of entertainment for each evening. Conditions and circumstances govern these things.

9. If your hostess has no maid, lend a hand when you can, take the children for a walk, read or tell them a story.

10. Don't bring in a flock of bachelors after the dance, cook bacon and eggs, and make a general shambles of the kitchen—unless you are invited to entertain by your hostess. In this case, make the bachelors help clean up and restore things to order.

11. If your hosts live off the post don't expect them to take you to the theater, expensive restaurants and night clubs. They may be very short on cash, and are perhaps stretching their budget no end just having you for a visit.

12. Be particularly thoughtful and gracious to the friends of your hostess who are kind enough to entertain you. In addition to a prompt thank-you note when you return home, it is a nice gesture to send a tiny gift, such as enclosing a pretty handkerchief in your note.

To Parents:

13. Army couples are usually delighted to have their parents and close relatives visit them, but often the visiting older people aren't so happy over the prospect. The social aspect of Army life is unfamiliar to them, unless they have belonged to the Service or have had prior contacts with Service personnel. Just relax, be your own sweet selves and everyone will love you!

14. For the short-time guest, special teas and dinners are usually planned. An older woman should include one long dress in her wardrobe for evening parties at the Officers' Club. A simple dinner dress with sleeves or jacket is good. An older man should bring dinner clothes. However, a dark business suit is permissible for evening

parties. Many older people who have retired from social life have no need for formal evening dress at home, and it would be foolish to invest in a wardrobe of this sort. A dark business suit and an after-noon dress should suffice for the enlisted man's parents.

15. It might be wise to reserve your opinions if you are a pacifist and dislike everything military—except your son. An outburst will only embarrass him. Avoid asking leading questions of a military na-ture. There are lots of things about his work that your son isn't sup-posed to talk about.

16. Don't offer advice or make suggestions to your daughter-in-law about the management of her house and the children. Certain Army regulations and customs may account for her methods of house-keeping, marketing, and handling the children—and anyhow you can remember how you resented such gratuitous advice when you were young.

A cause of embarrassment to both hostess and visitor sometimes is the question of payment for a telephone toll call. Imposition is a poor way to thank one's host. As soon as the call has been completed, the person making the call should ask the operator the charges, then leave the amount with a slip, giving the date and number called. Or if one has made many calls during a long visit, the complete list of calls and telegrams sent, with the amount of each and the total, should be handed to the hostess when one says good-by. This is the only way a guest can feel free to telephone as often as he may want to. If you fear that your hostess may not accept it from you, leave full payment in an envelope where it will be found by her. Blessings on the guest who leaves a clean trail of graciousness and fairness in his wake!

Thank-You Letter

A day or so after your departure, a gracious thank-you note, some times referred to as a "bread-and-butter letter," is a *must*. Remember that even an elaborate, expensive gift does *not* take the place of this letter.

THANK-YOU TELEPHONE CALL

The day following a cocktail party, luncheon, or informal dinner, it is a nice gesture to phone your hostess, thanking her again for in-cluding you at the party and extending a few complimentary remarks in regard to the success of the party. You might mention her artistic flower arrangements, the delectable food, if such, and the good time you and all the guests had.

Chapter IX

RETURNING SOCIAL OBLIGATIONS

HOSPITALITY accepted from others *should be returned*, just as social calls and all minor obligations should be repaid. This does not mean that the hospitality shown you should be returned exactly in kind. *Juniors are not expected to entertain on the scale that senior officers and their families are able to afford.* Entertaining beyond a scale appropriate to the officer's grade and pay, both commissioned and noncommissioned, is definitely frowned upon. Owing to this unwritten law there is little competition among hostesses, and the junior hosts should strive to make their parties as simple, yet as enjoyable, as possible.

INFORMALITY IN ENTERTAINING

For most people, giving a party means doing it unassisted. In this changing world, formality and well-staffed homes are on their way out; instead informal living and informal entertaining are the new order. As Carolyn Coggins says, "People are fun, parties are fun, living is fun," so with that feeling shared by most Army people it looks as if we will continue to live and have parties and fun even in a maidless world.

Science has come to the rescue with its increasingly well-packaged foods and mechanical aids; the present-day time-saving, streamlined equipment all add up to more leisure, gaiety, and happiness for the hostess. However, informality at its best requires more common sense and planning than servants. So if you have a first-class, sharp mind, put it to work on your home. I assure you there is a lot of groundwork and planning to being a good hostess.

The Army is full of good hosts and hostesses . . . but not full enough! Remember that informality does not mean a sloppily run home, badly prepared food, or such casual entertaining that guests feel neglected. But it does mean that any hostess with her wits about her can serve delicious meals, placing the emphasis on quality, quantity, and flavor rather than on the service and number of courses served.

Be good to yourself. Let your friends help you in your preparations and serving; this will give them a larger share in the fun, provided you never impose upon them and are not too exacting. Fun is good for all of us and any excuse you care to cook up for a party is fine.

YOUR FIRST TEA

If a lovely tea service was among your wedding gifts, your easiest party will be a tea. The number of guests may be from two to a round dozen or more, and you may choose to serve in the living room before an open fire, or perhaps in the garden, or to convert the dining table into a tea table. Your loveliest cloth will cover the table, and at one end will be the tea service. A pretty flower arrangement will be in the center of the table, flanked by candlesticks or candelabra holding lighted white candles. To carry out certain color schemes, colored candles are often used, but white or ivory tapers are really in better taste. Have all silver shining. If you can't have it gleaming, then don't use it. Substitute crystal or china. If there is no servant, prepare everything beforehand except boiling the water for the tea.

Near the tea service arrange the required number of cups and saucers and teaspoons, or cups and salad plates. The latter are more satisfactory, as sandwiches may be placed on them. Arrange tea napkins near by.

Place small loaf sugar in the sugar bowl, and provide both cream and lemon. A pitcher of ice water and several goblets may be placed on a serving table or on the buffet.

Trays of sandwiches, cakes, and mints are placed on the table or passed by one of the younger guests you have asked to assist you. It is customary to ask the commanding officer's wife, or some older person, to pour tea.

Three Suggested Menus for the Informal Tea

Bread-and-butter sandwiches—cinnamon toast—tea
Toast or muffins with jam or marmalade—tea
Water-cress sandwiches—cookies—tea

YOUR FIRST BUFFET SUPPER

Beloved of the maidless for Saturday or Sunday night entertaining, beloved of everyone who enjoys the casual, a buffet supper is a sensible way to entertain a large group with little effort.

Right from the start, you must learn to let other people help you.

Don't let all your guests jump up to help. Pick one or two and work them hard. They won't mind and it won't break up the party.

By this time your husband may feel that he would like to take a hand in the entertaining and have some of his bachelor friends in; so it is a tossup between a cocktail party and a buffet supper. Both are expensive, as they call for liquor, but the buffet supper is the less expensive of the two. Formal dinners given by ranking officers are often returned by buffet suppers given by junior officers.

For your first buffet supper, limit your guest list to twelve. By this time, if you have really applied yourself to learning to cook, you must have some specialty. Perhaps you are a past mistress at making "country captain" or Italian spaghetti, or have brought from home a very fine recipe for baked beans. If you are really proficient, and can turn out a superb product, then serve it over and over again and become famous for it! If your husband is a salad tosser, or one of those male maestros who love to cook, give him free rein and your party giving will be different, successful, and original.

Suggested Menus for Buffet Suppers

Roast turkey	Creole shrimp	Chicken à la king in patty
Wild rice	Rice	shells
Peas	Molded salad	Asparagus
Salad	Sherbet, cake	Tomatoes stuffed with celery
Hot rolls		Dessert, coffee
Dessert, coffee		

Mexican Supper
Chile con carne
Mexican rice
Frijoles
Enchiladas
Tomato stuffed with guacamole
  salad
Frozen fresh pineapple soaked
  in rum
Coffee

Southern Supper
Country captain
  or
Southern fried chicken
Grits or spoon bread
Asparagus au gratin
Frozen fruit salad or
Green salad
Coffee

Chinese Supper
Chop suey
Rice
Sweet-sour
  spareribs
Green salad
Dessert, coffee

Curry
Chicken curry
Rice
Condiments
Salad
Dessert
Coffee

Rehearse everything you're going to try on your guests beforehand, from butter balls to sauces. To pep up the menu, try "chicken in the rough." It's crisp fried chicken, and you serve it forth wrapped in damask, like the rolls, in a big wicker basket. It is crispest if you fry for five minutes in very hot fat-and-butter, then reduce to low heat to finish. Another fillip or attractive note to your menu is to serve interesting bread, such as Finnish rye, brioche, French bread, pumpernickel, Italian sesame seed, Swedish bread, or bread sticks.

Always set your dinner late so as to allow yourself plenty of time for last-minute touches. Don't rush through cocktails; it spoils the atmosphere conducive to a leisurely evening of good conversation. Note that the above menus are all of the "supper can wait" type and the *pièce de résistance* will not be spoiled. The C.O. and his wife are always invited into the dining room first at a buffet supper.

IF YOU SERVE LIQUOR!

Let's agree that you don't have to serve liquor if you don't wish to, but having a drink is fun and, for those who like it, liquor adds to a party. It is an excellent mixing agent!

Never insist even gently upon anyone's drinking. Certainly no one need drink at any time unless he wants to. Today, people usually do as they please. There are many who have never indulged in strong drink, and neither do they belong to a temperance union! Some of the older boys and girls who cut their adolescent teeth on bathtub gin bottles have given up the habit entirely. It could be that they are watching their figures or their ulcers. Sometimes, even without hypochondria, they see the folly of their ways.

By and large, few people include liquor in their budget, and the price of liquor plus mixers is something one seldom sits down and faces. For those who cannot afford to keep a stock on hand, it seems easier if a visiting fireman arrives unexpectedly to send up to the club for a bottle of Scotch. It is charged, of course, and forgotten until the first of the month; but there is always a day of reckoning, and if an influx of visitors occurs several times during the month, not even Einstein could balance your budget.

These suggestions were compiled with the help of a famous bartender of long experience and are taken from *The Household Manual* (p. 223):

1. Find out the cost of bottled drink and the different kinds just as you know the current price of butter and eggs.

2. Select what you can afford to serve, if any. Big stores often have special sales on standard brands. Watch for them. Decide before a party what you will serve and stick to it.

3. Serve drinks in adequate glasses but not oversized ones. If you do, you are asking for trouble!

4. Own a jigger. The professional bartender whistles softly at the idea of putting more than a jigger of hard liquor in a drink. Don't depend on that belated "when."

5. Without being obvious about it, see to it that you or your husband pours the drinks. It is the host's place to do so, anyway.

6. Keep the bottles preferably in another room. If you set the bottles down beside the visiting firemen, nothing can be done to space the drinks properly.

7. Finally, to be definite, if you cannot afford Scotch, don't apologize or feel embarrassed about it. The person serving the drinks should state: "We have Martinis and Old-Fashioneds" or "Manhattans and Scotch."

8. If your guests come to your home for dinner and are offered chicken, they do not ask for turkey; well, it is the same idea.

9. It is very unfunny to "load" a guest's drink, particularly if she is *usually* a lady!

To sum it up: price the drinks
plan the drinks
measure the drinks
space the drinks

and never serve more than two rounds before dinner.

How to Give a Cocktail Party

Unless a large number of guests is expected, it is better to have the cocktails mixed in the pantry and passed on trays. Should the guest list be large, set the dining table as for a tea, using either a novelty cloth or an elaborate one. Appropriate decorations should grace the table. Both the food and refreshment tables may be placed in the garden.

The first requisite for a cocktail party is good liquor. "Good liquor is not cheap and cheap liquor is not good." Everything for mixing drinks should be set up on one table. The six most popular mixed drinks are Bacardi cocktails, daiquiris, dry Martinis, Manhattans, old-fashioned cocktails, and whisky sours. Usually, and for even a fairly large party, provide dry Martinis, whisky and soda for highballs, sherry, tomato and iced fruit juices, plus milk for those on diets who like to go to parties just the same. Offer something for everyone.

Be sure that hot canapés are served very hot. Cold things should be chilled and banked in ice when possible. An Old English silver hot dish keeps hot canapés at the proper temperature. Potato chips served hot in wooden bowls are tempting, as are hot roasted nuts.

Canapés should be small enough to pop into the mouth in one bite. They should be crisp, never soggy.

Twenty-Five Suggested Appetizers

Pepitas, Mexican pumpkin seeds
Shrimp, onion, or chile Krispies
Oysters wrapped in bacon—broiled
Olives wrapped in bacon—broiled
Seasoned cream cheese wrapped in dried-beef funnels
Seasoned cream cheese thinned with mayonnaise for sauce in which to
   dunk cauliflower knobs, carrots, shallots, potato chips
Single spring onion rolled in bread-and-butter sandwich, held by
   toothpick, with green top of onion protruding from one end
Tiny hot biscuit with sautéed mushroom
Tiny hot biscuit with ham
Broiled chicken livers impaled on toothpicks
Large pecan halves sandwiched together with anchovy paste
Celery stuffed with Roquefort
Caviar, anchovy, hot cheese canapés
Spiced deviled eggs
Cheese, crackers, cold cuts, olives
Freshly roasted almonds, hot chestnuts
"Hush puppies"—made of water-ground meal mixed with finely
   ground bacon and onion. They originated at old-fashioned southern
   fish fries, when a busy cook would hurriedly throw a corndodger
   to the barking hungry hounds that were always underfoot. "Hush
   puppies" (or tiny hot corndodgers) are delicious!

Room temperature is an important feature in giving a party of any kind; but particularly at a cocktail party be sure to open a window which will not create a direct draft. An open fire is fine if there are only a few people, but it can make guests uncomfortable if it isn't controlled carefully. In giving a tea or a cocktail party, it is important to be space conscious. Remove all but two or three chairs, so that the guests when tired of standing will circulate. People like a crowd to be a crowd, and they don't mind being almost suffocated if the party is gay and they are having fun. But if it is to be a small intimate group, then be sure to provide a seating space for each person invited.

If servants are to be hired for the party, it is wise to get the help all lined up before you issue your invitations. Remember, it is easy to get guests but not so easy to get servants. No one ever knows what a cocktail party will turn into; it is a safe bet that it will run on into the evening. If you feel so inclined, have a baked ham or a roast chicken with rolls and coffee ready in reserve.

Whatever you do or whatever kind of cocktail party you give, avoid being tricky or cute about yourself, your house, your drink, or your food.

THE COCKTAIL SUPPER

The cocktail supper is becoming increasingly popular since it is given usually preceding a dance, a reception, or some social function at the club. This type of party is to be encouraged; it starts the ball rolling and everyone gets in the spirit of the evening. It is a stand-up party!

It differs little from a regular cocktail party except that it is not necessary to serve a great variety of food. An elaborate party table might be planned with a turkey at one end, a ham at the other, and plates of thin bread-and-butter sandwiches beside the platters. Also celery, olives, pickles, cheese, and coffee.

ENTERTAINING AT BREAKFAST OR BRUNCH

A brunch or breakfast is simply a stand-up luncheon, but the food is simpler. Provide large pitchers of orange juice, tomato juice, and pineapple juice, or a large, deep silver tray piled with cracked ice in which pieces of melon, luscious grapes, oranges, and other tempting fruits are kept chilled. The latter makes a pretty centerpiece.

Sausages and waffles; bacon or ham and scrambled eggs; or fried chicken and spoon bread are a few of the combinations you can serve. Have plenty of good hot steaming coffee. In winter, hot Tom and Jerrys served before a blazing log fire put everyone in a jolly mood, and in summer iced drinks may be served before brunch or breakfast is announced.

One of the simplest yet most congenial ways of entertaining is to have friends drop by after church for coffee, a piece of Danish pastry or coffeecake and that's all . . . period!

How to Give a Formal Luncheon

By this time you may feel experienced enough to attempt a formal luncheon. The buffet luncheon is far easier, unless you have a good servant. If you have a service for eight, then two servants are necessary to keep things going smoothly. In the setting of the luncheon table, the same service should be observed as for an informal dinner except that candles are not used.

Place arrangement is the same as for dinner, except that bread-and-butter plates are used at luncheon. Four courses are usually served: fruit cup or soup, the main course, salad, and dessert. If there is only one maid, and the plates are served in the kitchen, the salad is often included on the main course plate. However, this places the luncheon in the informal class. At a formal luncheon each dish is served individually.

Setting the Table

Having arranged a low centerpiece of flowers or tempting fruit, place your service plates, if you are using them, in the middle of each place doily. The napkin, folded in a picket-shaped point, is placed on the left of the service plate. A teaspoon or bouillon spoon should be placed at the right of the luncheon knife, a luncheon fork for the main course and one for salad at the left of the service plate, and a bread-and-butter knife across the bread-and-butter plate at right angles to the other flat silver. The bread-and-butter plate is placed on the left, and the goblet and wineglass at the right. The dessert silver is brought in on the dessert plate with the finger bowl, the fork on the left of the finger bowl, the spoon at the right. A violet, peach blossom, or any small fragrant flower placed in the finger bowl adds charm to the service.

Butter balls add a distinctive note, and may or may not be placed on the butter plate before luncheon is announced.

A formal luncheon calls for place cards, particularly if there are eight or more guests. Plain white cards with the monogram of the hostess in gray, gold, or silver are smart. Plain cards are correct. At one very fancy luncheon I attended, fresh ivy leaves with the names written in white ink evoked considerable interest and conversation.

The fruit cocktail glass is placed on a salad plate, which is set on the service plate. The idea of a service plate is to have a plate in front of one during the entire meal. The waiter removes the cocktail glass and its attendant salad plate from the right, leaving the service plate in front of the guest. When he returns with the luncheon plate, he removes the service plate from the right and, with practically a sleight-of-hand performance, places the luncheon or dinner plate before the guest from the left. All serving of foods is from the left, and throughout the meal all dishes are removed from the right. The dessert service may be brought in and placed before the guest as the main course plate is removed. The guest removes the doily and finger bowl and places them at the left, where the bread-and-butter plate has previously been. The dessert silver is put on the plate doily by the guest.

Wine at lunch is a matter of choice and not at all necessary. If served, it should be a light Rhine wine, and in this case cocktails should not be served before. Or you might serve a glass of dry sherry before luncheon, but be sure to have tomato juice or fruit juice for those who do not take alcohol. Don't mix wines unless you know what you are serving, and please remember that your luncheon may go off better without any alcoholic beverages at all.

Suggested Luncheon Menus

One hot course at a meal is always a wise procedure, as many people dislike cold food and it may not agree with them.

Borsch	Hot or jellied madrilene	Iced melon
Lobster tails	Squab	Lamb chop
Tiny roasted potatoes	Peas	Spinach ring
Tossed salad	Frozen fruit salad	Hot rolls
Vanilla ice cream	Hot rolls	Baked Alaska
Crème de menthe sauce	Coffee	Coffee

Mushroom soup	Vichyssoise
Cheese soufflé	Shrimp or crabmeat salad in half
Fresh fruit salad, French dressing	of avocado
Whole-wheat muffins	Shoestring potatoes
Iced tea or iced coffee	Rolls, coffee
	Raspberries with raspberry sherbet

The food you serve and the way you serve it are just as revealing of the kind of person you are as the house which is your background and the clothes you wear. It is fun to dream up new color combinations both in decorations and in foods. For instance, fancy a dinner of creamed chicken, mashed potatoes, and creamed cauliflower served on

a white plate. How deadly dull! Even if the food were perfectly seasoned, it would all taste the same; with such an unimaginative hostess
I dare say the evening would be equally colorless. Develop a line of
surface props that will add color to your food . . . simple little
things like paprika, pimento, green pepper, parsley, water cress,
chives, celery, eggs, tomatoes, sliced fruits, and relishes. Invest in
individual pottery casseroles and three or four large earthenware baking dishes with handles. Regard each dish, platter, or bowl you serve
as a still life you are creating.

Get in the habit of experimenting with condiments, herbs, and
spices. For instance, add a grating of nutmeg to chicken soup just
before serving, or a pinch of ginger to chocolate icing. It has been said
that "the discovery of a new dish does more for the happiness of a
man than the discovery of a star."

Simplicity in food is the credo of the day, and more and more new
canned foods are appearing on the grocery shelves. Excellent vichys-
soise can now be bought in jars and needs only complete chilling; delicious canned black-bean soup can be doctored just before serving
with sherry and lemon juice; hot green-turtle soup out of a can needs
only a spot of sherry added to it. Or it can be served thoroughly
chilled from a crystal bowl at the table; this goes for borsch, too,
which is put up in large jars and can be kept conveniently in the refrigerator. The best madrilene comes in jars and cans. A delectable
fruitcake-like garnish for ice cream is aptly named rum crumbles.
Frozen foods are a boon to the housewife, and a great saving in time
and labor. The newest culinary gibe about brides is "Can she melt
ice?" The latest news on frozen foods is that electric ranges are being
designed with food-thawing compartments to unfreeze food in a frac-
tion of the time now required. Frozen coffee is available. It appears
in tiny paper cups, each containing enough concentrated coffee to
make six cups when added to that quantity of boiling water. Frozen
grapefruit sections, cantaloupe balls, and sea foods of all kinds in addition to frozen vegetables and meats make cooking problems easier
for the brides of today. Exercise your ingenuity, study your cookbooks
and the latest recipes in magazines, and plan your menus so that there
will be a minimum amount of kitchen work at the last moment.

Two other pet ideas of mine: Try a few dashes of Angostura bit-
ters on your morning grapefruit or in orange juice or a scant tea-
spoonful of it in your applesauce; for old-fashioneds (this I learned
in Hawaii) keep a can of pineapple sticks and a bottle of cherries on

hand. Somehow the long fingers of pineapple give an impression of lavish hospitality!

DINNERS, FORMAL AND INFORMAL

For gay little informal dinners to which you invite one or two couples or several bachelors the table appointments may be very simple. Candles appear at dinner, and bread-and-butter plates are omitted. Cream-soup plates are used instead of bouillon cups; otherwise, the service is the same as at luncheon. At the informal dinner the host may carve the roast or fowl at table; at the formal dinner the carving is done in the kitchen and all dishes are served by waiters. The use of place doilies for informal dinners is accepted, but regulation-size dinner napkins are preferable to luncheon-size napkins.

Seating

Ten is considered the ideal number for a seated dinner. Multiples of four—eight, twelve, sixteen, twenty and twenty-four—are awkward numbers if one has the usual rectangular table. It is impossible to escape having two men or two women at each end of the table. To avoid this embarrassing situation the only solution is for the host and hostess to be seated at the middle of the table facing each other. Any formal dinner of more than sixteen moves up into the pretentious class and usually takes place only in high social, diplomatic, or political circles.

Although a hostess may prefer to seat her guests on the basis of congeniality, at an official dinner especially in Washington or in capitals of other countries she must observe the immutable laws of protocol. At a formal dinner, the names in full are written on the place cards in script writing. The order of precedence for members of the Armed Forces follows the order of precedence of the Services: Army, Navy, Air Force. Officers of equal rank in separate Services are placed accordingly. For example, a captain in the Navy, although of equal rank with a colonel in the Army, is seated below him at the table. A lieutenant general in the Air Force should be seated below a vice admiral in the Navy. Officers of equal rank in the same Service are placed according to the dates of their commissions. Here is where you need a *Register* of all three Services at hand!

It is important to remember in seating officials that the husband and wife are treated as equal in rank. In our country, the woman guest of honor is seated on the host's right; if a man, to the right of the hostess. But in some European countries the guest of honor is seated on the left. In Denmark, in addition to seating the guest of honor on the host's left, the hostess always enters the dining room last, and is the first to leave the table so she may stand at the door. As each guest passes, he thanks her for his meal.

The Formal Dinner

Formal entertaining with an eye to being impressive seldom brings favorable results. The word "formal" is a synonym for ceremonial, and a formal party is always conducted according to rules or established forms of ceremony. Very few people outside diplomatic circles are truly formal any more, as formality is really a sort of artificiality.

However, if you are eager to give a formal dinner, think three times before you plunge unless you are a victim of circumstances and it is part of your job. Remember, it has to be done perfectly—with the correct silver and china, and well-trained servants—or it will be a headache even to the guests. If all goes well, it is at best very likely to be dull.

Formal dinner service demands menservants and that is that! No dinner can be said to be formal if women serve it or assist in its service. Many hostesses when faced with giving a formal dinner take recourse to a hotel or private club, or call in a reputable caterer. When the dinner is to be given in a private home, it is quite a different matter.

Don't attempt a formal dinner unless you have an experienced cook, a butler, and two experienced servingmen for the evening. It is better to give a semiformal dinner, which is probably the most comfortable, the most practical, and the most pleasant way of entertaining.

At formal dinners the table should be covered with either an elaborate dinner cloth or a faultlessly laundered damask cloth, with a heavy silence cloth underneath. Even the most formal dinners of today consist of no more than five courses, and four are preferred.

1. Soup	1. Soup
2. Roast	2. Fish or entree
3. Salad	3. Roast
4. Dessert	4. Salad
	5. Dessert

Demitasse and liqueurs

The centerpiece, if it is a flower arrangement, should be kept low. See that the table has been extended enough to give the guests elbow room—twenty inches between places—and that there is enough space for the servants to pass the dishes. The dinner napkin, folded square, should be placed in the middle of the service plate, and if place cards are used they should be put on top of the napkins. The center decoration, candelabra, compotes holding salted nuts, salts and peppers, and individual ash trays are the only extra silver, besides the flat silver, on the table. Salts and peppers should be at every other place at table.

Suggested Menus for a Formal Dinner

Clear soup	Clams or oysters on half shell
Fish hollandaise	or
Filet mignon	Clear turtle soup with sherry
String beans	Roast duckling with orange sauce,
Carrots glacé	or quail or squab
Rolls	Green peas
Aspic salad	Artichoke hollandaise
Ice cream	Coffee ice-cream mold
Coffee	Coffee

At a formal dinner, the appetite should not be dulled by a heavy cream soup; a thin clear soup or some type of sea-food cocktail is more appropriate. Highly flavored Spanish, Italian, or Indian dishes are not appropriate for a formal dinner but are popular at an informal dinner or buffet supper.

Suggested Menus for Traditional Holiday Dinners

Thanksgiving	*Christmas Buffet Supper*
Tomato bisque	Hot strong bouillon
Roast turkey, gravy	Cold roast turkey, sliced
Chestnut dressing	Pickled peaches, cranberry jelly
Sweet-potato pumpkins	Creamed oysters with ham and
Creamed onions	mushroom either en casserole
Avocado-grapefruit salad	or in individual ramekins
Mince or pumpkin pie	Hot biscuits
Coffee	Aspic fruit salad, relishes
	Eggnog ice cream
	Christmas fruit and nut cake
	Coffee

New Year's

Fresh tomato soup with chives
Wild duck, black currant jelly
Wild rice, string beans not cut
 or sliced, but whole in neat
 little bundles
Apple and celery heart salad
Pineapple sherbet with choco-
 late leaves
Coffee

Easter

Tomato juice
Baked ham
New peas in cream or in
 potato nests
Molded vegetable salad ring
Angel food cake with
 fresh strawberries or
 strawberry shortcake
Coffee

Fourth of July

Jellied madrilene
Broiled fresh salmon
New potatoes, green peas
Cucumber salad, French dressing
Watermelon
Iced coffee

New Year's Reception

Eggnog in large punch bowl
Beaten biscuit, Smithfield ham
 or ham spread
Sandwiches, celery and carrot
 sticks
Olives, salted hot pecans
Miniature mince pies—
 size of fifty-cent piece

The Semiformal and Informal Dinner

At a seated dinner be careful not to invite more guests than you can seat comfortably at your dining-room table. Nothing is more awkward than to try to eat a meal without sufficient elbow room, or with a table leg between one's knees when wearing a narrow skirt. With more than six people, things will be greatly expedited by place cards.

One detail that distinguishes a formal from an informal dinner is the question of carving and serving at the table by either host or hostess. If the host carves at the table, the dinner is informal. It is customary to place the required number of hot plates in front of him, and the maid or waiter carries each plate to the guest, removing the place plate as she serves the meat course. This service is naturally slow, but if a second maid passes the vegetables to each guest served, the food will not grow cold. Another informal custom is for the host to carve at table and serve the dressing and gravy, then for the guests to pass the plate along to the hostess, who serves the vegetables. During this procedure the maid may pass the rolls, celery, and olives.

When the host is carving, family and guests should forget him. If he is in trouble, it will not help to give him the hypnotic eye. Carving is truly an art and calls for a few essentials on which the man of the house has a right to insist. First, he should have good tools—a standard carving set of good steel. If game is the *pièce de résistance*, a pair of poultry shears is a bit of required cutlery. The anatomy of a duck defies logical dissection, but shears make it easy. An acceptable Christmas present sometime!

A steak set also has its place. The knife should be razor sharp, and anyone caught cutting cord or the laundry line with it should be scalped! The platter should be large enough so that the guests will not shudder when the roast or chicken looks as if it is coming their way. A small platter garnished with potatoes, carrots and onions may make a beautiful magazine advertisement but it is an abomination to the carver. Skewers and cords should be removed in the kitchen, unless the rolled roast threatens to explode without them.

For the salad and dessert courses, if one maid is doing the serving, naturally the service will be slow, but it will not matter as these foods are served cold. Coffee is generally served in the living room at an informal dinner.

At semiformal seated dinners rank is observed, though not so rigidly on most posts as in Washington. The first and second of rank are given the seats of honor, and after that the guests may be seated according to congeniality.

Menus for Informal or Semiformal Dinners

Clear soup	Shrimp bisque	Consommé
Leg of spring lamb or crown	Roast prime ribs of beef	Roast duck, turkey, goose, or chicken
	Yorkshire pudding	
Mint jelly	Franconia potatoes	Dressing, gravy
New potatoes	Fresh asparagus	Wild rice
Fresh peas	Escarole, endive, chickory salad	String beans
Lettuce salad, water cress		Currant jelly
Cold lemon soufflé	Meringue with crushed fresh raspberries	Mixed green salad
Coffee		Hot rolls
	Coffee	Tangerine sections in sherry
		Coffee

One more thing about seating: If you want to be the family favorite, don't forget to place your husband's mother at the right of her darling boy and your father-in-law on your right. Remember, the first family dinner is the hardest. Serve good food, spread good cheer, but don't attempt anything too fancy that might not come off just the way you planned. If it is a traditional family dinner at Christmas or

Thanksgiving you are serving, and his family is of the school that goes all out for celery stuffing while you prefer chestnut dressing such as your mother makes, then fill the bird with celery stuffing, and in the upper part up to the neck include your chestnut dressing. Everybody will be pleased and your husband will be proud of you.

If the suggested menus are not to your liking, you can always add or subtract a course. Personally, I like the California custom of serving at the beginning of the meal a generous salad which takes the place of a soup or even a fish course. If the host has carving to do at an informal dinner, he can start while the guests are leisurely finishing their salad.

How to Set a Dinner Table

The fundamentals of table setting include orderliness, neatness, cleanliness, harmony, beauty, and suitability. Orderliness means places carefully set, dishes correctly spaced, and good balance maintained. Salts and peppers should stand at attention between every two place settings; they should be immaculately clean and, of course, always filled. Individual ash trays, even if they come from the five-and-ten, are a necessity. Place an ash tray at the top of each plate to the left of the water glass, and in it put two or three cigarettes and a book of matches . . . unless, of course, you have scruples about the propriety of smoking at the table.

1. What kind of cloth will you use? The best you have. (A cotton felt silence cloth should be used to keep hot dishes from marking the table.) A white damask cloth is preferable, but if a lace cloth is used then a dark-brown silence cloth should be used under it. Sheer doilies are much used today, but the runner is no longer fashionable unless two are used horizontally on each side of the table. Round, square, or triangular mats are popular; they do not always remain completely on the table surface, but a portion of them hangs over the edge.

2. What will you use as a centerpiece? Flowers are always correct, but a bowl of fruit or vegetables can be arranged attractively as a centerpiece. A small high vase of flowers does nothing for the table, and all arrangements should be low enough not to interfere with conversation. If you have ever played peekaboo with your host at the table, you will know what I mean. Shells have a distinct charm when attractively arranged with flowers. A copper bowl filled with oranges and bay leaves makes a colorful arrangement but is more appropriate for a buffet table than a formal or informal dinner table.

3. When should candles be used? There are two schools of thought on the subject of candles, but dinner tables whether formal or informal call for candlelight. It is soft and flattering and naturally women approve. Men are usually the dissenters, but remind your husband of the days of his ancestors when candles proved entirely adequate. Candles should always be above eye level, but they should never be combined with overhead lighting as one nullifies the other. If the using of candles on the dinner table becomes "a family issue," concede the point gracefully. Candles are nice but not essential. Remember that they are never used in the daytime even if the room is darkened. Ivory or white candles are always in better taste unless a particular theme is carried out. Have additional ones on the buffet so there will be sufficient light. If there are wall lights, use these too.

4. How should the silver be arranged for dinner? Stand first before your own place and arrange the flat silver correctly. Place the plate which will be on the table when you and your guests sit down. Put the dinner fork at the left of the plate and the dinner knife at the right, blade in, handles even at the bottom, about an inch and a half from the edge of the table. The soupspoon is placed outside the knife, its handle even with that of the knife. The salad fork goes inside the dinner fork, that is, next to the plate. The butter knife (not spreader), if bread-and-butter plates are used, is placed on the bread-and-butter plate. If an oyster fork or fruit-cup spoon is used, it is placed next to the soupspoon on the right. Looking at this arrangement, one can see that you use those on the outside first and work in toward the plate. The dessert fork and spoon are not on the table but are placed on the dessert plate—the spoon on the right, the fork on the left.

5. How should the napkin be folded and placed? Napkins are folded lengthwise or in squares or triangles, but never in fancy shapes, such as cocked hats. The napkin is laid either on the plate or at the left of the fork.

It is a good plan to check the table when it is set to see if the centerpiece is pleasing, all silver and glasses are in place, napkins and candles are properly placed, salts and peppers are arranged, and cigarettes and ash trays are in order.

Certain items of food are on the table when you sit down. One is butter, if you use it. Butter balls or squares are placed on the bread-and-butter plates, if used, and just before dinner the water goblets are filled. The water is iced, but ice cubes are never placed in glasses.

Bread sticks or crackers may be placed on the bread-and-butter plates; silver or crystal dishes of nuts and mints may also be put on the table in advance.

Setting the luncheon table is the same as for the dinner table except smaller knives and forks are used—if you own two sizes. Bouillon cups take the place of soup plates. If you haven't bouillon spoons, use dessert spoons. A luncheon napkin is smaller than a dinner napkin.

What Does the Hostess Wear?

The hostess wears whatever she pleases in her home. It is permissible for her to wear a long dress, and she may dress a bit more formally at a tea, buffet, supper, or dinner than she would ordinarily. She should never attempt to outshine her guests. A hostess should not wear black, but some color that is becoming to her. A bright-red dress during the holiday season or a sky-blue job at any time is the sort of thing—if you can take those colors. Most hostesses prefer street-length dresses in a high color, or a ballerina dinner dress for after-five parties.

Club Parties

Most Officers' Clubs have attractive Sunday-night buffet suppers or specially nice suppers on bingo nights. These are the answer for juniors who live in a motel, a trailer, or a tiny apartment. Invite a small group—a couple, two couples, or even three or four couples, if you have chairs enough in your two-by-four—for cocktails before the supper. Your invitation, either verbal or on an "informal," might be that "we thought we'd make it between four and six, so if you planned to go to the club supper you could make it."

This means that you can do as you wish about taking your guests on to the club for supper. If it is within your budget and you wish to ask them for supper, reserve a table in some corner of the club beforehand, put some flowers or fruit and candles on it, add place cards, not to make it formal but to make it easier for everyone, and your party will be a success. Serve two rounds of drinks, no more, with salted nuts or some simple appetizers if you are not going on to the club.

Parties before a club occasion should be encouraged because they draw members to the club and take care of the after-dinner lull . . . for the hostess. Sometimes two couples entertain together at the club.

If the party is held in the larger of the couple's homes, it will ease the silver, plate, and money shortage.

RECEPTIONS AT THE CLUB

If the C.O. is entertaining some VIP at the club function, junior officers and their wives should be courteous enough to make a point of going over to speak to the C.O. and his wife, who in turn will introduce the honored guest. When I say "make a point," I mean you should drift up casually, and after being pleasant and exchanging the social amenities, you should depart, to allow room for others. In this way you are graciously helping the C.O. to entertain, and it gives him a chance to introduce his personnel, of whom he is proud. Avoid sitting shyly in a corner at any party where the Army is trying to show a pleasant social side. If you have any qualms about this, just remember that if such social procedure were not desired the C.O. would entertain the guest in a private dining room or in his quarters.

The New Year's Reception which on some posts is a "command performance" is being outmoded on others. The guest list has got completely out of hand for the pocketbooks of most C.O.'s, and unless the Officers' Club is rich enough to stand the expense, the reception will probably be broken down to individual parties. There is something very jolly about a New Year's Day party with eggnog, whether one can stand the stuff or not, and it is a custom here to stay, we trust, and an old Army tradition.

Many NCO Clubs hold open house on New Year's Day, serving eggnog and Yuletime cheer to members of the club and their wives.

CLUB DANCES

Most Officers' Clubs have formal dances several times a year. Others have monthly and even weekly dances. There is a certain tradition to this formal type of entertaining in the Service, and it most definitely has its place.

Clubs which tolerate or promote only informal dances with jukebox music border on the honky-tonk variety of roadhouse entertainment and are certainly not up to standard for officers and their wives. Every officer should be able to afford a tuxedo. If not, he should feel free to wear uniform. If the price of an evening dress staggers you, invest in a long or ballerina-length black skirt and several evening blouses. Pretty young wives can make their own evening clothes or patronize inexpensive shops, since after all the proper type of dress and the effect is what matters in this case, rather than quality.

At a formal dance there are a few rules of etiquette which should be observed. If there is a receiving line, you *must* go through it with your escort, presumably your husband. He will give your name to the aide, who in turn introduces you to the first officer's wife and the officer. This will be the C.O., probably, and if an introduction is unnecessary, you shake hands and exchange some pleasantry or merely smile and say "Good evening." To each new person in the receiving line to whom you are introduced you say "How do you do?" and *smile*. Courtesy to elders is a sound social investment. Don't greet the C.O. and his wife as if they were inanimate objects; neither is it necessary to gush. Simply be natural, pleasant, and sincere.

Never thank a man for dancing with you, but always say you enjoyed the dance, even if your feet feel as if they will never be the same again. At this point your husband has certain definite social obligations besides dancing the first and last dance with you, his bride. If you have attended a dinner party before the dance, his next obligations are to his hostess, the lady guest of honor, his dinner partners on each side; after that he may return to you or dance with any other guests he chooses. But a whirl with his hostess and the guest of honor is considered a must. It is up to you to remind him, should he be remiss. Remember that club parties and dinner dances are not USO parties; they are dignified forms of entertainment where all of the social amenities, including proper dress, are observed.

A wife whose husband is away should not attend a dance or reception alone, but it is quite permissible for her to go with a couple or a group of friends. Comments may be made if she arrives with a bachelor, even though he is her husband's best friend, and not in the company of others. A nice gesture if you do not attend is to call on the honorees when your husband returns, or, if that is not feasible, to write a note of explanation. Never just fail to appear. A note is always courteous. While the omission of it may go unnoticed in a large command, the reception of it will be marked with appreciation as an evidence of your good breeding.

EIGHT RULES OF SOCIAL CONDUCT
(Taken from *NCO Manual*)

1. At a dance your primary mission is to show attention to your partner and see that she enjoys herself. You should introduce her to your friends

and see that she dances as often as she wishes. You should not leave her entirely with your friends, but should dance with her at least several times.

2. You should dance at least once with your hostess.

3. After a dance with a woman who came with someone else, you should escort her back to her partner, or to her table, thank her for the dance and leave.

4. Be sure to thank your hostess when you leave a party. You might say, "I have had a fine time here, Mrs. Jones. Thank you very much for everything," or anything along that general line. (Complete honesty is not always recommended in this case.)

5. Keep your voice low. Never be loud or boisterous. If you have had some drinks, try to remember that they may be making you talk too loudly and too much.

6. Never whistle at a woman. Leave that to the drug-store cowboys.

7. When you ask a woman for a date, give her a chance to get out of it if she wants to.

8. Avoid overstaying your welcome when visiting anyone.

These are all everyday customs in all parts of the United States. They help to make things go smoothly and in a friendly manner. If you have been in the habit of doing some of these things differently, it won't hurt you any to change. You don't *have* to. But the best all-round noncommissioned officer forms the habit of acting like a gentleman. And these are good, simple rules of conduct which you probably know already.

Many NCO Clubs have weekly Saturday night dances, tea dances, cocktail parties, and dinner dances. They are usually well attended and prove the center of social life. Their membership is limited to the first three grades of sergeants and corporals.

SERVICE CLUBS

Service Clubs on a post provide entertainment in the form of dances, bingo parties, suppers, beer parties for the enlisted men and their wives.

THE CORPORAL AND HIS BRIDE ENTERTAIN

There are so many adjustments to be made at one's first station that your first attempt at entertaining, Connie, will probably be some spur-of-the-moment affair that will come off much better than if you had planned for it.

On the social side, beer and the G.I. are practically inseparable, so one of the quickest and easiest ways to launch a friendly evening is

as follows: Ice enough beer for the guests far enough in advance to
assure its being icy cold. Fix big mixed trays of the "four P's" . . .
pretzels, peanuts, potato chips, popcorn (cheese and plain buttered).
Hard-boiled eggs may be added, and pickles. Let the guests do the
rest.

Variations on the Theme are as follows:

Substitute or add hamburgers.

Prepare a dressing into which potato chips may be dunked.

Set out the makings of "Dagwood sandwiches" and turn the guests
loose on their own.

Fix some submarine sandwiches in advance.

A dish of assorted cheeses might be arranged with crackers.

With beer, cold roast pork sliced paper-thin, laid on a platter, and
sprinkled with salt and lots of pepper, with a companion plate of
buttered bread will please the men.

There are two kinds of entertaining: one you plan; the second is
usually wished upon you. If you have a job, time (or the lack of it)
may be the vital factor in your entertaining program. If you have a
baby or babies, and washing is on your daily agenda, then effort and
the strength expended may be vital factors. Let your conscience be
your guide. Remember, you are not expected to return social obligations in kind, but it is important that you do something, no matter how
simple. It all depends on your attitude, your sincerity, and your
friendliness.

A Cup of Tea or Coffee

To ask a neighbor, a newcomer on the post, a young mother you
met out baby-pushing in the park to drop in for a cup of tea is an
easy, inexpensive, and simple way to make mere acquaintances into
friends. A thin bread-and-butter sandwich with a dish of jelly or a
pot of jam adds a festive note. You might invite your guest to bring
her knitting or sewing.

If you favor serving coffee, then invite your new neighbor for a
cup either in the morning or in the afternoon. You need not serve
anything with coffee, though Danish pastry, small doughnuts, or
cinnamon coffeecake is a nice addition. If your guest is unable to
return the courtesy to her original hostess, she will pass it on by inviting in someone else. Should you be the guest, be gracious and
appreciative. Don't go reluctantly, and then early in the conversation
apprise your hostess of the fact that you do not like to "neighbor."

That is exactly what one newcomer did on a certain post. Such crude behavior will probably not evoke a second invitation.

Certainly, everyone's privacy should be respected, and "running in" on friends at any hour is not to be indulged in or encouraged; but that is not being neighborly in the true sense. That is being a nuisance and a busybody.

In the *NCO Guide* special mention is given to the acknowledgment of courtesies: "It is rude to accept the hospitality of one's friends without expressing appreciation. As a general rule, obligations may be satisfied by a personal thanks, by calling or by writing a letter of appreciation."

The Buffet Luncheon, Dinner, or Supper

If you have never given a buffet, you will soon discover how easy it is. You will assume a three-in-one role as cook, waitress, and hostess, but it will be fun.

Serve simple, well-prepared food and plenty of it, and your guests will have a good time. A pretty, colorful table goes a long way. White tablecloths are reserved for the formal dinner table, so use a bright plaid or a high-color cloth on your buffet table. Greater space can be had by placing the dining table against the wall or across the door into the kitchen like a counter. Arrange the silver in military precision with some semblance of balance. If you use paper napkins, buy the heaviest and largest you can find.

The food should be of a nature that can be served on one plate; nobody wants to balance two plates unless he has had previous juggling experience.

Four Suggested Buffet Menus

Italian spaghetti	Boston baked beans
Meat balls	Tossed salad
Green salad	Hot apple pie, cheese
Hot French bread with	Coffee
garlic butter	
Fresh fruit	

Baked ham or meat loaf	Broiled chicken
Au gratin potatoes	Spring salad
String beans	Crisp French bread
Hot rolls	Berry ambrosia
Dessert, coffee	Coffee

Desserts are optional, but if you serve them, keep them on the light side and make them interesting. Hot coffee and plenty of it in man-sized cups is the final touch.

Some of the most pleasant ways of entertaining today are with a Texas or California barbecue, a New England clambake, a Florida fish fry, a steak fry, or a wiener roast. In fact, any kind of party where the food is cooked out of doors and eaten in the yard, on a terrace, at the beach, in a patio, or next to the barbecue pit or broiler is bound to have an informal zest that is hard to duplicate indoors.

SOME GENERAL SUGGESTIONS ON ENTERTAINING

1. Avoid cliché entertaining. I know it is hard not to invite your best friends every time, because you enjoy them, but remember, you have social obligations, too.

2. Keep your menus simple, and above all don't make entertaining a chore. If possible, plan to have a maid or a cleaning woman in to do the dishes and set your quarters in order, so that the party will be only a pleasant memory to you.

3. Have one knockout menu, guaranteed to impress any visiting celebrities or relatives, then *relax!*

4. Have plenty of food; in fact, be on the generous side. But your party will be more of a success if you are on the sparing side with liquor. If you do serve liquor, plan for two well-iced strong cocktails or drinks, then have dinner announced.

5. Don't experiment or try out new dishes when you have guests. A new or unusual dish to surprise your guests is fine, but watch out . . . you may be surprised yourself. Try it on the family first.

6. Don't invite too many people. It is wise to be space-conscious when planning a tea or a cocktail party, and while people like a crowd to be a crowd, still there are limits.

7. Try to make up congenial guest lists. If your guests don't enjoy each other, your goose is really cooked.

8. Your seating plan for a dinner party is as important as your menu. You can't afford to indulge in fuzzy thinking, and if you want the party to get off to a good start, seat your guests yourself by arranging place cards. There will be no shy, odd, or leftover people and this will break the ice.

Your party begins with you! Plan it so that you and your husband will have a good time, and the guests will have the time of their lives. If you feel that it is going to be fun, there will be an infectious gaiety in the air and your husband will fall into the spirit of it. A good book on giving parties is *Entertaining Is Fun,* by Dorothy Draper.

The wise bride will keep a social calendar and a record of social engagements. Also, it is a good plan to give a few small parties each month, unless you prefer to "save up" as your obligations pile up and then give one large, wholesale wing-ding. The latter method has its advantages, but it is much more sociable and more of a compliment to your guests to entertain them at a small party in your own home.

QUESTIONS CONCERNING ENTERTAINING

1. Must we ask the commanding officer and his wife to every party? Indeed not. Once is enough, unless you really wish to go further. The initial exchange of invitations of any kind is enough. Refuse tactfully further invitations from other couples if you do not wish further intimacy.

2. If we invite a couple to a party and they cannot come, must we ask them again? No, not unless you particularly wish to.

3. Whom shall we entertain? This is a broad one! Avoid blanket invitations, but invite your commanding officers and wives if they have come on the post since you arrived, provided you have exchanged calls or a reception has been held. Ask junior officers and their wives in your husband's outfit. If you have a tiny house with a yard, invite a couple in once a week to share hamburgers and potato salad picnic-style in your back yard. Or have one couple at a time for a card-table dinner, even if the stove is on one side and the other side is fenced in by an icebox. This is one time you can invite the C.O. and his wife to eat with you in the kitchen, and they will admire you for your honesty and hospitality if you don't apologize or explain to them that you were "used to better before you married in the Army." Your explanation will only embarrass your husband and your guests, and your mentioning the fact might cause them to mentally question your background. Never be guilty of giving the excuse that you are waiting to entertain until you have "nice things." Live now, and forget about "things." Your guests, if they are worth while, should be more interested in you as a person than in your accouterments such as silver, china, and linen. Be a realist, and carry on from there!

4. Should children be included in an invitation? That all depends. Certainly, children have no place at a luncheon, informal dinner, bridge party, or evening entertainment. Never assume that the invita-

tion includes your children unless specifically stated. If an invited guest phones to say, "I'm afraid I can't come because I can't get a baby-sitter," you should feel free to say, "Well, another time, then!"

WHEN YOU HAVE HOUSE GUESTS

In Chapter V a comfortable guest room was discussed, but here is a list of things about which no good hostess is ever neglectful. There is an old saying that "comfortable guests are happy guests and that makes happy hosts."

1. Have you ever shivered over a week end? Then see that there are enough blankets; an electric heating pad is an added luxury. Place it on the blanket at the foot of the bed in fall or winter.

2. A bed light for those who are accustomed to reading themselves to sleep, a few interesting books or current magazines, a thermos of cold water on the bedside table—these are thoughtful touches. Have the guest-room closet empty except for six to twelve dress hangers, two hat trees, two pairs of shoe trees and one or two luggage racks. Add filled cigarette box with matches and ash trays if the guest smokes.

3. In the room there should be a wastebasket, a mirror in good light, and a clock which does not tick audibly; in the bathroom plenty of towels, soap, bath cloths, bath salts, body powder, cleansing tissue, toilet tissue, hairpins, and bobby pins. A fresh toothbrush in pliofilm case is a really perceptive addition. (Forgetting to pack toothbrushes is a fairly common human failing and a supply on hand will save the guest a trip to the drugstore.) In the dressing-table drawer provide an emergency sewing kit with scissors, straight pins, and assorted safety pins. Supply an electric fan if the weather is hot, and a screen will prove a great comfort in a guest room for those who like to sleep late and are disturbed by light. A plate of tempting fruit with a fruit knife and small napkin is a nice touch.

4. For one guest, it is often easy to serve breakfast on a tray taken to the guest room. Your visitor feels flattered, pampered, and luxurious; and in the meantime, while she is reading the morning paper and taking a second nap, you have a chance to set your house in order and do any chores that are easier to do alone.

The tray is no trouble at all compared to serving breakfast in the dining room, and trays, in their little compass, can be charming. Nothing makes them look more attractive than a flower in a tiny vase. Use your best china, and perhaps, from a wedding check, you may have bought a pretty pastel wicker tray, the stationary kind, with pockets at either end for newspapers and mail. The folding wobbly type can prove disastrous. One trick I learned from a maid I had in Alabama is this: In carrying a tray, look straight ahead where you are walking, forget the tray, and it will remain steady enough for you to arrive with it at its destination, intact.

5. A thoughtful hostess plans some uncrowded hours when she and her husband can have an uninterrupted visit with the guests. After all, the guests may enjoy parties, but they really came to see you. Also, a guest should remember that a host and hostess require some time to themselves in order to take care of personal responsibilities. Make it easy for them by taking a walk, writing a letter, or reading a book!

Chapter X

ARMY JUNIORS—TEEN-AGERS TOO!

Here's to the man who wins the cup,
May he be kind and true,
And may he bring "our godson" up,
To don the Army Blue.
—"Army Blue"

THE Army is a wonderful place to bring up children. The nomadic life, with the constant changing of schools and adjustments to varied types of environment at home and abroad, seems to advance rather than retard the average "Army brat." Children develop a cosmopolitan and gregarious outlook which tends to make them self-reliant the rest of their lives.

In the West Point cadets' slang an "Army child" is described as a cadet whose father is in the Regular Army. Further note, from the West point *Howitzer*, that "one can always tell these Army children. They ride well, know all the Army answers . . . and outside of being high ranking and wanting Blue Uniforms, they are pretty regular kids."

Today an Army wife is assured of the best in prenatal care by competent medical officers, complete hospitalization, and excellent medical follow-up and postpartum care of the baby and herself. There is no need for the "planned parenthood" that young couples in civilian life, owing to economic conditions, sometimes feel necessary. Army juniors early in their young lives learn to sleep in a dresser drawer, and like it as well as a downy cradle.

It matters little to them whether their father is a major or a sergeant, and that is the way it should be. Certainly, there is no rank among the children of soldiers, NCO's, and officers. They attend the same schools, belong to the same Scout and pre-Scout organizations, and in general have a good time together.

Army children are accustomed to frequent moves; by the age of ten years they may have seen more of the world than their grandparents have in a lifetime. It is not unusual to hear a five-year-old roll off such jawbreaking names as Zamboanga, Guantánamo, Bogotá, Guatemala, Berchtesgaden, and Wiesbaden or the Zug Spitz. Their geography is firsthand, and their speech often has a little Japanese, German, French, Hawaiian, or maybe Tagalog in it. They know all about earthquakes, typhoons, pythons, and air raids, and in childlike fashion they like to tell wild hair-raising stories, some of which they have picked up from tales told by their elders.

Little boys enjoy making collections of guns, shrapnel, or war trophies; but their greatest delight is to get a collection of Air Force squadron insignia, chevrons, and flight caps. These kids are tough, resilient, self-reliant youngsters. Early in life they learn to solve their own problems, to get along with all classes and all kinds of people, and to make necessary social adjustments. The ability to make adjustments readily to changing conditions is characteristic. It is no small thing for an adolescent boy or girl well established in a good school with pleasant connections and congenial friends to be transferred suddenly to a foreign country where the entire setup is different. Yet this happens every day to Army families and they learn to take it in stride.

"Man Proposes, but God Disposes"

Wise young couples have their children in the early years of their married life if that is at all possible. Sometimes, when young couples plan to have their families at some future date—for instance, "When Jim gets to be a staff" or "When Bob is promoted and we have captain's pay"—"Man proposes, but God disposes." The couple may lose the wonderful chance of fulfillment with which heaven endowed them. The best advice is, don't delay.

A childless marriage is always incomplete, no matter how compatible a couple may be. The woman who goes through life without a child is robbed of one of life's greatest joys, and I am strongly in favor of adoption in cases where it is impossible for a couple to have children. One seldom sees a man or woman so inflexible that he or she cannot learn to love almost any small child who comes as a permanent guest. An old Moroccan proverb says: "If a man leaves children behind him, it is as if he did not die." General Lucius Clay on greeting his first grandchild proudly said, "We can touch the future with our children's hands." No one ever achieves all his hopes and aspirations. No one is ever sure, in looking back, that he has played his full part in making a better world. But as we live again in

our children and our children's children, we do not need to be afraid.
We can look to them to correct our failures, to achieve many of our
hopes and aspirations.

WHEN JUNIOR IS EXPECTED

Bearing a child is a perfectly normal function, and you have nothing to fear but fear. Pay attention only to your doctor, and discard
all superstitions, strange ideas, and advice from well-meaning relatives and friends. You are performing the most important and the
most magnificent job of your life, the one for which you were designed.

The waiting period should be filled with plans for the new baby,
which you and your husband will find pleasure in sharing together.
Don't forget it is his child too. There will be days when you are not
too comfortable. If you feel your sense of humor dwindling, by all
means invest in a copy of Rory Gallager's *Ladies in Waiting*; this will
make you smile again and maybe even laugh *with*, not *at* yourself.
Having a baby isn't exactly a laughing matter. When it gets tough,
grit your teeth and hang on. Eventually you can look back and smile
—for babies do have a way of getting born.

THE CHRISTENING

The parents may wish to send out engraved announcements, which
consist of a calling card, either the mother's or one that reads:

Captain and Mrs. James Theodore Worthing

and at the top of this card a smaller one which reads:

James Theodore Worthing, Jr.
May first

or

Collins: Born at Post Hospital, Fort Sill, Oklahoma, 25 March 1953, to
   Technical Sergeant and Mrs. Thomas James Collins, a daughter,
   Mary Ellen.

Of course, if the publication uses official abbreviations such as T/Sgt.
or M/Sgt. you cannot help it, but be sure to send the announcement
in correctly.

Another form is:

Barr: A son, James Thomas Barr, born to Mrs. Barr, wife of Captain
   Robert Louis Barr, A.F., at 11th Field Hospital, Stuttgart, Germany,

5 May 1950. The baby is the grandson of Major General and Mrs. Alan Courtney, and Mr. & Mrs. James Thomas Barr of Louisville, Ky.

The first form is the preferred one used by the *Army, Navy and Air Force Journal* in their facetiously called "Hatched" (birth), "Matched" (marriage), and "Snatched" (death, obituary) columns, which are widely read by both active and retired personnel.

Invitations to christenings are informal and may be extended verbally, or by telephone, since only intimate friends are invited.

The first step in the plans for a christening is the selection of a name for the baby. This is something about which an outsider should not even make a suggestion or venture an opinion. Next comes the matter of godparents, who should be chosen from among one's intimate friends. Should they live at a distance, proxies may take their place during the ceremony. The idea of godparents is that, if the child should be left alone in the world, the godparents would become its protectors. In Europe, godparents assume great responsibility, but somehow in this country they take their obligations more lightly and consider their duty accomplished if they give the infant a silver porringer, a christening cup, a lovely Bible, or a substantial check.

In the Catholic Church, the christening takes place usually before the infant is two weeks old and is always performed in church, if possible. The average christening in the Protestant churches takes place between the ages of six months and one year and may be performed at home or in the church.

Arrangements with the post chaplain, if he is to perform the ceremony, should be made in advance; he will probably suggest Sunday morning or afternoon as an appropriate time. If the ceremony is held at the chapel, the nurse or someone will take charge of the infant until time to hand it over to the godmother, who holds it during the baptism. It is very necessary that the godmother pronounce the baby's name distinctly; otherwise the child may carry through life a name not intended for it. A common practice is for her to hand to the minister a card on which the baby's full name is typed or clearly written. At a Catholic christening a certificate of baptism is given to the parents. The chaplain also forwards the original certificate to the Military Ordinariat, 451 Madison Avenue, New York City. Parents of the child should keep their copy of the certificate with other important papers in their personal file or lockbox, since it is necessary for a Catholic to have proof of baptism before entering into a marriage covenant. Should the baptismal certificate be lost, a copy can always be obtained at the Ordinariat.

As soon as the ceremony is over, the godmother hands the baby back to the nurse, who carries it immediately to the waiting car, and she and the baby return home. Should there be no nurse in attendance, the godmother or a member of the family carries the infant. The baby is dressed all in white. Exquisitely dainty christening robes are sometimes handed down in families, a lovely custom; however, the long christening robe is now almost entirely out of fashion and babies wear any kind of pretty, simple white dress.

It is far easier to have the christening at home. The baby can be brought into the room at the last moment, which is safer because he is not so likely to catch cold. The quarters may be decorated with flowers—pale pink rosebuds and baby's-breath are pretty as a centerpiece on the tea table.

The font is always a bowl of gold, silver, or crystal. It is placed on a small, high table. The table should be covered with a dainty cloth and everything placed in readiness for the chaplain. In Hawaii, the baptismal water might be taken from historic Pearl Harbor, later blessed by the chaplain, of course. In Panama, it might be obtained from both the Atlantic and the Pacific or the Panama Canal.

After the ceremony, which is usually held about four or five o'clock, the party resembles an afternoon tea. The mother or the nurse may hold the baby for everyone to admire, but the poor little dear should not be tired out or forced to endure too much. Before the first whimper, he should be returned to the nursery!

Christening "caudle," which is hot eggnog punch, or even champagne, may be served, as this is an occasion which rates something special. An old-fashioned custom is to pass around a loving cup from which everyone drinks as he makes a wish for the baby.

If gifts are brought, they may include a silver knife, fork, spoon set, a silver cup or mug, silver porringer or, for a tiny girl, a wee string of dainty pearls. Gold rings and bracelets are no longer considered fashionable for infants. One of the most acceptable gifts is a savings bond, baby or larger, depending upon your purse! Gifts are not expected, and whether you bring one or not depends upon how much you love babies in general and this baby in particular.

A baby can be christened without any festivity at all, of course, but most mothers like to have this opportunity of showing off their "little bundle from heaven" in a pretty way.

Your First Baby's Nursery

Most young mothers grow enthusiastic about furnishing the nursery the first time, and everyone appreciates your interest as long as you do not become sentimentally sloppy or a bore on the subject. As for decorations, you realize, of course, that it is an adult scheme since it is many months before a baby is aware of color or form except as connected with his own person.

Linoleum is the ideal floor covering, but that is seldom practicable. Small washable rugs are better than a large rug. Frequent launderings will be in order, and they can go right into the washing machine.

The essentials are: a clothes chest of drawers (if you buy it new, select one with a hanging compartment so that the child can get his own clothes when he is old enough); a low, comfortable chair or rocker to use while feeding the baby; a portable bath-dressing table; a disposal unit for diapers; a fitted wicker basket or tray for bottles to hold cotton, oil, and such necessities. A weighing scale may or may not be a necessity—certainly it is a comfort. A clothes tree is convenient and a bottle warmer is useful but neither is an essential.

"His Majesty's" bed is important; however, it can be a deep dresser drawer or a sturdy clothes or market basket mounted on wheels, so long as it has a firm pillow as a mattress. Lacy, beribboned bassinets are lovely but frightful dust catchers, and the baby grows out of them in a wink. It is more practicable to buy a full-sized baby bed at the start, in which he will be able to sleep until he is four or five years old. The screened folding variety of Kiddie-Coop remains popular.

Washable walls of cream color or white with one or two simple pictures make a good starter. Of course, there are inexpensive nursery prints galore, which charm the adult but have little or no meaning for a child. Keep in mind that it is your cherub's room, not yours!

When he learns to toddle, gradually you will remove all of the little-baby signs from the room—the diaper-disposal unit, bathinet, bottle warmer, bottles, and jars. This makes him feel quite grown up, and it has a marked psychological effect on acquiring good toilet habits.

For a while there may be a play pen; then he progresses to the creeping stage, when he will be ready for low shelves which you will provide for his toys and big blocks. Large blocks, even if home-made, are very important in these early years of muscle building.

I should advise you never, never to install one of those fiendish inventions called a "toy box" as nursery equipment. They only teach a child to keep his toys and possessions in the utmost disorder. A little child easily acquires a love of order, and if you have patience you can teach him to have a place for each toy. Believe it or not, he will enjoy putting each toy in its proper spot. It gives him a pleasant sense of achievement!

Standard nursery-school furniture is a good investment as it stands up well under the punishment inflicted by its little user. As soon as your prodigy shows an interest in creative decoration, it will be wise to provide him with a blackboard or, if space permits, a pin-board installed at a convenient height on an unbroken wall. A broad piece of wood-bound cork, on which can be thumbtacked or stapled cheap newsprint paper, will be a joy to him and to you and your landlord, too! He can use chalks, crayolas, or paints and give his creative instinct ample scope. If the scene isn't set for such activities, don't be surprised if energy turns into what you term naughtiness. With patience, if not with ease, you can teach him that this room is his, that his decorative talents belong only here, and in no other room in the house.

PREADOLESCENT AND OLDER CHILDREN'S ROOMS

If at all possible, each child should have a room to himself. Everybody, no matter how gregarious, has need of one place which for him is sacrosanct. There should be an understanding that when the door of a room is closed, no one should enter without being invited to do so in answer to a gentle knock. Mother might have a family understanding that when her door is closed she is not to be disturbed except in case of fire or an emergency. There are people who go through life without the slightest idea of respect for the privacy of others. They are pathetic people, but so insensitive they never know it. This is one thing that children should be taught early.

Although a desk is an adult accessory, even a seven- or eight-year-old will appreciate having a place to keep his schoolwork and supplies that he sometimes brings home; later, he will learn the correct use of a desk. Meanwhile, let him enjoy having nails in one drawer, drawing paper in another, a mouse trap in a third, and what not.

The real desire for privacy develops in the preadolescent years— ten, eleven, and twelve—when both boys and girls go all out for separate group and club activities and develop a great sense for possessions. They express their desires for privacy in strange and original ways, sometimes with signs printed on the door: "Enter at Your Own Peril" or an abrupt "Keep Out. Strictly Private" or a hotel admonition card filched from a visit which warns, "Do Not Disturb."

One week a Brownie's room may represent Alice in Wonderland, the next week, if she shares the room with an older sister, they may produce a medieval castle which the Girl Scout is studying at school. The interest span is short lived, at best, which helps a mother to encourage, and bear with, its odd variants.

Almost overnight, your little tomboy girl may develop into a junior miss and ask to have her room changed so she can invite her best friend, Suzy, over to spend the night. Don't wonder why the room has to be done over suddenly when Suzy has practically lived in it by day all summer; just accept it and put all the zeal into it you can to make the room attractive. Ostentation is definitely in questionable taste; no adult dressy satin or taffeta bedspreads or chairs—which aren't good taste any time, even for adults. Maybe I am prejudiced on the side of simplicity.

Let your daughter in on the planning, shopping, and buying; then surprise her with a peppermint-stick slip-covered chair or a canopy for her tester bed. She will love a pair of low slipper chairs which are just right for whispered confidences between girls. Think back! And she may prefer twin beds to the old four-poster, but they will be no guarantee against giggles that often go on far into the night. Provide a comfortable worktable or desk, a full-length mirror, a fruit bowl and cookie jar, and you won't have to refurnish until her college days.

For the teen-age boy, skip all the frills and fancies. Provide him with a he-man menu of sturdy fabrics and bold colors when he shows symptoms of asking to change to a young man's room. Don't underestimate his pride and interest in his own room or his thrill over a bunk bed, although he may say little. He will love a large pin-board on which he can put up pictures, clippings, football scores, and such. His clothes closet should be arranged for quick action. Boys need a large desk or table with a good light, on which they can construct planes and study without having to move either books or construction materials. As for a radio, that decision is up to you and your child. Personally, I can concentrate better if soft music is coming in on the radio, but parents often feel that this form of entertainment is detrimental to concentration in studying.

If you wish to foster good grooming in your children, provide hangers for their clothes, hat trees, shoe trees, and shoe racks within easy reach for whatever age. If possible, have them match the decoration of their rooms or the accessories in their closets. Your interest will do much to arouse a desire for neatness and attractive surroundings, even though it may take years to burst into full bloom! There will be a new pride in entertaining their overnight guests.

Children should hang up their own clothes and straighten their own rooms even if they have to wait until after school to do it. On weekdays, children or any job-holding members of the family should not be asked to make their beds. It is just one thing too many when everyone is trying to make a bus or train and not be late. The beds are given no time to air and are usually made carelessly, resulting in an uncomfortable night of sleep which isn't good. On holidays and week ends everyone should make his own bed if there is no maid.

EDUCATIONAL INSURANCE

This is a type of insurance that is becoming increasingly popular, because all parents are interested in a college education for their children. It is also a means of saving, and a convenient way to meet the real educational needs of your children. If taken out when the child is very young, the policies involve only small premiums. The plan is that the policy matures when Junior is sixteen, seventeen, or eighteen, and there will be ready cash to send him to either a good preparatory school, if he plans to enter the Military, Naval, or (proposed) Air Academy, or a standard college.

NURSERY SCHOOLS

So little is really known of the wonders accomplished by a good nursery school! However, a poor school with inefficient and inexperienced teachers is worse than no school at all. If you can possibly afford it, by all means send your child to a good one. Two years of age is not too young for him to enter nursery school although some parents prefer to wait until he is three or even four.

The young child is learning constantly, and what he learns may be desirable or undesirable. Character is taking shape, habits are being formed, skills and attitudes are being developed for better or for worse.

The expertly staffed nursery school is designed to enrich the child's day with a wealth of experiences conducive to desirable learnings, and to reduce to a minimum situations fraught with undesirable responses. The shy child learns to greet his companions cheerily. The helpless child acquires self-reliance in donning his play clothes, buttoning, lacing, tying knots and bows, and independently selecting his activity materials. The disorderly child discovers the pleasure of opening his locker door on a neat array of personal possessions—play shoes on shoe trees, playsuit on a hanger, art brushes clean, toys and toilet articles in their places—all arranged there by himself the previous day. The retiring child learns to stand up for his rights. The child whose table talk consists of silly noises and giggles is given through educational excursions an incentive to converse and worth-while experiences to discuss. The destructive, the inconsiderate, the selfish, the rude, the crybaby, the unsanitary learn the error of their ways through the anguish of unpopularity with their playmates. The child is exposed to the finest in art, music, and literature, thereby developing a taste for richer, fuller living and learning to create beauty himself.

The average busy mother is distracted by many other duties, whereas the child-training specialist becomes mother-teacher, a playfellow, a companion, a storyteller. To her is accorded this privilege of shaping the lives of the most wonderful of all creatures, little children.

To sum up, a few of the advantages of training in a modern nursery school are as follows:

1. Companionship with children near the same age
2. The development of proper attitudes—so very important
3. The forming of good health habits—eating, sleeping, toilet
4. The sharing of possessions with other children—toys, books
5. Learning to follow directions, take orders, obey
6. Learning to live and to play in a group

After all, one of the most important lessons in life is getting along with our fellow man, and the age of two years is the best time to start developing the proper attitudes and traits of character.

Kindergartens or Preschools

The word "kindergarten" has become obsolete with the advancement of knowledge about child psychology, health, behavior, and mentality. However, to the average parent "kindergarten" still denotes preschool training.

Personally, I feel that if the little child has two years in a good nursery school, where the important habit and attitude foundations of his future are laid, he can skip a year before starting to preschool or kindergarten. At the age of three or four, his mind is open to knowledge. He becomes acquainted with the world through his senses, and he is impelled by them to activity that further educates him. This is the question-asking stage, the imitation period, the imagination stage. His information is increased by the great number of questions he asks. To the mother and to the kindergarten teacher comes the rare privilege of unfolding to this plastic little mind the truths the child is so eager to know. The unhappy concepts some children receive are the result of bungling language used by adults and ugly attitudes toward one another and toward life. Health and happiness should be the first aims in all work with the preschool child.

The average child with the two-year nursery-school background seems to get the most out of kindergarten between the ages of five and six. In a modern, up-to-date kindergarten the curriculum is well rounded and planned, with special emphasis and freedom given to the child's initiative. Units of work that are related to the child's experience are the basis of his learning.

Don't let your parental pride and ambition push Johnny into the first grade! Many people are mortally afraid that because of their moving around in the Service, or because of the poor educational facilities on duty in the occupied countries, Junior may get behind in his studies and be considered backward.

For some reason Johnny must start school at six. Why? Simply because his parents did in their youth! What earthly difference does it make whether the child postpones reading and writing until he is six and a half, seven, or older! The most important phase of Johnny's life is the first seven years, in which he learns and develops the numberless qualities and habits which go to build his character. For instance, a child who has had his own way, or very nearly his own way, from infancy to the age of seven is so far on the wrong road that he is an almost hopeless problem for his first-grade teacher. Johnny has to unlearn the impossible things that are already fixed habits in order to become a member of the group. At this time, in the transition period, he develops complexes and attitudes that may give him a very distorted and unhappy outlook on life. The child who has attended a good nursery school, where he has learned the rudiments of the formality of the schoolroom, definitely has the edge on poor little Johnny, as you can see.

Elementary grade teachers quickly note the difference between children who have had preschool training and those who have not. Educators agree that a delay of six months or so in entering school makes little difference to a child. Many states will not accept a child for the first grade until after his sixth birthday, and in some localities the age requirement is seven. Cheers for the latter!

Medical surveys have shown that the muscles of a child's eyes are not properly developed for reading until the age of six and a half. His muscles for writing are naturally stronger at seven. We don't need to worry about Johnny; he will learn to read and write, and he will be a stronger student later if he is not pushed. Let us not mistake his desire to read for brilliance. Reading is perhaps the most important subject in the elementary curriculum, because the child has to read to learn arithmetic, language, history, geography, and all other subjects. Poor reading ability often causes failure in these subjects. And why is Johnny a poor reader? Because he started to learn to read before he was physically or mentally developed for this most important process.

SUNDAY ON AN ARMY POST

The Service provides a chapel and a chaplain for each of its posts of moderate size. Where the chapel has not been constructed, transportation is always available to take children to Sunday school and personnel to church in the nearest town. A chaplain is a member of the command, a qualified officer who needs the moral support of all post personnel and particularly of the commanding officer and his staff.

Many C.O.'s attend Sunday services regularly; others make it a rule to attend once a month. There is something in the spiritual character of a day of rest that is important to any person, but it is particularly important to children that they have a strong spiritual influence in their formative years. It helps to make them better citizens and gives them something which enables them better to cope with the world problems of our age.

I am not suggesting any particular religious belief, certainly; any belief which makes humanity better is good! Some husbands and wives continue to go to church on Sunday just as they did when they were younger, and this is the best possible example you can set for your children. Sunday should be a day of real rest, recreation, and relaxation, and children should be taught that rest and uplift can be found in the hallowed quiet of a church or chapel just as it can in the cool reaches of a forest or the windswept peaks of a mountain.

Little children love to attend Sunday school just as you did in your day, no doubt, and they like Bible stories and the extracurriculars that go along with church attendance today. It may take a bit of doing to get up on Sunday and get the family off to church with you and your husband in the lead, but it is far more satisfying than nursing a hangover from the Saturday night party or settling down to a morning of reading moronic comics to your small ones!

PREPARATORY SCHOOLS

For boys who wish to enter the United States Military Academy, there are several good preparatory schools.

The Sullivan School	The Bullis School	The Braden School
2107 Wyoming Avenue	Silver Spring	Cornwall-on-Hudson
Washington, D. C.	Maryland	New York

There are many other good ones, known as "tin schools," but the list is too long to publish here.

A booklet, *Information Relative to the Appointment and Admission of Cadets*, may be secured from the Adjutant General of the Army, Washington, D. C., by those who have their hearts set on entering West Point. There are a few basic requirements: The prospective candidate must be at least seventeen years of age, and not more than twenty-two, at the time of admission. He must not be married, nor can he have been married. He must be at least 5 feet 4 inches tall, and not more than 6 feet 6 inches. There is a long list of physical requirements. The standard method of admission is by appointment from a Senator or Representative in Congress, or by presidential appointment. An appointment is not a guarantee of admission; it is merely a chance to take a very stiff competitive examination.

TEEN-AGERS

Army teen-agers seem to have come into their own, most of the groups being sponsored by the Women's Clubs on the respective posts. In addition to Brownies and Cubs, junior and senior Boy and Girl Scout groups, special social activities are planned by the teen-agers themselves. Dances, hay rides, wiener roasts, candy pulls, golf and tennis tournaments, picnics are some of the activities enjoyed on various Army posts.

One very active group which is doing fine work is the Barksdale Teen-Age Club. The "Bar-Teens" (Barksdale, Louisiana), as they call themselves, have drawn up their own constitution, and members range in age from thirteen to nineteen years inclusive. The motto of this club is: "Better youth makes a better world."

One of the private dining rooms of the Officers' Club is reserved for the teen-agers' dancing classes, where instruction in both ballroom and folk dancing is given. In the fall the club attends local football games as a body; in the summer they take a Red Cross lifesaving course. Very definite projects are planned, and the teen-agers are responsible for cleaning their clubhouse before and after their parties. They have their own lending library.

Each teen-age club has a counselor, and usually a younger officer and his wife are asked to be sponsors. Dues average about fifty cents a month. Such a club gives the adolescents of the post a definite interest in their Army community and makes them feel as if they belong. Their energies are directed and juvenile delinquency is at a minimum. As a wise counselor said, "The parents are the real delinquents usually, not the children." Throughout the Army, teen-age clubs are being given the interest and co-operation they need to function successfully.

TRAINING FOR BABY-SITTERS!

Baby-sitting sounds so attractive that thousands of teen-agers—and older people, too—go into the business each year. Almost anyone can be a baby-sitter, but not everyone can be a good one. And only the good ones make a success of the job. Baby-sitting is not child's play. It requires know-how in child care and in employer-employee relations. Here are some of the qualifications:

1. Do you like children? Well enough, that is, to clean them when they're dirty, humor them when they're difficult, and comfort them when they're unhappy? Successful sitting requires a genuine love of children. The person who dislikes or fails to understand children has no business being a sitter.

2. Are you mature enough to sit with children? The sign of maturity is said to be the ability to think of others before yourself. This is important in taking care of children since young children are self-centered and concerned only with getting *what* they want *when* they want it. When you sit, you must be prepared to *work* for your money.

3. Do you have a strong sense of responsibility? When you sit, you alone are responsible for the safety and well-being of your charges. This means putting the children ahead of your own comfort and convenience.

4. Can you cope with an emergency? Of course, you are not going to meet with emergencies every time you sit but it is a good idea to know how you would act if the electricity suddenly failed, if Junior took a bad tumble or little Mabel threw a temper tantrum. Presence of mind and the ability to act are two qualities you should possess as a sitter.

At a post I visited recently, a baby-sitter pool with a course of instruction was being offered to teen-age boys and girls. Here are some of the highlights of the course in guidance . . . entitled:

What Every Sitter Should Know

1. Have the parents brief you on their full names, address, and phone number where they can be reached. Get all three facts. If they are going to the theater or a movie, get the name and phone number of the movie, or if they plan to go "out on the town," suggest they call you at least once during the evening. It is better than wondering, "Where, oh where have the parents gone?" should an emergency arise.

2. Equip yourself with a loose-leaf notebook and assign two pages to information about each of your clients. This is very businesslike, and on your second sitting you will have the permanent information. It will impress your employers. Arrive a few minutes before schedule so as to allow time for briefing.

3. Ask your employer to take you on a Cook's tour of their house. You should know the floor plan, where the child's room is and where his things are. . . . [Find out] where the telephone is located and lay the telephone book beside it. They won't think you are nosy, only smart.

4. You will be expected to know how to diaper a baby, prepare bottles, feed Donny, and under no circumstances must you ever spank him.

5. Never sit more than three nights a week and never more than one school night.

6. Talking financial turkey is often hard for a teen-age sitter. Remember, sitters should be businesslike in setting their rates, but they should be reasonable. Find out what other sitters in your community

are getting; ask your parents and check your own conscience. Fees vary, are usually higher in cities. Most parents and sitters agree that between 35 and 50 cents an hour is a reasonable rate.

(Note: An excellent booklet, *Baby-Sitters' Handbook,* by Judy Flander, can be ordered from Science Research Associates, Inc., 57 West Grand Avenue, Chicago 10, Illinois.)

7. If you are interested in baby-sitting, you owe it to the baby and yourself to read and study this pamphlet.

ADVANTAGES OF BABY-SITTING

1. It is valuable job training for your future career. You will learn to accept responsibility and make decisions on your own; you will learn to get along with adults of differing outlooks and personalities, which is fine preparation for future employer-employee relationships.

2. Baby-sitting prepares you for your future as a parent.

3. It is pleasant and easy way to earn money, under pleasant working conditions.

4. You can work at your convenience.

5. You have plenty of leisure time on the job. Time to read, study, or relax.

Baby-sitting is a rewarding job opportunity for boys as well as girls. More and more high-school boys—and college fellows, including football players and basketball stars—are becoming baby-sitters. It is no job for a sissy; if you think so, try to dig up that old movie, *Sitting Pretty,* in which Clifton Webb starred as a baby-sitter! This is a job that requires ingenuity, intelligence, and the ability to think clearly and act decisively. If baby-sitting is good training for future mothers, it also has some valuable experience to offer future fathers.

AIR TRAVEL WITH CHILDREN

Travel by air is commonplace today in the Service. When orders come in, your husband may have to precede you. You are left to pack, give up the quarters or house, and follow with the children. You really have a bit of planning to do, regardless of how green the grass may appear to be at your next station. Let us assume that you are an experienced hand at surface travel, which includes train, boat and motor. Flying, however, is something new to you and especially so with a baby or babies.

If you are traveling on a commercial air line and not by MATS

1. Be sure to let the air line know the ages of your youngsters even though you do not buy a ticket for children under two years of age. If possible, the stewardess will let your nonpaying baby have the spare seat if one is available. (Of course, you can't count on this; you must be prepared to hold your baby all the way, even if he does weigh twenty-five pounds and resembles a wiggle worm in his acrobatics.)

2. Change planes only if absolutely necessary and make plane connections as close as recommended safe (as to time allowance) because stopovers in public air terminals are difficult with children.

3. When making your reservations, choose the fastest trip with the fewest stops, and if possible select a large pressurized cabin plane. The latter is easier on the babies' ears, and the fewer landings and take-offs, the less trouble you have on this score.

Air Travel by MATS

Briefing comes first: All immunization charts for adults and children must be checked; then about two hours before take-off time all baggage must be weighed in, and a regular MATS briefing for overseas travel is given. A movie is shown which is important as it outlines the procedure employed in ditching a C-54 or large passenger transport. A short lecture is given, and remember all of this is for no one's good but your own!

On dependents' flights there are two or more flight nurses, and everything possible is done for the comfort of the passengers. Families are usually seated together in a plane, particularly those with babies (as far as possible removed from VIP's).

MATS service continues to improve all the time, and dependents who have traveled recently have nothing but good things to say about it. Like commercial air lines, MATS even gives passengers a blank form to fill in suggested improvements in the service and your impression of the flight.

Wear a tailored suit, of crease- and spot-resistant material, if possible, and remove the jacket and your hat when you get on the plane. Black is a poor choice since it shows all lint from blankets and paper diapers! Let what may happen to your blouse because you can either change it or cover it later with your jacket. Tuck an extra sleeveless silk jersey blouse in just in case. Wear good-looking but comfortable shoes so you can carry your baby and walk too. Appearance is a great morale factor, and if you keep yourself as neat as possible you will not only look but feel better. If traveling by MATS you will be requested to wear slacks. Take a warm jacket or coat—it's cold at ten thousand feet and the heater may go out. Clothing carried over the arm is not counted against your baggage allowance.

Get a good night's rest the night before leaving because you will need all of your energy to devote to the children; always plan to be rested before you embark on a trip with children. If you have any fear of being airsick be sure to take the new drug, dramamine. The tablets are now an item of issue on all MATS transports. A sick mother is pathetic and the children of a sick mother are more pathetic! Try to keep cheerful and calm because your children's attitude and behavior will be dependent upon yours. Your pediatrician may give you a light sedative for the children, but if they don't relax and sleep don't let it worry you. Just be prepared to amuse them all night long! This takes long-range planning but here are some of the tricks:

1. Take plenty of little toys; you won't want to load your luggage with heavy wooden toys or dolls. Small plastic cars, a matchbox full of buttons and a blunt threaded needle will amuse a three-year-old for an hour or more. You can tuck in little jars filled with red and white dried beans, fill and refill the bottles and screw on the tops. What harm if a few are spilled?

2. If your child is old enough to cut, put a pair of blunt-end scissors in your purse and a small roll of Scotch tape. Magazines afford lovely pictures, and Scotch tape is never messy to stick up an art gallery on the window or the next seat. A small note pad and pencil come in handy for drawing pictures, but for obvious reasons beware of crayolas, clay, or paint. Crayons might be taken for coloring books for the child old enough to be trusted with them.

3. All ten-cent stores have a fund of tracing and cutout books as well as tiny books that can be read and pack easily, using up little space. Little fellows love to unwind a spool of thread or one of those crepe-paper "Surprise Balls" that have little favors all wound up in them.

4. Do take candy, gum, and cookies but buy wisely. Take only candy that can be eaten in one bite like jelly beans or gumdrops. Avoid gooey, messy candy bars. Hold back on the candy; dole it out as a reward or a surprise for good behavior. As for fruit, leave all juicy fruit like oranges, plums, peaches at home and instead select what can be sliced with a penknife and fed to the child bite by bite. Never give a child a whole apple to wipe all over himself, you, the

plane, and fellow passengers. For an older child take a few sandwiches because often meals aloft are strange or the child is too fasci-
nated to eat at an air terminal; his favorite peanut-butter sandwich
will be the answer when he announces that he is hungry at 3 A.M.

5. Nature calls: Would that this problem could be eliminated on
the trip, but it cannot! On any long trip, "piddling" or "pot-potting"
for babies just out of diapers is very difficult. If the child is young
enough, put it back into diapers for the trip. However, if you can't do
this, take a little plastic "piddling pot" for boys and a regular little
"pot" for girls (a small cardboard hatbox is a good disguise for the
latter).

6. Whether you like to fly or not, it is a good idea to appear enthusiastic about the trip, so that your children will not be frightened
and will enjoy flying. Hold small ones on your lap during the take-off
and landing so they will not be frightened. It is a good plan to talk
to them as the engines are revved up prior to take-off, and point out
the windows at objects to keep their interest stimulated.

7. Teach them to yawn or open their mouths and swallow on taking off, and when the plane is coming in to land to blow their noses.
This helps relieve the pressure on their ears. For older children chewing gum, of course, is in order.

Baby Foods and Formulas

(Written by Kay Andrus, wife of Colonel Burton Andrus, USAF,
mother of three Air Force fledglings under six.) *

Even though the air-line pamphlet announces that they have all types of
baby food available, don't take a chance! If your baby is still on a formula
do not change this formula just before or during a trip. If you know it
has to be changed, do so weeks ahead of the time you must travel so the
baby will be used to it. If your baby is on canned or powdered milk
formula you are lucky, and you can take enough formula for the whole
trip.

I use Even-Flo or Vita-Flo bottles because each bottle is self-sealed and
can be packed in a suitcase if necessary and will not leak. The sterile water
and sugar part of the formula can be measured into as many of these
bottles as you will need for the whole trip and then sealed and kept safely
without being put in the refrigerator. Then, as you need more formula you
can add canned or powered milk to one or several of the sterile water

---

* Mrs. Andrus specifically wishes to state that what has worked for her in air
travel is not to be taken as a standard, since other mothers may have better methods.

bottles. Then, of course, you use these right away. I also feed everything to a baby over six months old at room temperature and don't worry about having bottles or food heated. I either feed them out of the can or put the strained food into an extra bottle and use a nipple with a huge hole in it. I mix Pablum right into the formula, too, and with a big hole in the nipple for this gruel, a baby will drink down his whole Pablum meal with no muss or fuss. Try it out before you leave home, and if your baby prefers to eat from a spoon then put your dry Pablum in a little jar, mix formula into it and feed it that way.

Bags and Baggage

All of the above advice on what to take in this traveling commissary will make you ask the vital question, "What kind of bag shall I take?" Again, I ask my efficient, travel-wise Kay! She says:

As you know, regular luggage goes in the baggage compartment of the plane where it cannot be reached en route, but I always take one or two small bags with me. The first I call my "on-hand bag." And it is just that! It is the bag of essential supplies for the children that I must be able to reach with one hand at all times—in terminals, in taxis or aboard the plane. It is small enough so that, if necessary, I can carry the baby, my purse and the "on-hand bag" and walk a mile. [What a girl!] It is sturdy leather and able to hold formula bottles, diapers and supplies without everything sticking out the top and without danger of breaking them. Flimsy, plastic diaper bags just aren't large enough or secure enough for the valuable formula you need at your side for your baby. My "on-hand bag" stands steadily alone when full and has a zipper top which I can open with one hand. These may seem mere trifles to consider; but picture a DC-6 over the Pacific with some thirty or more sleeping passengers, subdued lights and the stewardess busy in the rear of the plane. Suddenly the little cherub in your lap begins to scream. You need to reach that essential he is screaming for in a hurry in the dark. You will bless your careful planning and packing then!

Kay's check list may help you pack your first "on-hand bag" (for two children, four and a half and one and a half):

3 Even-Flo bottles of mixed formula
3 cans baby's favorite food
A turn-type can opener and a beer-can opener to open milk cans, tied with strings and pinned to bag
A small sharp paring knife
Baby's spoon, cup and bib
Small jar of dry Pablum

A few favorite cookies in foil paper
2 peanut-butter sandwiches
1 apple
Several kinds of jelly beans, candy and gum
12 or 14 disposable diaper fillers (Kleinert's)
2 Kleinert's pad-pants
½ box loose Kleenex
1 small jar of tap water (for clean changes)
1 small roll of toilet paper (also for clean changes)
1 wet washcloth in waterproof bag for hands and faces
1 tube of Diapereen ointment to prevent chafing
6 extra safety pins, pinned near top of bag
A cotton twill harness (anchors a sleeping baby to seat; helps harness
  an active squirmer)
1 small lap pad
Baby's favorite small blanket (helps Baby sleep, smells familiar)
1 complete change of dress for baby
Heavy sweater for each child

If your baby is old enough to know a stranger is strange, don't force it to stay with someone different if you can possibly help it. Plan the whole trip with the baby at your side. In terminals and hotels an aluminum stroller that folds up and weighs only nine pounds is worth its weight in aluminum—if not gold! Well, happy landings and may all of your flights with your youngsters be happy ones.

A MOTOR TRIP WITH CHILDREN

It is to be hoped that you will recover from this flight before you have to take an automobile trip with your children, but it just might happen that your husband will meet you at the air terminal—say, at Fairfield Suisun—with a new family car to complete the cross-country trip to his new base. For an officer under orders, automobile travel with his family is the cheapest way he can go. The head of the family draws eight cents a mile, he is allowed four cents a mile for wife, and two cents a mile for the children over five.

The following notes were supplied by Kay Ascani, wife of Colonel Fred Ascani, Jr., who made the trip across the continent by automobile with her four children, all under six years of age. She suggests the following:

1. Have AAA or one of the oil companies plan your trip with reference to shortest routes, best roads, preferred lodging and eating places.
2. Motels are easier than hotels: the car is at the door, many tips are

saved; only the luggage you need as you need it is unpacked. No one likes to drag or carry three or four tired little children through the lobby of a hotel. Even the family dog or cat is welcome at most motels, if it sleeps in the car.

3. Don't overload the car.

Another convenience: Take your shoebag, hanging on your closet door, and fasten it over the back of the front seat, so the compartments will be handy to the back-seat travelers. Fill the compartments with the things the family needs from time to time—road caps, magazines, toys, paper cups, napkins, fruit, and a thermos bottle filled with your favorite beverage.

4. For yourself choose packables for traveling—suits or sweaters and skirts with extra blouses.

5. Include Lux, a collapsible ironing board which fits into your suitcase and a Pak-away electric iron as part of your laundry gear. For the more difficult laundry, stop at a Laundromat and have it washed and dried one day while you and the family have lunch. It can be done and is just that easy.

6. Light diets for children while traveling are recommended, although there is usually one passenger who can't get enough to eat. If possible, eat only at recommended restaurants. Always insist upon pasteurized milk for children.

7. Never use restaurant silver for small children. Paper spoons and cups are preferred; each child should have his own plastic bib to save clothes from spots and for easy cleaning.

8. After several days of restaurant dining, stop at a delicatessen, select food for a picnic lunch, then stop at a roadside park or an inviting picnic ground.

9. Give the youngsters as much exercise as time permits. They will love sightseeing from five on, and it is amazing how much little ones remember about the historic spots they have visited. This all adds up to the pleasure of the trip, and automobile trips can be very educational as well as fun.

10. Plan the children's clothing with care. Be sure not to burden them with heavy clothes or long coats. Short jackets or sweaters worn with corduroy or seersucker slacks and washable T-shirts, depending upon the weather, will prove satisfactory. Remember that children become ill more easily from being overdressed than they do from being lightly dressed while traveling. Dress them as you yourself feel comfortable. Three or four changes for a week's trip should be adequate if you do a bit of laundry as you go along.

Luggage

Suitcases which will not be needed en route can be packed between the front and back seats, and with the baby's crib mattress placed on top will give additional sleeping space. Children tire easily and frequent cat naps improve their dispositions. Sleeping children while traveling in the car depends, of course, upon their ages. Small canvas car beds, convertible to car seats, are on the market, but a bed made of blankets and pillows will also prove satisfactory for children over two years.

Baby rates a zippered bag of his own which will contain only his changes and clothes. This will probably go on the floor in the front of the car. Bottle warmers attachable to the dashboard are a real convenience. A small bag or box containing a one-burner hot plate, and utensils for formula-making placed in the trunk of the car will enable you to make the baby's formula in any motel or hotel room. You'll be glad you took this along!

A "Fort-niter Bag" will hold enough for a family of six if you pack just those things needed at night and for two or three day changes. Pack it in the trunk in the most accessible space so that the car does not have to be unpacked every night.

There will be another bag or perhaps a basket for sheets, disposable diapers, rubber pants, socks, Kleenex, baby oil, cream, soap, socks, extra overalls, towels, washcloths, and in one compartment a can opener, bottle opener, paper cups, spoons, straws, and bibs.

No experienced mother will start on a motor trip without the little sprout's toidy seat, if he is used to it. It can be camouflaged with a plastic cover, and baby's routine need not be disturbed. Many mothers find it easier to feed the baby in the car before taking the family into a restaurant to eat. The car seat serves as a high chair and you have your formula or baby food, cups, and spoons at hand. This type of planning often prevents restaurant scenes. A baby does not like changes of environment at feeding time; if fed in the car first, he will go along and keep happy in a high chair with his favorite toy or perhaps a cookie while the family enjoy their meals.

To keep the older children occupied is important too. Take along crayons, coloring books, push-out puzzles, beads to be strung. When they become restless, bring out a new trinket. The whole family can enjoy guessing games or favorite stories.

A FEELING OF SECURITY IS IMPORTANT

Owing to the itinerant life an Army child is forced to lead, he misses the feeling of security in a permanent home in an established town or community to which most civilian children are accustomed.

Parents should realize that there is a definite psychological effect upon a child each time he is uprooted. It would be interesting to analyze a small child's thought processes, emotions, fears on each one of these moves. Certainly a hurried, hectic automobile trip with worried parents will not contribute to his sense of security. Of course, on the move is a fine way to learn geography and history firsthand, but it does not give a child a feeling of permanence.

Security is an important factor in children's development. Children have great faith; they feel their parents are eternal, fixed and unchanging. That sense of safety that they feel in their fathers and mothers is an overwhelming force for their good, and they usually follow in their own lives the example of love and companionship set for them by their parents.

Thus, Army children, perhaps more than others, need the security of knowing that they have the love of their parents regardless of what happens. A child may have to be disciplined or may be temporarily out of favor, but loved he *must* be *always*.

CHILDREN ON AN ARMY POST

Each post has its own regulations in regard to the deportment of children, but here are a few general rules:

1. Don't fail to acquaint your child with local rules in regard to the swimming pool, golf course, tennis courts, and the Officers' Club.

2. Don't permit your child to impose upon neighbors; discourage frequent calls, picking flowers, teasing pets, playing in driveways and garages.

3. Don't allow vandalism, such as defacing, destroying, or injuring government property or private property.

4. Don't permit a child to deface quarters, write on walls, break windows, dig holes in lawns.

5. Don't allow impertinence to soldiers or guards, or tolerate misconduct on school bus.

6. Teach obedience to traffic rules in regard to crossing busy intersections on posts, proper riding of bicycles, scooters, etc.

7. Children or their pets should not be allowed near hangar lines, picket lines, gun sheds, or firing ranges.

8. Try to control unnecessary noise, crying, or any play that is annoying to neighbors.

9. Teach respect, consideration, and courtesy for older people of the garrison.

10. Remember the old saying that "little pitchers have big ears." Be careful not to discuss anything of an official nature before children; they may not get the true meaning and repeat something very different from what was said. What is sometimes worse, they repeat all too accurately what was said, and to the wrong person.

11. A positive effort should be made by parents to explain to their children that rank should never be mentioned, even casually. For instance, never say, no matter how it is meant, "Oh, she's a colonel's daughter!" "His father is a sergeant."

12. Don't feel that an invitation includes your children, unless they are specifically mentioned in it. Never take your children with you on a formal call, even if they remain in the car. Stretch a point and hire a baby-sitter if the call is a must. Arrange for your children not to be in the living room when you are receiving formal callers or having dinner guests.

13. Wise parents ignore children's quarrels; you should be too adult to let your children's quarrels become quarrels between parents, even if *your* child is *right*.

14. Neither is it wise for parents to criticize the behavior of other children. Have a care! Yours may be guilty of the same conduct tomorrow.

15. In general, impress upon your children the fact that their misbehavior can cause their father to suffer official humiliation.

It might be well for a wife to realize that her husband may be judged by the neighbors largely on how the children behave. This is true whether you live on a post or in a civilian community. You would not like to have your husband passed over as chief of staff of an important command simply because the general couldn't stomach the idea of having your children living next door to him. It could happen. Or the C.O. might think that an officer or NCO with such "Army brats" for children must be lacking in some essential quality of leadership and discipline, even though the behavior might be due to your laxness and misguided mother love in spoiling Junior.

Most people love a well-mannered, courteous child, but no one enjoys a rude, spoiled "little monster"! Army children on the whole are usually well disciplined, orderly, and courteous, but always remember they reflect you and their home training.

Chapter XI

CHANGE OF STATION

O RDERS are always exciting, even if the move involved is only of a local nature. By "local" is meant from one post to another, in the Zone of the Interior. "Foreign duty" may be in any foreign country, where the Army is represented or established, and where we are serving as a partner in a mutual defense effort. Army families may be compared to nomads or gypsies in the true sense of having no fixed abode, or never remaining for a long time in any one area; yet even the carefree gypsies have the advantage of deciding *where* they will pitch their tents, and it is up to their chief *when* they will pull up stakes.

Not so with Army families, as the *Officers' Guide* specifically states: "Any time and to practically any place on earth, a member of the Army may be dispatched by orders of the Department of the Army."

Whether or not dependents are permitted to accompany or to join the officer or enlisted man depends upon various conditions, hinging on the availability of quarters at the new station and the state of the world's peace at the moment. There is no law that forces dependents to leave the good old U. S. A., or to move from one post to another, for that matter, provided they vacate quarters and do not remain on the post indefinitely.

BE A COSMOPOLITE!

It usually takes a few hours, sometimes a few days, to adjust oneself to orders that involve a change of station, but *take it easy, adjust you must*. In the past few years, geographical boundaries of countries have changed radically, and as for boundaries of race and creed, these, too, are undergoing revolutionary changes on every part of the globe. After the first shock, you will learn to welcome orders, love a change of station which will involve meeting old friends and making new ones. You will enjoy learning the customs of strange countries and strange people, and in a short time you will be enough of a world traveler and a cosmopolite to look at people not only with your eyes but with your mind and heart as well. Never fret about official orders; let your husband worry about them. When the orders come, smile and pack. The next station is never as bad as you think it might be; it's all one Army.

PACKING AND MOVING

Our friends the gypsies may or may not have system when moving day arrives but most Army wives develop an individual system, applicable only to herself and family, after three or four changes of station. Rule One is to do nothing until your husband actually receives his official orders. Of course, if the curtains need laundering and the rugs are ready for the cleaner's anyway, you might have this done ahead of time. The Transportation Section which packs all household goods and arranges transportation to the new station is not authorized to start packing until orders have been received by the officer or noncommissioned officer.

MOVING BY VAN

If the distance between stations is not too great, and the transfer company's bid is lower than rail rates, your move may be made by van. From the housewife's point of view, this is an easy way to move.

The disadvantages are: If at your new station you are to be on commutation, you will have to either place your household goods in storage, or rent a house sight unseen. Vans have been known to burn up, and to suffer complete loss by accident; but of course you will be wise enough to protect yourself with insurance. These hazards are simply a possibility in moving, and serious accidents are rare.

The transfer company employs experienced packers, and they prefer to do all the packing themselves, even to taking down the pictures and curtains. It facilitates matters for them if, for instance, all of the bric-a-brac is assembled on a table, all of the glassware placed in another space, and your best china segregated. No doubt you will prefer to pack your clothes and personal belongings yourself, and perhaps your flat silver and valuables.

When the move is to be made by rail, Supply lists and tags each article of furniture at the quarters, then removes it to the warehouse for packing and crating. Glassware, dishes, and silver are packed at the quarters in barrels, supposedly by experienced packers but sometimes by raw recruits who may be pressed into service in emergencies.

Just try not to watch when one of your Wedgwood cups is tossed across the room from one packer to another. It is easier on the nerves to busy oneself with personal packing in another part of the house. On a permanent change of station the baggage allowance is as follows:

Grade	Net Pounds
General	9000
Lieutenant general	9000
Major general	9000
Brigadier general	9000
Colonel	9000
Lieutenant colonel	9000
Major and warrant officer W-4	9000
Captain and warrant officer W-3	8500
1st lieutenant and warrant officer W-2	7500
2d lieutenant and warrant officer W-1	7000
Enlisted men (E-7, E-6, E-5)	4500

CLEARING THE POST

Before leaving a post on change of station, officers and enlisted personnel must receive various clearances. Having occupied government quarters, the housewife must see to it that they are left clean and in good condition. The woodwork, windows, and floors should be washed, and the housewife should inspect the refrigerator, baths, and closets to see that they are left in perfect condition. No foodstuffs should be left about, as the quarters may be unoccupied for some time, and food will attract animals and vermin. The final inspection before clearance will be made by the property officer, or one of his assistants, when he comes to check the property. Every article of property must be accounted for, from furniture to door mats and electric bulbs.

Army hospitality is famous when orders are received. *Despedidas*, alohas, or farewell parties, depending upon the individual's popularity, begin as soon as an officer or enlisted man receives orders. Between the parties and the strain of packing, most families leave their station in a sort of daze due to exhaustion. However, it is all fun, and part of Army life. Thank-you notes should be written promptly in return for parties and courtesies extended at your departure.

Transportation of Dependents

The government pays the cost of transporting legal dependents of officers and noncommissioned officers upon permanent change of station. If TPA or automobile travel is preferred to transport dependents, a claim for payment may be made after the journey is completed. This payment is about equal to the cost of railway fare on the shortest usually traveled route. You can see how this would eliminate side trips to Yellowstone or the Grand Canyon at government expense!

Allowance for air travel of dependents between stations is computed on a different scale, while railway transportation may be procured prior to making the trip by requesting transportation in kind.

Your New Station

If possible, it is advisable to report at a new station before noon. In any event, try to avoid arriving after four in the afternoon or on a week end. After a few years in the Army you will always find friends or at least acquaintances to make you welcome at any new station.

If time permits, it is a good plan to write the local chamber of commerce in advance for information concerning the town near the post. It will give you a good feeling to have some knowledge of the locality next to your new home, and sometimes small towns really "roll out the red carpet" for a newcomer in the Army who shows enough interest to write for an information brochure.

Unless you have arranged to stay with intimate friends, it is best to go into quarters and eat at the club or Post Exchange or put up at a hotel until your household goods arrive. Should you be forced to accept proffered hospitality even from strangers, accept it graciously. Never impose longer than necessary, and move into your own quarters at the very first opportunity.

Some Army posts have guesthouses; others have converted barracks made into "Hotel de Ginks" where transient Army families may stay for a short time.

At every post there will be new adjustments to make, new friends to meet; life will be interesting and different. Comparisons are usually odious, and it is well not to start out comparing quarters, social customs, and the personnel at your last station with those of your new station. A saying in the Army asserts, "To some, the last station is always the best, the present one very undesirable, and the future one the most desirable of all." This is just another way of saying, "Distant fields are always greener."

Regardless of how undesirable a station may appear at first, if you look closely enough you will discover some advantages. If you are so fortunate as to draw a good station, enjoy it while you may!

ASSIGNMENT: OVERSEAS BY MSTS

(Military Sea Transport Service)

The travel of dependents to join Army personnel is operated under a priority system, which provides that one credit is established for each month of service on the current tour of oversea duty computed from the date of the sponsor's departure from the United States. If you do not understand the point credit system for oversea duty, get your husband to explain it to you.

In addition to the priorities system, there is one other method of dependent travel. This, covering only a small minority, is concurrent travel, where a family sails together (usually limited to personnel going to attaché assignments).

Since March 1, 1950, all former Army transports operating out of ports within the United States have been operated, in conjunction with the Navy transports, by the Military Sea Transportation Service. This organization is under the control and management of the Secretary of the Navy. The ex-Army transports bear the designation USNS (United States Naval Ship). Thus the former USAT *Fred C. Ainsworth* is now the USNS *Fred C. Ainsworth*. All Army personnel have been replaced by Navy personnel and the former title of TC or Transport Commander is now the Commanding Officer of the Military Department. Thus all military ships are now operated exclusively by the Navy under MSTS.

To accomplish its mission MSTS has a fleet of C-4 and P-2 class ships in service including some completely air-conditioned passenger liners like the USNS *Barrett, Upshur,* and *Geiger.* However, all are clean and modern and relatively fast and comfortable.

The names of some of the more important MSTS ships are:

USNS *General Daniel Sultan*
USNS *General Nelson M. Walker*
USNS *General William O. Darby*

USNS *General Edwin D. Patrick*
USNS *General Frederick Funston*
USS *General A. E. Anderson*
USS *General J. C. Breckenridge*
USNS *General James O'Hara*
USNS *General Fred C. Ainsworth*

There are four ports in the United States from which personnel are shipped overseas: New York, San Francisco, Seattle, Hampton Roads, Virginia. Persons going to Europe, Africa, the West Indies, and the Canal Zone leave from New York; from San Francisco go passengers to Japan, Okinawa, Guam, the Philippines, and Hawaii; Seattle operates vessels to Alaska and Japan.

It is well to keep in mind that a government-owned vessel is a military post and that regulations are strictly enforced. For instance, in your packing don't include intoxicating liquors since the introduction, possession, or use of these aboard government transports is prohibited.

PREPARATION FOR FOREIGN DUTY

The first step is for your husband to make application through his commanding officer or through the proper channels at his station for his dependents to join him. It is infantile to become impatient about "orders," and under no circumstances must you write to the Chief of Staff of the Army, to your Congressman, or to your husband's commanding officer requesting transportation overseas. You might as well save your postage since the handling of transportation for dependents isn't done in this fashion.

Once your orders have been authorized, you will receive a sheaf of travel orders. Guard these with care for eventually you may be required to show or to surrender each of the dozen or so copies of the original order. This is part of the tape that is known as *red*; however, you will find that one of the mimeographed sheets will prove an open-sesame when you arrive at your port of embarkation.

By telegram or by letter from the transportation officer of the Army headquarters in which you reside you will be advised as to the date, port of embarkation, and place where you should report for your transportation overseas. You will be furnished commercial rail, air or motor transportation between your home and your port of embarkation, unless you prefer to drive your own automobile or travel by commercial means at your own expense. If you choose to go by train the transportation officer makes your reservation and presents you with your ticket. Your railroad ticket permits you to check up to 350 pounds of baggage, and a half-fare ticket permits 175 pounds. Should your baggage be in excess of these weights, you must pay the charge.

Again, may I remind you to carry your travel orders with you on the entire journey. Various officials will require copies to authenticate many acts of assistance.

Three Important Don'ts on Port Call

1. Don't "jump the gun" and report to the embarkation port until you have been notified.

2. Don't fail to notify the transportation officer of the Army headquarters in which you reside should illness or some unavoidable circumstance make it impossible for you to report.

3. Don't fail to notify the transportation officer immediately should there be any change in your address.

Port call. . . . When it comes, you go!

Medical Certificates

All persons traveling on MSTS transports must present medical certificates showing that they have been inoculated against smallpox, typhoid, and paratyphoid (within twelve months prior to departure). Typhus immunization is also required, and certain additional inoculations, particularly diphtheria and whooping cough, are advisable for children.

Infants under one year of age are exempt from smallpox vaccination. On South American travel, a medical certificate is required on trachoma, and if one is traveling in the Orient, cholera shots are advised.

As soon as you receive your travel orders, you should arrange for these immunizations. They are given free at U. S. Army dispensaries, but you must pay for any given by a private physician.

The present regulations are that no female dependents who are beyond the end of the seventh month of pregnancy at the time of scheduled arrival at the overseas port will be carried by the MSTS. Infant dependents between six weeks and six months old may travel in transports if accompanied by the mother and father or the mother alone or even by another responsible person who is over eighteen. Dependents over six months old may travel with the mother, father or another responsible adult.

Passports and Visas

There are four classes of passports: diplomatic, special, regular, and dependent. If you travel beyond the continental United States, Alaska, Hawaii, Canada, or Bermuda, a passport is required.

To apply for a dependent passport you must submit a letter of authorization from the oversea commander to whose area you are going. This letter arrives before your orders so that you will have sufficient time to apply and to have your passport at the port before you arrive. Complete instructions are given, and you must follow them or you won't get a passport. Without a passport you will not receive a port call.

You may apply at a State Department office in Washington, D. C., New York, Boston, Chicago, New Orleans, San Francisco, or at a state or federal court authorized to naturalize aliens.

You must submit two passport photographs of yourself, $2\frac{1}{2}$ by $2\frac{1}{2}$ inches, full face. If you have children under twelve years of age, they will be included on your passport. Your picture should include all minor children.

You must submit a birth certificate or other birth evidence for yourself. Your birth evidence will be retained by the State Department. Forms of birth evidence other than a birth certificate are a baptismal certificate with the seal of the church imprinted on it, and a notarized affidavit executed by a parent, guardian, or the physician who attended your birth, or by a reputable person who has knowledge of the facts which enables him to testify as to date and place of birth.

If you are a naturalized United States citizen, you must submit your naturalization certificate with your application. Your naturalization certificate will be returned to you by the State Department.

You must also pay the fee of $1.00 for having your passport application executed. This means you take an oath of allegiance and sign your application before a State Department agent or a clerk of a state or federal court authorized to naturalize aliens.

Your passport application and supporting documentation will be sent to the State Department in Washington. This is the last you will see of it until you reach the port of embarkation, and a complete passport with visas, if necessary, will be handed to you before you board the ship or plane.

When your passport is issued it will be picked up at the State Department by the Passport and Visa Division, Military District of Washington, Department of the Army. They will have visas affixed when necessary and forward your completed passport to the port specified in your orders.

EMBARKATION PORTS

As stated before, the principal ports of embarkation are Seattle and San Francisco on the west coast and New York and Hampton Roads, Virginia, on the east coast.

WELCOME TO NYPE (New York Port of Embarkation)

Military and dependent personnel who are port-called directly to Brooklyn have their choice of staying at Fort Hamilton or at the Henry Hudson Hotel, West 57th Street, New York City, or Hotel St. George, Clark and Henry Streets, in Brooklyn, New York. Processing teams are on hand at these three places to conduct the necessary administrative processing pertaining to passports, identification cards, final medical checkup, and hold baggage. They will also furnish information in regard to orientation, final temperature check, handling of cabin luggage, and subsequent movement to shipside or airstrips. Rates are reasonable for family accommodations. For an additional charge a roll-in bed or crib may be procured. The government pays your travel expenses to Fort Hamilton, if your travel orders so authorize.

If you wish to stay at the Hostess House either telegraph or telephone Fort Hamilton, but do not try to make your hotel reservations through Fort Hamilton. Fort Hamilton, Brooklyn, is a beautiful Army post located at 96th Street and Marine Avenue. It may be reached by subway from Manhattan (one hour) by taking BMT express train marked "Sea Beach . . . Coney Island" to 59th Street Station, Brooklyn, then the Fourth Avenue local train from that station to the last stop, which is just a few blocks from Fort Hamilton. Taxi service is expensive; however, don't dismiss the taxi at the gate of Fort Hamilton. Have your driver take you to Operations Building No. 28.

Accommodations at Fort Hamilton are limited, so it is not possible to provide space on the post for all personnel reporting for shipment overseas. Every effort is made to make your stay at this port as pleasant as possible. Your expense at the port can be estimated, based on the following, though all prices are subject to change. Lodgings for adults and persons over six years of age, $1.00 per day; 50¢ per day for children under six. For adults, meals average $2.20 per day; for children, $1.30.

You should plan to have sufficient funds with you, in addition to the amount you plan to take overseas. You may want to plan on a little extra to cover local transportation fares and perhaps some shopping and sightseeing in New York. There may also be expenses involved for the use of such other facilities as Post Exchange, beauty shops, tailor shops, barber shops, and theaters. Dependents are obligated to pay in advance for meals on board ship. Approximate charges per day and number of days' voyage from New York are as follows (*all prices subject to change*):

Destination	*Meals*
Europe, 8–9 days	About $1.65, adults
Mediterranean, 12–13 days	Half adult rate
Caribbean, 4–6 days to San Juan	for children
Canal Zone, 7 days	under six

Note: Should your port call indicate air transportation overseas, read "Travel by MATS," later in this chapter.

A Few Musts

1. Locate the Bulletin Board in your building immediately after checking in.
2. Be on time for lectures and briefings.
3. Read your Bulletin Board frequently.
4. Participate in the fire drill; locate the nearest fire exit.
5. Take notes during the orientation lecture.
6. Don't miss the boat!

Seattle, a Pacific Embarkation Port

Seattle will be your embarkation port if you are sailing to Alaska or Japan. Fort Lawton is a military reservation in the city of Seattle and is located on a strip of land bordering on Puget Sound. It is about five miles northwest of Seattle's city center.

In Seattle, port calls are issued by Dependents Travel Section of the Port of Embarkation, and the dependents are gathered together and quartered at Fort Lawton Hostess House three days prior to sailing. Here they are briefed or are given orientation lectures on their forthcoming trip and facts about their new homes.

The Hostess House at Fort Lawton has a limited number of rooms. They are adequately but simply furnished. Boys over seven years of age are quartered in the boys' dormitory. The charge at the Hostess House is $1.25 per person for each day. Meals are obtainable at the Hostess House cafeteria with prices well below those of commercial dining places. A special nursery and playground are provided for the children. The Hostess House is equipped with laundry facilities and is near the city bus line.

Overflow dependents are sent to the New Richmond Hotel in the downtown area of Seattle. Rooms vary from two to six dollars a day, and in addition to a coffee shop in the hotel there are good restaurants near by. A regular processing section of the Seattle port of embarkation is installed at the New Richmond Hotel.

Port	Meals	Destination
Seattle	About $1.65, adults	Whittier, Alaska, 3 days
	Half adult rate	Kodiak, Alaska, 3–4 days
	for children	Adak, Alaska, 6 days
	under six	Japan, 12–14 days

FORT MASON AND CAMP STONEMAN

To do its job, the San Francisco port of embarkation has three major installations: Fort Mason, Oakland Army Base, and Camp Stoneman, a Sixth Army Installation located forty-four miles from San Francisco.

Fort Mason is the port headquarters and the fountainhead and nerve center of the port. Oakland Army Base is primarily for shipside storage and movement of overseas supplies. Here is located the APO or Army Post Office, through which moves all outbound mail addressed to APO's in care of Postmaster, San Francisco. Camp Stoneman is mainly a personnel center, designed for both outward and inbound flow of vast numbers of personnel.

Fort Mason is rich in historic lore, with almost a century of Army service. Aside from the dock area, Fort Mason at first glance resembles a typical Army post. There is a chapel—a handsome structure in Spanish style—a P.X., a theater, a dispensary, a hostess house, a nursery, motor pool, utility shops, and warehouses. Facilities offered by the Officers' Club include commercial cleaning with one-day special service, four-day regular service; a post tailor for mending needs;

and a post shoe-repair shop. The Post Exchange offers a completely equipped beauty shop in Building 251, a barber shop, and a watch-repair shop.

OFFICERS' CLUB ANNEX

Owing to the extremely limited housing facilities at Fort Mason, accommodations are limited to dependents and to military personnel with dependents. Priority is given to unaccompanied wives with small children. Requests for reservations are recognized, but no acknowledgment or confirmation is made.

The daily rate is approximately $1.25 per person, varying slightly with the type of quarters available. The Hostess House is adequately equipped for a short stay. It is Building 257. The lounge has a good library. For the children there is a playground in the rear, also a supervised nursery where on the days of individual processing mothers may leave their children in charge of a responsible attendant.

The hostesses on duty are ready to assist you in any problems you may have. Safety makes sense, so be prepared for one fire drill while you are in residence. There is a cafeteria where breakfast, luncheon, and dinner are served daily.

Port	Meals	Destination
San Francisco	$2.55, adults	Hawaii, 6 days
	$1.80, children	Guam, 12–14 days
		Manila, 15–20 days
		Okinawa, 14–16 days
		Yokohama, 12–18 days

BAGGAGE—YOU CAN TAKE IT WITH YOU

The first thing you should decide is what you need to take with you and how you are going to pack it! Take everything you need and *only* what you need. The trick is to avoid duplication, yet provide for a versatile wardrobe. If you take two suits instead of four, or five dresses instead of ten, and a minimum of comfortable shoes, you'll have more space for accessories and the little extras that are so convenient.

The fifth freedom for travelers everywhere is "freedom from baggage worries," so pack sensibly, taking a minimum of luggage. If you have traveled to any extent by air with a baggage allowance of sixty-six pounds, you will have small difficulty on water transport. Each member of your family is limited to two pieces of standard hand luggage (not foot lockers), which will go into the cabin. In addition, you are allowed a train or make-up box for toilet articles, and you will be wise to select a roomy one to include essentials which you may need should your other baggage be checked through and not be available immediately upon your arrival at the embarkation port.

It will greatly simplify matters if you make a check list for each piece of luggage. I speak from experience on this score. I have traveled extensively and lived out of suitcases for so many years that my clothes practically leap from their hangers in the clothes closet into their assigned places of luggage at the mere mention of a trip! Here are my check lists:

Overnight Bag	*Shoe and Hat Trunk*	*Big Case*
Bottles, jars	Hats (stuffed with nylon	Dresses, belts
Toilet articles	slips and panties)	Jackets
Perfume, manicure kit	Furs (around hats)	Handbags
Sewing kit	Shoes in pockets	Girdles
Silk robe	Hose in pockets	Baby pillow
Nightdress	Lingerie tray	Folding umbrella
Travel slippers	Brassières, gowns	Travel iron
Comb, brush, soap	Gloves	
Toothbrush, jewel case	Spare stockings	

Cabin Baggage, Hold Baggage, and Household Goods

Personal baggage is divided into *cabin* and *hold* baggage. Your cabin baggage, which will be available to you during the entire trip, is limited to two pieces of standard luggage per person, including children's luggage.

Hold luggage includes the additional trunks, baby cribs, and other miscellany (such as dishes, kitchen utensils, small amount of linens needed upon arrival). This baggage will not be accessible to you during the voyage, but will be available within a week after your arrival. If you want to send other less imperative items for which you can wait two to four months, these should be designated as "household goods" and should not take up the weight allowance of hold baggage, which is 350 pounds for adults and 175 pounds for each child under twelve.

A good plan is to inventory and to keep lists as you pack; alphabetize or catalogue what is in each trunk and it will prove a great help when you are madly searching for Junior's ear muffs or your electric heating pad. One of the most convenient articles with which you can equip yourself before sailing is an ordinary cretonne shoe bag or, better, an apron of this sort. There will not be wall space to which you can thumbtack a shoe bag on a crowded transport, but you can always tie it to your bunk or around your waist. It is ideal for holding toilet articles or manicure equipment and may serve as a sewing kit. It deserves special mention because it is a standard article of equipment to the experienced Service woman when traveling. Soldiers used the khaki apron idea during the war.

Another indispensable item is a small bag, the knitting-bag type. Carried on the arm it will not be considered luggage, even if you are flying. It proves its worth in helping you keep small articles, such as sunglasses, hair nets, scarves, playing cards, bridge scores, books and writing material, with you when on deck.

Marking of Baggage

In order to avoid damage or loss of baggage, be sure your pieces are sturdy and durable. Easily identified baggage saves time for everyone so here are a few pointers:

1. Remove all stickers and travel labels; erase or paint over all old markings now on your luggage to be stored in the hold.

2. Stencil or paint, in letters one inch high or larger on side, top, and end of each container, your address as follows:

> TO: PORT TRANSPORTATION OFFICER
> SAN FRANCISCO PORT OF EMBARKATION
> OAKLAND ARMY BASE
> OAKLAND, CALIFORNIA
> FOR: JUDITH C. BRANDON
> CAPTAIN ROBERT L. BRANDON
> AO1230345
> MANILA, PHILIPPINE IS.
> PRIORITY 12345 JUNE

3. It is good to place a copy of travel orders for identification in each piece of luggage.

4. In case your cabin or hold luggage does not accompany you, it is recommended that you forward it by express prepaid to Port Transportation Officer, allowing plenty of time for delivery at least seventy-two hours before your reporting date.

5. A wise traveler carries his personal luggage with him and never permits it to get separated from him.

Remember, two pieces of luggage, but all women have hat boxes, jewelry boxes, and small packages which are allowed within reason. There is no better spot to apply the golden rule than on a transport. One inconsiderate, selfish person can ruin the trip for all of those with whom she shares a stateroom or compartment.

HOUSEHOLD GOODS AND AUTOMOBILES

This is a frigthening topic but don't worry, all will be taken care of for you except getting your car to the embarkation port. Privately owned cars are not shipped to the port at government expense; however, overseas shipment of one privately owned automobile may be made at no expense to the individual if space is available on an Army transport. This is fair enough, and you will probably enjoy the motor trip to the east or west coast.

Should you desire your car to be crated when you reach the port, that expense is borne by you; also, overseas shipment of automobiles may be made by commercial means at the owner's expense.

MAIL AND MONEY

Mail sent to dependents at embarkation ports should be addressed in care of military personnel, using the same APO number. For instance:

Mrs. James Burke
c/o Tech/Sergeant James T. Burke
Hq. & Serv. Group, GHQ AFPAC
APO 500, c/o Postmaster
San Francisco, Cal.

In order to avoid confusion, all correspondents, including magazine publishers, should be advised of the proper address before the departure of dependents from the United States. In time the address system may become less detailed.

It is suggested that banking accounts be maintained in the United States. You should plan to have sufficient funds to pay subsistence charges aboard transports and to cover all expenses while awaiting departure of the transport.

FIGURE YOUR FINANCES

Plan to have sufficient cash, traveler's checks or U.S. postal money orders to cover your daily expenses at the port of embarkation since personal checks cannot be cashed aboard ship or at the ports. Allow funds for at least two days' processing to include food, lodging, local transportation, entertainment, and purchases of personal items ashore and aboard ship.

Not more than fifty dollars in United States currency may be taken to overseas destination by each person. Do not purchase foreign currencies before your departure, since the Army Finance Department has adequate facilities for converting United States currency and dollar instruments into foreign currencies. Of course, additional funds may be carried in the form of traveler's checks or postal money orders.

THE TRANSPORT VOYAGE

If it is your first trip on an MSTS transport, you will find a few differences from travel on large ocean liners. A transport trip can be very interesting and a most pleasant experience; however, the first day out is always a trial and everyone is in everyone else's hair. After the first few days the passengers relax, settle down, and get together. Transport travel differs from the cruises of yesterday, when fine friendships were made at sea only to be casually forgotten as soon as the passengers landed or returned to their homes. Transport friendships have a happy faculty of lasting. There is something very personal and intimate about sitting at table three times a day with a group of people for fifteen to twenty days from San Francisco to Manila. You get to know their idiosyncrasies and their food preferences. Sometimes, perhaps, you get to know too much about them, but you can always skip a meal, you know!

And speaking of meals on transports: Unless you are a victim of *mal de mer*, or the old tub gets to romping too much in the waves, you won't want to miss many meals, because the food is exceptionally good. I like one old salt's description of passengers on transports. It isn't very refined, but it is expressive. He said that most passengers on his boat suffered from "t.b." One young bride looked startled at this remark until he explained "transport belly" as a very common ailment.

Don't expect eleven-o'clock bouillon, afternoon tea, or cocktails; and should you be more than fifteen minutes late at a meal, you automatically skip that meal. This regulation is strictly enforced. No meals are served in staterooms without special orders from the ship's surgeon.

PETS

A limited number of pets may be carried on MSTS ships. Pets are limited to dogs and cats. They must be declared when you request booking and they usually will travel on the same ship with you. Owners are required to furnish their own shipping crates according to specifications, furnished at booking. Animals must be cleared medically and must be taken care of by the passenger while aboard. Food must be furnished and the animal fed by the owner. Exercise areas are prescribed, but dogs must be muzzled and leashed while out of the cage. Necessary policing is the responsibility of the owner.

MSTS transports are equipped with automatic washers and some have driers. Laundry soap or flakes must be furnished by the individual. All ships have some electric irons available; however, a great number of ships have D.C. current, which will burn out the normal electric iron. The number of furnished irons is never enough, so it is suggested that if you buy a travel iron be sure it will operate on either A.C. or D.C. I might also add that it is wise to pack your radio as *hold* baggage. Often it will not work because of the D.C. current, or the steel hull, and even portable radios will be good only for a day or two. In many cases they cannot be played because of interference with the ship's electronic gear.

As soon as you go aboard, go to your stateroom and get things more or less oriented before the sailing hour. Keep your children with you during the excitement of sailing and exercise special care in keeping them off and away from railings, portholes, or any open area. If the ship strikes the pier or a tug strikes the ship there may be an unexpected lurch and children perched on the rail may be hurled over the side. Baggage or furniture should not be placed where children can climb on it to reach a porthole. Little ones should be instructed not to extend their arms or heads out of ports because of the danger of falling articles or swinging ropes; and older children for their own safety must observe all "Off Limits" and "Restricted Areas" in the ship.

The wise mother includes a harness for the toddler, and at all times parents are responsible for the control of their own children. No supervision is available, nor will any be furnished.

Bon Voyage Gifts

Boxes of assorted nuts, crackers, cookies, candy, books, magazines, and small baskets of tempting fruit are always appreciated. Baskets containing surprises for children, with written instructions about when they are to be opened, have a great appeal for the small fry. In Honolulu, candy leis made of lollipops or even of miniature toys find great favor with youngsters. Games, puzzles, and interesting juvenile stories appeal to mothers as well as to the children.

Fire and Boat Drill

There are very strict regulations in regard to fire and boat drill on the MSTS ships. The ship's captain is required by U. S. law to see that all passengers participate, and this includes *all* infants. Usually drills are held at regularly announced times.

Care of Infants

Every effort is made to safeguard the health of infants aboard ship. Formulas are prepared and dispensed by a gradute nurse at specified hours, in the formular room in the sick bay. Navy nurses are aboard to prepare and issue formulas for all infants. Any special formula must be brought aboard and the ingredients should be delivered to the nurse soon after you report aboard. Bottles are furnished by the ship, but additional ones should be taken for a day's supply when debarking. Canned baby foods are available aboard all ships. Adequate medical care is available for all passengers, each ship having a complete medical staff and a hospital suitable for almost any emergency. None of the ships has children's dining rooms, but some stewards will make special sittings for mothers with children.

The ship's load will be the limiting factor. All MSTS transport meals are served at dining-room tables, with four to six at a table, by waiters, as in any first-class restaurant. High chairs are furnished.

Entertainment

Passengers provide the major portion of their own entertainment. Gambling is strictly prohibited, including bridge tournaments. All entertainment is free, including bingo. This program is supported by the profits from the ship's service store (P.X.).

Liquor is not allowed, nor is it served aboard MSTS ships. You will have to sign a statement that you do not have any aboard. The sign saying "To the Saloon'" means dining, not liquor. In most sailings there will be no bon voyage parties aboard. Ships sail shortly after loading, and usually no visitors are allowed aboard, so farewells must be said hurriedly on the dock.

Some ships show three or even four movies per day, and have afternoon teen-age showings, or children's cartoon movies. However, this depends on the size of the lift and the number of children.

Cabin passengers with talent are urged to get into the amateur shows, and often a cabin-troop-class show is worked up. Some voyages will get a passenger list that will contain a good dance band, so four or five dances may be held. Dances are usually dependent upon the degree of passenger participation. No orchestra is furnished by MSTS ships. Usually a Special Services officer is appointed, who with the chaplain organizes programs. Religious services are held every Sunday and on weekdays, if so specified in the ship's bulletin. Read your ship's daily newspaper; it is for your enjoyment and entertainment.

CLOTHES

Travel light, but travel sensibly! You will not need all you think you will. Take few clothes, wear them often, and relax. The over-all atmosphere of MSTS ships is one of informality. Slacks are recommended, as well as low-heeled shoes, particularly for boarding with high gangways, and during rolling days at sea. Slacks are acceptable at breakfast and lunch. For evening meals a dress is required, and standards are maintained similar to those of any good restaurant ashore. You will have no need for a formal dinner or evening dress. In urging the wearing of low heels, slacks, etc., for boarding, one ship's officer used this phrase at pre-embarkation briefings: "You don't have to dress to impress us. We'll see you in housecoats, hair-curlers and bedroom slippers before we part, and we'd rather see you that way than visit you in the hospital." Shorts, sunsuits, bathing suits are allowed on ships in certain restricted "sun areas" but are not permitted for general wear.

Transport travel shortly after World War II was rugged, but today there are few creature discomforts or inconveniences. Two of the Atlantic Fleet ships are even air-conditioned, and crowded conditions have been relieved to a great extent. Passengers are all quartered in cabins, the sizes running from two to six occupants, plus a crib if necessary. Most have portholes and separate "heads" or toilets. Linen is changed regularly and table linen is maintained in clean condition, and napkins are furnished. Cabins are still shared by women and children of different families, but six is the maximum unless a crib has been installed. You must be prepared to clear your cabin from 8:30 to 10:30 each morning, so that the room stewards can clean. This does not mean that the steward will perform individual service or come on call. He will not pick up clothes, or perform personal services, but he will make up the bunks and do general housecleaning. Ninety-five per cent of the Army wives are unaccompanied by their husbands. Sometimes it is necessary to separate families because of berthing requirements. Husbands and older male children may not always be berthed with their families, although these cases are the exception rather than the rule. In some instances in the case of enlisted Army wives, husbands may even be forced to travel troop class, while wives travel cabin class (this is particularly true in the case of enlisted men of the lower pay grades, not entitled to transportation for dependents, and when dependents are accommodated on a space-available basis). In common practice now are the coffee hours, usually at 1000, 1400, and 2000 hours, on most transports (although the hours themselves may differ).

AIR TRAVEL BY ARMY DEPENDENTS—BY MATS

The Military Air Transport Service was organized June 1, 1948, by the late Secretary of Defense James Forrestal. The new command was a consolidation of the Air Force's wartime Air Transport Command and the Navy's Air Transport Service.

From its headquarters at Andrews Air Force Base, near Washington, the MATS global air-route command operates three major transport divisions: the Atlantic, the Continental, and the Pacific.

MATS has a fourfold mission. It provides global transportation of personnel, mail, and essential cargo for the entire defense establishment. It is charged with the evacuation of the sick and wounded. It maintains the official AWS (Air Weather Service), which furnishes complete, accurate forecasts, climatological information, and special weather studies for the Army, Navy, and Air Force. It operates the ARS (Air Rescue Service), which is responsible for the search and rescue activities needed to locate and assist any aircraft, military or civilian, reported missing or in distress at points remote from established air bases. The AACS (Airways and Air Communications

Service) provides a global net of radio communications, navigational aids, and transmission of vital flight information as well as control of air traffic. The FS (Flight Service) monitors military aircraft in flight and co-ordinates flying safety.

PORTS OF AERIAL EMBARKATION

Dependents traveling on MATS aircraft to and from foreign stations are processed at the embarkation port. Ports of aerial embarkation are located at Westover Air Force Base, Massachusetts, for Europe; Travis Air Force Base, California, for the Pacific; McChord Air Force Base, Tacoma, Washington, for Alaska; Brookley Air Force Base, Mobile, Alabama, for the Caribbean and South America; National Airport, Washington, D. C., for all foreign areas.

PRIORITIES

There are four priority classifications. The precedence with which you will travel is determined by your command or a higher one and your priority is included in your orders. In this way everyone is assured a fair share of available airlift.

A number One priority is granted in cases of national emergency and when the time element is vital to the welfare of the country.

A Two priority is granted to cover movement considered urgent and vital to the Armed Services or in case of serious illness.

A Three priority is granted to members of the Armed Services and other federal agencies to cover travel of interest to the national security.

A Four priority is granted for all air travel authorized when no other means of travel exists and for urgency in transportation.

MATS takes pride in making air travel a pleasant and memorable experience for its passengers; it is a carrying agency only, and does not decide what moves in its planes over its routes.

PROCESSING OF DEPENDENTS FOR OVERSEAS AIR TRAVEL

Dependents arriving at any one of the aerial embarkation ports for overseas air travel are welcomed by the processing clerk in the Embarkation Section. Here is the procedure: Present a copy of your orders so that the clerk may check all the pertinent details. If you are going where warm clothing will be needed, the clerk directs you to the Supply Section with a copy of your orders, and necessary warm clothing is issued.

The dependent, or the person responsible for the dependents if there is a mother with children, then signs *three very important cards*: a baggage certificate (one hundred pounds is your allowance per person); a blue card (complete with detailed information which eventually becomes a permanent record. It is used to compile the manifest, so guard this with your life. First you will present it to the doctor for medical clearance. Dependents must have taken all required shots and physicals before reporting to the port); a white card, giving your mailing address and the person to be notified in case of emergency. When properly filled out, it is forwarded to the base post office, which assumes the responsibility of forwarding all mail to the family's new address.

If you applied for a passport to be picked up at the port of aerial embarkation, you will be directed to the Passport Section. A clerk must verify the passport picture, and if it is valid, you sign it in his presence and receive your passport.

Your blue card, having been initialed by each section you have cleared through, is now returned to the processing clerk, who turns it over to the Passenger Service Section, where you receive your plane reservation and a ticket stating flight number, date, and pickup time.

After being ticketed, the passenger is free until the trip is set up. The SOP or standard operating procedure of processing dependents is basically the same at all ports of embarkation. Currently passengers clear through the port in one day and go out the following day; however, the procedure is very fluid, and length of stay depends on the amount of traffic flowing through the port and on one's priority for travel.

In order to acquaint dependents fully with the accommodations available at the port and to give them an idea of the general routine while awaiting departure, the processing clerk gives a briefing on such things as accommodations, where to get meals, where to secure baby foods if needed, the amount of money to carry, how and where to get traveler's checks. The passengers, in turn, have an opportunity to ask about anything that is still puzzling them.

Enlisted men traveling with their families are informed of the consolidated mess available to them. Women traveling with children are briefed on the use of the nursery and available transportation. Everything possible is done to make the waiting period as comfortable as possible.

Information concerning the country to which the dependents are going is usually furnished at the time port calls are issued. Such data ordinarily originate with the overseas commands, and enclosed brochures are issued by each headquarters. But don't let it stop there. If you have an inkling in advance, go to the library. Reading is a handy device for gathering information.

Passengers are called four hours prior to take-off and brought to the passenger terminal for final processing and flight briefing. This preflight over-water briefing is given by the flight attendant. It includes an explanation of the emergency equipment, emergency flight procedures, flight times, and anticipated weather. One important point to remember is that passengers cannot be posted for shipment until all phases of the processing have been completed.

Information on trip accident insurance is available at the Passenger Service Counter in the terminal.

FACILITIES AVAILABLE IN FLIGHT

The motto of MATS traffic personnel is "Passenger service is second only to flying safety," and every effort is made to keep all passengers as comfortable as possible. Of necessity, MATS aircraft operating on world-wide air routes are not as luxurious as commercial liners, but in-flight meals, hot soup and coffee, milk, and fruit juices are available. Pillows and blankets are also provided. The flight clerk has a hot cup that can be used to heat babies' bottles or to warm milk for older children.

It is suggested that you take an adequate supply of magazines and a book or two on the flight. Air travel with children has been covered adequately in Chapter X.

MATS PACIFIC AIR ROUTES

If your overseas orders are to Honolulu, Guam, Okinawa, Tokyo, or Manila your aerial port of embarkation will be Travis Air Force Base, California. The processing of dependents follows the general procedure already given, but the following specific notes may be useful.

The air base is located seven miles east of Fairfield and its twin city Suisun. It played an important role in war years as the "jumping-off" base for operations in the Pacific. Converted to a more stable role, it is now an important MATS terminal in addition to carrying on strategic reconnaissance.

Located in the heart of the Solano Valley amidst an evergreen wonderland of orchards and hills, the base is surrounded by the beauty of the California hinterland. It is the largest air base on the west coast and is the aerial gateway to the far-flung Pacific and Near East military installations which are so vital to the United States.

The following facilities are located within the passenger terminal:

1. Baggage check room (Room 25). Baggage must be rechecked every forty-eight hours.
2. Cafeteria (middle of building).
3. Travel Bureau (across from cafeteria). Passengers may purchase commercial rail, bus, and air-line tickets.
4. Post Exchange (Terminal Store). Tailor shop (next to P.X.).
5. Barber shop (Room 43). Beauty shop (Room 43-a).
6. Red Cross (Room 40).

On the base, shuttle busses leave from in front of Terminal Building every twenty minutes for all points of the base. Commercial taxis are also available in the Terminal parking lot.

It is suggested that passengers accomplish processing as quickly as possible in accordance with instructions received from the clerk responsible for the processing. When completed, your processing card is turned in to the Port Control Counter. As emphasized before, a passenger *cannot* be posted for shipment until all phases of the processing have been completed.

Alert bulletins are posted twice daily at specified times, and all passengers are required to check these bulletins in person. Should you not be alerted for departure within a reasonable length of time (one to four days), it is advisable to inquire at the Port Control Counter the reason for the delay.

Officers' dependents may eat at the Officers' Club, which also has a snack bar, or in any of the post cafeterias.

Both officers and enlisted men will be issued a mess pass at the Port Control Counter which will permit them to eat at the Consolidated Mess, Building P-7.

Dependents and female officers are billeted in Building P-30. Female enlisted personnel and dependents are billeted in WAF quarters.

How to Dress

Female passengers are advised to wear slacks when boarding aircraft, but ladies are not permitted to wear slacks in the Officers' Club at any time. MATS usually requires slacks so that Mae Wests or life preservers and parachutes can be worn decently; but unless you are specifically requested at the time to wear slacks, I think, for a flying start, a simple basic dress under a flaring short jacket travels better than a suit. If you find the high altitudes cool, you can slip off the jacket and roll up comfortably in your blanket. It might be hard to look glamorous in Alaskan flying apparel, outfitted in G.I. oversized trousers, Mukluks, parka, and mittens, but for a short flight to Hawaii of ten hours, you can arrive at Hickam Air Force Base looking very well turned out with a bit of planning.

Air travel tests your clothes sense. Wear a well-mannered girdle, not a new, stiff, uncomfortable one—if you come in the girdle category. Wear stockings that fit, low-heeled shoes, a taffeta petticoat to keep your skirts from "sitting out," and a smart print tie-silk or packable in a light color. This, with either a small or a large hat and a gay short coat over your arm, plus a roomy handbag, the shoulder-strap type if you like, will see you off the plane smartly anywhere in the tropics.

The trick, of course, is the co-ordination of everything to a master plan . . . a color plan. White, beige, all shades of green, bright blues, and yellow are your basic colors in the tropics accented with any exotic shade becoming to your natural style of beauty!

A hat with a separate veil so you can pin the veil on first and stay kempt even when hatless will be a delight, and be sure to choose a handbag more than big enough for your needs. Your handbag check list will include an American-money wallet, a foreign-money wallet, passport case, flying pen, pencil, small pocket diary with combination address book, a mirror, compact, lipstick, perfume flask, comb, sunglasses, cigarette case, lighter, and handkerchief. You will add six other incidentals peculiar only to you, if you are like most of us.

If you are the slender type for slacks, and "orders are orders" whether you are the type or not, invest in a well-tailored pair in gray or a dark color. Pastels are not to be desired, and certainly white slacks are appropriate only for sailing or yachting. A bright-colored silk blouse, or white with a gay scarf, plus a topcoat will see you off.

As for luggage, you will be allowed one hundred pounds, so carry light bags. Commercial air lines carry excess baggage at about $1.25 per pound; MATS may accommodate if the excess is slight or they may ship excess by cargo, but don't count on it. Weight-saving canvas or aluminum luggage is available. Another travel trick is to substitute a cardboard hatbox for your heavier make-up case for a short flight.

If you travel by air to Okinawa from the States, it takes thirty-odd hours with various stopovers. Today, the majority of military personnel sent to the Philippines is Air Force, with home station at Clark Air Force Base, sixty miles north of Manila. Clark is located on the site of old Fort Stotsenburg, originally a cavalry post, first established in 1903. After the Liberation in 1945, the whole installation became primarily an air base.

MATS PACIFIC DIVISION

The Pacific Division, with its headquarters at Hickam Air Force Base in Hawaii, has its terminal at Dhahran, Saudi Arabia. This division operates scheduled air routes across India and Siam from the Philippines, with refueling stations at Bangkok, Calcutta, New Delhi, and Karachi.

THE ATLANTIC DIVISION OF MATS

Transport operations of the Atlantic Division are directed from headquarters at Westover Air Force Base in Massachusetts, the northeastern port of aerial embarkation. Atlantic Division routes spread generally east and south, with stops at Harmon Air Force Base, Newfoundland; Keflavik, Iceland; Kindley Air Force Base, Bermuda; Lagens Transport Station in the Azores; Burtonwood, England; Paris; Frankfurt; Rome; Athens; Tripoli; and Dhahran, where it connects with the Pacific Division.

WESTOVER AIR FORCE BASE

Dependents arriving at Westover Air Force Base to be processed for overseas travel follow the procedure described on pages 261-263. At the conclusion of their briefing they are directed to the "Westover Hotel," which was established to billet transients traveling to and from overseas stations or on domestic flights. VIP quarters are made available to general officers, diplomats, and high-ranking government officials of this nation and foreign nations, and dependents' quarters are readily available for occupancy.

Two-room suites and single rooms with baby cribs have been set up; at times entire families are billeted in these quarters. Small but adequate kitchenettes with all necessary equipment needed for the care and feeding of children are located in these quarters and are at the disposal of the guests. The billeting officer maintains a twenty-four-hour registration desk, a locator system, and a flight notification system for the convenience of guests.

An additional feature to keep the dependents comfortable right up to departure time is the lounge in the terminal. It is equipped with a refrigerator, eight bassinets, one baby bed, and several strollers. It is open on a twenty-four-hour basis with an attendant on hand during the day.

THE CONTINENTAL DIVISION OF MATS

With headquarters at Kelly Air Force Base, San Antonio, Texas, domestic schedules are maintained by the Continental Division. These flights link the three ports of aerial embarkation at Travis, Westover, and Washington or Brookley. In addition, the Continental Division provides airlift for military forces in Alaska. Other Continental Division flights based at Brookley link the Canal Zone, Puerto Rico, and South America.

Chapter XII

DUTY OVERSEAS

NEVER in the history of the United States Army have American troops been allocated on such a global basis. During World War II small children spoke of their fathers serving on Saipan, in Guadalcanal, or at Casablanca as if these bases were near by. And indeed, they are becoming nearer with each speed invention that is perfected. The airplane can come from anywhere and it gets everywhere. Whether we like it or not, Des Moines, Iowa, and Moscow, Russia, are on the same aerial beam, and oceans, ports, and armies are no real barrier.

After our so-called global war, we need global thinking. "Foreign service" is really a misnomer as applied to duty in the United States territories and possessions. But since it is the Army's and Department of State's way of expressing a tour of duty in Hawaii and Alaska, which are territories, and service in the Panama Canal Zone and Puerto Rico, which are possessions, it is probably best to use it. In time it is to be hoped that the very word "foreign" may be deleted from our diplomatic and political language. To apply it to a friendly neighboring country might be classed as a provincialism on our part because today we are obliged to live with and among other nations.

Army wives today expect their husbands to be ordered outside of the continental limits of the United States, and if you have longed always to see other countries, the opportunity is now yours. But with this wish go certain responsibilities! Orders may take you to Rio de Janeiro, Copenhagen, Cairo, London, Addis Ababa, Helsinki, Teheran, Baghdad, Dublin, Ramat Gan, Beirut, Tripoli, Tangier, Oslo, Karachi, Madrid, or Ankara. Your husband may be ordered to serve on a Joint U. S. Military Aid Group in Athens or on a Joint U. S. Military Advisory Group in Manila. The Army also has Military Assistance Staff and Advisory Groups in Brussels, Santiago, Bogotá, Quito, Taipeh, Paris, Saigon, The Hague, Rome, Lima, Dhahran, Bangkok, and other places throughout the world. Orders may also take you to Okinawa, Japan, Germany, Austria, Greenland, or Fairbanks, Alaska, plus a score of other places. If it's "greener fields" for which you are looking—and who isn't?—they say that somewhere over the rainbow troubles melt like lemon drops, and dreams really do come true.

ARMY SERVICE IN THE TROPICS

It is no longer possible in this book to give detailed information on each tropical station or each arctic station, so it seems practical to give general suggestions with special emphasis on the places where more troops and dependents are stationed.

Panama, Puerto Rico, the Virgin Islands, Hawaii, Bermuda, Saipan, Guam, and the Philippines are considered tropical stations and the following may be of help to you.

First of all, don't sit around and grumble about the rain or moan about the heat. It won't do one particle of good, and if you keep busy you will forget about the weather. Bridge won't be enough to fill your time, and you will find yourself counting boats pretty soon. Take up the study of Spanish, or some other language, start collecting something, even if it is only sea shells. Go sightseeing in spite of the rain and learn everything you can about the customs of the place. Do something to keep yourself interested. Cultivate any worth-while civilian contacts that may come your way and, above all, don't be so provincial that you fail to appreciate and recognize the fine qualities of the natives. Make social contacts outside of the Army circles when you can. It is broadening.

A thousand Army wives might spend three years in Panama, Puerto Rico, the Virgin Islands, Honolulu, Guam, or Manila, and it would be interesting to hear their impressions; their complaints, gripes, and pleasant memories. There would be some, by the law of averages, who never venture out of the Army colony of bridge players; others who only transported their bodies and are mentally still living in the good old U. S. A. Certain groups will have become proficient in Spanish, while others will have mastered Oriental flower arrangement and Japanese art. This is only human nature!

HOW TO KEEP COOL DESPITE THE THERMOMETER

Keep as cool as an ice cube, and cultivate a cool temperament. By that I mean laugh at the thermometer in thin cottons you have brought from the States or feather-light Shantung. Look cool in short hair-dos, use iced cologne, and of course leg make-up instead of stockings if nature hasn't already sun-tanned you. Indulge in large straw hats or carry colorful parasols, the Japanese oiled-paper kind, if you must be abroad in the heat of the day. Make the most of the daily siesta period and relax.

If it is sizzling outside, try to keep the inside of your quarters cool by keeping them darkened. Have the shutters closed (if you have this blessed protection) or the Venetian blinds or awnings drawn. Insist upon as little furniture as practicable and dispense with useless bric-a-brac. Bare, highly polished floors are preferable to rugs and are much cooler. Overstuffed furniture is impractical. If you have brought it with you, cover it in white slip covers or some light-colored material. Work out a cool, cool color scheme. You can't go wrong, ever, on nature's own choice of green and white. Or perhaps you have in mind some combinations such as lemon yellow and gray that are equally effective.

Pianos that are built for the tropics can be rented reasonably at leading music stores. If you are musical and just had to bring your piano, be sure to buy an item called "Damp-Chase." It sells for about $6.00 in most piano stores.

You won't want pictures, as the dampness and mildew ruin them. In the Philippines blinds, curtains, and draperies are not used. The sliding windows, made of small shell squares, are very effective.

Government furniture, such as the dark unattractive steel dining sets, can be brightened by light slip covers made for the chairs, and unattractive bed ends can be slip-covered in some light, cool material.

Pots and boxes of ferns, hanging air plants, cool-looking flowers like gardenias, white gladioli, water lilies, pale pink queen's crown, light yellow hibiscus, delphinium, and carnations will strike a cool note. Carnations have a refreshing, spicy perfume. Large containers of dark green leaves look cool.

Dine on the porch or in the garden, if practicable. If the porch is screened, you will enjoy your meals more wherever there is a cool spot and an attractive view. Serve the coolest foods you can imagine. If your appetite deserts you, then the next time you dine at the Manila Hotel, the Candado, Caribe, or the Washington Hotel ask if you may take one of their menus. It will prove a lifesaver on a hot day, and will more than repay you for the embarrassment you may have felt in asking the maître d'hôtel for it. Serve long iced drinks, and skip the cocktails and heat-producing drinks.

Running water—a spray in full play on the garden just outside your window—will give a cool sound, and should you have a fountain in your garden, turn it on in the morning and evening even if the charges are extra for the water.

In the tropics government quarters are usually designed for comfort. Some are equipped with ceiling fans, and almost all include a dry closet. An electric light must be kept burning in a dry closet, but even so, the efficient housewife has the servants air all woolens on sunny days. Mold, moths, and mildew are a constant source of annoyance and ruin. Leather goods should be kept polished, and aired often.

Termites will eat the floor right out from under you, believe it or not! And what they won't do to books! Better leave those rare editions in the States, or varnish the pages.

In the Philippines and Hawaii you will have to accustom yourself to white ants and small house lizards from one to three inches in length that play hide-and-seek on the screens and have a field day on the walls of your living and dining room. The little lizards are harmless, and in time you will grow accustomed to them and even become quite fond of them. They eat the mosquitoes, and for that you will be grateful. One family in Manila had a lizard they called Algernon, and he became quite tame; so tame, in fact, that at a dinner party, while he was executing one of his figure eights on the ceiling above the table, he fell into the soup of one of the guests. The hostess was far more distressed at the loss of Algernon than at her guest's misfortune. That is the story, anyway!

The ants are harder to deal with. After an exterminator has done his best, you will still have to put the legs of the stove, refrigerator, tables and beds in small cans of water containing kerosene or some disinfectant.

Wild animals and snakes! You will hear all kinds of hair-raising stories about the python in the Philippines that squeezed a six-foot man into a mass of pulp twenty feet long, and others equally appalling about bushmasters, tarantulas, crocodiles, fierce tigers, sharks, and the horrible octopus in Panama. No doubt they are true in a measure, and undoubtedly the jungle and tropical waters are alive with monsters of one kind or another; but generally speaking there is not much danger unless you go looking for it. There are very strict regulations about women riding horseback alone, and few would be so foolhardy as to stray off into the mountains or jungle.

What to Take to the Tropics

Any reed or wicker furniture you may have

A sewing machine

A washing machine (nonautomatic) (In many places water is rationed, or the pressure is not strong enough to operate the automatic kind.)

Kitchen utensils (Iron rusts on Guam and Okinawa.)

Flat silver and china, inexpensive crystal or glassware

Inexpensive lamps (both floor and table)

Rain gear and umbrellas

Plastic raincoats and hats for each member of family

Baby cribs and children's beds

Electric iron, toaster, mixer, waffle iron, radio, lamps with new extension cords

Electric roaster

Before packing any electrical equipment it is best to consider the current system. Electric current varies. In some places 110-volt, 25–cycle alternating current (A.C.) is in contrast to 60–cycle current usually available in the United States. Electrical appliances containing motors or transformers wired for 60–cycle current cannot be operated in the Canal Zone and therefore should not be shipped to the area. Heat-generating electrical appliances (irons, toasters, vibrator-type razors, etc.) are not affected by the differences in cycles and should be brought to the area.

Some Things Not to Take to the Tropics

Overstuffed furniture

Antiques (meat for the termites)

Expensive lamps, curtains, or hangings

Fine rugs

Pictures and valuable books

Furs, woolen clothing, or blankets

Pianos and string instruments

Veneered furniture, expensive mirrors

Leather equipment

Iron utensils (rust)

Housing Conditions in the Tropics

Generally speaking, government quarters range from permanent cement structures and prefabricated wooden structures to Quonset huts. Because of the tropical climate these quarters do not require heat and the housing is designed to permit the breeze to circulate. Each set of quarters is furnished with a stove, refrigerator, and sufficient furniture to meet the minimum needs. Off-post housing is not available because of the substandard living conditions in the Philippines, Panama, and other tropical stations.

As for Hawaii, the Army was never in better shape so far as housing is concerned, the solution for government housing being the Wherry Act. Everyone lives in government quarters, thereby losing his commutation. The reduction in troops stationed on Oahu has greatly relieved housing in Honolulu. At Schofield quarters are old, but they have been well kept up. As to household goods, take everything you can ship within your allowance. The climate is perfect and you can use anything that you can use in the States.

QUARTERS IN P. I.

Sufficient bachelor-type government quarters are available for all military personnel arriving without their dependents. Ordinarily, off-base housing is not available owing to the substandard living conditions in near-by towns, so for this reason dependents are not authorized to travel to the Philippines to occupy off-post housing.

On-post dependent housing is adequately furnished to meet basic needs; however, for more comfortable living it is suggested that in your *hold baggage* you include radios, phonographs (converted to 50 cycles), linens, dishes, silver, china, glassware, cooking utensils, cribs, play pens, and high chairs, if there are children; also a supply of toys.

In your household goods, it is suggested that you ship a mattress with springs, a nonautomatic washing machine, materials such as chintz and cretonne for seat covers.

LIFE IN PUERTO RICO

Puerto Rico lies in the path of the trade winds, and the climate is tropical. Living conditions are good, and the quarters are desirable. The only fly in the ointment is: There aren't nearly enough quarters to go round. If you have to be on commutation status, then enjoy the experience. The exteriors of old Spanish houses are often deceiving. Behind moldy walls that look as if they are about to crumble you may find a charming old Spanish *casa* with a patio of incredible beauty. In Puerto Rico you really have to explore to find an interesting place to live, and exploring may lead you into fascinating avenues of life.

American electrical appliances can be used without being converted. Gas appliances cannot be used.

SERVANTS IN THE TROPICS

"The old order passeth" as far as servants are concerned, even in the tropics.

In Panama, domestic servants are available at wages averaging from $35.00 to $45.00 per month. They also may be engaged on a daily basis with salary at about $2.50 per day. Since there are no employment agencies in the Canal Zone for hiring servants, it is necessary to contact them through newspaper advertisements or by recommendations from residents. The supply is plentiful, although for the most part unskilled. Most servants are English-speaking Jamaicans or Spanish-English-speaking Latins. Occasionally good Jamaican or Panamanian seamstresses can be located. Army wives owning sewing machines will find them a valuable asset in the Canal Zone.

Servants in Puerto Rico

Servants in general throughout the area are mediocre, and most of them are untrained. They are far better in the English colonies than in Puerto Rico. Virgin Island natives are imported to work for Army personnel, and the wage scale varies. The Puerto Rican servants make very little effort to speak English, and many Army wives find it easier to do their own cooking and to let the servants do the cleaning. Servants are not too expensive.

If you can speak Spanish (a language every Army wife should make an effort to learn), it will be a great help in all dealings with Puerto Ricans. We are in *their* country, so we are the ones who should make the greater effort to speak *their* language.

Servants in Manila

One of the joys of living in the Philippines, now as formerly, is the ease of obtaining servants. Wages have increased since the war, but there is a fixed price on military posts varying according to the size of the family.

The average family has a "combination" cook and houseboy or housegirl, a *lavandera*, and an amah or nurse if there are small children.

The servants on the whole are kindly and willing, loyal and loving. Most of them weep when the Americans leave for home. Many wives do their own cooking but have a housegirl to clean and care for the children, a second girl to wash, and usually a gardener once a week.

To an old-timer it is always amusing to watch newly arrived Americans attempt to hurry the Filipino. It can't be done. The natives are too smart to speed up in the hot climate; they just keep at the job slowly and consistently and it gets done.

The servants formerly ate fish and rice mostly, but now many of them have acquired a taste for American food and will eat what the family does. Those who like United States dishes are usually easier to teach to cook.

Servants on Okinawa

Servants should be hired through the billeting office. Local Okinawan housemaids are available, as are yardboys and gardeners. Wages range from $9.00 to $13.00 monthly.

SCHOOLS IN THE TROPICS

A complete school system, which includes nursery, kindergarten, elementary and high school, is set up by the U. S. Army at most stations. The schools are fully accredited; many of them have American teachers. The school calendar in the Philippines, which was formerly from July to March, has now been changed to a better schedule for tropical weather—August to April.

In Hawaii many Army people prefer to send their children to private schools. Punahou, the oldest preparatory school west of the Rockies, is the most popular for Service children.

In Puerto Rico the public schools are out of the question for American children, but there are twenty private schools in San Juan, including several good Catholic convents. Most of the Army posts have grade-school facilities giving instruction from kindergarten through the sixth or ninth grade. The University of Puerto Rico is located at Rio Piedras and specializes in agriculture and engineering; it also has a graduate school of tropical medicine. The latter is located at San Juan.

The Panama Canal operates a superior school system including a junior college. Elementary and high schools are located on both sides of the Isthmus and are readily accessible to all posts. The junior college is located in Balboa on the Pacific side.

Tuition and books are free through the high school. Tuition for junior college is fifty dollars per year, and students are required to furnish their own books. The schools are fully accredited by the Middle States Association of Colleges and Secondary Schools.

CLOTHES FOR THE TROPICS

Cottons, of course! Or any material that tubs easily and looks better after its bath. Packables or noncrushable linens, washable silks, and cottons will give the most satisfactory service. Velvets, sequin-trimmed dresses, or fur-trimmed coats are not for the tropics. Often good native dressmakers are to be found, and sometimes Oriental tailors to make your linen suits, shorts, and slacks, so the clothes problem is reduced to a minimum.

For Hawaii, take your entire wardrobe, although today you can buy real island clothes in Honolulu. Many of the island prints are featured in sun-back dresses, pake-mus and holo-mus. A pake-mu is a combination of the Chinese straight dress and the old Hawaiian muu-muu. It is tight fitting with a stiff inch-high collar, like the Chinese dress, then has the loose, flowing, lined sleeve of the muu-muu. Holo-mu is the modern version of the holoku and muu-muu; usually low necked and often sleeveless, it does not have the long train of the holoku, but hangs just to the ankles. Hats are seldom worn, even in church; most of the women go bareheaded except in the Catholic Church. There are lots of good dressmakers in the islands, where you can have clothes made at a reasonable price.

The weekly fashion show featuring tropical styles during luncheon at the Royal Hawaiian on Tuesdays is very popular. On Thursdays the Halekulani stages a fashion show at the cocktail hour, showing beach clothes.

On Okinawa and Guam hats are rarely worn, though bandannas or scarves are a necessity because of the wind. There are few stores on Okinawa, so your shopping will be limited. Hosiery is seldom worn, though it is well to take a few pairs of nylons for trips. Cotton underwear outwears silk, nylon, or rayon. Be sure to take cotton clothes of all kinds: sun suits, play suits, bathing suits, sports dresses, afternoon dresses of organdy, voile, swiss, and formal evening dresses of cotton or washable materials.

Ten to one, you will wear a larger size in shoes after a tour of duty in the tropics. Anyway, take plenty of shoes, and don't depend upon the shoes that the native shoemakers produce. There should be a law against them, because more Army women have ruined their feet by wearing ill-fitting footgear produced in the Orient than Chinese women have bound feet, today! I know from experience, because one of the most embarrassing and painful of all times was when I returned from Manila with a pair of reptile shoes. They were made from a baby python caught in a playful mood in someone's woodbox at Nichols Field. I even had a large envelope purse and belt to match, though I must admit I never carried the purse or touched it with my bare hands without flinching. There was just something too personal between me and that baby python to ever fasten the belt around my waist.

You will understand my feeling, perhaps, when I tell you what happened to the shoes. Apparently, the skin was not treated properly because the first time I wore the slippers in Los Angeles on an extremely hot August day, the python skin started to contract. I was startled, my toes started pinching more and more, then finally the heels and toes looked as if they were bound to meet in their drawing-up process. It reminded me of the story of an Indian girl who "did wrong once" and was sewed up in a snakeskin and left to die out in the Oklahoma sun. With great effort I hobbled into a shoe store, and the salesman could hardly remove the torturous shoes from my feet. I left the shoes where they lay, and walked out in a pair of good States shoes. You guessed it, the purse contracted too and the belt curled up into a little infant snake. I shudder yet when I think of the python story of the officer on Corregidor and the chance I took with my waistline.

But getting back to shoes. Take all kinds with plenty of the play or sport shoe variety. Serviceable white linen, duck, or gabardine shoes that will clean well are preferable to suedes and leather. You want nothing that will mildew, because if it will mildew anywhere, it will in the tropics, I assure you. Include a generous stock of white shoe polish, your favorite kind.

For the Philippines you will want the same kind of sports clothes as would be good in Florida or California. Sunback dresses, if you like them, lots of play suits, shorts, slacks, and all the cotton evening dresses you can manage. Six will see you through a season if you take a good stock of material along for replenishing.

Take a variety of rain gear; the rainy season lasts from two to six months of the year sometimes. Be sure to have several colored plastic umbrellas, raincoats or capes of bright shades, light in weight and color, but the serviceable kind that won't stick together. Of course you will want several bathing suits, caps, and a beach coat or so.

In the tropics clothes do not seem of great importance and little by little, day by day, month by month, and year by year you will become less and less interested. Bits will disappear from your costume, depending upon your size, age, and occupation. First you may discard your earrings—why wear the silly, cumbersome things in the heat? Next you will decide that stockings are too expensive, and besides you have been told you have Grable legs, and you can see for yourself that your sun tan is perfect. Why all these arguments with yourself, you wonder! Girdles and slips have fallen by the wayside long ago, and finally some morning you will wake up and suddenly decide that you have missed too many boats or planes.

The coolest attire possible is worn during the day, but the government requires even children under seven years of age to wear at least *one* piece of clothing! The mischievous small Tagalog boys choose to wear large Baliwag hats; the Igorot waiters at the rest camp at Camp John Hay in Baguio decide on a G string, and there is a naughty parody on an Army song, something about the "Ladies in Manila," another one about "the men they wear no pants in Baguio." Ask any of your older Army friends, and they will sing it to you, maybe . . . with all the verses!

TRANSPORTATION AND PRIVATE CARS

A private car is almost a necessity at all posts. Automobiles should be in first-class condition prior to shipment. A bicycle or a scooter is a fine thing to include and will more than pay for itself; also, any vehicle can be sold, usually at a profit, when you are ready to leave the station.

In Puerto Rico the posts are large, but you will find a small car with a short wheel base that can be maneuvered on the narrow, winding streets of San Juan much better than a larger automobile. All cars must be licensed and insured to be operated on stations in Puerto Rico. State licenses can be used. The roads are not too good, and no one in his right mind would risk his life in the public cars or *publicos*, as they are called. Their rates are low, about thirty-five cents for a twenty-mile trip, but a conveyance built to hold eight persons usually carries sixteen with all sorts of freight. A passenger may hold a bird in a cage, or a farmer struggling with a wriggling young pig whose feet are secured with ropes may be your seat mate. The drivers are breath-takingly reckless. If life should grow monotonous, you might try a trip around the island in a *publico*!

In Panama an automobile is a necessity at all posts except Fort Sherman. A driver's license and license plates are required by both the Canal Zone and the Republic of Panama. The costs are low. Closed cars are recommended because of the additional comfort during the rainy season, though an open car has more resale value. Taxis are not cheap in Panama. It is fun to ride in the old horse-drawn Spanish *carromatas* of yesteryear, and pretend in the romantic moonlight that you are a Spanish queen riding in state or at least a ravishingly beautiful señorita of the old days! But the springs are not too good, and horses have a tendency to forget what they are doing. Yes, a private car is a necessity.

In Hawaii there are beautiful motor trips, and the roads are excellent. Taxis are high—in fact, much higher than in New York and Washington or any city on the mainland.

ARMY LIFE IN THE ARCTIC . . . ALASKA, NEWFOUNDLAND, LABRADOR, AND GREENLAND

You never dreamed you might go to Anchorage, Alaska; Halifax, Nova Scotia; to Labrador or to Greenland, did you? Alaska is a territory, as you know. Newfoundland is the tenth province of Canada and a triangular island extending across the mouth of the Gulf of St. Lawrence. Labrador is a dependency of Newfoundland. Greenland is a colony of Denmark and the largest island in the world. Only its periphery is habitable, however, since more than four-fifths of the island is covered by a great glacier known as the inland ice-cap. An ice-free belt of 100 miles extends inland on which three air bases and Army stations are located. In summer, brilliant flowers grow profusely in the hills and valleys. The air bases on all of these islands are held under the ninety-nine-year lease arranged by President Roosevelt and are to that extent permanent bases; the Army maintenance units and detachments are also operated on a permanent basis.

Newfoundland is in the same latitude as France, with a climate similar to that of Maine. Greenland enjoys a climate modified by the Gulf Stream with severe winds, occasionally exceeding 100 miles an hour. Weather conditions in Labrador are perhaps the most severe as temperatures reach thirty-five degrees below zero in the winter and ninety-nine degrees above zero in the summer.

HOUSING

Limited government-type housing is available for officers and the top three enlisted grades. Private rentals are available in St. John's, Newfoundland; also, St. John's offers the only modern hotel accommodations. Transient military personnel may be accommodated at military installations.

CLOTHING FOR THE ARCTIC

First of all, your wardrobe should be adequate for the tour and it should include suits, afternoon dresses, cocktail and evening dresses. Take a complete shoe wardrobe, oversoes, stadium boots, and rain apparel for each member of the family. Hats and gloves are important items. Casual clothing should include sweaters, skirts, and slacks. Cotton dressses are appropriate for summertime wear.

Each child should have snow suits—several pairs of snow pants and a jacket with hood. Children's caps with ear muffs are recommended for protection against the wind. In general, heavy clothing, including warm woolen socks, is desirable.

The exchanges carry children's necessities, and an excellent special order department is operated by the Air Force exchanges at the following air bases: Pepperell, McAndrew, Ernest Harmon, Goose, and at Narsarssuak.

Be sure to take personal kits for the care of your hair—curlers, shampoo and permanent supplies. A few beauty shops are available on or near installations in Newfoundland but dependents going to Labrador or Greenland will have to be prepared to "roll their own." Include plenty of creams, lotions, toilet soaps of all kinds.

NEWFOUNDLAND

St. John's is the seat of the government, and the governor and his family reside in Government House. The members of the American consulate are active participants in the social life of the post.

Servants of average ability are available, and the wages are reasonable. The commissary and post exchanges are well stocked, and the base supports its own dairy. Of course, all prices are higher than in the States.

As to clothes: Tailored suits are practical and are much worn by the British women in St. John's. Excellent British woolens are available. A full-length fur coat is almost a must, or a warm coat such as an alpaca pile or one lined with alpaca is necessary. An adequate supply of shoes should be included in your wardrobe, but all types of overshoes can be bought in St. John's.

There are many interesting motor trips, and the Newfoundland Railway connects all the principal towns. The roads are poor, but beautiful scenery is at your finger tips. In the summer, with the boat trips available, one is reminded of the fjords and scenery of Norway.

Newfoundland itself is a very poor country. Before the air base was set up, the people around Stephensville earned their livelihood in the woods by chopping down trees and cutting pulp. The additional work at the base gives them more money than they have ever had before, though there is a strict wage scale set up by the Newfoundland government to which the Army must adhere.

While the Newfoundlanders speak English as we do, some of their words, phrases, and expressions sound strange as, no doubt, ours do to them. For instance, instead of saying, "Where are you going?" they say, "Where you to?" Perhaps this economy is due to the cold and they like to save their energy instead of expending it on verbs which seem useless to them. Before the Army arrived, these hinterland people had never seen a typewriter, an electric stove or an electric refrigerator. The last-mentioned still intrigues the maids, and they want to place everything in it, including fresh-baked pies, bread, etc.

Quarters range from three-room to eight-room abodes and are quite comfortable, even to steam-heated garages.

ALASKA

Alaska not only is the key to the defense of the United States but is said to be the most strategic piece of property in our hemispheric defense. As our last geographic frontier, it is a focal point for world airways and serves as a vital military base.

The territory's strategic location, close to Asia, both across the Bering Sea and over the North Pole, caused far-seeing General Billy Mitchell, who lived there in his youth, to regard Alaska as "the Achilles' heel of American defense" and now his warning is being heeded. The Army, which has maintained at least a token force in Alaska since 1897, is now present in strength.

Alaska covers a lot of territory, and it has climates as varying as those found in the continental United States. You may be surprised to know that it is one-fifth as big as the entire forty-eight states; in fact, Alaskans discussing statehood for the territory often claim that Alaska can be divided into several counties, each as big as Texas.

There are three distinct climates in Alaska. Along the south coast, the winters are generally mild and the summers cool, with considerable annual rainfall. This region includes Anchorage, Juneau, Ketchikan, Seward, and a few other cities, but in this climatic zone most of the Army people are in the Anchorage area. There the average January temperature is 20 degrees above zero, although there may be a few days and nights of 20 degrees or more below. The snow is rarely more than a foot deep. During the summer the nights are cool, the days in the 70's and 80's.

The second climatic region is the interior, where both summer and winter temperatures are more extreme. At Fairbanks, Eielson, and Big Delta, all Army stations, the thermometer drops to 50 degrees or more below zero every winter, although usually not for very long at a time. There are protracted periods of zero- to 20-degrees-below weather during January and February at both places. In the summer, on the other hand, temperatures often rise into the 90's.

The third region is the true Arctic, north of the Brooks Mountain Range on the coast of the Arctic Sea, but you won't be stationed there. This region, populated almost exclusively by Eskimos, has an average year-round temperature of only 10 degrees, and has only fifteen frost-free days a year, between the first and the fifteenth of July.

Schools

The public school system in Alaska is excellent, ranking with the best in the States, except in the rural areas where the population is extremely scattered. The schools are supervised by a Territorial Board of Education, with school boards in the incorporated cities performing the same function as those at home, and rural schools administered directly by the Territorial Board.

Housing

No, igloos are reserved for the Eskimos.

Alaska's cities, which have practically burst their seams since the end of World War II, are only just beginning to catch up with the housing problem. Off-post housing is generally quite expensive, and not always up to Stateside standards. Especially in the summer, when the construction workers and tourists create an extra demand, your husband may have to look long and hard to find a house or apartment you will like at a price he can afford to pay. The situation is getting better every year, with the addition of many-storied apartment buildings and single or duplex houses, but there will probably be a scarcity of good housing for a long time.

If you are entitled to government quarters, you will probably have to wait several months before they are available even at the larger posts. The quarters are fairly small—usually consisting of living room, dining ell, and kitchen downstairs, and three bedrooms and bath upstairs—but they are new, and adequate for most families. They have electric stoves and refrigerators and the usual basic government furniture. Full basements have electrical and water connections for washing machines and clothes dryers.

You should consider carefully before shipping all your household goods to Alaska. There is little or no government storage space available, and commercial storage is very expensive. If you have more furniture than you can use in quarters, you'll be better off to leave it in storage in the States. As a minimum, you should plan to ship your living room furniture, beds, and all your kitchen utensils. What you don't have, you can buy in the stores if you are stationed near one of the larger cities—although you will find the prices slightly higher than in the States because of the freight charges. The majority of Alaskans, and most Army people as well, do much of their shopping from catalogues.

Eskimos are quick to catch on, and once initiated into the charm of gadgets, outboard motors, and radios they, too, order from the Flomgommee Ward catalogue, as they pronounce Montgomery Ward. They also take great pride in dancing to the latest jive tunes.

Services

The post exchanges and commissaries are well stocked, and there is little in the way of food and household supplies that you will not find. At the larger stations, post laundries will take care of your family laundry at reasonable prices. The post exchanges also have dry-cleaning concessions which will give you expert work and fast delivery, although at prices that are higher than you are accustomed to in the States. Servants are nonexistent. Nurseries and baby-sitters are available at most stations to take care of your children while you shop or play. Modern theaters show recent movies, both on the posts and in the larger cities. There are beauty parlors on most posts, and your favorite cosmetics are on sale at P.X.'s and stores in the larger cities. Local commercial banks, on and off post, offer checking and savings accounts and other banking services. Post chapels have regular services for all faiths, and Sunday schools for the children. Many Army families belong to the civilian churches in the surrounding communities and take part in the social life of the church.

Transportation

If you have a car, you will want to take it to Alaska with you. With the exception of a few isolated stations, most Servicemen in Alaska are located on the excellent highway system that connects Anchorage and Seward in the south with Fairbanks and Big Delta in the north, and runs eastward through Canada to connect with the United States in Montana. The roads are crowded on Sundays with the usual "Sunday drivers" looking at Alaska's magnificent scenery, picnicking, and taking pictures. Automobile maintenance costs are higher than in the States, and in the winter precautions must be taken against freezing, but if you don't bring your car you will miss much in the way of enjoyment.

The train ride on the Alaska Railroad from Anchorage to Fairbanks and from Anchorage to Seward offers an experience no traveler should miss. If you go by ship from Seattle, as most families do, you will have a pleasant three- or four-day sail to Whittier, the Army's all-year port in southern Alaska, and then a short train ride to Anchorage or an all-day trip to Fairbanks on a modern streamlined train through some of Alaska's most beautiful scenery.

Almost everybody in Alaska flies. Because of the great distances and the limited road and rail system, Alaska has more planes per capita than anywhere else in the world. Anchorage, a city of about 20,000, has one of the fifteen busiest airports in the United States, ranking with New York City and Washington, D. C. It is not uncommon to hear housewives shopping in Anchorage comparing notes on trading in their old planes for new, much as most of us talk about our cars.

Clothes

In the cities of Juneau, Sitka, Fairbanks, and Anchorage one sees fashionably dressed women. The cities are very cosmopolitan, and anything can be bought, but luxuries come high. Inflation hit Alaska during the gold rush and prices have soared ever since. A fur coat is not a necessity, but if you have one, take it along. A warm cloth topcoat with a removable parka and inner lining will prove sufficient. Wonderful bargains are to be had in furs, such as reindeer, fawn, sealskin, silver fox, and ermine, but the cost of making up the furs is something else. A fur coat will be less expensive if bought in the States. It is suggested that lightweight woolens be included in your wardrobe, over which you can wear a very warm coat. Take a good supply of sweaters and skirts, woolen dresses, afternoon dresses, and evening dresses. A pair of lined overshoes or galoshes and a pair of fur-lined carriage boots for evening should be included. The sportswoman should take along a ski suit with a windbreaker, and ice skates.

Equip yourself with plenty of warm slacks and warm underclothing. Be sure to include rain gear, a trench coat with hood. You may take a trip into the interior by dog sled or go up to Fairbanks to attend the winter Ice Carnival; so be prepared by taking warm but not heavy apparel.

Recreation

If you like to fish or hunt or ski or take pictures, you will find Alaska made to order for you. If you don't, chances are you will learn before you leave. Moose, caribou, mountain sheep and goats, bear, game birds, and rabbits have long provided some of the best hunting on the continent, as well as being a major source of food for the native population. Salmon and trout abound in the streams away from the major cities. However, game laws are strictly enforced as a conservation measure, and for the first year of your stay, when you are classed as a nonresident, you will find big-game hunting an expensive sport. Winter sports are excellent in most parts of Alaska from about December to April, and you will find as many skiers on the slopes near the larger cities as you will find in the major ski resorts in New England and the Rockies. Ski tows, lighted slopes, and good access roads with frequent bus service make skiing a pleasant sport for a winter Saturday or Sunday afternoon. Ice skating, snowshoeing, and tobogganing are also popular, as is sledding for the younger set. There are the usual facilities for indoor sports, including "Alaska's favorite game," bingo, weekly dances at the Officers', NCO, and Service clubs, bridge, and many more.

Just about every Alaskan, and every visitor and Serviceman, has a camera and uses it constantly. Alaska's mountains and lakes remind one of Switzerland, and the southern coastline, with its deep fjords and towering glaciers, resembles the coast of Norway. At many points in Alaska the sun is visible at midnight on the longest day of the year, in June, and in the long, dark winter nights the northern lights brighten the sky with their indescribable beauty. Film is available in all sizes and types, and photofinishing facilities compare with those in the States.

Tourist attractions are everywhere, and there are several trips you can take to see the Alaska of the Eskimos and the gold-rush days. In the summer, you might take a steamer trip through the famous Inside Passage, where you will see dazzling white glaciers, huge mountains, and valleys filled with exquisite flowers. Visit Sitka, the old Russian capital, and Skagway, where you can follow the gold-rush trail of '98 through Dead Horse Gulch, past Inspiration Point and Pitchfork Falls. At Ketchikan and Wrangell you will find Indian tribes, many of whose homes are decorated with totem poles. The Tlingit and Chilkoot tribes still hold their potlatches, or big feasts and dances, right in town. If you have the opportunity, you should also see Juneau, the capital. From Anchorage you can drive to the village of Hope, site of the first gold strike in Alaska, where there is still gold to be panned in the streams, and to the ghost towns of Ernestine and Copper Center.

Anchorage and Fairbanks have two outstanding social events in the winter, the Anchorage Fur Rendezvous and the Fairbanks Ice Carnival. Eskimos, Indians, miners, hunters, and just plain people crowd the cities for the big festival week, with native dances, dog-sled contests, and other reminders of the past.

While you are in Alaska, you may want to visit Nome, Kotzebue, St. Lawrence Island, or some of the coastal villages, but few Army families do, because of the time and expense involved.

The Army Wife in Japan

As far as Army personnel is concerned, Japan has acquired a reputation as "good duty," and the wives find their stay pleasant. It is well to remember that each American is an ambassador of the American way of life, and that the reaction of the Japanese is to a great degree influenced by the personal actions of the wives and children as well as the men of the military forces.

When you enter Japan, you enter the Orient and a country with an ancient historical background founded upon a feudal system, which only in the last century has been subjected to advanced Western civilization. However, the Japanese are most adaptable and have in the more urban communities adopted Western dress and mannerisms.

It is well to remember that the Japanese people are products of a totally different cultural background and ideology. To them an American family is as much of a novelty and object of interest as the Japanese are to the Army wife and her children.

As a nation, the Japanese set great store by ceremony and avoidance of giving offense. They are extremely polite, and there is much bowing from the waist and smiling; Americans, in turn, should keep their voices low and avoid in every way possible making an Oriental "lose face" by causing him embarrassment.

In January of 1946 General MacArthur severed the connection between Shintoism and the state, and at that time the emperor renounced his claims to divinity. In addition to the right of freedom of worship, Japanese women have been given the right of suffrage. In 1946 they voted for the first time in history. The breakup of the Zaibatsu, setting up of labor unions, and decentralizing of police are some of the further reforms intended to put the government in the hands of the people as a step toward a democracy.

General Information

1. For travel to Japan a passport is necessary.
2. Embarkation port by boat for Yokohama is San Francisco or Seattle.
3. Embarkation port by air for Tokyo is Travis Air Force Base. Baggage accompanying dependents by air must not weigh more than a hundred pounds.
4. All personnel must have a series of immunization shots.
5. Dogs and cats are the only pets which may be taken to Japan.
6. Normal full medical care is available to Army dependents. All emergency cases beyond the capacity of medical facilities in the theater are flown to the United States unless the patient specifically refuses to fly. General health and diet of dependents are closely watched in the Far East.
7. Dependents are under military law from the time they sail from the United States until they return. Air police, military police, and Japanese police protect American families during their stay in Japan.

8. If possible, an automobile in first-class condition should be taken to Japan with some extra parts. Speed limits are lower than in the United States and are strictly enforced. Driving is on the left side of the road. Gasoline is rationed, but the ration is more than adequate for normal use.

9. Walking in Japan differs from walking in the United States. Sturdy shoes with low heels prove more serviceable than open-toed, high-heeled footgear for shopping tours and walking. Japanese etiquette requires shoes to be removed before entering houses. One pair of walking shoes that can be slipped on and off readily will find many uses.

Climate and Clothes

Cabin baggage, regardless of the season, should include some winter clothing, since most ships travel the great-circle route to Japan through cold northern waters.

Japan's climate includes a variety of weather and temperature changes with hot, humid summers and long, pleasant falls with some rain as fall is the typhoon season. Spring is rather foggy and hazy though beautiful days are interspersed, and winters are sunny and clear, with frequent snows in the northern part but snow only once or twice during the season in central and southern Japan.

As a result, winter as well as summer clothing is needed, plus an adequate supply of rain gear. The P.X. stocks a good supply of clothing, including adult wear, children's and infants' clothing, and layettes. However, stocks are limited as to sizes and variety of items, and it is not always possible to obtain particular articles of clothing when they are needed, especially for children. Shoes that fit are the biggest problem along the clothing line for Americans in Japan. Well-known brands of shoes, such as I. Miller and British Walkers, are among those stocked but it is hard to get one's size. Most of the clothes are labeled "Californians" and the prices compare with Stateside prices.

Housing Areas in Japan

Sendai, Misawa (northern Honshu). The climate is comparable to that of North Carolina.

Tokyo-Yokohama, Tachikawa (central Honshu). The climate is similar to that of South Carolina or Washington, D. C.

Kobe-Osaka-Kyoto-Nagoya (southern Honshu). Similar to Tokyo.

Sapporo (island of Hokkaido). Warm summers, long cold winters.
Fukuoka, Itazuki (island of Kyushu). Summers oppressively hot and
humid at sea level, winters mild and clear.

Housing Conditions

Dependents were first allowed to go to Japan in July of 1946. Conditions are constantly changing and have improved, but there still
remains a shortage of housing facilities.

Army families sometimes rent Japanese residences, which are often
large, rambling structures, complete with picture windows and se-
cluded rock gardens. However, few Japanese houses have central
heating systems, and in most the American occupants must rely entirely on electric heaters during the winter. In some cases the Army
family occupies the entire house; in others the Japanese owners live
in one wing or section. In Tokyo a few families get permanent housing in apartments, which come in one-, two-, and three-bedroom sizes.
The housing situation in the Tokyo-Yokohama area is serious.

Japanese native houses are of flimsy structure with no solid foundations. The partitions are of paper screens with the usual sliding windows, sliding doors, sliding screens, and sliding planks to cover the
windows in case of typhoons. Storage space is the most remarkable
places—over the windows, under the windows, in closets in every
room and small ones above them. Most of the houses have delightful
gardens with tiny dwarfed crooked trees. If you wish to get on with
your Japanese gardener, include many ten-cent packages of vegetable
and flower seeds which will delight his horticultural soul and guarantee you flowers the year round.

Various developments have been built for military personnel. Notable among them are Washington Heights and Grant Heights in
Tokyo, which are in effect United States communities.

What to Take to Japan

Electric coffee pot	Steam iron
Electric fans	Iron skillet (essential)
Electric iron	Strainers, sifters, pans
Electric heaters	Sharp kitchen knives
Electric toaster	One good can opener (a must!)
Electric vacuum	Rotary egg beater
Radio, converted	Wash cloths
(and tubes)	Cotton material

Phonograph, converted	Zippers, findings
(and records)	Shoes (to last for tour)
Electric roaster	Mattress and pillows

The electric current in Japan is 100 volt, 60 cycle. Most electric appliances operate slower than in the States, so electric clocks and television sets do not work properly. Radios in Japan must be converted unless you live in one of the United States housing developments.

Almost every move is accompanied by breakage and loss, but maybe an overseas move is just a bit more difficult. However, wherever you are at the moment is your home in the Service and you should be as happy and comfortable as possible, so forget about your things. I like the philosophy of a musical Air Force wife who wrote me recently, from Japan: "We brought our piano and when it arrived, it was in four sad pieces with the keyboard dangling on the floor. However, a factory in Tokyo rebuilt it, and I'd say it is as good as ever. The chance I took was a long one but it has been well worth it to me."

Servants in Japan

Many servants speak some English as they have been employed by Americans before but their comprehension is limited. Many speak excellent English; some speak and understand just enough either to infuriate you or to make you laugh. They work slowly and are very kind, especially to children. If they like you, they give you presents, and if you treat them with consideration, they are more than grateful and go to far extremes to show it. As a race, the Japanese are extremely emotional. They cry very easily and, if embarrassed, will laugh to hide it.

The most important rules to follow when supervising Japanese servants are: (1) Be patient. (2) Speak slowly and distinctly. (3) Use pantomime. (4) Demonstrate how things are to be done. (5) Don't shout or display exaggeration. (6) Treat the servants courteously.

Schools

The schools are strictly Stateside, with imported books and teachers. Schools ranging from kindergarten through high school are located in every military area. Mothers should request a transcript of credits for schooling already accomplished before returning to the United States. The schools in Japan also require transcripts from the United States.

Food

Splendid commissaries are maintained at all major installations, and the larger ones in Tokyo and Yokohama are excellent. Reconstituted milk, produced in American-operated recombining plants in Japan, is sold. In addition, several bases have garden projects, producing a wealth of fresh vegetables and fruits in summer.

Every inch of possible land in Japan is cultivated and in the shortage of chemical fertilizers human excrement is used as a substitute; therefore no food should be procured from anything but approved sources. Most dining is done in private homes, since Japanese restaurants, with the exception of a few located mainly in the Tokyo area, are off limits to military personnel.

Sukiyaki is the most famous Japanese dish. It is made of strips of beef cooked with vegetables over a small brazier; the guests take turns in attending to the cooking. At the last, two raw eggs are broken over the top of the mixture. *Eels* are a great delicacy and the Japanese eat large quantities of seaweed. Another popular native dish is *tempura*, made of various kinds of shellfish, lobsters, and shrimp fried in batter; it is served very hot.

Yen and Sen

Within forty-eight hours after an Army wife arrives in Japan she is required to exchange all her United States currency for Military Payment Certificates (M.P.C.), which are the authorized medium of exchange on military installations in Japan. Printed in denominations from five cents to ten dollars, the certificates are referred to as script.

What to Buy in Japan

You can buy silk, but not in the selections and quantities you may expect. Look for beautiful scrolls, brass, kimonos, chow tables, tea sets, Noritaki china, lacquer ware, bamboo ware, tortoise-shell and ivory articles, jade, pearls, furs: mink, sable, and stone marten. Linens, and grass linens for kitchen towels, are a good buy; and porcelains, cloisonné, Satsuma, and silverware are coming back as in prewar days.

Recreation

Entertainment is on a high level in Japan; there is always something of interest going on in the cities and at military installations. All types of athletic contests take place on the bases, while the Japanese also entertain with judo matches, sumo wrestling, and kendo, an ancient type of fencing which uses long bamboo poles.

Within easy motor or train distance there are mountain, lake, and seashore resorts where the military operates hotels. There are also golf courses and tennis courts, and fishing (both salt and fresh water), boating, mountain climbing, and skiing are popular.

Army movies and stage shows are scheduled, and Japan's leading symphony orchestra and opera company occasionally make appearances at base theaters. Every village has its own festival, and all Japan turns out in gay kimonos and holiday attire for New Year's Day, the cherry-blossom festival in April, and a long list of traditional and religious holidays.

Famed Mount Fujiyama is sixty miles west of Tokyo and rises to 12,425 feet above sea level.

Try to visit *Nikko*, famous for its shrines, located in the mountainous Honshu lands of Japan. The temples and shrines, elaborate in architecture and adorned with artistic carvings lacquered or painted in red, black, or gold, have a singular beauty.

Kyoto is known as the classical city, the center of fine arts. Also, it was the first capital of Japan. It is here that the annual cherry-blossom festival is held.

Nagoya, where headquarters of the Fifth Air Force is located, is an important railway center, and also the center of the porcelain industry.

Osaka is the most modern industrial city of Japan, while *Kobe* is the main seaport of central Japan.

Foreign visitors regard the Tokyo Ginza as one of the most interesting spots in all Japan.

Observations in Japan

Japanese babies are usually carried papoose fashion on the mother's back.

The geisha is a subject of great interest to Americans. She is not, as popularly supposed, always a prostitute, although many geishas have special admirers with whom they live. The chief requisite is that they be pretty, and their primary objective in life is to entertain the male.

To visit a teahouse where geishas perform for mixed company is an experience not to be missed.

PREPARATION FOR SERVICE IN THE EUROPEAN COMMAND (EUCOM)

So you're ordered to Europe! However thrilled you may be, and while friends are envying your good fortune, you must at the same time seriously consider living conditions in Germany, France, Austria, Italy, or the United Kingdom; also, that great problem of what to take with you.

Because of the limited housing available at overseas bases, dependents are not normally permitted to travel with their sponsors. However, upon arrival at assigned stations overseas, all officers, warrant officers, and enlisted personnel (with seven years' service and above) who meet overseas command requirements may apply through their commanding officers for dependent travel authorization. Should you be permitted to accompany or travel with your husband, this is termed "concurrent travel."

Overseas commanders have established a priority system whereby lists are submitted to the Department of the Army periodically for the movement of dependents. Relative priority is based on longest cumulative service overseas and the length of separation of dependents from the sponsor as of his date of departure from the Z. I. (Zone of Interior, the U. S.) on his present overseas tour.

"HURRY UP . . . AND WAIT"

Of course, excitement will reign in your household when your husband receives his overseas orders, but be prepared. It will probably be one of those cases where "Hurry up and wait" is applicable. He will take off, and you and the children will do the waiting! Again it is the availability of quarters and the requirements of the priority system which determine whether you will be allowed to join him in two or three months or, in some instances, fifteen or more months.

The Army's mission overseas is really a hard one and dependents who are permitted to go overseas are, in a sense, guests of the Army. The Army of course realizes that men in the Service are more satisfied and generally do their jobs better when they can have their families with them. That is why it goes to such lengths to send as many dependents overseas as possible.

As an Army family you will have tremendous influence overseas and this influence should at all times be helpful to our national objectives. Army children also are just as much ambassadors of good will as you are. Courteous, loving, well-mannered children can be a tremendous help in showing foreigners a better picture of American life. Spoiled wives and children, on the other hand, hamper our best efforts at promoting good relations abroad.

American women should be very careful as to their appearance, particularly in public. Dungarees or blue jeans with loud Western shirts worn on the streets give the same bad impression that Europeans receive from some of our poorly done movies. We should be extremely careful in our dress to leave a good impression of the American way of life.

THE ARMY WIFE IN GERMANY

The primary mission of EUCOM today is the defense of western Europe. The West German Federal Government is located at Bonn, while the United States High Commissioner for Germany maintains his headquarters at Frankfurt. The mission of the Office of the High Commissioner, in conjunction with its French and British counterparts, has evolved, during the past few years, from one of complete control of German political and economic affairs to one of guidance and advice to the West German Federal Government in managing its internal affairs. The headquarters command of all U. S. military forces in Germany is located in Heidelberg. The Commander-in-Chief of EUCOM exercises operational control over all U. S. Army, Navy, and Air Force units assigned to the command.

Germany is a country of quaint, Old World charm—one of the historic spots where ancient customs still prevail. In addition, the region's colorful past is reflected in the beauty of the Black Forest and the sunny vineyards framed by the snow-capped Alps. Throughout Germany, Army dependents are looked upon as products of democracy. Consequently, the individual American's every speech and action makes a direct and lasting impression upon the German people.

If your orders read by boat, you will travel MSTS from New York to Bremerhaven, Germany; if by air, from Westover Air Force Base by MATS to Frankfurt Air Force Base or to one of the air bases in

Germany. Sometimes, owing to the scarcity of rail accommodations, dependents are required to pass a night in Bremen after their arrival by transport. Accommodations are provided on the transport or at hotels.

The time of year you arrive in Bremen will determine the type of clothes in which you should land. The winters in Bremen and Berlin are severe, but the year-round climate is similar to that of Pennsylvania.

Housing in Germany

So many apartment housing projects have been completed on the *Kasernes* or posts that the average family is now billeted in a two- or three-bedroom apartment. These apartment projects are, in most cases, convenient to an exchange-system shopping center or commissary.

The type of house will naturally vary in each community. All billets, family or bachelor type, are equipped with adequate sanitary facilities, electricity, and either central or space heating. For the most part the fuel is coal. All family-type quarters when available have as a minimum a living room, dining room, at least one bedroom, kitchen, and bath. Each room is also equipped with the necessary items of basic furniture, but at the present time there is a serious shortage of rugs, lamps, curtains, draperies, and kitchen equipment.

While it is not advised that fragile or expensive items of furniture and equipment from the United States be shipped to Germany, basic items, the loss or damage of which can be tolerated, can always be used and will make you more comfortable.

The following are recommended to be included in the household goods you ship to Germany:

Linens: table, bath, and bed
  including bedspreads
Silver
Card tables
Lamps
Pictures
Crystal
China, to augment that
  which is issued
Vases

Electric appliances including
  a refrigerator, toaster, iron,
  heater, mixer, radio, phono-
  graph (and records). German ovens are small and
  an electric roaster helps.
Kitchen utensils
Small scatter rugs
Knickknacks
Nursery furniture

Again, television sets and electric clocks are not advised. If you require a "Beauty-Rest" mattress, take your own; German mattresses are not the most comfortable, but you may like the feather beds.

Electric current in the European Command is both 220 volts A.C. and D.C. and 110 volts A.C. Transformers and reducers which will permit the use of Stateside electrical equipment can be bought in the Post Exchange and in German stores. Electric clocks seem to lose time consistently, but phonographs play satisfactorily although the tone is slightly distorted.

Servants

There are various reports on servants; for the most part German servants are satisfactory. At times, streaks of stubbornness are exhibited, which may be a national characteristic. Also, English-speaking servants have a superior attitude and take too many things for granted. The majority, however, have been working many months for Americans and have become oriented to the American manner of accomplishing things, such as cooking, tricks in cleaning rooms and doing general housework rather than only one type of work. Maids are plentiful and the average wage is from 100 to 200 marks ($25.00–$50.00) per month.

Schools

Nursery, kindergarten, elementary, and accredited high schools are now in full operation in Germany for the children of military personnel. American schools in Heidelberg, Wiesbaden, Frankfurt, Bremen, Nuremberg and other installations look like and are operated like full-fledged schools in the United States. School buildings are requisitioned former German schoolhouses, and excellent teachers have been secured from the States.

Competent accredited substitutes or "fill-ins" are recruited from the ranks of officers, noncommissioned officers, and the State Department civilian wives. In addition to the regular subjects the German language is taught in grade and high schools by licensed German teachers. German tutors may be hired on the side for all subjects including German and music.

There is a strong spirit of competition among the various American schools in athletics. A school annual which embraces the activities of all schools is published yearly. Parent-teacher associations are active in promoting the welfare, recreation, and education of school children and in providing money for extracurricular activities.

Newly arrived grade and high-school students soon feel at home with the American children in the American schools in Germany. Teen-age clubs for social activities have been initiated in several localities.

Shopping

The European Exchange System, commonly known as EES, is excellent, as are all of the well-stocked government commissaries. German stores now offer many commodities, and the manufacture of civilian clothing has improved remarkably. However, at this time the quality and price do not compare favorably with those of American goods. Dependents should take enough clothes to last one year or more. Yardage taken over may be fashioned by competent seamstresses and tailors. British woolens may be special-ordered.

Clothing is now fairly plentiful. The local German stores and shops are well stocked at higher prices. Children's clothing, especially for ages one to five, is scarce, and bringing a supply along is suggested.

Fresh milk is now available and is delivered to the quarters by the commissaries.

Recreation

There is a normal amount of entertainment in the homes of Army personnel. Clubs have the usual activities for officers and their wives and noncommissioned officers and their wives while there is an abundance of theater-wide Special Services entertainment with troupes of entertainers engaged from European circuits.

Many stage and screen celebrities from the United States take special shows to Germany for the troops. There are local Theater Play groups, musical groups, and the German Opera. Theater Special Services operate three famous resorts, Garmisch, Berchtesgaden, and Chiemsee, famous for skiing and bobsledding, as recreational centers for military personnel.

Special Services co-operate with AMEX or American Express Company in publicizing European, Mediterranean, and Scandinavian tours, for all military personnel and their dependents. The tours are devised to give the maximum in pleasure and enjoyment at a greatly reduced travel rate.

Recommended: an Automobile

If at all possible, take the family automobile to Germany. Many bases are relatively isolated and most Americans abroad wish to travel and to see everything possible.

Automobiles may be purchased in the European Command if you prefer through private agencies, such as Ford and Chrysler. Automobiles of foreign make are also available: the Italian Fiat; the British Austin; the French Renault, Citroën and others, the German Volkswagen.

Gasoline and oil, purchased through the EES, are inexpensive. The EES attempts to keep replacement parts for cars for models from 1947 on. Numerous German garages work on American cars; however, the service is not completely like Stateside service and sometimes the work does not stand up. This is also partially due to the highways in Germany, some being made of cobblestones. There are a number of main roads across Germany, called *Autobahn*, which are made of concrete and compare favorably with good roads in the United States.

Having made several tours about Europe with AMEX so as to get oriented, what fun it would be for a family to take off in their private car on a vagabond tour to revisit the places which most appealed to them!

A Few Travel Tips

1. The more knowledge you take to a foreign land, the more you will be able to appreciate the beauties of the country and its people.

2. Know in advance what art works, shrines, and landmarks are worth seeing, and learn the stories related to them.

3. Armed with knowledge, you will have an intelligent viewpoint, which is an unmistakable sign of a seasoned traveler. Don't transport only your body from place to place; travel with your mind, too.

4. An understanding of the language will open all sorts of doors to you. You will find a foreign-phrase book with four or six languages in parallel rows a valuable help.

5. To take the children costs little more and Darwin says, "Travel changes places from names on maps to pictures in the mind." The plastic minds and memories of childhood retain impressions a lifetime.

6. American boisterousness conceals from others the finer qualities of Americans.

7. Foolish spending leaves a trail of inflation. Americans have given the idea that everyone is a millionaire and also in some instances have earned the dreaded phrase, "those horrible American tourists."

8. Have respect for the Europeans in whose country you are traveling. Americans have a tendency to order everyone around in high-pitched voices.

9. Don't sound off about the superiority of everything American; making constant comparisons is crude.

10. Travel with the idea of promoting a better understanding, and of making other nations respect and like Americans.

American Express arranges tours to Paris, the Riviera, and the United Kingdom, taking care of every detail from transportation to hotel accommodations with tips, including the organized tour itinerary and program. If you are new to European travel, these conducted tours under the wing of an intelligent and witty conductor will give you a wonderful bird's-eye view, which is all you can expect on a first trip. Then, the next trip, go back and concentrate on the Alps, the château country, or the section that appeals most to you. The only way to really know a country is to spend some time living there, mingling with the people, not rushing through on a tour.

ARMY LIFE IN VIENNA, AUSTRIA

Austria is one of the key countries in Europe, and much is being done toward its rehabilitation. You will find it profitable and informative to study the history of this fine country and the part your command is playing in its present progress.

Should you be fortunate enough to have a tour of duty in Vienna, by all means take advantage of all the city has to offer. Vienna is occupied jointly by military forces of Great Britain, France, Russia, and the United States. Each of the occupying powers has assumed supervision of a section of the city, using existing Bezirk (district or ward) boundaries. Bezirk Number One is international.

Housing

American Army families live in the United States Zone and are assigned quarters in officially secured houses, apartments, or hotels. Many of the houses have beautiful gardens, both floral and utility.

Although it is up to the individual occupant, the Austrian owners are usually allowed to harvest their gardens.

Shopping

Army personnel do much of their shopping at the United States Army Stores, consisting of Sales Store, Post Exchanges, and Beverage Store. Austrian shops are well stocked with virtually all items, most necessities and luxuries. Americans make many local purchases of all types.

Identification

A special identification card for residents of Vienna known as the "Four Powers Pass," written in three languages, is recognized by all four occupying powers and should be carried at all times. Holders of this pass may travel throughout twenty-one Bezirks of Vienna and along the Vienna-Tulln Road.

Health

Army medical facilities are available at the 110th Station Hospital.

Government Motor Transportation

There is Army bus service to virtually all Army installations. While Vienna transportation systems were badly damaged during the war, all have since been restored. There are plenty of taxis of ancient vintage, but indestructible and not too expensive.

Schools

There are four categories of schools established in Vienna for the education of American children: nursery, kindergarten, elementary, and high school. The school building is located at 85 Gymnasiumstrasse. An exceptionally well-qualified staff of American teachers is in charge. Teachers of foreign languages and of arts and crafts are qualified Austrian professors.

Recreation

In Vienna there is a varied program of year-round activities: music, art, entertainment, tours, and sports. There is an American motion-picture theater which shows the latest films. Within the United States Zone of Austria there has been established a fairyland of vacation sports for week-end excursions or holiday leaves. Untouched by the war, these rest resorts have been selected for their scenic beauty, comforts, and seasonal activities. Picturesque hotels high on snow-capped mountains, others on shores of large lakes, locations world famous for skiing, boating, hunting, fishing, and mountain climbing are available to Army families.

THE ARMY WIFE IN FRANCE

Should your husband be ordered to France, you will find an entirely different kind of living. It is necessary to arrive with an attitude that you will accept things as you find them. The French are just as proud of their country and its traditions as we are of ours, and they have no intention of changing. You can make yourself miserable, chafing over the many inconveniences, or you can take them in your stride and enjoy to the full the many, many wonderful opportunities available to you. Your enjoyment of your stay in France will be largely up to you.

There are many tricks to selecting a house or an apartment in Paris, and it is wise to take your time. Desirable quarters are scarce and rents are high. Heating is very expensive and most houses are very hard to heat. In apartments a charge is made for heating over and above the monthly rental. It is helpful to rent a place previously occupied by Americans because not only can they better explain the advantages and disadvantages of living conditions but in most cases they have improved the comfort of the quarters.

Whether to live in Paris or the suburbs depends largely upon your own taste. Families with small children or teen-age boys usually prefer the suburbs. Make sure that you locate near to transportation; life can be very complicated if you are not reasonably near the train, bus, or *Métro* (subway). You can estimate the average rent to be around $200, and this does not include utilities.

Regardless of what you have heard about Paris shops, unless you can afford the *haute couture* fashions, you will find clothes very expensive. Lingerie and nylons are good at the P.X. Be sure to include plenty of *warm clothing*. Except for a short period in the summer, Paris is damp and cold. Many women find winter-weight cotton underwear practical. Take sufficient pairs of shoes to last throughout your stay as French lasts are different from ours, and also French shoes are expensive. Walking shoes, preferably those with crepe-rubber soles, to ward off the dampness, will be useful. You are advised to take suits, a warm coat, sweaters, wool dresses, raincoat, galoshes, umbrella, cocktail dresses (black and dark colors should dominate), dinner dresses, and evening clothes. Naturally the number of evening clothes you will need will depend largely on the nature of your husband's assignment. For your children take plenty of warm clothes. It is well to open an account with a U. S. children's shoe store, so that shoes may be reordered as needed.

Household Effects

Articles that will make life more comfortable:

Lamps—a must
Rugs—small scatter variety
Furniture—no, but small tables, perhaps your favorite bed and chair
Refrigerator—yes, even if you have to put it in the living room
Washing machine—nonautomatic
Vacuum cleaner—very useful
Stove—yes, gas is preferable
Radio—yes
Television set—no
Dishes—yes
Blankets—definitely!
Pillows—yes, French pillows are larger than ours and do not fit our pillow slips
Electric appliances, such as an iron and toaster—yes

Medical Attention

The Army operates a dispensary complete with hospital and dental care. All emergencies, general illnesses, deliveries, shots, etc., are taken care of in the American Hospital.

Servants

You will find it necessary to employ one or more servants. Finding good help is one of the keys to an enjoyable stay in Paris. Again, if you are lucky enough to find servants who have previously worked for Americans, you will have a head start.

Here are some of the headaches: Finding accommodations requires diligent searching; living in hotels is very expensive; commissaries carry a restricted variety of stock; and sometimes it is necessary to travel for a distance of 55 miles (110 miles round trip) to make commissary purchases. Coal is expensive (approximately $35.00 per ton). Bathroom facilities are antiquated but passable. Public transportation is nonexistent between some housing areas and duty stations. Travel by private automobile is expensive.

However, just walking through Paris is an exciting experience, not to mention living there. Somebody once said that "To study Paris is to gain a window that opens out onto the history of Europe." Nostalgically my mind runs back over past days there . . . to the gay, painted shutters . . . lilacs in bloom in the Bois de Boulogne . . . the lacelike shaft of the Eiffel Tower . . . the bookstalls along the Seine . . . crêpes suzette at the Café de la Paix . . . Mass at Notre Dame . . . an afternoon at Versailles. There is no city in the world like it.

Bon voyage, et bonne chance!

THE UNITED KINGDOM

(For the following interesting account of "The U. S. Army in England" I am indebted to Captain Quentin Keith, Sig C[MI], U. S. A.)

Although the "sceptered isle" is host to larger numbers of American airmen, the U.S. Army has a fair contingent of antiaircraft artillery personnel who serve as a protection for the air bases in the vital area of East Anglia, near the North Sea. Having a headquarters in Maidenhall, Suffolk, a typical English market-town dating back to Roman times, Army personnel can move about freely (especially in small cars) with no language barrier in mingling with the hospitable dairy-farmers and horse racing enthusiasts in this region. For close by is the famous racing center of Newmarket, and many old towns such as Ipswich, Sudbury and Bury St. Edmunds offer shopping centers and entertainment. Handy for intellectual stimulus is the great university town of Cambridge, and London is only a few hours by train.

An assignment in England is considered especially fortunate because of the similarity of British life to ours. However, English weather is perverse and requires great patience of its American guests. Tweeds and suits are more practical and necessary than frills and feathers, if one expects to keep warm. English roads were not built to sustain American cars; if one wishes to explore the beauties of the English countryside, including the little spots on the road with thatched roofs, it is best to travel in a British or French automobile. It is also much cheaper. Human nature being what it is and conditions as they are now in England, the price automatically goes up when a Cadillac approaches the old inn yard.

Like everywhere else outside the United States, females in dungarees are not appreciated. Slacks are tolerated only if they have a feminine cut;

otherwise, the American woman is apt to be embarrassed by being hailed
before the local "m'lud" for impersonating a male. This has happened to
more than one innocent wife who thoughtlessly marched into the shopping
battle in blue jeans and was returned to her husband by Scotland Yard.

The core of English life centers around that wonderful and unique institution called "the local pub," which offers much pleasure in communi-
cating with all types of Britishers. Thankfully enough, no juke boxes,
pin-ups, or chromium bars interfere with the simplicity and homeliness of
its friendly atmosphere.

England is famous for its fine schools, especially for boys. You will find
that the local "council" schools for both sexes offer a substantial and
sturdy environment for the teaching of the "three r's," and for very little
money your son may have the advantages of a "public" school education,
which is the model for intellectual leadership in England. Many Army
fathers have found the discipline and emphasis upon self-reliance to be
excellent experience for their young hopefuls. A year or two at Marl-
borough, Clifton, Charterhouse, or Winchester can be of immense benefit
to your son. Likewise there are schools for girls which measure up to the
highest standards of the American mother.

Fortunately you will not be required to live solely on British rations.
That would be too much to ask of any American wife who is used to
bountiful markets. However, in dining you will find the English table to
be in essence a most refined and elegant work of art. It only lacks proper
food. If a little American meat and spice is added to the party, the results
will be a marriage, not of convenience, but of love.

England is a small country but the city of London covers 700
square miles. In fact the whole of Great Britain—comprising England, Scotland, and Wales—is scarcely larger than Minnesota. More-
over, no part of England is more than 100 miles from the sea.

The climate compares with that in Seattle or Boston, and cold and
dampness prevail three-fourths of the year. Days are long in summer
and very short in winter.

The normal tour of duty is three years, and dependents are permitted to join individuals on permanent assignment in the United
Kingdom.

Housing

Furnished houses and apartments suitable for the average family
come high. When you are looking for a house to rent, it is advisable
to take along an English friend. Most of the British people make
every effort to be friendly to Americans. Again, may I stress: "Every
American who goes to England is, in a sense, an ambassador for the

United States." Even though the language is the same in Britain, remember that the British have different ways of doing things. This is all by way of prefacing a few don'ts:

1. Don't expect a kitchen like the well-equipped ones in the U. S. An electric refrigerator in England is something of a luxury.

2. Don't look for a place with central heat. Be prepared to provide your own system for heating.

3. Don't expect your electrical household appliances to work without checking the type of electric current before you sign a lease for a house or flat. You may have to buy a transformer.

4. Don't complain about the time it takes the British laundries. It usually takes from one to two weeks for laundry since it is necessary to use some type of chemical in the water. The chemical with the lime in the water tends to shorten the life of clothing about 25 per cent, it is said.

As an Army wife you may find it necessary to revise your sights downward on housing and your housing expenses upward if you are going to live in London. It is well to consult a legal adviser and officers who have experienced the local customs on leases before making final arrangements on housing. Rent is always payable in advance, and often three months' advance rent is required. Agents' fees and dilapidations deposits frequently add to the high initial cost. You may be surprised to find that leases for five years or more are frequently required.

As Captain Keith mentioned, "English weather is perverse." The cold is penetrating because of high humidity, so this situation can best be met by dressing, as the English do, in woolen underclothing and heavy suits. In summer there is an occasional wave of high temperature, but it does not usually last for more than two or three weeks. Take plenty of warm clothes such as sweaters and stoles to wear around the house. Heat in most cases comes from a small coal grate in each room. One wife suggests including a pressure cooker, since you may find it useful for tenderizing tough cuts of meat. One other tip is this: If you are planning to take your car, you might buy a small British car instead. Cost of maintaining the large American car is very high.

Entry of Pets into the United Kingdom

It is suggested that you think twice before you plan on taking household pets to England. There are various restrictions and require-

ments imposed by the British customs authorities which make such
transportation rather impractical. The general cost is $400 per pet,
and this naturally varies with the breed of pet being transported. In
addition, all pets entering the United Kingdom are required by
British law to be detained for a period of not less than six months in
a registered Veterinary Quarantine Kennel.

ARMY DEPENDENTS IN FRENCH MOROCCO

Morocco, to many of us, is associated with the Sahara, but Army
people who have been stationed there describe it as a "cool country
with a hot sun," meaning it is hot in the sun and cool in the shade.
Morocco is much like California—like living in San Francisco and
visiting Death Valley and Palm Springs. There is a critical housing
shortage and most of the housing available is below American standards. Officers and enlisted men occupy temporary-type "dallas huts"
and tents.

It is almost impossible to obtain hotel accommodations unless
reservations are made well in advance. The rates are usually lower
than in American hotels, but accommodations are not comparable.
Private baths are considered a luxury.

Household Goods

If you wish to be comfortable, you should ship your own household goods and furniture, particularly ironing boards, kitchen cutlery,
household linens, and all equipment to take care of infants and small
children. You will find rugs useful on the customary tile floors. Of
course the stores in French Morocco are well stocked with household
goods and furniture (there is no dearth or shortage), but the prices
exceed those of the U. S. by 50 to 300 per cent. Children's toys are
very expensive. In the furniture line, beautiful French and Spanish
antiques can be purchased; Moroccan rugs are also worth buying.
Rabat is a famous rug center. French, Spanish, Jewish, and Arabic
servants are available at wages ranging from 55¢ to $1.50 a day.
Again, there is the language barrier.

Clothing

In general, it is suggested that complete summer and winter wardrobes for all members of the family be secured before leaving the
United States. Women wear hats for all occasions other than extremely
informal or formal affairs. Raincoats are a must, and again, complete

your shoe wardrobe before leaving the U. S. Women's low-heeled shoes can be purchased, but high-heeled shoes should be ordered from or purchased in the United States. Yard goods can also be purchased, but at high prices. Cotton goods should be shipped from the U. S., and if you plan to sew, you should include sewing notions and patterns.

Schools, Medical and Recreational Facilities

Service-operated schools providing for grades one through eight have been established.

Dependent care in French Morocco is limited to emergency cases. Seriously ill dependents or those requiring care and treatment are evacuated to the nearest adequate Armed Forces Medical Facility.

French Morocco offers swimming and bathing at the beach resorts, skiing at mountain resorts, fishing, and hunting. During the winter months Casablanca and Rabat offer horse racing and dog racing. Two golf courses are also available. Also, the intense bright sunlight, plus the unusual scenery and local life, makes Morocco an ideal country for camera enthusiasts. Officers' Clubs and NCO Clubs provide a variety of social activities.

ANKARA, TURKEY

Not many, but a few Army wives may have the experience of living in the Middle East. It is hard to describe Turkey, so I shall give only a few pointers as related to me by the wife of an Army attaché.

First of all she suggests that you take everything you can within your baggage allowance. Most of the entertaining will be done in your home and you will need all your nicest things from the sofa to the silver service. In addition, everyday china and glassware will be needed because the servants smash it with the greatest of ease. She says, "I personally would never come to Turkey without everything I own." It seems the windows are unscreened and are very wide. Also, there are many French doors. A bolt of window material; another bolt for draw drapes, as there are no window shades; and the drapes help keep the cold weather out. A roll of wide-width window screen will prove a joy, and should you find a place previously occupied by Americans, you can easily dispose of the screen at no loss. Other fixtures needed will be curtain rods with extensions, towel racks, and all sorts of things from the dime store, such as picture hooks, picture wire, tacks, etc.

An electric refrigerator, a nonautomatic washing machine, and a small bottled-gas cooking stove will make your life happier. Don't bother to take electric heaters; they are too expensive to operate. A 2000-volt transformer is needed to handle such things as toasters, irons, and waffle irons. A Halicrafter radio with short-wave band is fine if you want news from home.

Ankara is cold in winter. The houses are poorly heated, so warm clothes and dresses with jackets or sleeves are really essential. Warm slacks are all right for indoors but are not worn on the streets. Include plenty of jerseys, sweaters, and warm house slippers. Again, your entire shoe wardrobe. Most wives order clothes from magazines or a professional shopper.

A school is in progress using the Calvert system, but since Calvert doesn't go farther than the first year of high school your teen-ager may have to be tutored. There is a Teen-Club in Ankara and Boy and Girl Scouts are being organized, plus a newly formed Wives' Club with all the usual activities.

Dhahran, Saudi Arabia

Even though on the underside of the world, life for the Army wife in Arabia goes on just about as on a Stateside post. There is a definite winter season from November to March, comparable to California's or Florida's. Standard equipment for winter should include a warm topcoat, a raincoat, sweaters, gloves, and jackets.

You will need an unusually large number of cotton dresses for the summer season, which lasts from May to October. Include two or more swim suits and a beach robe. The extreme brine of the water plus Old Sol at his best tend to fade suits and they deteriorate quickly. Sunglasses, both for yourself and your children, are a must, owing to the unusual glare from the sand. If you wear glasses, take at least two pairs and make arrangements with your oculist to handle requests for replacement or repairs since there are no facilities therefor.

Quarters

The houses are made of rock with concrete floors throughout. One-bedroom houses have a small dinette as part of the kitchen; two-bedroom houses have no dinette or dining room but ample space in the kitchen for a breakfast table; three-bedroom houses have a dining room and two baths. The windows are all of the same unusual size—

28½″ x 54″— and 85 inches from top of rod to floor. Round wood curtain poles are furnished, but no window shades!

The quarters are equipped with electric stoves, refrigerators, and the usual G.I. furniture but no rugs. Because of sand native matting is used and a vacuum cleaner proves a definite aid in housekeeping. Because of the shipping distance involved, it is best to ship inexpensive dishes and glassware. These can be obtained locally but are very expensive.

All quarters and offices are air conditioned. Quarters on the post are for key personnel only, and there is no off-post housing.

You should take your flat silver, linens, cooking utensils, and all miscellaneous kitchen equipment such as an egg beater, orange juicer, flour sifter, can opener, and Chore-boys (rustproof type). You might include coat hangers, wooden clothespins (sun softens plastic ones), bathroom plunger, alarm clock, hot-water bottle, ice bag, needles, pins, thread, buttons, snaps, gift wrappings, Christmas cards, Christmas tree ornaments, and personal stationery.

As always include a generous supply of shoes, particularly low-heeled ones in white or light colors, as you will be walking in soft sand much of the time. Children need more than the usual amount of shoes, since the sand wears them out so rapidly.

Personal Items of Which There Is a Dearth

Costume jewelry	Artificial flowers
Cologne	Children's books
Cosmetics	Toys
Manicuring equipment	Reading material
Hand mirrors	Children's clothes

Adequate dry-cleaning facilities are available, and there are two laundries, one on the post and one at Aramco. The extremely hard water handicaps them and all white things tend to yellow quickly.

Because of the frequent wind and blowing sand you will be glad if you take scarves for your hair, and include plastic garment bags to protect your best clothes from sand which filters into clothes closets.

Electric power is 60 cycle, 110 voltage, so standard household appliances can be used. A portable electric heater and fans for summer will increase your comfort. You will enjoy a radio-phonograph if you care to send one, especially a receiver with short wave. It is well to change your address for magazine and home-town newspaper subscriptions, allowing plenty of time, since you will enjoy them as much in Arabia if not more than at home. Take plenty of playing cards, if you enjoy bridge, canasta, or gin rummy.

Recreation

Swimming and beach parties are popular, while fishing in the Persian Gulf heads the list of sports. The Aramco Club House activities include bowling, tennis and dancing, and there are movies at two theaters. There is a well organized Woman's Club and as always teas and the usual round of cocktail parties.

Shopping

Beautiful brocades from Damascus, silver and jewelry from Iran, and ivory and brass from India are available but all are higher in price than in those countries.

THE DOROTHY ROBINS SHOPPING SERVICE

Mrs. Robins is the special shopper for the personnel of the Armed Forces, handling all mail orders for Joske's in San Antonio, Texas. Since most Army personnel at some time or other are stationed in San Antonio, Joske's, owing to its fair dealing and courtesy toward Service personnel, is an institution familiar to most Army families.

If your favorite store in the States has a shopping service, it might be well to get in touch with the Personal Shopper concerning any special requirements you might have, and to open a charge account for use while abroad. Mail-order houses which send catalogues are also helpful. Items shipped by boat from New York require from three to six months for delivery, so it is best to send all things via parcel post, which should insure their arrival in four to six weeks. All parcel-post packages should be less than 100 inches in combined length and girth, and weigh less than seventy pounds. Be sure to emphasize the necessity for careful wrapping to avoid breakage during the long trip, and do not forget to include your husband's APO.

A SUMMING UP

To attempt to cover the many, many stations today where Army dependents are living is a stupendous task, and much too great a feat to be covered in one chapter of this book. Here are a few general hints, in the broad sense of the term, which should be helpful on any overseas assignment.

1. Whether or not you are a mail-order advocate, you should procure the latest Sears Roebuck, Montgomery Ward, Spiegel, and Lane Bryant catalogues. Best's and Altman's also are good mail-order houses furnishing catalogues.

2. Again and again and again: Take plenty of comfortable shoes, particularly walking shoes.

3. Visit the dime store, stocking up on notions and gadgets, children's toys, storybooks (the latter of course you will save for Christmas, birthdays, or occasionally dole out for good behavior).

4. It is well, before taking electrical appliances on foreign duty, to check the voltage at the station to which you will be assigned.

5. Wherever the Army sends dependents, you can be assured that some type of housing is available. This is why, on overseas orders, dependents are not allowed to join their sponsors until suitable quarters are made available. It is very unwise for an Army wife to arrange commercial travel to a foreign station unless she can provide her own quarters. The Army also makes certain to establish adequate elementary-school facilities at each foreign base. Likewise, medical and dental facilities are always made available for emergency cases, with evacuation facilities in case of serious illness.

6. On the serious side: Learn to be philosophical. Accept people and their country as they *are*. Respect their customs and religion, be understanding and tolerant.

7. Above all, if you don't have a sense of humor, develop one *pronto!* You will need it to carry you over the rugged spots in your Army life.

8. The emphasis placed on the fact that you, your husband, and your children are official and unofficial "ambassadors at large" on an overseas assignment may strike you as redundant. Even if I repeated it for each country, each city, and each post, it could not be emphasized enough. IT IS *THAT* IMPORTANT!

Chapter XIII

HOSPITALIZATION—DEATH AND MILITARY FUNERALS

Hospital Facilities for Dependents of Army Personnel

MEDICAL care of dependents is not part of the military mission but was authorized by Congress in 1884, when a substantial part of the Army was stationed on the then undeveloped Indian frontier. It was authorized in order to allow the families of officers and enlisted men to obtain benefits of the medical service provided for them by the United States, which in most instances was the only medical service available at that time in those areas. This practice has extended through the years as a custom and a privilege of the Service provided adequate facilities and personnel were available for dependent care. During an emergency, it is impossible for the Medical Department to administer to personnel other than enlisted men, NCOs, and commissioned officers, except in cases demanding immediate attention.

The ranking medical officer or post surgeon is assisted by a staff of doctors and an especially trained staff. There is always an O.D. or medical officer of the day who is on call or on the alert at all times. The post surgeon has certain calling hours, and these hours should be respected except in cases of immediate danger, emergency, or a definite relapse in a patient's condition. For instance, if Junior has been running a slight temperature all day, do not wait until ten o'clock at night to phone the hospital to send an O.D. "at once." Doctors, even though they are O.D.'s, appreciate consideration; however, should something serious develop, such as convulsions, by all means telephone for the O.D. Medical officers are more than willing to serve, and they regard legitimate calls not only as part of their duty but as an opportunity to serve their fellow man.

If a patient is at all able, he should go or be taken to the hospital during outpatient clinic hours, which vary on different posts, though the usual hours are from nine to twelve in the forenoon or from one to three in the afternoons. This information will be covered in *Post Regulations*. Light, cheery waiting rooms, equipped with magazines and current newspapers, are usually available. Upon entering the Outpatient Service, give your name and the required medical data or case history to the orderly or nurse in attendance. Then wait your turn and, except in emergency cases, never try to get special service or earlier attention. Everyone in the waiting room is probably as anxious as you are to get away to other tasks and duties. "Pulling rank" for special service causes decidedly unfavorable comment.

Infants and small children who need scheduled medical attention should be placed in the hands of a good civilian pediatrician if you can possibly afford it. Army doctors are entirely too busy to attend to weighing babies, changing formulas, and the hundred and one needs of infants and small children. If you go regularly to a good pediatrician, you will feel free to call upon him for advice or service at any hour of the day or night. Please do not misunderstand or misconstrue this suggestion! Army doctors can and will render pediatric service, if time and their duties permit; but, remember again, except in cases of sudden illness or extreme emergency, women and children still come in the category of "camp followers" and should not expect service from busy Army doctors. Dependents must necessarily be cared for only after the needs of the enlisted and officer personnel have been administered to, as soldiers rank first service. It is decidedly unethical to go to a civilian doctor during the day and then call an Army doctor at night. It looks as if you were pitting the skill of one doctor against that of the other, which is very unfair.

Note: Most Army hospitals have qualified pediatricians available today.

Dental officers cannot find enough hours in the day to take care of the molars of Uncle Sam's fighting men, let alone take time out to straighten Johnny's teeth or do the intricate and time-taking work required for fillings, bridgework, and inlays. If an emergency arises, however, Army dentists are willing to give service. Since the war, the Army provides competent dental care for dependents when facilities are available. If they are not, consult a good dentist in town, not the most expensive, but a reputable one with whom you can arrange to make monthly payments if there is to be a long-drawn-out piece of work, such as putting bands on Johnny's teeth. If you were in civilian life, you most assuredly would expect to pay for this service, and so it is in the Army. Of course, you may be fortunate enough to be stationed at a small garrison not overcrowded with troops; in such case often the Medical Department will administer to all types and kinds of requests; so accept its services and be thankful.

ARMY NURSES

The Army Nurse Corps of the Medical Department is composed of graduate nurses who have the same rank as commissioned officers in the Army. Having passed a satisfactory examination to determine her efficiency, the Army nurse is appointed to the corps and is commissioned as a second lieutenant.

She is accorded the same obedience from enlisted men and patients in and about military hospitals as is accorded commissioned officers of grades corresponding to their relative rank.

While Army Nurses are not eligible as members of courts-martial, they may prefer charges against any member of the military service. They are entitled to the same privileges and allowances, except mileage, as are prescribed for commissioned officers of grades corresponding to their relative rank.—*Army Regulations*

An Army nurse enters the Service as a second lieutenant, and the requirements are, in addition to being a registered nurse, that she be between twenty-two and thirty years of age, a graduate of an accredited high school, unmarried, and a citizen of the United States. The highest office in the corps is that of chief, which position carries with it the rank of colonel. All other appointments are made by the Surgeon General.

The reason for quoting regulations in regard to the status of Army nurses is this: Many Army wives do not know that Army nurses are commissioned officers of the Army, and these fine women deserve all the consideration and respect that is their just due. Army wives, who receive the best of care in the hospitals, are sometimes not too thoughtful or courteous to the Army nurses outside in the social circles of the post. They are definitely a most important part of the Army and should be included in the social life of the post. I am sure this attitude is not intentional, but since it is one of thoughtlessness and ingratitude, it should be corrected.

The Army Nurse Corps established a magnificent record by its heroic services in World Wars I and II. The top strength of the corps was 57,000 nurses, and over 1,400 nurses received military decorations in World War II. Seventeen nurses were killed in action. Five hospital ships have been named for nurses, and one general hospital bears a nurse's name.

ARMY HOSPITALS

Army hospitals necessarily have a set of regulations as long as a Canal Search Warrant, but a few general tips will suffice to acquaint the Army wife with the general requirements. The general hospitals are:

Army and Navy Hospital, Hot Springs, Arkansas
William Beaumont Army Hospital, El Paso, Texas
Brooks Army Hospital, San Antonio, Texas
Fitzsimons Army Hospital, Denver, Colorado
Percy Jones Army Hospital, Battle Creek, Michigan
Letterman Army Hospital, San Francisco, California
Madigan Army Hospital, Tacoma, Washington
Murphy Army Hospital, Boston, Massachusetts
Valley Forge Army Hospital, Phoenixville, Pennsylvania
Walter Reed Army Hospital, Washington, D. C.
Tripler Army Hospital, Oahu, T. H.
Osaka Army Hospital, Osaka, Japan
Tokyo Army Hospital, Tokyo, Japan
Ryukyus Army Hospital, Nabo, Okinawa
97th General Hospital, Frankfurt, Germany
98th General Hospital, Munich, Germany
Rodriguez Army Hospital, Fort Brooke, San Juan, Puerto Rico

Each large command or post has its own station hospital, and each small post has a dispensary or clinic, with medical officers in attendance.

If you are to be a patient in an Army hospital, there are several things you should know before entering. Should you not be a bed patient, and are able, you may be asked to make your own bed. This is no hardship, yet some Army women object strenuously, even when they can see that the busy nurses need a helping hand. The meals are served at the most unusual hours; in fact, after a week's sojourn in the average Army hospital, you will find yourself losing all track of time. Breakfast varies, but it is early enough to remind you of your convent boarding-school days; dinner follows the natural hour of mid-day, and you will receive the light collation called "supper" any time between four and the usual cocktail or tea hour. Large hospitals employ expert dietitians. The cost of food varies from $1.50 to $1.75 per day; so, naturally, on this limited amount a patient cannot ex-

pect anything very individual, special, or fancy to tempt his appetite.
The food is wholesome, well cooked, and nicely served, though inclined to be on the heavy side.

With obstetrical cases or surgical cases, each patient should provide
her own special nurse if she can possibly afford it. With one nurse
to a ward, it is impossible for a really sick patient to receive the attention she may need. In obstetrical cases, the special nurse should be
engaged in advance, and many young mothers arrange to take the
nurse home with them from the hospital. This is wise, because if the
hospital is crowded, obstetrical patients are often sent home at the
end of five or ten days, and certainly the services of a qualified nurse
are needed at this time.

As a patient, your general attitude toward hospitals, doctors, and
nurses is important. If you "hate" hospitals, are "afraid" of doctors
and nurses, "dread" anesthesia, "can't take" medicines, you have two
strikes against you! Sounds infantile, but intelligent people often
have such phobias, which are hangovers from a badly conditioned
childhood.

If there is an operation on your calendar, one of the planned kind
and not an emergency, it's smart to ask your doctor what you can do
before and afterwards to get well speedily. Once you are in the hospital, and out of anesthesia, there are many specific ways of speeding
your recovery. Your doctor will tell you after he has finished your
particular piece of tatting and embroidery.

Remember that food is therapeutic, and don't think you are being
dainty and delicate when you pick at the food on your tray or ignore
it. Of course, I'll admit the soup may taste like diluted library paste
at first, and the solids may resemble sawdust but nevertheless, it's
part of your recovery and being a good soldier to eat your rations
. . . so tuck it away.

Drink the water the nurse brings you while it is fresh, and don't
feel you are doing her a favor. It's your health, not hers. That goes
for all fruit juices, too.

As soon as possible, put on make-up, particularly lipstick; and it
will improve your morale to wear a ribbon in your hair. Reading is
one of the best ways to keep your mind off discomforts; the less you
dwell on the pain, the better off you will be. If you make up your
mind you are going to be the sickest woman in the Northern Hemi-
sphere, you'll probably come close to that unhappy state. This is what
is known as "the law of expectancy" and it seldom fails.

Enlisted men in the Medical Department are called corpsmen, orderlies, or ward attendants. They assist the nurses and do most of the cleaning and the menial work connected with the hospital; so don't be surprised when a sprightly young soldier enters your sickroom with your tray or comes in to sweep and dust. Don't ring for the nurse unless it is absolutely necessary for you to call her. She is a busy person.

It is a gracious thing to give the nurse or nurses who have given you special care a small gift though, of course, this is not expected. Some patients prefer to wait until they return home, then invite the nurses to dinner or to some social affair later. Nurses appreciate these little courtesies, as their social life is limited at best because of their strenuous hours and arduous duties. Why not make the effort to know the nurses on duty at your post? Patients who receive an abundance of flowers usually ask that some be sent to other patients or to the various wards, and this is often done when a patient is leaving a hospital.

Visiting Army Hospitals

There are definite hours for visiting patients in Army hospitals, and visitors are required to observe the regulations. Morning visits are seldom allowed, owing to the fact that the doctors are making their calls and inspections and the nurses are occupied with changing dressings, giving baths, and attending to the general care of the patients. The visiting hours are usually from two to four o'clock in the afternoon and from seven to eight in the evening. In corridors you will see signs requesting "Quiet . . . No Loud Talking," and you are required to observe these rules.

Either send in your name or ask the nurse if it is convenient for you to see the patient, and under no circumstances barge into a sickroom unannounced, as Army people are wont to do sometimes in Army hospitals. Confine your visit to only a few minutes. Doctors prefer that the visitors do most of the talking but keep the conversation in a light, cheery vein. Patients who are recovering from operations, however, often like to relate the grim and gory details as they imagine them; so if you must, listen sympathetically. Avoid launching into a long dissertation on an operation that *you* once had. If the patient is bent on talking about her operation, give in gracefully and listen! After all, she fancies herself the martyr and heroine; let her enjoy her moment.

It is unwise to ask a patient, "How do you feel?" If she looks well, she will probably resent being told so, and if she looks ghastly, you should be too tactful to tell her so.

If you take flowers, it is well to have the florist arrange them in an inexpensive container, because Army hospitals do not go in for charming flower receptacles, nor do the nurses have time for flower arrangement. Small blooming potted plants are preferable, but even they require care and someone has to water them and set them out of the sickroom at night.

An amusing book, or the best seller of the moment, provided it is not morbid or terribly exacting, would be an acceptable gift to one convalescing. Several of the latest magazines, or a box of sweets or a tempting basket of fruit similar to a bon voyage basket might be welcome. Attractive small jars of jams, marmalades, and jellies often give an invalid a lift. Any little novelty, or any gift that shows a kind thought, will be appreciated.

Army hospitals have strict rules concerning visiting maternity patients. Don't ask to have the baby brought in unless the mother and nurse suggest it. It is quite all right to take gifts to the hospital, but if many arrive, something may be lost in the confusion, and it is better to wait until the mother and infant return home. Common sense should warn you never to visit anyone who is ill if you have a cold or are recovering from one.

DEATH AND MILITARY FUNERALS

*May we find a soldier's resting place beneath a
soldier's blow,
With room enough beside our graves, for Benny
Havens, Oh!*
—"Benny Havens"

Army people are like one big family, and in times of sorrow and stress they draw even closer together and prove themselves wonderful friends. Upon the death of a soldier, an NCO, or an officer at an Army post, every consideration is shown his widow and family, though there is little outward show of mourning and grief. The commanding officer or his representative assists in making funeral arrangements, supervises the conduct of the funeral, and takes care of all official reports. To be relieved of all these trying details means much to one in sorrow.

Should an officer die under unusual circumstances, such as in a train wreck, an automobile accident, or an airplane crash outside an Army post or hospital, his widow should send radiograms or telegrams immediately, as follows:

1. Telegraph the deceased officer's Commanding Officer, stating the details and requesting instructions.
2. Telegraph the Adjutant General of the Department of the Army, Washington, D. C., giving the deceased's full name, rank, and branch of service; date, place, and cause of death; cemetery where burial is desired; and request instructions as to burial arrangements.
3. If burial is to be in a national cemetery, the widow should apply by telegraph to the Quartermaster General, Department of the Army, Washington, D. C., for a burial lot in the national cemetery desired.*

Excited though she inevitably is, she should be careful to *give definitely the address where the reply will reach her!*

Should the widow be living on a post, all of these items will be taken care of by either the commanding officer or the post adjutant. On the death of an officer at a military post, the flag is displayed at half-staff and so remains between reveille and retreat, until the last salvo is fired over the grave.

ARMY ETIQUETTE TOWARD PERSONS IN GRIEF

In Army circles, when death occurs, there is no outward display of mourning except in the observance of the military customs of the Service. There are no drawn shades, crepe-hung doors, muffled bells, or hushed voices, despite the deep sorrow of the family of the deceased. There is a certain *esprit!* Death is accepted as an inevitable happening, and while everything possible is done to show consideration to the bereaved family, post life goes on in an uninterrupted manner except during the actual funeral services.

Calls

If death is sudden and unexpected, as happens on occasion, then usually a medical officer, accompanied by the post chaplain and the commanding officer's wife, or the widow's most intimate friend, go to break the sad news. It is wise for a doctor to be in attendance in case the shock should prove so great that the bereaved wife needs medical attention. No one, except the most intimate friends, should call at a time like this, and even intimate friends should not call un-

* Reprinted from *The Officers' Guide*, Military Service Publishing Company.

less they can be calm and collected. Acquaintances on a post usually send in a note of sympathy, or some flowers from their garden with a note of sympathy, or simply leave cards. Should you know the bereaved family well, you might offer your services in a note or offer to call, if and when they would like to see you. If there are young children, kind friends often ask if they make take care of them. A very intimate friend might send over tempting food. Persons in deep grief usually feel that food is not for them, yet it is better for them to eat, otherwise physical weakness only adds to their general depression.

A close friend should be at the door to receive callers, to accept cards, and to take messages. Under no circumstances should the bereaved person be expected to carry on a telephone conversation. Army women are so schooled in being practical that when bereaved they often purposely busy themselves with their personal affairs as soon as possible. It is unwise to be alone with one's thoughts at a time like this, and immediately they begin to make necessary adjustments and to work out future plans.

A house funeral or a funeral at the quarters is something that is entirely unheard of in the Army. Whether there are any regulations on this subject I have not been able to find out, but the lying-in-state is always at a funeral establishment, or special arrangements are made for the body to be taken to the post chapel for a short time before the ceremony if that is the wish of the family. Sitting up with the dead is no longer an essential tribute of veneration, unless the lying-in-state is a public ceremony for a deceased personage.

FUNERAL DIRECTORS

The director in charge of a military funeral is one who has obtained a yearly contract with the government; in other words, he has been able to secure the contract by making the lowest bid. Once in a while an unscrupulous racketeer type of director will secure the government contract, and this type of individual is crafty. He will find out to the penny exactly how much insurance the widow will have at her disposal; then he tries to work on her sympathy, and encourages her to invest in the most elaborate and expensive funeral possible. By omitting to give an itemized list of costs, which he knows no one wants to bother with at a time like this, he will order his own automobiles for the funeral procession; he will prevail upon the family to invest an unreasonable amount in a casket (money that, in later years, the poor Army widow may need desperately) and in every way possible increase the expenditures of the funeral. Someone who knows the widow's taste and circumstances, preferably an officer's wife, should go personally to the funeral establishment with the officer in charge and make all arrangements and plans. It is not a pleasant errand, but one that is very necessary. I am glad to say that funeral directors of the type here mentioned are few.

MOURNING CLOTHES

Mourning clothes to be worn to the funeral do not receive the regard and formality of past years. An Army widow looks through her wardrobe, and usually has on hand a plain black dress, suit, or coat. If there is any colored trimming, it can be removed. Stores and all dressmaking establishments will always give precedence to mourning orders and will often open their shops on holidays and after hours to accommodate a customer. Nearly always friends or acquaintances will offer to lend wraps and veils.

It is a matter of choice and taste whether or not the widow wishes to wear mourning after the funeral; however, in the first throes of grief, she should avoid disposing of her entire wardrobe. If she decides to wear mourning, then many articles of wearing apparel may be dyed successfully.

Mourning or the emblem of black gives a woman a certain protection when she is in the depths of real sorrow. On the other hand, a person in mourning should observe all mourning conventions. Conspicuous attire, exaggerated fashion, and boisterous manners are highly inconsistent for one in sorrow.

An officer in mourning may, if he wishes, wear a crepe sleeve band of from three and a half to four and a half inches in width on his uniforms and civilian clothes.

CERTIFICATES OF DEATH

A widow should obtain from the doctor in attendance on her husband at his last illness a *Certificate of Death*. A copy of this certificate must accompany various claims, including settlement of commercial insurance policies. She should also ask two officers who intimately knew her husband, to identify his remains before the casket is closed. They will then be prepared to furnish the affidavit required by commercial insurance companies to be filed with the claim for insurance due.*

* Reprinted from *The Officers' Guide*, Military Service Publishing Company.

MILITARY FUNERALS

A military funeral ceremony is based on a few simple customs and traditions. The following are the foundation of all military funerals, whether last rites are over a private's casket or final honors are being paid at the grave of a general officer.

> The casket is covered with the American flag.
>
> The casket is usually transported to the cemetery on a caisson.
>
> The casket is carried from the caisson or hearse to the grave by six military body bearers.
>
> Honorary pallbearers usually march to the cemetery alongside the caisson.
>
> At the cemetery, the casket is placed over the grave and the body bearers hold the flag-pall waist high over the casket.
>
> After the committal service is read by the chaplain, a firing party fires three volleys.
>
> A bugler stationed at the head of the grave sounds taps and the military funeral is completed.
>
> The body bearers fold the flag and present it to the next of kin.

Customs

The ceremonial customs of all military funerals are rooted in ancient military usage. In many cases they are based on expedients used long ago on the battlefield in time of war. For example, the custom of covering the casket with a flag probably originated on the battlefield where caskets were not available, and the flag wrapped around the body served as a makeshift pall in which it could be buried. Later, these customs assumed a greater significance. The fact that an American flag is used to cover the casket now symbolizes service in the Armed Forces of the United States, and is a nation's recognition of the debt it owes the deceased's service and sacrifice. The use of the caisson as a hearse is an obvious improvisation.

At the funeral of an Air Force officer, an escort of planes is timed to fly over the funeral procession. A V, five- or seven-plane formation, usually has one position unoccupied, signifying the place of the former comrade. This is the salute and farewell to a former flier. At the funeral, the three volleys are fired from rifles.

ORIGIN OF CERTAIN CUSTOMS AT MILITARY FUNERALS *

Firing Three Volleys at Military Funerals: In the funeral rites of the Romans, the casting of the earth *three* times upon the coffin constituted the burial. It was also customary among the Romans to call the dead *three* times by name, which ended the funeral ceremony, after which the friends and relatives of the deceased pronounced the word *"Vale"* (farewell) *three times* as they departed from the tomb. Today, when a squad of soldiers fires *three volleys* over a grave, they are, in accordance with this old Roman custom, bidding their dead comrade *Farewell, Three Times!*

Taps

This practice involves a deep-felt sentiment. . . . "Rest in Peace." In the daily life of the soldier the sounding of taps at eleven o'clock at night, signifying "Lights Out," announces the end of the day, implying that the cares and labors of the soldier are ended for that day. So does the sounding of taps at his funeral signify the end of his day . . . his "Rest in peace!" There is no other call so beautiful, no other call that arouses so much sentiment, so many emotions in the soul of the soldier as the sounding of TAPS.

> *Fades the light;*
> *And afar*
> *Goeth day,*
> *Cometh night;*
> *And a star*
> *Leadeth all*
> *To their rest.*

MILITARY FUNERAL WITHOUT CHAPEL SERVICE †

When the services at a chapel are omitted, the escort for a military funeral forms at or near the entrance of the cemetery. The officer in command supervises the transfer of the casket from the hearse to the caisson. During the transfer of the casket, the family and friends remain in their automobiles until the funeral procession is formed. The funeral services proceed then as outlined above.

Graveside Service

All military elements participating in a graveside service should be in position prior to the arrival of the remains. Should troops not be available,

---

* Reprinted from *The Officers' Manual*, by Colonel James A. Moss, George Banta Publishing Company.

† From *The Officers' Guide*, Military Service Publishing Company.

or should the family wish to eliminate any military elements, the following
will suffice:

1. Clergy
2. Pallbearers or casket bearers
3. Firing Party
4. Bugler

Ceremony Prior to Shipment of Remains

In cases where the remains of a deceased officer or soldier are moved to
a railway station or other point of shipment to a distant place for interment or final disposition, funeral services, modified as necessary, may be
carried out. If no further military honors are anticipated at the place of
interment, the volleys of musketry may be fired and TAPS sounded at the
discretion of the Commanding Officer and dependent upon local conditions.

Often a military service is held at the funeral establishment, before the body is shipped to its destination. If military honors are anticipated at the place of the final disposition, the firing of volleys
and the sounding of taps is omitted.

Cremation Services

In cases where the remains are conducted to a cemetery and the ashes
are to be interred with military honors at a later time, the ceremony will
consist only of the escort to the crematory. Arms are presented as the remains are borne into the crematory. The firing of volleys and sounding of
TAPS are omitted.

In case the funeral ceremony is held at the crematory, and no further
military honors are anticipated, the volleys may be fired and TAPS may be
sounded at the discretion of the Commanding Officer and dependent upon
local conditions.

In all phases of the funeral where the cremated remains are carried by
hand, one enlisted man will be detailed to carry the receptacle holding the
ashes. Four enlisted men will also be detailed as flag bearers. When the
receptacle has been placed on the stand before the chancel of the chapel or
when placed in the conveyance, the flag will be folded and placed beside
the receptacle. Remains are cremated only on written request from relatives.

MEMORIAL SERVICES

In case of death or burial on foreign shores, or loss of life at sea, in
any disaster or air accident when no burial services have been held, it is
customary to hold memorial services in honor of the deceased. The services

are conducted according to the religious procedure that has been requested. A memorial service is a painful ordeal for the bereaved to undergo but it often brings consolation and helps to assuage grief to a small extent by honoring the memory of a loved one.

EXPENSES OF BURIAL . . . MONUMENT OR MARKER

Should circumstances be such that a widow might have to employ a local undertaker, then she should obtain an itemized bill to support proof of expenditures. The limit of reimbursement in the case of a Regular Army officer varies between $75.00 and $125.00 depending upon the circumstances. When remains are shipped to a funeral director selected by the next of kin, and subsequently interred in a private cemetery, an interment allowance, not to exceed $125.00, is authorized. When remains are shipped to a funeral director selected by the next of kin, and subsequently interred in a national or post cemetery, the government will reimburse the person who paid any expenses incurred prior to interment, for such expenses up to but not in excess of $75.00. In both cases, any expenses over and above the amount specified must be borne by the person who incurred the expenses. In case of the death of an officer of the National Guard or a Reserve Officer, the amount does not exceed $100.00 for both burial expenses and transportation.

If the widow or family does not provide a private monument in a national cemetery, the government erects a white marker headstone of regulation pattern inscribed with the rank, name, and branch of the deceased. The widow or family should not contract for a private monument until both the design, material, and subscription have been submitted to, and approved by, the Quartermaster General.

FUNERAL ESCORT

Army Regulation 30-920 provides "that transportation, including return when required, may be issued to a relative or friend, to accompany remains to the home of the deceased or to a national cemetery for interment, when the relative or friend is at the place of death and desires to accompany the remains." With an unmarried officer, a brother officer is usually asked to escort the remains to the home of the deceased, but in the case of a married officer, it is customary for the widow and children to act as an escort to the place of burial.

In the case of an enlisted man or an officer, the military escort chosen is always one grade higher in rank than the deceased. For instance, in the case of the death of a private first class, a corporal is chosen as the military escort. Should the deceased hold the rank of corporal, then a sergeant is chosen to accompany the remains.

Breaking Up the Army Home

Circumstances determine how long an Army widow may occupy quarters after the death of her husband, but a generous allowance is from two weeks to a month, if the commanding officer of the post approves. Two weeks is usually long enough in which to pack household goods, make adjustments, and attend to all official business before clearing a post. However, on foreign service a family may have to wait for a transport or, as the other extreme, a widow may wish to close her affairs, pack, and clear the post before leaving for the funeral.

Whatever the circumstance, it is one of the most difficult of undertakings! She feels now that her life with the Army is over. Friends of long standing, years of service together . . . how she will miss them! She will probably find upon going back to the home of her girlhood that she has lost contact with the friends of her youth. Her interests are different, and she finds it very difficult to adjust herself to her home surroundings and environment. This is why so many Army widows settle in Washington, San Antonio, and San Diego. Their contemporaries usually retire in or near one of these Army cities, and they long for Service companionship.

If affluent, which few are, the Army widow should travel a bit before deciding on a permanent home. The quartermaster will store a deceased officer's household goods for one year, and in this time she should be able to make a decision. If she is able and capable, her salvation will lie in finding some suitable work. If she has not been trained for a profession, then there is no time like the present for her to equip herself whereby she can make her own livelihood. A special talent of any kind, no matter what, should be developed.

If the desire to be connected with Army personnel is still strong, she can perhaps make herself valuable in some capacity. Today there seem to be more opportunities than ever before. Army hostesses are in demand, and the remuneration is good. All types of positions are available in the civil service field, and the nursing corps is crying for Army and Navy nurses. The widow answers that all positions mentioned here require special training. True, but what worth-while position today doesn't? The Army widow should be in a position, financially, to take courses and work to equip herself. Of course, where there are small children who need a mother's care, that is a different matter. But nature has partially solved the problem here, as the mother must keep so busy that she has little time to think of herself and her loneliness.

After the first break with friends at the last post is made, things should be easier, though there will be days of heartbreak and loneliness when she will long for the companionship of Army friends who sympathize and understand. She should try to interest herself in some worth-while work as quickly as possible, and avoid feeling sorry for herself.

ARMY CHAPLAINS

Army chaplains are on call to help the bereaved spiritually, or in any way they can. Friends are essential but if there are no friends, always remember the chaplain is your friend. It is well for the bereaved not to fight their grief or repress it, and they will feel better, perhaps, to talk over their loss and to talk about their loved one to an understanding, sympathetic listener. Any other feelings related to the deceased should be brought out and discussed since it is better to bring emotions out in the open rather than to have trouble from them later on.

Army chaplains are wonderful in the work they perform. Remember, in addition to being a minister of God, the chaplain is a trained psychologist, and ethically any conversation you have with him is treated with the sacredness of a medical conference. When the time comes to settle your personal affairs he will act as the Casualty Assistance Officer; it is he who will follow through until all government or insurance claims are established and payments are made. He is always ready to render assistance or advice, and is not only concerned with the claim forms but sincerely desirous of helping the widow during the difficult period of readjustment.

ARMY MUTUAL AID ASSOCIATION

If an officer or enlisted man belongs to the Army Mutual Aid Association, his widow or dependents will need no outside legal help in the filing of necessary claims. Upon official notification of a member's death, benefits are paid without awaiting request; also papers and instructions regarding other claims are sent out by the association's office. Practically all widows have to ask help in filing and securing their various claims, if they do not receive it from the Army Mutual Aid Association or the Army.

Letter of Condolence

Many find a letter of condolence difficult to write, yet a truly sincere note at a time of sorrow is always appreciated. The letter need not be long. A person in grief, whose eyes are dimmed with tears and whose heart is aching, does not feel up to reading a long philosophical dissertation.

The letter of condolence should show admiration of the character and fine traits of the deceased and express genuine affection. If you cannot honestly say anything of this nature, don't give false praise to the dead, but write a sincere word of sympathy to the bereaved ones. Avoid harrowing the feelings by too familiar allusions to the deceased and sentimental allusions to the good times you used to have together.

Abraham Lincoln's famous letter of condolence to Mrs. Bixby, the mother of five sons who died for their country, is a classic. It is simple, sincere, and dignified.

Letters, telegrams of condolence, and floral tributes should always be answered with a personal note. Only a line is necessary and there is no immediate rush about answering. A personal card with "Thank you for your kind sympathy" will suffice. The answer to a note of condolence is another letter whose message must be sincere. In the case of a notable person, engraved cards of thanks are sometimes sent out by the family, but this is an impersonal way of thanking those who have thought enough to write a letter or send a telegram or flowers.

Important Information Every Army Man
Should Discuss with His Wife

Every Army wife should have written information concerning:
1. Where her husband desires to be buried
2. The six months' death gratuity to which dependents are entitled
3. Collection of accrued military pay after death
4. Pensions to dependents
5. Benefits according to the provisions of insurance policies

It is an unpleasant and complex subject but you should face up to the fact that you must know enough about your joint affairs in case of your husband's sudden death or serious injury to have some idea what to do and what you have to do it *with*. You can work this out much better *with* your husband now than you can stand having all the problems dumped on you alone when you are suffering from shock.

BENEFITS FOR WIDOWS AND DEPENDENTS

Six Months' Gratuity

As the name "gratuity" suggests, this is a gift equal to six months' base pay in a lump sum and includes longevity and flight pay. Gratuity does not include allowances. It is payable to widows, or, if there is no widow or children, to certain other dependent relatives. Upon notification of an officer's or enlisted man's death in line of duty, a form for six months' death gratuity pay will be forwarded to the beneficiary, *without* request, from the Settlement Division, Finance Center, U.S. Army, Indianapolis 49, Indiana.

Government Insurance

Within two or three weeks after the death of the insured, the beneficiary should receive claim forms from the Veterans Administration, Washington 25, D. C.

General information on the National Service Life Insurance will be given by the Casualty Assistance Officer, normally the chaplain.

Arrears in Pay: Any unpaid pay and allowances remaining to credit of deceased; to legal heirs, whether dependent or not. Application Standard Form 1055 for officers on active duty. Letters testamentary if claim is filed by executor of estate. Receipted itemized undertaker's bill, if claiming reimbursement of funeral expenses. Write to *Claims Division, General Accounting Office*, Fifth St. and Judiciary Square, N. W., Washington, D. C.

Move of Household Goods by Government

Dependents of deceased or missing military personnel are entitled to one move of household goods at government expense.

State Benefits

The veterans' associations in local communities have information on state benefits. Likewise, all questions regarding civil service benefits must be referred to the local civil service commission.

PENSIONS

Explanations are far too lengthy to list here. However, it is *important* to know that payments do not begin until after all necessary papers to substantiate claims are filed and approved. The dependent should write to Central Office, Veterans Administration, Washington 25, D. C., asking for forms covering claims procedure as soon as possible after the officer's or enlisted man's death. (Again, the chapplain will help with this.)

DEPENDENTS' COMPENSATION

The Veterans Administration is authorized under existing laws to provide compensation to dependents of enlisted men who die while on active duty providing the enlisted man's death is *in line of duty* and not the result of willful misconduct. Widows and children become eligible for compensation regardless of their income.

Eligibility is as follows:

1. Widow must have been married to the officer or soldier at the time of his death and must have lived continuously with him from the date of their marriage until death. Compensation ceases if the widow remarries.

2. Child or children must be unmarried and under the age of eighteen.

3. Child: legitimate, legally adopted, stepchild providing he was a member of the deceased Serviceman's household, or an illegitimate child of an officer, enlisted man, or WAC, providing the required evidence is submitted to the Veterans Administration.

If death occurs in line of duty during wartime service, the following amounts are awarded:

1. Widow .... $ 75.00
2. Widow and one child 121.00
3. Each additional child..... 29.00
4. No widow, one child..... 67.00
5. No widow, two children.. 94.00 (equally divided)
6. No widow, three children. 122.00 (equally divided)
7. Each additional child..... 23.00 (total to be divided equally)
8. One dependent parent.... 60.00
9. Two dependent parents... 35.00 each

The Veterans Administration has ruled that dependents of Servicemen who die in flight during peacetime if flight simulates combat conditions or is of an extra-hazardous nature are entitled to wartime rates.

If death occurs in line of duty during peacetime, amounts are:

1. Widow $60.00
2. Widow, one child 96.80

3. Each additional child. $23.20
4. No widow, one child 53.60
5. No widow, two children. . 75.20 (equally divided)
6. No widow, three children. 97.60 (equally divided)
7. Each additional child. . . . . 18.40 (total to be divided equally)
8. One dependent parent. . . . 48.00
9. Two dependent parents. . . 28.00 each

In addition to the chaplain, the following Army officers assist an Army widow to settle her personal affairs before clearing the post:

The Summary Courts Officer. Obtains all personal property of decedent and certifies to all items. (In turn and if possible this personal property is delivered to legal next of kin.) Collects all personal monies owed to decedent and pays all claims against the decedent. When necessary, can be authorized to sell any personal effects. If money is not turned over to a legal representative, it must be turned in to finance department for credit.

Regimental or Battalion Commander. Forwards the personal effects of the deceased to the place and person the deceased has designated. This is usually in the case of an unmarried officer or enlisted man except in time of war.

The Transportation Officer. Arranges for transportation of the remains. Also arranges transportation of dependents and shipping of household goods.

The Escort Officer. An officer or Serviceman, usually the closest friend of the deceased, is appointed by the immediate commanding officer and accompanies and delivers the remains to the person designated to make the interment. If the family is in need of financial assistance, the escort will give such information to the Red Cross or Army Mutual Aid Society at the nearest Army installation.

It may be possible that the widow and children of a *Reserve* officer are eligible for a sizable benefit under the Federal Employees Compensation Act. The Bureau of Employees Compensation in the Department of Labor should be contacted for information concerning this benefit.

It is also possible that the widow and children of *any* Reserve who dies while on active duty in the Air Force may be eligible for a sizable benefit from social security. The local social security office should be contacted for full information. If it is not available there, contact the central social security office.

Chapter XIV

SERVICE IN THE NATION'S CAPITAL

ARMY wives, as a rule, look forward to their husbands' having a tour of duty in the nation's capital, regardless of the fact that living conditions may be difficult. Rents are high, houses are at a premium, and servantless "cliff dwelling" or apartment life has little appeal; but to offset this, the Army wife considers the cultural advantages: the concerts and musicales, art groups, lecture courses, interesting statesmen and notable personages one meets or almost meets . . . all those experiences that are an integral part of Washington. Most of all—and we might as well face it—there is a tremendous excitement and stimulation that comes from being at the nerve center of the nation.

In former years, service in Washington carried with it definite rules and regulations in regard to official and social life. Knowledge and observance of even trifling rules of etiquette were of great importance. "Protocol" and "Washington" were synonymous; "precedence" and "who ranked whom" were the Nemesis of every Washington hostess whether in official or social spheres. These rules and regulations still hold after a fashion in the higher echelons, but all Washington hostesses whether in social, official, or diplomatic circles know that they can play safe by submitting their guest list to the Chief of Protocol at the Department of State should they get in a spot. This office knows all the answers in regard to protocol, seating arrangements, who ranks whom and will be glad to tell you where to seat Queen Elizabeth, the Premier of Thailand, or the Sultan of Sulu.

In official circles there are a few points necessary for the Army hostess to know. Remember that the Secretary of Defense ranks the Secretaries of the Army, the Navy, and the Air Force. The Secretary of the Army ranks the Secretary of the Navy, and the Secretary of the Navy ranks the Secretary of the Air Force. Why? Because the Army is the Senior Service and the Navy is older than the Air Force.

In addition, it is important today to learn the uniforms, insignia, and ranks of officers and men serving in NATO. There are also many

Allied soldiers training in this country under the MDAP (Mutual Defense Assistance Program). It is well to be able to recognize their ranks.

WASHINGTON SOCIAL LIFE FOR JUNIOR OFFICERS' WIVES

Don't worry your pretty head about the above-mentioned protocol; the thing varies considerably with your husband's duty and position. If he is on duty at the Pentagon, and he probably will be, his working hours will normally parallel those of the average civilian, from eight-thirty in the morning until five in the afternoon with Saturdays and Sundays free. In times of national emergency you and he forget regular hours. No doubt he will be a member of a car pool and will need the car one day or more a week. Transportation is a major problem for those on duty at the Pentagon.

A young wife coming to Washington for the first time often is lonesome. Distances are great; traffic is a problem; the lack of a central club or meeting place and the discontinuance of social calling tend rather to isolate her. Unless she exerts her initiative, she will remain lonely as no one calls.

The best way for you to become acquainted is to offer your services to one of the many volunteer organizations: Red Cross, Soldiers', Sailors', Marines' and Airmen's Club, Jangos, or the Armed Forces Hostess Association.

Should you be invited to an informal morning coffee by the wife of your husband's commanding officer, by all means attend. Some wives of officers in command give informal coffees for newly arrived wives and this may be considered as a call and a return. Cards are left; one of your visiting cards for your hostess.

Today there is almost no calling, even by senior officers. What calling is done is the result of the personal choice of an officer in command of a branch division or section and his wife.

Though no policy concerning calling by the military at the White House has been publicly announced, the Department of the Army has been notified that calling is *not* necessary. At any time, calling at the White House is merely a form of respect, as neither the President nor the President's wife returns the call, or seldom if ever sees the callers.

There is not much social life in Washington except for high officialdom and the Diplomatic Corps. Cocktail parties usually are the extent of entertaining. No-host parties are popular—when several young couples have dinner and an evening of dancing at one of the many fine hotels. Evening clothes are rarely worn but a smart cocktail suit that can be dressed up or down with accessories will prove quite satisfactory.

THE HOUSING SITUATION

How to get a place to live in Washington is the concern of every Army officer and enlisted man ordered to duty there. The housing situation is critical; however, the Armed Forces, being cognizant of conditions, has set up the Armed Forces Service Center located in Room 1A876, the Pentagon.

The best plan seems to be for a member of the immediate family to visit Washington before the reporting date specified by the orders. As part of the Armed Forces Service Center a joint Armed Forces Housing Office is maintained complete with a Housing Counselor. In order to give efficient service, it is necessary for the counselor to have specific and pertinent data, such as: Where will the applicant be stationed? How many, if any, children does he have? What is the sex and age of each? Will they want public or parochial schools; grammar or high-school level? Are furnished or unfurnished accommodations required? An apartment or a house? What is the maximum rental that can be paid? Are there any pets? Will the applicant drive to and from his office or depend upon public transportation?

The applicant should be a member of the family who can file the request for housing, obtain the listings, examine the properties, make the decision, sign the lease and give the customary one month's advance rent.

In the event an advance visit cannot be made, you will probably have to stay in a hotel from two to six weeks while an agent locates a suitable place for you.

Many Army families live on the Virginia side, south of Washington—in Rosslyn, Falls Church, Arlington, or Alexandria. There are many new housing projects and in Arlington alone over one hundred such apartment communities. The Virginia side is most accessible to the Pentagon and for one big reason: the traffic. A network of broad four-lane highways leads directly into the Pentagon parking areas from all sections of Virginia. Intersections have been eliminated by underpasses so that traffic moves swiftly over these highways.

The District itself runs mostly to hotels and furnished apartments converted from old houses, except for Georgetown, which will be described later.

The Maryland area north of the city includes Chevy Chase, Silver Spring, and Bethesda. It is a lovely residential section offering primarily individual homes. It has the disadvantage of being on the far side of the city from the Pentagon and traffic going through the city and over the bridges in the morning and evening is very heavy.

GOVERNMENT QUARTERS

A small number of government quarters is available for junior-grade officers and NCO's of the first three grades, but the waiting lists are lengthy. In the apartments at Arlington Farms, near the Pentagon, priority is given to junior officers with the greatest number of dependents. Nearly all of the larger apartment developments will take children.

Several apartment developments rent apartments by the day, the week, or the month. Presidential Gardens in Alexandria is a very popular one, ten minutes from the Pentagon. Glass Manor near Bolling Air Force Base is also popular for transients. Junior officers can afford both of these. Lower ranks, captains, lieutenants, and warrant officers can apply for quarters at South Post, Fort Myer, or at Arlington Farms.

You are advised to keep an eye on the extensive classified ad sections of the *Washington Post,* the *Times Herald,* and the *Evening Star.* It is even advisable to insert an ad yourself.

While the Armed Forces Hostess Association has nothing to do with billeting, if the going gets too rough the Hostesses will be glad to give you information about baby-sitters and practical nurses, doctors and dentists, seamstresses, shopping service, furniture repair, schools and camps, transportation, and similar questions pertaining to the various sections of Washington, Virginia, and Maryland. Their primary mission is to welcome you as a newly-arrived wife to the area and to answer questions about Washington.

AN INVITATION TO THE WHITE HOUSE

Should you be fortunate enough to receive a formal invitation to the White House, it should be answered within twenty-four hours. Good form decrees that replies to White House invitations should not be mailed, but delivered in person or by messenger. If you receive an invitation to lunch or dine at the White House, it amounts to a command and takes precedence over any other engagement. The President is addressed as "Mr. President"; the First Lady as "Mrs. ———."

The wife of the Vice-President is the second most important lady in the land. She makes only a few official visits, and she receives as do the wives of other executives.

Should you receive a dinner invitation to the White House, Carolyn Hagner Shaw suggests in her *Official List of Washington* that you accept "to dinner" not "for dinner." On an invitation for an informal dinner "Black Tie" is written in the lower left-hand corner, indicating that a woman should wear a dinner gown and a man a tuxedo or uniform.

Men invited to dinner with the President and the First Lady usually have the impulse to wear tails, but a dinner jacket is in order. Presidents are men, too; and they find black tie more comfortable and quite correct.

Ladies invited to Blair House would do well to think twice before wearing that divine little imported décolleté number; save it for the country club dance as cover-up dinner dresses are the rule and a dress with a suggestion of sleeves, stole, jacket, or cape is more appropriate.

BLAIR HOUSE

Diagonally across from the White House stands Blair House, a home with historic memories which in the last few years has taken on a new interest since it serves as the official guesthouse for the nation. As a caravansary it has had an imposing guest list of visiting notables, and during the period of repairing of the White House President Truman and his family resided there.

No one seems to know when Blair House was built, but it was erected by a distinguished Army surgeon of the War of 1812, Dr. Joseph Lovell. In 1836 the property was purchased by the man whose name it has borne ever since—Francis Preston Blair of Kentucky.

Since Blair House has been acquired by the government, it has been refurbished and now houses a priceless collection of Americana. Should the Rajah of Rajputana-Hyderabad, the President of Patagonia, or the Queen of England arrive for an official visit he would after his first night in the White House be transferred to Blair House for the remainder of his visit.

The Beauty of the Nation's Capital

You will be charmed by the physical beauty of Washington and the somewhat ponderous magnificence of its public buildings. The site for the nation's capital was selected by President Washington, and the city was planned by a young French engineer, Major Pierre Charles L'Enfant. Everything fans out from the Capitol like the spokes of a wheel into the four sectors—Northeast, Southeast, Northwest, Southwest.

Life in Washington is overshadowed by politics since it is the workshop of political leaders, and it is therefore an exciting if somewhat unreal place to be. Retired career men like to linger in the capital close to the swirl of events, as is evidenced by the retired military men who live at the Army and Navy Club or congregate there to reminisce and talk shop. Washington today is the capital of capitals, in addition to being the capital of the world's most powerful democracy. It is a white-collar town since there is no industry, and continues to be the loadstone which attracts thousands of career-minded girls who wind up as government workers ranging from State Department consultants to file clerks in remote and forgotten departments.

Washington is truly a city of paradoxes. For instance, take Georgetown with its pillared old mansions, beautiful gardens, and iron porch railings. Georgetown gives one a socially desirable address with the slums literally next door. The city itself was founded as a meeting place of northern and southern sectionalism but a southern influence has flavored its atmosphere from the beginning. A longstanding local witticism has it that Washington is "the city that runs on southern efficiency and northern charm." Regardless of how the climate is berated, either for its beastly hot summers or below-zero winters, you will love the springtime with its cherry blossoms and the gorgeous autumns that are all too short but beautiful beyond description.

If this is your first visit or residence in Washington, there are certain national shrines and definite beauty spots you should see in your early enthusiasm. Provide yourself with a 35¢ map, the kind that folds flat but opens up into something almost as big as the Pentagon, and get halfway oriented. You will soon discover that the avenues are named for states and territories and have the most confusing way of intersecting one another, while the streets are numbered. Don't try to do it all in a week or even a month or with two pairs of walking shoes.

It is best to plan so that the sights fall into groups. If you start with the Capitol building, along with pages, other tourists, and politicians who crowd the corridors you will want to see the House which is usually in an uproar though most of the Representatives who are present seem to be chatting or reading newspapers. It is said that the important business gets done in committees. You will also see the old Senate chamber before taking a walk through the tunnel or riding the little electric subterranean railway to the Senate Office Building where you might be lucky enough to have an appointment with your home-state Senator. Having started your walkathon, you might as well step over to the Library of Congress, where it is said a copy of every published book is to be found. To enter the reading room in the great central rotunda one must procure a card. Perhaps you might end your first day with a visit to the Supreme Court, which is also within easy walking distance.

Then for another day you will enjoy the Monument circuit of the tidal basin, where you will see the Washington Monument, the Lincoln Memorial, and the Jefferson Memorial. The Smithsonian Institution is also a must even though it has been called "Mother America's Attic." There you will see early experiments of the Wright brothers, Lindbergh's *Spirit of St. Louis,* and Wiley Post's dapper *Winnie Mae.* The White House, of course, will be on your list, now that it is reopened to the public, and there will be Arlington and a visit to Mount Vernon. By this time you will be an old hand at sight-seeing and will want to read *Washington, The Cinderella City,* by William O. Stevens, which will give you a charming picture of Georgetown, some old houses and their legends, and a firsthand picture of capital life in the past and today.

Most of the entertaining in Washington is done at home, but a great many Service people use private clubs. Some of these are:

The Army and Navy Club. The main lobby, lounge, library, and writing rooms are restricted to the use of officers, though ladies are welcome to dine at the club. The cocktail lounge is smartly decorated. Aviation dioramas cover the walls, and the furniture is modern. By far the the most famous A & N dish is curry. Always on Mondays a curry is featured but it can be ordered à la carte at any time.

The Army and Navy Country Club. Located three miles from Washington, it always has a long waiting list. Initiation fee is $188.00 plus tax with $12.00 monthly dues including tax. It affords swimming, a good twenty-seven-hole golf course, weekly dances, popular Sunday-night buffet suppers, and many social advantages.

Bolling Officers' Club. Located on Bolling Air Force Base six miles from Washington, it has no initiation fee and monthly dues are $4.00. The club has been redecorated recently. There are frequent dances, bingo parties, and a swimming pool.

Fort Myer Officers' Club. This club is largely for personnel living at Fort Myer. It has a good swimming pool and the usual club facilities.

Fort McNair Officers' Club. The old War College Club. There is no initiation fee and dues are $5.00 monthly. It affords swimming, golf, bingo once a week, and frequent club dances. The food is better than average and it is popular for private parties.

Washington Golf and Country Club; Kenwood Country Club. These have good golf courses and swimming pools.

Chevy Chase Country Club. This club is expensive and exclusive and has a long waiting list.

Belle Haven Country Club. A good family club for those personnel who live in its vicinity, it has a good golf course, pool, frequent Saturday night dances, and Sunday buffet.

Other club facilities available are located at Andrews Air Force Base, Walter Reed, and at Fort Belvoir. Clubs for NCO's are also located at each base.

Washington is full of good restaurants and hotels that are popular for dining and dancing. Service personnel seem to be partial to the Shoreham, but the Mayflower is an attractive place for luncheons and also has a popular cocktail lounge. The Carlton and the Statler have favored dining rooms, and the Shoreham has dancing on the terrace in summer. The Sheraton Park is always a favorite with all Service personnel. The newest Washington hotel is the Dupont-Plaza on Connecticut Avenue and Dupont Circle. For luncheon the Crown Room is the place to go, and for cocktails the Circle Room. The Caribar at the Sheraton Park Hotel, with food specialties imported from the Caribbean, is popular for dinner and supper dancing.

Pierre's and the La Salle Du Bois are two of the best French restaurants for luncheons. There one sees the best-dressed women in Washington. They are also favorite spots for dinner.

It is interesting to go down to the wharf for some of the best sea food you have ever tasted. Among the famous restaurants are Herzog's, Hogate's, O'Donnell's, and Hall's. The last-mentioned stays open late for dining after cocktail parties, is very old, and has its original *décor*. Terrace dining at Hall's is popular in summer.

In the center of the business district, try the Occidental Restaurant, one of the oldest in Washington. It specializes in lobsters, cherrystone clams, oysters, and sea food in general and the famous rum buns. Autographed pictures of celebrities and military brass who have dined there are one of its features. Harvey's on Connecticut Avenue is another Washington landmark, famous for oysters. Normandy Farms on Route 189 between the Potomac and Rockville, Maryland, also the Water Gate Inn on the Potomac at F Street serve special parties.

For quaint charm and good food try the Iron Gate Inn, 1734 N Street, N. W., a transformed stable on the estate of General Nelson A. Miles. The hayracks, feedboxes, harness hooks, and saddletrees around the inn were in actual service as stable accessories. General Miles was one of the most colorful figures of his day in Washington, and his prancing horses were familiar sights to old and young. The stalls in the inn retain the original name plates of the General's horses. From 1895 to 1903 General Miles was the Senior Officer, Commanding, United States Army.

Collingswood-on-the-Potomac, between Alexandria and Mount Vernon, stands high in favor. It is an old estate converted into an inn.

In Georgetown, on Wisconsin Avenue, be sure to try Billy Martin's Carriage House.

EQUIVALENT RANKS OF OFFICERS OF UNITED STATES ARMY AND AIR FORCE AND THE NAVY

General of the Army (and Air Force)	Admiral of the Fleet
General	Admiral
Lieutenant general	Vice admiral
Major general	Rear admiral
Brigadier general	Rear admiral
Colonel	Captain
Lieutenant colonel	Commander
Major	Lieutenant commander
Captain	Lieutenant (senior grade)
First lieutenant	Lieutenant (junior grade)
Second lieutenant	Ensign

How to Distinguish the Rank of Army, Air Force, and Navy Officers

General of the Army
  (and Air Force) .... five stars
General .... four stars
Lieutenant general .... three stars
Major general .... two stars
Brigadier General .... one star
Colonel .... silver eagle
Lieutenant colonel .... silver leaf
Major .... gold leaf
Captain .... two silver bars
First lieutenant .... one silver bar
Second lieutenant .... one gold bar
Admiral of the Fleet .... one 2-inch stripe with four ½-inch stripes above it
Admiral .... one 2-inch stripe with three ½-inch stripes above it
Vice admiral .... one 2-inch stripe with two ½-inch stripes above it
Rear Admiral .... one 2-inch stripe with one ½-inch stripe above it
Captain .... four ½-inch stripes
Commander .... three ½-inch stripes
Lieutenant commander ..... two ½-inch stripes with one ¼-inch stripe between them
Lieutenant (senior grade) ... two ½-inch stripes
Lieutenant (junior grade) ... one ½-inch stripe with one ¼-inch stripe above it
Ensign .... one ½-inch stripe

Air Force ranks and designations are the same as those in the Army.
The Marine Corps is part of the Navy, but the rank is the same as that of the Army.

SERVICE MEDALS AND BADGES—DECORATIONS

The newcomer into the Army may wonder about the Service medals and badges and decorations worn on state occasions by officers in uniform. These are authorized by the government in recognition of an outstanding act of heroism or some especially noteworthy service rendered by individuals. Deeds of high valor on the field of battle have been rewarded in all wars. In case of posthumous awards, presentation of the decoration is made to the next of kin.

The Medal of Honor is the highest and most rarely awarded decoration conferred by the United States and was established by act of Congress in 1862. It is awarded for gallantry and intrepidity at the "Risk of Life Above and Beyond the Call of Duty." The medal is a five-pointed star, surrounded by a laurel wreath, suspended by a bronze bar bearing the inscription "Valor" and surmounted by an eagle. The ribbon on which it is suspended is light blue, with thirteen white stars. Whenever practicable the recipient of this decoration is ordered to Washington, and the presentation is made by the President of the United States.

The Distinguished Service Cross was instituted by Congress in 1918. It is awarded for "Extraordinary Heroism in Military Operations Against an Armed Enemy." In rank of awards it is number two. It is a cross of bronze with an eagle on the center. Below the eagle is a scroll bearing the inscription "For Valor." Its ribbon is a broad band of blue, bordered on both edges by narrow bands of red and white.

The Distinguished Service Medal, dating also from 1918, is awarded to those who distinguish themselves by exceptionally meritorious service to the government in a duty of great responsibility. The coat of arms of the United States in bronze, surrounded by a circle of dark blue enamel, bears the inscription "For Distinguished Service" and the year of award. The ribbon is composed of a band of scarlet, a stripe of dark blue, a band of white, a stripe of dark blue, and a band of scarlet.

The Silver Star—a silver star superimposed on a bronze star, the rays of the two coinciding—is given for gallantry in action.

The Legion of Merit is awarded for "Exceptionally Meritorious Conduct in the Performance of Outstanding Services." The design of the Legion of Merit, developed from the great seal of the United States, was approved by Congress in 1942. Awarded to members of foreign friendly nations as well as members of the Armed Forces of the United States. The front of the badge is a five-pointed American star of heraldic form in red and white enamel, centered with a constellation of the thirteen original stars on a blue-enameled field breaking through a circle of clouds.

The Distinguished Flying Cross is awarded for "Heroism or Extraordinary Achievement while Participating in Aerial Flight." On a bronze cross patée is a four-bladed propeller. On the reverse side is engraved the name of the recipient.

The Soldier's Medal was instituted in 1926. This decoration is given for "Heroism Not Involving Conflict with an Enemy." On a bronze octagon is displayed an eagle standing on a fasces between groups of stars and a spray of leaves. On the reverse side is engraved, "Soldier's Medal, for Valor." The ribbon is composed of two outside stripes in blue, with the center containing thirteen white and red stripes of equal width.

The Bronze Star Medal was authorized February 4, 1944, by President Roosevelt. It is awarded for "Heroic or Meritorious Achievement or Service against an Enemy not involving Aerial Flight." The bronze star has superimposed on it a smaller and raised bronze star, the center lines of all rays of both stars coinciding. On the reverse side is the inscription "Heroic or Meritorious Achievement." The ribbon is of Old Glory red with a one-eighth-inch vertical stripe of royal blue in the center.

The Air Medal is given for "Meritorious Achievement While Participating in Aerial Flight." This medal is given in cases where the act of meritorious service does not warrant the award of the D.F.C. This is a beautiful decoration. Pendant from a ribbon striped with the Air Force blue and gold is a compass rose. In relief on the rose is a swooping American eagle with lightning bolts clutched in his talons.

The Commendation Ribbon with Metal Pendant was authorized in 1945 to be awarded to members of the Armed Forces of the United States who distinguish themselves by meritorious achievement or service on or after December 7, 1941, not sufficiently outstanding to qualify them for one of the afore-mentioned higher awards. The medal is a bronze hexagon on which is superimposed an American bald eagle with wings displayed horizontally grasping three crossed arrows and bearing on its breast a shield paly of thirteen pieces and a chief. On the reverse, between the words "For Military" and "Merit" is a panel, all above a sprig of laurel. The medal is suspended by a ribbon composed of two stripes of green within a selvedge of white, with the center containing nine white and green stripes of equal width.

The Purple Heart is given for "Wounds Received in Action Against an Enemy of the U. S." Originally established by George Washington, it was discontinued for many years but was re-established in 1932. On a purple heart of enamel within a bronze border is a profile head of Washington in relief in military uniform; above is his coat of arms between two sprays of leaves in green enamel. The ribbon is purple with white edges.

There are badges too numerous to mention for the different branches of the Service.

Medals go back to the Indian campaigns and to the Civil War. While few people know them all, it is quite a compliment if you recognize those of World War II. Certainly, you should be able to recognize those earned by your husband, and to know a bit of their history, also the order in which they are worn.

Undoubtedly there will come a time when you will have to serve as valet and you should know how to arrange your better half's insignia and decorations. It isn't easy, and what those sharp pins and rugged edges won't do to a manicure! Be sure to collect for your services: this one should rate a dinner at your favorite restaurant "come the first of the month." Don't become too expert at this valet service or you will have the job permanently!

Many wives are hard put to it to find a way or a place in which to display their husband's war decorations. Army men do not care for an ostentatious display, and seldom like them set under glass in coffee tables or on trays. Believe it or not, I have seen this done! The cleverest medals case I have seen was an old-fashioned spool case, the kind small department stores used to have for spools of thread. The drawers were relined with purple velvet, and the decorations and many beautiful awards of foreign countries were nothing short of regal in their smart setting. The case rested on a table in the library, the medals out of sight unless there was reason to display them.

Service medals worn indicate that the individual participated in the particular campaign, such as Spanish War Service Medal or Mexican Border Service Medal.

Badges worn on the uniform include aviation badges and badges for marksmanship, gunnery.

Service ribbons and miniature replicas may be worn on prescribed uniforms on certain official occasions.

The Medal of Honor is worn pendant from the ribbon placed around the neck, outside the white collar and inside the coat collar. It is an honor to be authorized to wear decorations and medals, and under no circumstances should they be worn by anyone except the rightful owner.

Chapter XV

THE ARMY ATTACHE'S WIFE
IN FOREIGN CAPITALS

The diplomat is quite restrained
    In his official life.
But deeper is the tension that
    Surrounds his loving wife.
She has to be a portion of
    The diplomatic team,
With every hospitality
    From salad to ice cream.
She has to smile and say hello
    With every little drink,
And often say the opposite
    Of what she wants to think.
Her grace and poise and manner are
    A part of his career,
And more than any other task
    She has to sound sincere.
And while her husband strives to solve
    The world and all its ills,
She has to figure out a way
    To pay the family bills.
                    —James J. Metcalfe

ONE of the most interesting, glamorous, and important assignments in the Army is duty in a foreign capital as an Army Attaché. Sometimes a bachelor is selected but more often a married officer receives the plum because in this way the government gets the full-time services of two people for the pay of one. In the Diplomatic Service a wife plays an integral part in representing the government and is considered a most important member of the diplomatic community. For that reason, in the selection of Attachés considerable weight is given to the ability of the wife to meet the requirements of this duty.

.There is a widespread impression that a diplomat's wife is a pampered darling of fortune, that she has a rollicking life made up of an unending round of amusing parties all at the government's expense. It is true that there is a fascination to the life, but it is not all champagne and caviar, and along with these good times there are definite responsibilities. The successful diplomat's wife must accept her share of them.

When an officer is selected for Attaché duty, he becomes a member of a very distinguished Service with a justifiably high morale. His life is bounded by the discipline of the Service and his obligations to his country. He is on duty twenty-four hours a day; he is the living representation, not of the average American, but of America as a world power.

His conduct is circumscribed by international custom and usage, and he must weigh every act in the light of the effect it will have on the reputation of the country which he represents. Just as in the Armed Forces, the higher the officer's rank, the more of a public figure he becomes and the more his conduct is scrutinized in all its details. When he commands the highest post in the Diplomatic Service he is the personal representative of the President of the United States. The diplomat's wife moves right along with her husband and is just as much in the service of the government as her husband.

It takes time and effort for the diplomat's wife to make things go smoothly; she is expected to make her home a center where government officials and colleagues of the Diplomatic Corps like to come on easy and friendly terms. She is expected to take an active interest in all sorts of local enterprises, American and foreign, such as hospital, church, and school openings and benefits. At all these affairs she demonstrates a friendly attitude. She is also expected to attend and to take an interest in cultural and sporting events with the idea of winning and keeping friends for America.

There is a steady stream of visitors, both official and unofficial. VIP's arrive in droves. Three or four Congressmen descend for a few days' visit—usually on very short notice. Plans immediately have to be made by the embassy for a series of dinners and luncheons and perhaps a reception. If you should have any personal plans, as a diplomat's wife you must be prepared to shelve or discard them. The amusing part is that each visitor looks upon his own sojourn as an incident apart, a pleasant interlude for the diplomats, and a breath from home for the exiles. To the diplomats this is no more than a steady stream; however, successful diplomats have notably gracious manners, otherwise they would not be diplomats.

THE DEPARTMENT OF STATE

Just for your own background, I think an Army Attaché's wife should know that the Department of State was created by the First Congress in 1789. It is the highest-ranking department of the government, and the Secretary of State is the Number One cabinet member.

The State Department is often referred to as the nerve center of the government. It is charged with preserving peace by diplomacy when possible and establishing our foreign policy among other nations as two of the first among its many missions. In addition to looking after foreign affairs, it issues passports and visas, sets up protocol, makes commercial treaties and agreements, establishes international communications and cultural relations, directs Foreign Service personnel, and takes over the translating of all communications and records.

The career diplomat is trained in diplomacy and is hidebound in certain particulars. He has definite inhibitions about making easy promises, and flowery public speeches are not in his line. If he attended the Fletcher School of Diplomacy and International Law, a graduate school of political science and history jointly staffed by Harvard and Tufts College, he learned languages, international law, diplomatic usage, public administration, political theory, economics and finance, international economic relations, history, maritime law, law of the air, and other subjects too numerous to list.

THE FOREIGN SERVICE OF THE UNITED STATES

The Foreign Service of the United States, to which your husband is assigned as an Army Attaché, operates under the direction of the State Department in carrying out the orders of the Chief Executive and acts for all government agencies with overseas interests. It is organized on a geographical basis and functions much as does a military organization with a clear and a distinct chain of command.

The Secretary of State, as the President's operational representative, issues the orders through the Department of State. The orders are transmitted to the Chief of Mission within any major political area, who in turn handles, with the help of his staff, all United States interests in that area. The only exception to this procedure occurs when, in time of war, a military commander may become the President's representative.

The Ambassador or Minister is the highest-ranking American on the diplomatic staff in a foreign embassy or legation.

The work performed in a Foreign Service post is divided generally into four categories:

1. The political work in which the Ambassador, the counselor, and various sections of the legation or embassy participate. This work is the conduct of international relations on the political level and includes the negotiation of treaties. This section may also include the cultural and informational attachés.
2. Work of the economic section, headed by an economic counselor, which is concerned with international trade.
3. Work of the consular section and the administration section, which handle the vast flow of correspondence, citizenship problems, issuing of visas, and general administration.
4. Work of other departments and agencies, which includes that of the Army, Naval, and Air Attachés.

Normally an officer in the Foreign Service starts his career as a vice-consul. For obvious reasons, personnel is hand picked. "Men, like bullets, go farther when they are smoothest."

GENERAL INFORMATION

When your husband receives his orders to report to a mission in a foreign capital, literature concerning the country to which he is being sent is forwarded along with a suggested list of things to take along.

For instance, it is generally suggested that each of you take two hundred personal visiting cards and two hundred joint cards. Yes, calling is very much in order in diplomatic life, even today. Also, take along a good supply of engraved "informals" for simple tea invitations and notes.

If you leave from Washington, you and your husband will probably be briefed on the essentials you should know by a member of the State Department staff. You will be told that there is a trend throughout the world in diplomatic circles toward more formality.

You will be wise to include plenty of hats and gloves for luncheons and receptions, and your wardrobe should contain several formal evening dresses, one of which should be white. If a lady is presented at court to royalty only white is considered appropriate, and long white gloves are worn.

PREPARATION FOR ARMY ATTACHÉ DUTY

More and more, the State Department recognizes the need for trained career diplomats. Since Army Attachés come in this category, special training is now being given Army officers ordered to foreign duty. Provision is also being made for their wives to attend lectures on life in foreign capitals and briefings concerning the country to which their husbands will be assigned.

Officers are trained from twelve to eighteen months. The Army maintains a Language School at Monterey, California, which many Army Attachés are required to attend. Since an Army Attaché's duty will be of a different type from any you and your husband have previously experienced, you must realize that he will begin an intensive program of study for his assignment in the Army Attaché system.

You will be sent a booklet that will guide you in preparing for your role as an Army Attaché's wife. The station and housing reports will give you a general picture of living conditions in the country to which you will travel. From your perusal of the station reports you will get the rosy side, but—"forewarned is forearmed"! Be prepared for the seamy side and a few thorns as well. Later in this chapter I will explain what I mean by the thorns. No doubt you are already wondering exactly what will be expected of you and, in turn, what you may expect from the assignment.

RESPONSIBILITIES AND OBLIGATIONS

It cannot be overemphasized that American official personnel stationed abroad are guests of the people of the countries in which they are stationed. Remember the following; have it printed and framed; hang it beside your mirror and read it out loud every morning of your stay in the country where you are assigned or visiting:

"NEVER COMPLAIN ABOUT THE COUNTRY OR THE PEOPLE"

Your actions will be scrutinized not only by the people of the country but also by compatriots traveling or residing abroad. The degree of attention given your conduct by compatriots abroad far exceeds that which it would receive in the United States. Acting in a dignified and proper manner will naturally preclude any suggestion of excessive drinking, or of undue familiarity and effusiveness in public.

In days past, French was the accepted diplomatic language officially, but today English is the major language of the world. It is understood by countless persons everywhere. One should resist the temptation in foreign countries to make disparaging remarks in public, either about the country of residence or about the United States, under the delusion that no one can understand. It is not unusual for an American tourist to cudgel his brain and go to great lengths in explaining directions in his faltering French only to have a Paris taxi driver answer in excellent English!

An Attaché's wife must be willing to attend social functions and reciprocate. She must have a real interest in the people and country to which her husband is assigned and, above all, she must be considerate of her husband's free time.

A successful wife can assist her husband in the following ways:

1. Remember to be a good mixer. Don't be clannish. Make friends among the foreign groups.

2. Think of the possible consequences of something you are about to say before you say it.

3. Look your best at all times. One never knows when a formal call may be paid.

4. Look ahead and make plans for family get-togethers and for social functions that will not conflict with other parties.

5. Look always at your engagement pad before accepting another engagement. (Carry that extra little black book.)

LANGUAGES

It is impossible to say enough of the importance of knowing the language of the people. To be an accomplished linguist is one of the greatest assets a wife in a position like this can possess. Use the foreign-language records, go to class, have a tutor, and read as much as possible of the history and customs of the people.

Servants are necessary, but they are also a problem. The Attaché's wife must be able to talk to them in order to: (1) have a personal understanding of their problems and situations; (2) have harmony in the household; (3) have a smoothly run household; (4) have the ability to make out menus and get what was intended; (5) have her husband's best tux shirt washed and ironed for a certain important night.

Socially, if an Attaché's wife cannot converse with the majority of guests at a cocktail party or dance she will find herself alone. She will find it very embarrassing, too, at a dinner party if her partner, after his first pleasantries, devotes the rest of his time to the lady on his other side who speaks his language!

SOME OF THE THORNS!

You will probably find plenty of *real* complaints but always remember *you are a guest*, and in addition recall the American feeling and our typical expression, unspoken or verbal, to foreigners: "If you don't like it here, go back where you came from." It works both ways!

Your big problem may be the electricity. It will go on and off, will dim, then have a surge and blow all your delicate electrical appliances. Or perhaps the plumbing won't work. The plumber and electrician will promise on their sacred word of honor to come tomorrow, but they won't show up for three weeks. When they do show up they will do only half the job, then they won't come back for another month. Perhaps the elevator won't work. You will have dysentery, and at first it will make you sick to go to the native markets, see the meat hanging in the open with flies swarming over it. Guests will drop their cigarettes on your best rugs instead of on a conveniently placed ash tray.

As for automobiling, at first you will think everyone drives with his horn and often on the left-hand side of the street. Your maids will pull every conceivably silly stunt and you may have to fire and hire dozens of them before you get a good team, and before you learn to handle them. The answer: Relax, grin and bear it! Every time you and your husband start to complain, make a pact between yourselves and remind each other with an understanding smile, "You never had it so good!" And it will be true.

Keep in mind that the people, your hosts, are as proud of their country as we are of ours and they are quick to resent criticism. However, many of them think all Americans are out to drain their economy dry. A few may resent seeing your shiny, good refrigerator and high scale of living; seeing you drive a new car through their streets. The important thing to remember is that you are more than a guest, you are an official representative of the United States government and its people. So . . . you never, never criticize, even among yourselves.

CALLING

Twenty-four hours after their arrival at a post, an Attaché and his wife should call on the wife of the Chief of the Mission (meaning the Ambassador or Minister), having inquired of her secretary if she would like to receive them in person or if they should only leave cards. In diplomatic circles the new arrival calls first on those of her husband's rank and above; the juniors in rank call on her first.

The correct number of cards is left, as explained earlier in this book. This means *one* "Mr. and Mrs." or joint card and one "Mr." card for a married woman, *one* joint card for each single woman. The upper right-hand corners are turned down to show that the cards were left in person and not sent by a servant. The address of the new Attaché should be written in pencil in the lower right-hand corner— never in ink. Likewise, all messages written on cards should be in pencil.

The call should be brief—lasting only ten or fifteen minutes. Cards may be left at tea or cocktail time in the afternoon but, of course, never at the luncheon or dinner hour.

In many countries calling is taken seriously and often people are extremely sensitive if their call is not returned. It is well to keep careful lists and to be punctilious in both making and returning calls. Inquiries should be made as to new arrivals and close attention given to promptness in discharging this social-official obligation. Etiquette in foreign capitals is far more exacting than in Washington.

One of the first things a new arrival at an embassy post should do is to learn the proper title by which each diplomat, government official, and military officer should be addressed. This is not nearly as difficult as it may appear, since each embassy has someone in charge of protocol who not only briefs you on where, when, and on whom to call but gives you factual information on the customs of the country. For example, in Denmark it is explained that it would be considered rude not to send flowers the first time you are invited to the home of a Dane.

Before calling, an Attaché and his wife should know about introductions. One presents a lady to the Ambassador or Minister, who is always spoken to as "Mr. Ambassador," or "Mr. Minister." The Ambassador's wife is "Mrs. Robertson," or "Mrs. Smith." A husband or wife always refers to "my husband," or "my wife," or "John," or "Mary," among friends. With servants he says "Mrs. Brandon," and she says "Colonel Brandon."

There is a great deal of handshaking abroad; be sure your clasp is firm and friendly. A lady extends her hand first.

INVITATIONS

Shortly after your arrival, in the gracious, hospitable fashion of the diplomatic set, invitations will begin to arrive. Again, this whole procedure has been covered fully in Chapter VIII so I shall merely summarize the essential points.

Formal invitations should be answered formally, never dated or signed. The answer is always written by hand, never under any circumstances typewritten.

A luncheon invitation by note should be answered by note, and your name signed

Sincerely,
Judith Brandon

Never Mrs. Robert Brandon, as you well know!

PROTOCOL

Mr. Webster defines "protocol" as "a preliminary memorandum, as of resolutions arrived at in negotiations, as a basis for a final negotiation or treaty." In diplomatic vernacular, protocol might be said to follow a mass of traditions, some based on common sense, others laid down in the Treaty of Vienna in 1815.

To the Attaché's wife and to most hostesses protocol means "precedence"—who ranks whom, and how to seat dignitaries and persons of conflicting rank. If the order of precedence becomes too involved, Washington hostesses consult the Chief of Protocl at the State Department. On foreign duty, the protocol officer at each embassy or legation will gladly arrange the seating for the new Attaché's wife, and someone at the "Foreign Office" (the foreign State Department) will arrange seating for larger miscellaneous groups.

Let us start with table seating, which in diplomatic circles, even for the smallest luncheon, is always planned according to the rank of the guests.

At formal dinners there is usually a seating chart either in the hall or the drawing room, or both, to show the guests where they are to sit. It is not the custom for all guests to be introduced to each other at a large dinner. At formal dinners the gentlemen take the ladies in to dinner and there are "take-in" cards to tell them their ladies' names. A gentleman usually takes the lady on his right according to

the chart, and if it is someone he has never met, he should ask to be
presented to her before dinner.

There are always place cards on the table, above each plate, with
the writing clear and large enough to be read easily by the guests on
either side. The ranking lady guest is seated on the right of the host.

Again according to protocol, the ranking lady guest is the first to
leave after dinner or luncheon. There is a definite time, and in many
capitals the hour after dinner is eleven o'clock.

PARTY GIVING

In giving any party of size, the date should be cleared with the embassy, so as not to run a competitive party with someone else. Always
offer your assistance or services at the embassy and ask to help with
parties; their success depends on the assistance of everyone on the
staff.

Another point to be emphasized is the duty of all the staff to see
that the Ambassador and his wife are not left talking too long with
people. As for yourself, tactfully avoid getting involved in gossip
about the Chief, his wife, and others of the mission. Always remember that you are a guest in the country where your husband is serving;
that everything you do or say is observed; and that the United States
is judged by your behavior. This cannot be stressed too strongly with
officers and their wives young in the Service since one unthinking
person can do enough damage to ruin the reputation of the whole
mission.

Wives should watch their drinking, or better still keep clear and
abstain. Often imbibing leads to undignified and improper manners
such as sitting on the floor, exchanging kisses at formal parties, and
various types of behavior which in themselves may not be essentially
wrong but are far from a foreigner's idea of dignity.

Another American habit which is much criticized abroad is smoking during meals. Do not smoke unless cigarettes are passed to you
or unless the host or hostess smokes or offers you a cigarette. It is
usually not done until after the salad or dessert course, and at some
British formal dinners not until after the Queen is toasted.

The question arises as to the repayment of social obligations. As
for ever asking the Ambassador and his wife to dinner, after being
entertained at the embassy, it should be carefully considered since
they are so very busy and are always pressed for time. If it is thought
advisable to extend an invitation, they should be offered two or three

dates quite a bit in advance so that the Ambassador may make a choice. It is not necessary to repay dinner with dinner or luncheon with luncheon; after a dinner the younger people can return the hospitality with a simple luncheon or cocktails. The gesture is the main thing.

After any luncheon or dinner, some gracious gesture of thanks should be made. The most correct formal gesture is to make a dinner call or leave cards the day following the dinner. This means leaving the same number of cards, with the corners turned, as on the initial call. If a post is more casual, a note of thanks can be written or flowers sent.

An invitation from the Chief of the Mission is in the nature of a command and takes precedence, the same as an invitation to the White House. If you have accepted another invitation, inquire as to whether the Ambassador prefers that you break it or keep it. The inquiry is made through one of his secretaries, of course.

Ladies and gentlemen both rise whenever the Ambassador and his wife enter the room. This applies to groups of up to eighteen or twenty people. Sofas abroad are regarded as seats of honor in family as well as diplomatic circles. Consequently, guests should not sit on the sofas unless invited to by the hostess. The right-hand corner is the ranking seat.

The Chief of the Mission and his wife always go through doors first; their car should be allowed to pass ahead on the street. But in entering an automobile, the procedure is the same as for Navy personnel entering a boat: the junior gets in first and sits on the left of the car, the ranking person enters last, sits on the right and gets out first. If they enter from the left side of the car, the Ambassador crawls over everyone's legs, or walks around the car!

DIPLOMATIC SUGGESTIONS

Always be exactly on time for engagements; in fact, at most American embassies the staff is supposed to arrive a few minutes ahead of time. As in the Army, Navy, and Air Force, no one is fashionably late.

Always speak to your host and hostess, then find your Ambassador and his wife. Never leave before they do unless it is absolutely necessary, and then excuse yourself and say good-by.

The hostess is never served first under any circumstances. The ranking lady guest of honor on the right of the host is the first to be served.

The host always accompanies his guests to the door. When a high-ranking guest such as the Ambassador leaves, he accompanies him to his car. At most posts all the staff stay until the Minister and his wife have left.

The wives of members of the nobility are always addressed by title —"Lady Astor," "Countess Simploni," "Baroness Von Kimball," "Princess Margaret"—but the wives of men holding official titles, no matter how exalted, are addressed as "Madame," or if British or American just as "Mrs. Jones" or "Mrs. Smythe."

There is one social custom at the English table which you should know, even though a few may find it irksome. That is the custom of "leaving the gentlemen to their port." If there is no port then it will be tea or cider or ginger beer. The point is not the drink but the occasion. It is a time when the gentlemen light their cigars, pipes, and cigarettes to indulge for a few seconds in masculine talk at the conclusion of the meal. It allows them to get the business and politics out of their systems before they rejoin the ladies; and it allows the ladies to indulge in fireside feminine chat which also would bore the gentlemen. Consequently, when the hostess rises and asks rhetorically "Shall we leave the gentlemen to their port?" it is best not to protest, for these gentlemen will join their ladies in a short time and will usually offer more to the mixed conversation by this little respite. By being gracious guests, the American officer and his wife will quickly appreciate the generous hospitality which characterizes the Englishman's "castle-cottage."

At first, as the wife of a newcomer to an embassy you may find the strain on your memory for names and faces great, but this will soon be overcome if you like people and are socially inclined. An Army Attaché, by virtue of his assignment, is usually the third- or fourth-ranking officer on the protocol list of each American embassy or legation. Consequently the social demands on his wife are exacting.

An innately well-bred Army wife has not so very much to learn and certainly nothing to fear if she is alert, is eager to fall in with the diplomatic policy, and follows the suggestions given in the briefings arranged by the Department of State. The prerequisites for a successful Army Attaché's wife might be summed up as follows: she should be gracious, diplomatic, well-mannered, but above all *American.*

BIBLIOGRAPHY

Boots and Saddles, Elizabeth Custer, Harper & Brothers, New York, 1885.

Reminiscences of a Soldier's Wife, Ellen McGown Biddle, J. B. Lippincott Co., Philadelphia, 1907.

Vanished Arizona, Martha Summerhayes, Salem Press Co., Salem, Mass., 1911.

Tenting on the Plains, Elizabeth A. Custer, Harper & Brothers, New York, 1895.

With Custer's Cavalry, Katherine Gibson Fougera, Caxton Printers, Ltd., Caldwell, Ida., 1940.

Old Days in the Old Army, Lydia Spencer Lane.

Following the Guidon, Elizabeth Custer.

Following the Flag, Alice Sargent, P. N. Barnett, Sidney, N. S.W., 1920.

History of the United States Army, William Addleman Ganoe, D. Appleton and Co., New York, 1924.

Army Letters from an Officer's Wife, Frances Roe, D. Appleton and Co., New York, 1909.

The Officers' Guide (no author), Military Service Publishing Co., Harrisburg, Pa., 1st edition, 1930, 19th edition, 1952.

Customs of the Service, Col. James W. Powell, The Franklin Hudson Publishing Co., Kansas City, Mo., 1905.

Army Posts and Towns, Charles J. Sullivan, Free Press Interstate Publishing Co., Fort Thomas, Ky., 1926–1935.

West Point Today, Kendall Banning, Funk and Wagnalls Co., New York and London, 1937.

The Fleet Today, Kendall Banning, Funk and Wagnalls Co., New York and London, 1940.

Annapolis Today, Kendall Banning, Funk and Wagnalls Co., New York and London, 1938.

Ups and Downs of an Army Officer, George A. Armes, Washington, D. C., 1900.

Who's Who in the Regular Army, John McDonald Thompson, San Antonio Printing Co., San Antonio, Tex., 1925.

Etiquette, Emily Post, Funk and Wagnalls Co., New York and London, 1937.

Social Washington, Anne Squire, Washington, D. C., 1929.

Naval Customs, Lt. Commander Leland P. Lovette, George Banta Publishing Co., Menasha, Wis., 1934.

Adventures in Alaska, S. Hall Young, Fleming H. Revell Co., New York and Chicago, 1919.

Travels in Alaska, John Muir, Houghton Mifflin Co., Boston, 1915.

Public Education in the Territories and Outlying Possessions, Pamphlet No. 16, Advisory Committee on Education, U. S. Government Printing Office, Washington, D. C., 1939.

Songs of the Army Flyers, courtesy of the Order of Daedalians.

The Book of Navy Songs, The Trident Society, Doubleday, Page and Co., Garden City and New York, 1926.

Songs of the U.S.M.A., Lt. Philipps Egner and Fred C. Mayer, Egner & Mayer, West Point.

The Blood of the Shark, Beatrice Ayer Patton, Paradise of the Pacific Press, Honolulu, 1936.

Soldiers in the Sun, William Thaddeus Sexton, Military Service Publishing Co., Harrisburg, Pa., 1939.

The Bum Bugler, Jane Comstock, The Mellen Associates, Honolulu, 1926.

Army Directory (published semiannually), Department of the Army, Washington, D. C.

Thomason Act, regulations quoted from *Army Regulations*, and regulations quoted from special pamphlets printed by the Adjutant General's Department, U. S. Army, Washington, D. C.

Army Register and *Army, Navy and Air Force Journal*.

Traveler from Tokyo, John Morris, Sheridan House, New York, 1942.

Noncommissioned Officer's Handbook and Manual, Combat Forces Press, Washington, D. C., 1952.

The Immortal Wife, Irving Stone, Doubleday & Co., New York, 1943.

Your Child, Frances Bruce Strain, D. Appleton-Century Co., New York, 1943.

Hold Your Man, Veronica Dengel, Coward-McCann, New York, 1945.

Personality Unlimited, Veronica Dengel, John C. Winston, Philadelphia, 1943.

Entertaining Is Fun, Dorothy Draper, Doubleday & Co., New York, 1944.

Inside Your Home, Dan Cooper, Farrar, Straus & Co., New York, 1946.

All About Modern Decorating, Mary Davis Gillies, Harper & Brothers, New York, 1942.

You Can Live in an Apartment, Dorothy Duncan, Farrar & Rinehart, New York, 1939.

The Entertaining Lady, Vera Bloom, G. P. Putnam's Sons, New York, 1949.

Table Setting, Amelia Leavitt Hall, Greystone Press, New York, 1949.

The Household Manual, Henrietta Ripperger, Simon & Schuster, New York, 1948.

Lunching and Dining at Home, Jeanne Owen, Alfred A. Knopf, New York, 1942.

Teen Age Manual, Edith Heal, Simon & Schuster, New York, 1948.

Your Manners Are Showing, Betty Betz, Grosset & Dunlap, New York, 1946.

Betty Betz Party Book, Betty Betz, Grosset & Dunlap, New York, 1945.

The Social List of Washington, D.C., C. H. Shaw, 1948.

Army, Navy and Air Force Journal.

Various travel and fashion articles appearing in *Vogue, Harper's Bazaar, Holiday, House & Garden, House Beautiful, Fortune, Seventeen, Mademoiselle, The Bride, Reader's Digest, Living,* and *Town & Country.*

Combat Forces Journal.

Officers' Call.

Armed Forces Talk.

Troop Topics.

INDEX